Youth at Work

This cross-national study of youth employment examines the composition and characteristics of the jobs held by youth in six industrialized market economy countries: Australia, the Federal Republic of Germany, Great Britain, Japan, Sweden, and the United States. The purpose of the study is to establish whether the nations differ in the amount and nature of the disparity between youth and adults, on the one hand, and among youth subgroups, on the other, in the types, conditions, and rewards of jobs held. Among the specific issues investigated are the existence of a distinct youth labor market, disproportionate shares of youth in "secondary" labor markets, "youth jobs," and labor market segmentation of youth. The analysis also considers school enrollment status, educational attainment, race or ethnicity, and place of residence as sources of differences between youth and adults or within the youth groups.

Conservation of Human Resources: 22

Youth at Work
An International Survey

Edited by
BEATRICE G. REUBENS

Foreword by Eli Ginzberg

LandMark Studies
ROWMAN & ALLANHELD Publishers

ROWMAN & ALLANHELD

Published in the United States of America in 1983
by Rowman & Allanheld, Publishers
(A division of Littlefield, Adams & Company)
81 Adams Drive, Totowa, New Jersey 07512

Library of Congress Cataloging in Publication Data
Main entry under title:

Youth at work.

  (Conservation of human resources series; 22)
(LandMark studies)
  Bibliography: p.
  Includes index.
  1. Youth—Employment—Case studies. I. Reubens,
Beatrice G. II. Series.
HD6270.Y67 1983   331.3′4   83-8631
ISBN 0-86598-101-9

83 84 85/ 10 9 8 7 6 5 4 3 2 1
Printed in the United States of America

Contents

List of Tables   vii

Preface   xi

Foreword by Eli Ginzberg   xv

1   **Perspectives and Problems**   1
    Beatrice G. Reubens

2   **Trends in Numbers Employed, 1960–1980**   17
    John A.C. Harrisson, Beatrice G. Reubens, and
    Pamela Sparr

3   **Occupational Dissimilarity by Age and Sex**   39
    Beatrice G. Reubens and John A.C. Harrisson

4   **Youth Employment in Australia**   86
    Paul Paterson and Keith Mackay

5   **Youth Employment in West Germany**   113
    Karen Schober

6   **Youth Employment in Great Britain**   149
    David Metcalf and John Richards

7   **Youth Employment in Japan**   185
    Shun'ichiro Umetani and Beatrice G. Reubens

8   **Youth Employment in Sweden**   232
    Anders Björklund and Inga Persson-Tanimura

9   **Youth Employment in the United States**   269
    Stephen M. Hills and Beatrice G. Reubens

10 **Overview and Implications**   319
    Beatrice G. Reubens

Index   342

About the Authors   349

List of Tables

2.1   Employment Growth, Employment to Population Ratios,   21
       and Unemployment Rates, 15 Years and Over, Both Sexes,
       Six Countries, 1960–1980.
2.2   Employment Growth, Males, by Age, Six Countries,   22
       1960–1980.
2.3   Employment Growth, Females, by Age, Six Countries,   23
       1960–1980.
2.4   Employment to Population Ratios, by Age and Sex, Six   24
       Countries, 1960–1980.
2.5   Shares of Total Employment, by Age and Sex, Six Countries,   29
       1960–1980.
2.6   Spearman Rank Correlations Between Youth Employment   35
       Growth Rates and Selected Variables, by Age and Sex,
       Six Countries, 1960–1980.
3.1   Most Common Occupations of Female Teenagers, Four   42
       Countries, Recent Census Year.
3.2   Most Common Occupations of Female Young Adults, Four   46
       Countries, Recent Census Year.
3.3   Most Common Occupations of Male Teenagers, Four Coun- 48
       tries, Recent Census Year.
3.4   Most Common Occupations of Male Young Adults, Four   52
       Countries, Recent Census Year.
3.5   Most Common Occupations of Male Adults, Four Coun-   58
       tries, Recent Census Year.
3.6   Most Common Occupations of Female Adults, Four Coun-   62
       tries, Recent Census Year.
3.7   Indexes of Occupational Dissimilarity, Detailed Occupa-   68
       tional Classification, by Age and Sex, Four Countries,
       Recent Census Year.
A3.1   Occupational Data in Censuses, Four Countries   75
4.1   Youth Employment, by Age, Hours of Work, and Student   93
       Status, Both Sexes, Australia, May 1981.
4.2   Youth-Intensity of Employment, by Industry and Sex,   97
       Australia, 1981.
4.3   Employment Change in Youth-Intensive Industries, by Age   99
       and Sex, Australia, 1971–1981.
4.4   Employment, by Industry, Age, Sex, and Hours of Work, 100
       Australia, 1981.

4.5   Employed Persons Who Changed Jobs, by Age and Sex,   102
       Australia, 1972 and 1979.

4.6   Award Wage Rates, Apprentices Relative to Skilled Work-   106
       ers, Both Sexes, Australia, 1971–1979.

4.7   Hourly Earnings of Juniors Relative to Adults, Full-time   107
       Employees, by Sex, Australia, 1966–1980.

5.1   General and Vocational Educational Attainment of Em-   116
       ployed Population, by Age and Sex, West Germany, 1978.

5.2   Working Population, by Age, Sex, and Employment Status,   130
       West Germany, 1961 and 1980.

5.3   Industry of Apprentices and Trainees Compared to Other   132
       Wage and Salary Employees, Both Sexes, West Germany,
       1979.

5.4   Indexes of Occupational Dissimilarity, by Age and Sex,   133
       West Germany, 1961, 1970, and 1980.

5.5   Most Common Occupations of Males Under 25 Years Old,   134
       West Germany, 1980.

5.6   Most Common Occupations of Females Under 25 Years   136
       Old, West Germany, 1980.

5.7   Weekly or Monthly Earnings of Youth Relative to Adults,   138
       by Age, Sex, Vocational Qualifications, and Type of Work,
       West Germany, 1962–1978.

6.1   Type of First Employment of New Entrants, 15–18 Years   160
       Old, by Sex, Great Britain, 1952–1974.

6.2   Occupations of Youth, 16–24 Years Old, by Race, Sex,   164
       and Socioeconomic Group, Great Britain, 1975.

6.3   Youth Intensity of Employment, by Major Industry Group,   167
       Age, and Sex, Great Britain, 1971.

6.4   Characteristics of Six Most Teenage-Intensive Major In-   169
       dustry Groups, Males, Great Britain, 1971.

6.5   Characteristics of Six Most Teenage-Intensive Major In-   171
       dustry Groups, Females, Great Britain, 1971.

6.6   Hourly Earnings of Youth Relative to Adults, by Sex,   173
       Great Britain, 1949–1980.

6.7   First Occupation and 1975 Occupation, Males, by Year   177
       of Entry to Labor Market and Socioeconomic Group, Great
       Britain, 1930–1975.

6.8   First Occupation and 1975 Occupation, Females, by Year   179
       of Entry to Labor Market and Social Class, Great Britain,
       1930–1975.

7.1   Flows from Education into Employment, by Educational   190
       Level, Both Sexes, Japan, 1955–1980.

7.2   Newly Hired Employees, by Prior Work Experience, Age,   198
       and Sex, Japan, 1955–1980.

7.3 Occupations of Employed New Graduates, by Educational 201
     Level and Sex, Japan, 1980.
7.4 Employment of New School Graduates, by Size of Enter- 205
     prise, Educational Level, and Sex, Japan, 1961–1980.
7.5 Relative Starting Salaries of New Graduates, by Educational 209
     Level and Sex, Japan, 1955–1979.
7.6 Monthly Earnings of Youth in Enterprises with 10–99 211
     Employees Relative to Earnings of Youth in Enterprises
     with 1,000 or More Employees, by Educational Level, Age,
     and Sex, Japan, 1958–1980.
7.7A Job-changers Within One Year, by Age and Sex, Japan, 214
     1959–1979.
7.7B Annual Separation Rates, by Age and Sex, Japan, 1955–1980. 215
7.8 Gainfully Occupied, by Size of Enterprise, Educational 221
     Level, Age, and Sex, Japan, 1979.
7.9 Duration of Formal Internal Training, by Type of Employee 222
     and Size of Enterprise, Both Sexes, 15 Years and Over,
     Japan, 1980.
7.10 Monthly Earnings of Youth Relative to Adults, All In- 224
     dustries, by Age, Sex, and Educational Level, Japan,
     1958–1980.
7.11 First Occupation and 1973 Occupation, Males, by Age in 227
     1973, Japan.
8.1 Type of Job, Permanency of Employment, and Earnings 245
     in 1979, Upper Secondary School Graduates of 1977, by
     Sex, Sweden.
8.2 Jobs Held in 1978 by Compulsory School Leavers of 1971, 248
     by Type of Upper Secondary School Program and Sex,
     Sweden.
8.3 Unemployment Rates by Labor Market Status, Age, and 252
     Sex, Sweden, 1975 and 1980.
8.4 Occupational Status of Employed Population, by Age and 255
     Sex, Sweden, 1965 and 1980.
8.5 Earnings of Youth Relative to Adults, by Age and Sex, 258
     Sweden, 1960–1980.
8.6 Distribution of Hourly Earnings in 1968 and 1974 of 260
     Persons Employed in Both Years, by Age and Sex, Sweden.
8.7 Unemployment During 1967 and 1973 of Members of the 261
     Labor Force in Both Years, by Age in 1968, Both Sexes,
     Sweden.
8.8 Degree of Job Security and Attainment of Supervisory 262
     Position in 1968 and 1974 of Persons Employed in Both
     Years, by Age, Both Sexes, Sweden.
9.1 Employment of Youth, 16–24 Years Old, by Enrollment 278
     Status, Age, and Sex, United States, 1953 and 1980.

9.2   Part-time Employment of Youth, 16–18 Years Old, by   280
        Industry, Sex, and Race, United States, 1968 and 1980.
9.3   In-School and Post-School Jobs of a Cohort of Noncollege   285
        Youth, by Occupation, Industry, and Sex, United States,
        1979–1980.
9.4   Annual Mean Number of Employers for Employed Youth,   291
        16–23 Years Old, by School Enrollment Status, Race, and
        Sex, United States, 1980.
9.5   Share of Out-of-School Youth, 14–24 Years Old, in Total   297
        Employment, by Major Occupational Group and Sex,
        United States, 1958–1980.
9.6   Median Usual Weekly Earnings of Full-time Youth Relative   302
        to Adults, by Age, Race, and Sex, United States, 1973–1982.
9.7   First Jobs of Youth, 16–24 Years Old, Leaving School in   306
        1968 and Jobs Held Ten Years Later, by Occupation,
        Industry, Sex, and Race, United States, 1968 and 1978.
9.8   Median Weekly Earnings and Average Annual Change,   309
        Youth 16–24 Years Old on Leaving School in 1968, by
        Age and Sex, United States, 1970–1978.

Preface

This book is the third product in a series of cross-national studies of youth labor market issues. When the project was initiated in the late 1960s, it appeared that the United States, beset by high and persistent youth unemployment, could learn much from Western Europe, Japan, Australia, and New Zealand where youth often had as low or lower unemployment rates than adults.

From the outset, the scope of these studies was broader than a comparative analysis of the levels, composition, and causes of youth unemployment in the various countries. Full attention also was directed toward those education and labor market processes and institutions that might in part explain differences among countries in the fortunes of young people, including their exposure to unemployment upon entering the labor force and changing jobs in the early years of working life.

This decision proved wise, inasmuch as the exemplary low youth unemployment gave way during the 1970s to sharply rising youth unemployment rates that greatly exceeded the elevated rates of adults in almost all of the foreign countries. It became clear that macroeconomic conditions play a decisive role in setting youth and other unemployment levels. Yet cross-national variation due to differences in labor supply trends and the effectiveness of basic educational and labor market processes remained important forces. Moreover, a new comparative subject was added: the efficacy of programs to ameliorate the adverse employment situation of youth produced by insufficient demand and the lessons for the United States.

Published in 1977, *Bridges to Work: International Comparisons of Transition Services* (Montclair, N.J.: Allanheld, Osmun, LandMark Studies) dealt with differences among countries in the orientation, information, guidance, placement, induction, and follow-up services provided to youth before they entered the labor force and during the initial years. While the impact of these services on youth unemployment was not great, the study placed a high value on effective services as easing the transition from school to work. It was followed by *The Youth Labor Force 1945–1995: A Cross-National Analysis* (Totowa, N.J.: Allanheld, Osmun, 1981). This joint effort (with John A.C. Harrisson and Kalman Rupp) explored the medium-term trends in 12 industrialized market economy countries in the absolute size of the youth labor force, youth shares of the total labor force, and youth labor force participation rates. Particular attention was given to the special problems of youth neither in school nor the labor force, youth both in school and the labor force, minority and immigrant youth, and females. Demographic movements and educational enrollment rate trends were shown to be major determinants of the medium-term trends in the absolute and relative size of the youth labor force and hence of youth unemployment as they interacted with forces on the demand side.

The present book, *Youth at Work: An International Survey,* concentrates on youth employment (not unemployment) in six advanced countries, comparing young people and adults and subgroups of youth, divided by sex, age, educational attainment, racial/ethnic background. Beyond throwing light on a relatively neglected subject, this study examines aspects of youth employment that may be related to differential unemployment experience within and among countries. The final output of this comparative youth project is tentatively entitled *Youth Programs: From Temporary Unemployment Measures to Permanent Reforms of Education and Training.* Reviewing the youth unemployment experience in a large number of countries over the past decades and the literature on its causes, the study will give detailed attention to youth unemployment programs in Great Britain and France where the utilization of the private sector was a key element, and their subsequent conversion and institutionalization of emergency programs into permanent methods of serving not only unemployed youth but youth who potentially might be exposed to unemployment upon leaving school. Lessons for the United States will be drawn.

In the present book, a new method has been utilized; separate country chapters were written by experts from the six countries, according to a uniform list of subjects and basic set of issues. There was a natural inclination of the country chapter authors to discuss matters that we had dealt with in our previously published studies or would consider in the final study. This produced a somewhat irksome intrusion by the editor, but it may be justified by the resulting fresh and full information on youth employment, most of it new even in the home countries, and by the more reliable basis for cross-national comparisons.

We provided introductory, background, and concluding chapters, in addition to an analytic chapter on occupational dissimilarities in four countries. We benefited greatly from the comments by the country chapter authors, to the point where we sought little outside aid. As always, Eli Ginzberg was available for consultation and wise counsel. On countless large and small issues, the editor profited from discussions with Edwin P. Reubens who, like all others who gave assistance, bears no responsibility for the final product.

Beyond his contributions to Chapters 2 and 3, John Harrisson gave valuable assistance in the editing and processing of the whole manuscript. Kalman Rupp supervised the extraction of the occupational information and construction of the measures for four countries in Chapter 3; George Winslow, Ahmad Hatami, Steven Horowitz, and Marcia Katzmar served as statistical assistants at various times.

Initial support for this comparative research on youth came jointly from the Department of Labor's Employment and Training Administration and the German Marshall Fund of the United States. Subsequently, the Rockefeller and Ford foundations provided funds to extend the work and the German Marshall Fund contributed again in the final phases.

Beatrice G. Reubens

Foreword

We are told with increasing frequency that a world economy is rapidly evolving and that the United States must act with all deliberate speed to adjust to the new realities, lest it be left behind in the accelerating race for markets, jobs, and profits. However one reads and interprets the trends—and I accept the conventional wisdom that internationalization is proceeding apace—it is also true, and this new book is a powerful reminder, that the advanced nations still differ considerably among themselves in various aspects of their economies, including the role of young people in the labor market.

Dr. Reubens's latest contribution to comparative studies of young people in school and in and out of work is a collaborative effort with experts from Australia, West Germany, Great Britain, Japan, Sweden, and the United States, and she is much more than the editor, being also the author or coauthor of five of the book's ten chapters. Moreover, her contribution as editor is considerable. She not only found competent collaborators in six countries, but she also provided an analytic design and persuaded them to follow it, thereby imposing a structure on what might otherwise have been a diffuse and inchoate collection of essays.

The first and last chapters offer a short guide to the book and should be read by anyone and everyone who desires to deepen his or her knowledge and understanding of a complex but important facet of modern labor markets—the jobs that youth get or don't get, and how the jobs held by youth parallel or diverge from those of adults. Further, the analysis in all chapters discusses job differences among youth subgroups and the possible interactions between type of job and the likelihood of being unemployed. Distinguishing between two groups of young people—teenagers and young adults—the authors present separate information for males and females, since their experiences are quite disparate. They also provide insights into the special difficulties that minority youth face in such diverse environments as West Germany, Great Britain, Sweden and the United States.

While Dr. Reubens and her collaborators have been most concerned with mastering the facts of youth employment and presenting a coherent story, they share a strong interest in the policy implications of their research. Perhaps the most important implication to be drawn from a careful reading of this significant work is that those who believe that the problems that young people encounter in the labor market reflect their personal weaknesses or faulty public policy, such as a high minimum wage, are constructing excuses largely out of whole cloth. The non-fit in the youth labor market is much more serious.

We are all indebted to Dr. Reubens and the other contributors to this book for providing us with rich fare that enables us to move from hunches to facts, from prejudices to policies (if we have the wit to do so) and, in the process, to add to the well-being of young people and of society.

Eli Ginzberg, Director
Conservation of Human Resources
Columbia University

1

Perspectives and Problems

Beatrice G. Reubens

We know much less about young people who are employed than we
do about those without jobs. The reasons are fairly obvious. Since the
early 1970s, youth unemployment has been a highly visible and persistent
problem in the industrialized market economy nations. In most countries,
youth account for a disproportionate share of total unemployment,
whether measured by the youth proportion of the labor force or by
historical records on unemployment. The result has been an outpouring
of studies on youth unemployment, to the relative neglect of youth
employment. Whatever has been true of the national tendency to
concentrate on youth unemployment is even more valid for cross-
national studies. The latter have focused on comparative studies of
youth unemployment rather than on cross-national analyses of the
composition and characteristics of youth employment, due to the
immediacy of the social problem of out-of-work young people and the
need to devise programs to assist them.

Yet, national and cross-national analysis of youth employment may
be inherently as, or more, important than studies of unemployed youth
for an understanding of the labor market problems of young people,
since youth unemployment is the outcome of the interaction between
the level and structure of the demand for, and the supply of, young
workers. At any given moment, cross-sectionally as well as longitudinally,
more young people are likely to be involved in employment than
unemployment, and what happens in periods of employment is likely
to be of greater consequence than periods of joblessness for differences
in lifetime work histories.

Moreover, the types of jobs youth hold may be directly related to
youth unemployment levels and patterns. Although we are familiar with
the adverse impact of rising levels of youth unemployment on the
number and type of jobs open to young people, there has been little
study of whether the types of jobs held by the youth groups most prone
to unemployment promote recurrent or prolonged unemployment. In

this connection, Bowers* (1981, p.21) points to the importance of obtaining information on youth's jobs, employers, wages, working conditions, number of employers and number of weeks worked per employer, and reasons for job separation as "critical to unraveling competing hypotheses about youth joblessness."

Among these competing, but not mutually exclusive hypotheses, are that youth have higher job turnover rates than adults, and hence higher unemployment rates, because they are shopping around for the most congenial and rewarding jobs (Mincer and Leighton 1982; Denton et al. 1980). Having fewer claims than older workers to the benefits of job tenure and fewer family responsibilities, youth feel freer to leave jobs. On the other hand, such job shopping by youth might be due to "the seasonal nature of the labor supply of many youth and/or the temporary jobs supplied by employers" (Bowers 1981; see also, Gregory and Foster 1981). It might also be that youth, more than adults, are limited to certain unsatisfactory, unrewarding jobs and hence move frequently from one job to another (Hall 1970; Piore 1978; Brown 1982; Osterman 1980). While accepting a role for high turnover in youth unemployment, others maintain that the heart of the problem lies in the concentration of unemployment on a small group of youth that experiences a great deal of joblessness (Clark and Summers 1982). Finally, some see changes over time in the youth labor market, making the main hypotheses more relevant to one period than another (Pollard 1982; OECD 1982a; Merrilees and Wilson 1979; Collier 1978).

Clearly, an understanding of the various interactions between employment and unemployment would give more balance to the picture of the youth labor market. Inquiries into the structure and trends of jobs and occupations by age group and the influence of the state of demand for labor relative to its supply may reveal whether there are significant patterns and cohort effects in the allocation of employment opportunities within youth groups and particular differences between young people and others. In addition, studies of the structure of youth employment may indicate how social and economic institutions and systems affect the jobs held by young people.

A cross-national framework is especially desirable in such studies, since it can offset cases of national myopia concerning the behavior of young people. If, for example, explanations of youth unemployment rest on inherent characteristics assigned to a nation's young people, or to certain groups of them, and such traits appear to be largely absent in the young people of other countries, the theories of the first country become suspect and other causes of the observed behavior may be sought. Another benefit of comparative study arises from the acknowledged analytic difficulty of separating the personal attributes of workers from the attributes of their jobs and places of work. Problems in

---

*Full references are given at the end of Chapter 3.

assembling and interpreting data to test the independent influence of establishment characteristics in earnings and mobility may be reduced if cross-national data are utilized, since they are likely to contain more independent variation among the two sets of characteristics than data for a single country (King 1979).

Apart from the intrinsic and social importance of investigating the diverse types and conditions of jobs held by young people, studies of youth employment, both nationally and cross-nationally, should contribute directly to an improved analysis of youth unemployment. It is in fact likely that a fully satisfactory interpretation of cross-national differences in the levels and trends in youth unemployment cannot be offered until account is taken of the impact of cross-national differences in the jobs young people hold, making due allowance for the heterogeneity of youth.

A few examples may suggest the relevance of youth employment as an explanatory factor in youth unemployment and the usefulness of cross-national approaches. When West Germans discuss how their nation has coped with youth unemployment, they do not dwell, as others do, on special programs to aid young unemployed people. Instead, the West Germans refer mainly to their apprenticeship system, the most important form of employment for teenagers. Through this system, and its expansion due to governmental pressure, the Germans maintain that they have had a smaller rise in youth unemployment than countries in which youth unemployment also was low at the outset. Similarly, in Japan, the special circumstances which govern the employment of young people as they leave the educational system are cited as factors in the relatively low unemployment of young people.

This favorable nexus between youth employment and unemployment is quite contrary to the situation observed in other countries, such as the United States, France, Belgium, and the Netherlands. As has been noted, some American analysts claim that the adverse conditions and types of employment open to youth, especially the more disadvantaged sectors of young people, actually breed high rates of job turnover and unemployment. Others believe that the main causes lie in the characteristics and behavior of young people. Some cite both factors—the unsatisfactory qualities of the jobs and the immature behavior of youth. In all cases, there is an unfavorable interface of youth employment and unemployment. These examples, drawn from a few countries, reveal an intimate though disparate relation between youth employment and unemployment and suggest that a deeper probing of cross-national differences in the levels, trends, composition, characteristics, and institutional background of employment by age group may be useful to national policy makers and analysts. Particular attention will be given to the most disadvantaged youth subgroups and those most vulnerable to unemployment.

Cross-National Sample

Six industrialized market economy countries have been selected for this comparative study—Australia, the Federal Republic of Germany,* Great Britain, Japan, Sweden, and the United States. These countries lend themselves to comparative analysis because they are all highly industrialized, have experienced substantial growth in the service sector, show a convergence of occupational patterns, have a high proportion of employment held by females, and, except for Japan, have had to adjust to an enlarged minority or foreign population. Along other dimensions, the countries display differences that should be noted, but need not impede the cross-national comparison. In regard to educational systems, youth employment practices, and related subjects, a deliberate effort was made to select countries which exhibit differences in laws, institutions and practice in order to assess their role in divergent employment outcomes for youth. The country chapters below discuss these factors and here we mention only a few outstanding.

Although the six countries vary little in regard to the legal age of leaving compulsory schooling, which is 15 or 16 in all six countries, they differ considerably in actual enrollment patterns and in the types of education provided (Reubens et al. 1981, ch.3). In three countries, a majority of youth leave formal full-time education when they are 15 or 16 years old (Australia, Germany, Great Britain), and in three a majority leave around 18 years of age, having completed upper secondary education (Japan, the U.S., Sweden). Japan currently has one of the highest educational retention rates, despite a legal leaving age of 15 which coincides with the completion of junior high school. In the Spring of 1981, about 97 percent of Japanese junior high school graduates were expected to continue their education and under 40 percent of prospective Japanese senior high school graduates indicated a desire to seek jobs immediately (Japan 1981a). According to OECD data for 1979, the proportion of 15–19 year-olds enrolled in full-time education was 75.0 percent in the U.S., 71.4 percent in Japan, 56.3 percent in Sweden (1976), 46.2 percent in the U.K. (1977),† 45.4 percent in Germany (1978), and 44.4 percent in Australia. These six countries also have diverse types of schooling, including one country in which upper secondary education has a large vocational element (Sweden), one in which a part-time school system plays a similar major role (Germany), and four in which the choices vary but an academic upper secondary education predominates over vocational (Japan, the U.S., Great Britain, Australia).

---

*Hereafter called "Germany."
†The United Kingdom includes Northern Ireland and Great Britain.

Employment systems affecting youth also vary among these countries. Germany and Japan have distinctive and noncompetitive employment forms for a substantial share of the youth age group, while Australia and Great Britain offer forms to a minority of males and an insignificant share of females; such provision for young people newly entering the full-time labor force is largely absent in Sweden and the United States. The practice of working during the school year is far more common among enrolled American, Australian and Swedish youth than in the other countries (Reubens et al. 1981, ch.5). Cross-national differences in occupational training methods and structures, the organization of production units, occupational titles, job hierarchies, the social structure of the workplace, and industrial relations cause significant impacts on the age distribution of employment and also complicate comparative analysis (Lutz 1969, 1976; Maurice et al. 1980; Sorge and Warner 1980).

Another important difference among the six countries concerns the existence of a legal minimum wage. Only Japan and the United States have such national statutes, applying to all age groups, though the Japanese law provides for area differentials, unlike the American uniform minimum wage rate. British law since 1909 has provided for Wages Councils which set separate minimum wage rates in selected low pay industries (Metcalf 1980). In the other countries, variable minimum wage rates by age and industry or occupation are set by collective bargaining agreements or other arrangements.

On the more general indices, the six countries vary widely. For example, the population of the U.S. is over 25 times as large as that of Sweden, the least populous country. Japan has the highest population density and Australia the lowest (Reubens et al. 1981, Table 1.4). With regard to the working age population (15–64) as a proportion of total population, all six countries fell within a narrow range of 64 to 68 percent in 1979; Japan had the highest proportion and the United Kingdom the lowest (OECD 1980a). Natural resource supplies are scanty in Japan, Germany, and somewhat less so in Great Britain because of off-shore oil, while Australia has much unexploited mineral wealth. Sweden and the U.S. fall between these two groups. According to OECD calculations (at market prices and expressed in U.S. dollars), per capita gross domestic product in 1980 was highest in Sweden, with Germany, the United States, Australia, the United Kingdom, and Japan following in that order. Even allowing for the effects of prevailing exchange rates, the gap between highest and lowest was very wide. Rank in GDP per capita does not correspond closely to country rank in the equality of income distribution within nations. Both before and after tax, an OECD study for the mid-1970s found Japan most equal, followed by Sweden, the U.K., Germany, and the United States (Sawyer 1976; see also, Japan 1979a). Australia, omitted from the study, probably ranked just behind or with Sweden.

Substantial cross-national differences characterize the rate of growth of the youth population and its share of the working age population.

The teenage (15–19) population grew most rapidly in Australia 1950–75 (3.2 percent compounded per year), followed by the U.S. (2.8 percent), Germany (1.1 percent), Sweden and the U.K. (1.0 percent) and Japan (−0.3 percent). Young adults (20–24) showed a somewhat lower growth rate than teenagers in each country except Japan where they registered a positive rate. A slightly different sequence of countries also appeared; Australia still led, followed by the U.S., but then came Sweden, Germany, Japan and the U.K. (Reubens et al. 1981, Table A2.6; Chart 2.4).

The youth (15–24) share of the working age population (15–64) in the late 1970s was largest in the U.S., followed in order by Australia, the United Kingdom, Germany, Sweden, and Japan (Reubens et al. 1981, ch.2). The trend in teenage shares was generally upward from 1950 to 1965, downward to the mid-1970s, and variable among the six countries thereafter. As a share of the working age population, Japanese teenagers were far in the lead of the other countries from 1945 to 1967, constituting over 15 percent in almost every year; thereafter, the teenage share in Japan declined, becoming one of the lowest. In most years after 1960 the U.S. teenage share was highest or second highest. Sweden's proportion was the lowest in 1945–55 and 1970–77 (9–11 percent). Germany also had a lower than average share of 9–10 percent from 1961–70, but otherwise followed the other three countries in showing shares close to the median (Reubens et al. 1981, Table A2.8, Chart 2.5).

Employment patterns have been converging in the six countries, although some differences persist. All six countries are highly industrialized with very important service sectors. A relative and absolute decline in agricultural employment, including forestry, fishing, and hunting, occurred in all six countries, particularly in Japan, Germany, and Sweden where the immediate postwar agricultural share had been high. By 1978, there was only a 12.8 percentage point spread between the highest (Japan) and lowest (U.K.) share in agriculture, contrasted with a range of 33.4 percentage points in 1954 (Reubens et al. 1981, Table 1.4). OECD data for 1980 show further reductions in the shares in agriculture, ranging from 10.4 percent in Japan, 8.8 percent in Germany, 6.5 percent in Australia, 5.6 percent in Sweden, 3.6 percent in the U.S., to a low (also among all OECD countries) of 2.6 percent in the U.K.; the spread was now only 7.8 percentage points between the highest and lowest countries. The shift out of agriculture was due to the creation of larger agricultural units, usually with some reduction in the number and size of family farms, increased mechanization, greater output per acre through improved crop types, fertilizers and management, and, in some cases, elimination of surplus farm labor. In part, the movement from the land reflected the superior attractions of alternative employment and urban living.

The industry sector, including mining and quarrying, manufacturing, construction, and electricity, gas and water supply, occupied a declining share of the labor force from 1960 to 1980 in four of the countries.

Japan had a marked and continuous rise until 1973 and then a slight leveling off, while Germany had a slight rise from 1960 to 1970 and then a decline to a level below that of 1960 (Hönekopp and Ullmann 1980, Chart 1, Table 2; Australia 1979b, p.103). The 1980 shares in industry, according to OECD calculations, narrowed the spread among countries. The U.K., with 38.0 percent, was highest, followed by Germany (35.9), Japan (35.3), Sweden (32.2), Australia (31.0), and the U.S. (30.6). Due to increased labor productivity, declines in the industry share of employment usually were not accompanied by proportionate decreases in the share of industry in the value of total output. The various employment shares reflected the loss of low level factory jobs to developing nations, as well as losses and gains within the six countries attributable to shifts in competitive position among the developed nations, notably Japan's ascendancy. However, trends in the shares of the other sectors also influenced the shares of industry.

By far the greatest absolute and relative increase in employment in each country occurred in the service sector, including wholesale and retail trade, restaurants, hotels, and places of entertainment, transport and communications, finance, insurance, real estate, business services, and community, personal, and social services. In 1980, over half of total employment was attributed to the service sector in each of the countries, and in the U.S., Australia, and Sweden it topped 60 percent, according to OECD data. The spread was 11.5 percentage points between the U.S. and Japan. If service jobs in the industry and agriculture sectors were included, the service sector share would be even higher (Goldstein 1980, Table 5; Kuwahara 1981). Service employment has risen absolutely and proportionately because of the growth of service activities, many of which are labor intensive, and because of the reduction of labor inputs per unit of agricultural and industrial output. While there is a common trend in industrialized nations, eventual uniformity in sectoral shares is not predicted (Hönekopp and Ullmann 1980).

In an examination of cross-sectional data for 25 countries, Fuchs (1980) found that the level of GDP per capita was positively related to the growth of service sector employment. In this analysis, differences in distribution of employment across the three main sectors were primarily the result of cross-national differences in the income elasticities of demand for various goods and services. Fuchs observed that changes in employment patterns also tend to feed back on the growth process; for example, a rise in the female labor force participation rate may lead to a demand for additional services for the household and child care, thus producing more service jobs. Other explanations are the smaller measured productivity growth rate in the service than the industrial sector and the rapid increase in public expenditure on services (OECD 1982a, p.30).

As expected, data by sex on the sectoral distribution of employment in the six countries reveal a greater concentration of females than males in service sector employment. Trends in the sectoral distribution of employment are, however, much the same for males and females in each country, revealing for each sex a decline of the share in agriculture and other primary activities and, in most of the six countries, a parallel decline in the share in industry.

We computed distributions of the total employed population by major occupational groups from the most recent available population census in Great Britain (1971), Japan (1975), Sweden (1975), and the United States (1970), and adjusted the major occupational categories to make data more comparable (Chapter 3, Appendix). Among employed males in each country, the occupational categories associated with manual work predominated, but the range was from a low of 43 percent in Japan (46 percent in the United States and 52 percent in Sweden) to the high of 59 percent in Great Britain. Reflecting the persistence of a traditional service sector, Japan's second most important occupational grouping for males was clerical and sales combined (26 percent), while clerical and sales occupations held a lower rank for males in the other countries, accounting for 14 percent in the U.S. and Great Britain, and 12 percent in Sweden. The combined group of professional, technical, managerial, and administrative workers was in second place in the U.S. (26 percent), Sweden (22 percent), and Great Britain (17 percent); it was 14 percent in Japan. The importance of agricultural occupations varied among the four countries; Japan had 11 percent, Sweden 8 percent, the U.S. 6 percent, and Great Britain under 3 percent. Service workers, on the other hand, formed a fairly uniform share of male employment, ranging from 6 to 8 percent, although the addition of the armed forces in the United States would somewhat strengthen that country's first place position.

Total female employment constituted a similar share of the total for both sexes in each country, 37–39 percent; the proportion would be higher today. The similarity in overall shares was not, however, repeated in the female shares of the major occupational groups. Among managers and administrators, for example, the female share of employment was 21.4 percent in Sweden, 16.6 percent in the U.S., 8.5 percent in Great Britain, and 5.4 percent in Japan. In professional and technical occupations, on the other hand, the female share was 40–41 percent in each country, except for Sweden where it was 47 percent. Sales workers also showed disparities, with a share of over 70 percent in Sweden and Great Britain and under 40 percent in the U.S. and Japan.

Turning from the female shares of total employment by major occupational groups to the distribution of total female employment among major occupational groups, we find a more even distribution than among males, with less spread between the highest and lowest categories in each country. Nevertheless, the countries varied. Reflecting the importance of the public sector services in Sweden, professional and technical occupations of women ranked first (26.7 percent), followed by clerical, service, and manual occupations. For American and British females, clerical occupations dominated, followed by service, manual, and professional and technical occupations. Likewise, in Japan clerical occupations were first (22.9 percent), followed by manual, agricultural, and sales occupations. Japan thus showed two categories of female employment, agriculture and sales, which did not appear in the top ranks of the other countries, probably because of the importance in Japan of unpaid female family labor in small farms and shops.

The distribution of the total employed population by such status designations as employer, self-employed, employee, and family labor also reveals cross-national differences. Non-employees, that is, employers, the self-employed, or unpaid family workers, are found relatively more frequently in Japan than in the other countries, with the result that in several fields of employment, wage and salary workers constitute a much smaller share in Japan than in the other countries. Germany and Australia also have had relatively low proportions of employees. In 1963, for example, only 58.2 percent of the Japanese labor force and 79.2 percent of the German labor force were employees, in contrast to over 90 percent in the United Kingdom, the country with the lowest proportion of employers, self-employed, or family workers. By 1972, the gap between Japan and the U.K. had narrowed, but Japan still had about one-third of its labor force outside of paid employee status (Maneval et al. 1976, App. Table 2; Australia 1979b, pp.98–100; OECD 1980a).

Although country patterns generally were closer to one another by 1978, Japan, and to a lesser extent Australia and Germany, continued to have a lower share of employees than the other countries. While all countries displayed a drop in the share of unpaid family workers, by 1978 Japan still had 11.8 percent in this category against under 1 percent in Australia, Sweden, the U.S., and the U.K. (estimated), and 4.9 percent in Germany. The proportion of employers and self-employed rose in Australia to 15.4 percent by 1978, second only to Japan's 17.8 percent. Sweden and the U.K. had under 8 percent in this category (OECD 1980a). Precise information about distribution by employment status is not available for the youth labor force, but it may be assumed that cross-national differences are somewhat smaller for youth than for the entire labor force, especially in regard to self-employment which currently is a larger category than family worker. Within the employee group, countries appear to have similar divisions between blue and white collar workers (Hönekopp and Ullmann 1980, Table 5).

Trends in unemployment rates separate the United States, with consistently high unemployment rates 1960–1980, from Japan, consistently low, and the other four countries whose low rates of the 1960s and early 1970s have risen considerably since; in the case of Sweden, the level of recorded unemployment should be adjusted for the large number of unemployed removed from the count by labor market measures. Youth unemployment, absolutely and relative to adult, has changed from a negligible or nonexistent issue in the 1950s and 1960s to a major problem in the 1970s and 1980s in Australia, Great Britain, and Sweden. The change was less marked in Germany and Japan. In the United States, where youth unemployment rates and ratios were much higher to begin with, the relative youth position did not deteriorate even as youth unemployment rates rose. Subgroups of youth, particularly black youth, however, experienced a worsening of their position vis-à-vis other youth and adults.

Cross-national differences in employment growth rates and employment/population ratios for various age-sex groups will be explored in Chapter 2, as will trends in the youth share of total employment.

Issues and Hypotheses

It is an assumption of this study that in each country the types of jobs held by teenagers and young adults differ in significant respects from those held by other age groups, and that the divergence between teenage and prime age males is especially marked. Support for the view that youth employment diverges from that of adults can be drawn from the models of the labor market that economists have offered in extension of or in opposition to neoclassical economic assumptions about the homogeneity, free mobility, and wage flexibility in the labor market. Whether these doctrines explicitly mention youth and whether they stress factors in the labor market or the attributes of individuals, they state or imply that young people are likely to have different and inferior jobs compared to adults. This situation of youth may be portrayed as natural and expected in the process of entry and progress in the labor market, as in human capital theory (Becker 1964; Mincer 1970, 1974; Psacharopoulos 1978) or life-cycle models (Loveridge and Mok 1979; Sleeper 1975). It may also appear as the outcome of rational employer reaction to rigidities in the wage and job structures and differences in the experience and trainability of workers, as in the "queue" model (Thurow 1969, 1975).

Other doctrines are based on outright discrimination against certain groups, of which youth may be one, or discrimination arising from perceived differences in prospective workers' qualities arising from earlier unequal preparation, or discrimination due to familial position and income needs (Marshall 1974; Bergmann 1971; Schiller 1973; Aigner and Cain 1977; Loveridge and Mok 1979; Stiglitz 1973; Ledrut 1966; Rubery and Wilkinson 1980). In segmented labor market approaches, the structure and characteristics of labor markets and the various clusters of jobs, whatever the sources of the segmentation, provide the setting for the assignment of young people, among others, to inferior, unstable jobs. Once in such jobs young people have a negative work experience that is unfavorable to upward mobility, in contrast to youth with identical characteristics who start out in job segments with internal labor markets and primary sector jobs (Harrison and Sum 1979; Edwards et al. 1975; Edwards 1979; Buchele 1976; Carnoy 1978; Cain 1976;

Doeringer and Piore 1971; Ryan 1980; Kalleberg and Sorensen 1979; Rosenberg 1975; Wachter 1974; Loveridge and Mok 1979; Freiburghaus 1976; Falkenburg and Vissers 1978).

Sociologists also offer occupational and earnings attainment models that specify or imply differential status according to age. Entry positions of youth in relation to adults are similar to those described by human capital theory, but the sociologists are concerned with the societal factors determining the range of entry positions and restricted mobility paths as well as intergenerational change (Blau and Duncan 1967; Duncan et al. 1972; Duncan and Featherman 1973; Featherman et al. 1974; Glass 1954; Rutter and Madge 1976; Sewell and Hauser 1975; Sommers 1979; Sorensen 1974; Spilerman 1977; Stewart et al. 1980; Lipset and Bendix 1959). Structural theories use the stratification of enterprises, occupational groups, and society to explain how certain groups, including youth, may be denied access to the favored enterprises or jobs "by purposive social action on the part of employers, unions, and other dominant groups" (Bibb and Form 1977, p.978; see also, Form and Huber 1976; Jackson 1970; Rubery 1978; Freedman 1976, ch.7; Beck et al. 1978).

Thus, our assumption of a divergence between youth and adults in types of jobs has considerable backing in the theoretical and empirical literature. To make such an assumption is not to deny the existence of decided variation within the youth group. Differences among youth, such as age, sex, marital status, educational level, training, aspirations, socioeconomic background, race, ethnicity, and place of residence, may be significantly associated with disparity in jobs. All that is needed, however, to sustain the proposition that youth jobs differ significantly from adult is a finding that the variations within the youth group are smaller than those between youth as a whole and adults. Ample room is left for substitutability among the age groups, and the complementarity of young to older workers is not questioned at all.

One need not maintain that a distinct and separate youth labor market exists in order to posit significant differences in the composition and characteristics of the employment of various age groups. Demonstration of a distinct youth labor market, implying that young people are a separate productive factor of low quality and output, would, of course, cinch the case. Such a market has been discerned in a study of the wage structure of industrial workers in the European Community nations:

> there is a separate market for juvenile labour which provides a pool of cheap unskilled labour for jobs often of a relatively short duration [Marsden 1980, p.92].

A youth labor market can also be defined as one in which the vast majority of all employed young people work in jobs or occupations in which a majority or significant proportion of all workers are young (Willauer 1974, pp.188–89). On this stricter definition, it would be difficult to establish the existence of a youth labor market in our countries (see Chapter 3).

Analysts may refer to a youth labor market without, however, defining it precisely or accepting its separate existence (Kalachek 1969b; Barton 1975; Osterman 1980). Osterman, for example, makes liberal use of the phrase "youth labor market" in his title, chapter headings, and text, but he also asserts that "there is no youth segment of the labor market" (Osterman 1980, p.22). While it is unnecessary to postulate a youth labor market, we find the concept of "youth jobs" or entry jobs of practical utility (Folk 1968; Kalachek 1969a). The characteristics of "youth jobs" are overlapping but not identical with the jobs held by youth.

A second major hypothesis is that within the youth group, there will be substantial differences in types of jobs, earnings, availability of training, ease of obtaining first and subsequent jobs, degree of job turnover, and related factors. While the emphasis is on youth who have permanently or temporarily left the educational system, separate attention will be given to students who work in the countries where this is relevant. Wherever possible, the two main youth age groups and all youth subgroups will be divided by sex. Differences in the composition and characteristics of employment by sex are hypothesized to equal or exceed those by other variables, such as age, education, socioeconomic status, family income, race, ethnicity, religion, immigrant status, and place of residence. These characteristics provide the chief bases for establishing the youth subgroups.

The following are the more important dimensions of employment expected to display disparities in jobs between youth and other age groups and within the youth group, separately for each sex:

Nature of the Job
Degree of skill, complexity, and autonomy; age requirements; nature of tasks; status and titles; degree of danger and exertion; quality of workplace physical environment; relations with supervisors and co-workers.

Wage rates; fringe benefits; methods of payment; paid vacations and sick leave; travel and other work costs.

Scheduled full week, full year work; availability of overtime; required shift, night, and holiday work; seasonal or temporary work.

Training and promotion opportunities; seniority provisions; lay-off and dismissal procedures; vulnerability to displacement; unionized job; coverage by social protection laws.

Nature of Firms and Industries
Firms: size of workforce and job hierarchy; age, sex, and skill composition; recruitment methods; age limits in hiring and promotion; ports of entry; promotion ladders; wage payment methods; fringe benefits; technology and capital intensity; continuity of

establishment, firm, and direction; profit rate; degree of market power; presence and activities of trade union; location relative to labor supply's residence; provision of transportation.

Industries: age, sex, skill composition of workforce; method of wage payment; type of product, average size of firms, growth patterns, profitability, technology, capital intensity, product market concentration, extent of competition, extent, type and role of unions.

Geographic location; distance from population centers; transportation facilities; physical aspects of workplace.

This less than exhaustive list of indicators might be used to distinguish youth from adult jobs as well as to establish job differences *within* the youth group, an equally important subject. We recognize the paucity of data on certain points, difficulties in quantifying some of the variables, and problems in separating the inherent from the acquired characteristics of jobs, resulting from an adjustment of jobs to the preparation, qualities, and desires of the available labor supply (Rumberger 1981). It also is possible that significant differences between young people and adults in attitudes, motivation, and behavior have a bearing on the jobs held by various age groups. The effects on young people of living at home, depending on parental financial support, and limited geographical mobility, especially of younger teenagers, are relevant, as are the changes accompanying marriage and family responsibilities.

While all of the above factors are relevant at any given time, their shape and character may alter over time, making an exploration of trends in youth/adult employment and in the jobs held within the youth group a subject of prime interest in each country.

In addition to comparisons between and within age groups based on cross-sectional data, longitudinal data and analyses of various youth cohorts will be utilized to document the hypotheses and establish the trends over time in youth employment.

Cross-National Comparisons

Variations among the countries in the composition of young people's employment can be attributed in part to overall differences in the structure and type of employment available. It would be unreasonable to expect that young people on the whole should have superior jobs to those provided by the economy as a whole. Thus, young people in a country whose total job structure contains a relatively high share of inferior or unrewarding jobs would probably display an unfavorable situation on a comparative basis. But, such a judgment should also take account of whether the youth in the first country have a smaller or larger share of these jobs than the youth of the other countries. Differences in the organization of work, staffing of firms, and nomenclature of jobs clearly affect such comparisons. Account should also be taken of special institutional arrangements or business practices that bear on the cross-national analysis of youth employment.

Cross-national differences in the average age and qualifications of a group of young people, their share of the population and labor force, and attributes or behavior also influence comparisons of the composition of youth employment. Even if youth attitudes toward specific jobs are similar to adult attitudes in each country, there may be significant cross-national disparities in youth attitudes. The size of the youth labor supply depends mainly on demographic trends, educational enrollment rates, and propensities to work while at school, with the two latter forces fluctuating with economic conditions (Reubens et al. 1981). Each country's distribution of jobs between youth and others will be affected by the overall level of demand for labor as it interacts with the relative supply of youth labor. In circumstances where the demand for labor is strong relative to the supply of labor in general, and to the youth supply in particular, it might be anticipated that the entering cohort of youth could have an easy time finding jobs, locating somewhat better jobs and advancing more rapidly than their immediate predecessors in a less tight labor market or than contemporaries in another country with a looser labor market. Evidence of this sort has been produced for the United States (Okun 1973; Vroman 1977; Thurow 1969; Thurow and Lucas 1972). Cross-national comparisons of the structure and characteristics of youth employment, therefore, must allow for differences in the tightness of labor markets, especially for youth.

Another variation across nations is in trends in the number and type of "entry level" jobs relative both to total employment and to the number of new entrants. Either demographic factors or changes in the educational attainment and qualifications of new entrants might be responsible for disparity, or there might be an independent change in the number of entry jobs. For example, institutional rigidities introduced through the job security provisions of legislation and collective bargaining agreements became increasingly common and widespread in some countries in the 1970s, and consequent changes in recruitment and work organization have worsened the employment position of youth vis-à-vis other age groups (OECD 1982a, pp.60–65). Youth is seen as part of

> the non-protected group of workers, the highly mobile and adaptable . . .
> The emergence of casual jobs with no stability, social protection or career prospects also implies a serious long-term risk: those who accept these types of jobs now will find it difficult to make the transition to better jobs later on. This is particularly serious in the case of young people who meet institutional and behavioral barriers on the market for "good jobs" and thus have no other choice than to "price themselves into the market" by accepting low-status, low-paid jobs. In the absence of serious and continuous work experience and on-the-job training the chances of these young people eventually being absorbed into the market for skilled labour are practically zero [OECD 1982a, p.65].

Whether countries are equally affected by these developments and the extent to which they concern all youth or only certain youth subgroups should emerge in a comparative examination.

Throughout the book certain common designations will be used. The total working age population and total employed exclude those under 15 years and have no upper age limit for the employed, except in Sweden where it is 74 years. Adults are those 25 years and over or 25–74 in Sweden. Youth as a whole are those under 25 years of age but not less than 15. At all times, a distinction is made between young adults, 20–24 years old, and teenagers who are 15–19 in Australia, Germany, Japan, and Great Britain (to 1972) and 16–19 in Sweden and the United States, and Great Britain (from 1973), according to the legal age to begin paid employment and to leave school. In teenage employment data, variations among countries in the starting age may impair some cross-national conclusions, especially those dealing with ratios between age groups or employment/population ratios (Chapter 2).

The book uses two different approaches to obtain a comparative view of youth employment. Chapters 2 and 3 analyze cross-sectional occupational data for a number of countries, drawn from similar sources. While sex and broad age divisions in these data are an essential part of the analysis, no attempt is made in Chapters 2 and 3 to study subnational aspects, whether they be geographical, racial, educational level, or other significant factors.

The second approach consists of six separate studies of youth employment in individual countries, using a common framework of inquiry (Chapters 4–9). Each chapter begins with an overview of the youth labor market since 1960 or earlier. As background information from which cross-national comparisons later may be made, each chapter presents a brief account of the national systems of education and training and the flows within and out of these systems. This is followed by a series of capsule statements on the chief statutory provisions and institutional arrangements of each country bearing on youth employment to be drawn on by the chapter authors subsequently and to aid the later cross-national discussion. The discussion of youth employment proper begins with a section on students who work during the term. Relevant only to some of the countries, such a section will document the extent, trend, and character of student jobs and provide the base for comparisons with the jobs of non-students of the same age. Next, the authors of the country chapters will delineate as many aspects of the employment of out-of-school youth as national data permit.

Comparisons of youth and adult jobs follow along the same lines in each chapter, but add sections on age differences and trends in hours of work, varied job characteristics, and earnings. Trends in the earnings of youth relative to adults can be interpreted both as evidence of age differences in types of jobs and as an influence on employers' willingness to hire and train youth. Finally, in those countries in which longitudinal data have been collected, descriptive and analytic materials will be presented to illuminate the later employment, unemployment, and earnings experience of cohorts of youth, divided according to their initial experience. A summary of the findings on youth employment will conclude each chapter. To the extent that data allow, the country chapters will utilize cross-sectional and longitudinal data, local studies, finer age breaks, and subnational divisions by race, ethnicity, educational level, and place of residence. Each country chapter will attempt to go beyond occupational data to the characteristics of the jobs held by young people and other age groups, as outlined earlier in this chapter. A more comprehensive and up-to-date view of youth employment in each country should emerge from the separate chapters than can be conveyed in the cross-national reviews of Chapters 2 and 3. Chapter 10 draws all of the material together into a comparative appraisal.

2

Trends in Numbers Employed 1960–1980

John A.C. Harrisson, Beatrice G. Reubens, and Pamela Sparr

This chapter examines the number of persons in employment, in aggregate and by age and sex, and in absolute and relative terms. Trends for the period 1960–80 are examined for Australia, West Germany, Great Britain, Japan, Sweden, and the United States. In addition to providing the background information for subsequent chapters, we will inquire whether a positive relationship exists between the magnitudes and directions of change in aggregate employment and change in the employment levels of the four age-sex youth groups.

The measurement of total employment over a period of time, even for a single country, raises questions about the temporal stability of various types of employment within the total. For example, it seems likely that part-time and full-time employment would grow at varying speeds, and that a composite employment figure might not mean precisely the same thing at the start and at the finish of the measurement period. Indeed, some Australian analysts regard part-time and full-time employment as aspects of separate labor markets and view them as exerting contradictory influences which tend to cancel out when aggregated. Total employment data are adequate for establishing how many and what share of the population are gainfully occupied, but for other purposes, it is desirable to have greater disaggregation of the employment data, along the lines indicated by a Swedish example of different rates of change in the components of total employment (Björklund et al. 1979, Table 5).*

---

*Full references are given at the end of Chapter 3.

The overall Swedish employment rate of the 16–74 year-old population 1965–78 showed a slight increase—from 65.5 percent to 68.7 percent of 16–74 year-olds, but the rate for full-time employment dropped from 48.6 to 40.8 percent, part-time employment climbed from 10.6 to 16.8 percent, and the temporarily-absent employed rate rose steeply from 6.3 to 11.1 percent. These divergent movements would be concealed by a single statistic on employment growth. Moreover, such a statistic would convey an inaccurate impression of total labor inputs to production. In fact, from 1965 to 1978, the total weekly hours worked in Sweden fell from 139.5 to 124.9 million, although part of the decline may be due to reduced work time per individual in full-time employment, in keeping with worldwide trends (Cain 1977).

Reservations in regard to a time series on total employment for a single country would be multiplied in a cross-national comparison. Even if the general tendencies were similar to those described for Sweden, the distribution at the start among the components and the rate of change for each component would vary among the countries (see Leon 1981b). These valid points notwithstanding, our comparative data refer only to total employment, chiefly because similar data to the Swedish were unavailable for the other countries and partly because age-sex comparisons would become unduly complex.

Whether they show the total hours worked per year or average weekly hours, the data confirm that countries varied at the outset and over time (Moy 1979; Japan 1980a; Germany 1980a, p.22; OECD 1981a). With regard to temporary absence from work, the Japanese rate is and has been far lower than in other countries (Shimada 1980). On balance, the series for Japan more nearly reflects changes in full-time employment than do the data for any of the other countries.

A further issue concerns cross-national variation in the statistical concepts, definitions, survey methods, and timing of the collection of employment data. These factors, however, create relatively minor problems of comparability, and fewer than in comparisons of unemployment statistics. The employment and population statistics analyzed in this chapter are generally drawn from similar types of surveys and follow consistent definitions in the several countries. Data for Japan and the United States are annual averages of monthly labor force surveys, while the Swedish data for 1963–69 reflect averages of quarterly surveys and thereafter of monthly surveys; the exclusion of certain summer months before 1970 possibly affect employment data, particularly for teenagers. We revised the U.S. data to include the armed forces in both population and employment, using data provided by the Bureau of Labor Statistics. West German annual average population data come from the Federal Statistical Service; German employment data are annual averages, drawn from the Federal Statistical Service, with age-group data estimated by the Federal Employment Research Institute and augmented by the authors. Australian data are from a revised series based on the August labor force survey which has been adjusted for revised population estimates and new labor force survey techniques; data have not been seasonally adjusted. The British series on population and employment each come from a different source, raising some problems of comparability. Moreover, the British employment series, a mid-year, seasonally unadjusted estimate, may not be fully comparable to those of the other countries, since the British data exclude employers, the self-employed, and family workers.

Annual employment data for Japan and the U.S. cover the entire period 1960–80, while West German data are for 1960–79. Swedish annual data begin in 1963 and Australian in 1966. The British annual series with age breakdowns run from 1960 through 1972, with an additional series for 1973–80 for all ages combined. Ideally, measurement of both employment and unemployment data would occur between cyclically comparable years in each country. Data limitations have, however, prevented such dating. The method used to calculate the annual employment growth rate—the least squares trend of the logarithms of the annual data—copes with the problem of giving undue weight to the first and last years. The age span of the population and employment data is 15 years and over in Australia, Germany, and Japan. In Great Britain, it is 15 years and over through 1972 and then 16 years and over, while in the U.S. it is 16 years and over throughout. Sweden, with a coverage of those 16–74 years-old, is the only country with an upper limit.

While the surveys vary slightly in their practice with regard to the inclusion in employment data of such groups as the armed forces, conscripts, unpaid family workers, those waiting to report to work, the temporarily absent from work, temporarily laid-off persons, and those in government training programs, the changes in practice within countries were not so marked 1960–80 as to invalidate the construction of employment trends. Nor is there much initial difference among the countries or change over time in the methods used to distinguish the employed from the unemployed, a factor that could affect comparative employment levels and trends. Similarly, the unrecorded employed are a relatively small group in all of these countries and too little is known about their precise numbers to cause the official totals to be rejected. Cross-national differences attributable to statistical or data practices will be pointed out where relevant but, on the whole, the comparison is based on compatible employment series; the national data series compared reasonably well with similar data adjusted to U.S. concepts by the U.S. Bureau of Labor Statistics (US 1978a, ch.2).

This chapter will be based on three data series: employment levels; shares of total employment held by various age-sex groups; and employment/population (E/P) ratios. While medium-term trends are the focus of attention, there will be some discussion of annual patterns, particularly where these show divergence or fluctuate significantly within the overall period.

Total Employment: Levels and Growth Rates

The three non-European countries led in aggregate employment growth in the period 1960–80 during which four of the six countries experienced positive growth (Table 2.1). In addition to employees, the employment totals include employers, the self-employed and family workers, except in Britain, and the armed forces, except in Australia and Britain. Averaging 1.9 percent aggregate employment growth a year, the U.S. was in first place, closely followed by Australia (1966–80). Next came Japan and Sweden. Great Britain experienced no measurable growth over the two decades, using a composite rate based on two employment series, while Germany displayed a small decline in the total number employed. British and German trends describe the experience of many Western European countries in the two decades; Sweden might be in the same category were it not for the advance of part-time employment. The Australian growth rate might have surpassed that of the U.S., if Australian data had included the armed forces and had extended back to 1960–65, a time of rapidly expanding employment (Australia 1979b, p.91). By comparison, the employment growth rates of Canada, another "new world" country, exceeded those of both the U.S. and Australia over a similar period, based on U.S. concepts (US 1978a, p.22). In all of the countries showing growth, the increased share of part-time workers in the total was notable.

Year-to-year growth trends followed two main patterns in the 1960–80 period. Total employment growth in the U.S., Australia, Japan, and Sweden registered increases in almost every year; only the 1974–75 recession produced a downturn, except for Sweden. Britain's employment peaked in 1966, declined to 1972 and then, according to an unpublished series, fluctuated slightly until it dropped below 22 million in 1980. After an initial rise between 1960 and 1965, Germany experienced oscillations in employment levels until 1973; an annual decline 1974–77 was reversed by 1978, but in 1980 there again was a drop. From 1979, the gap between the European and non-European countries tended to widen.

The vast disparity between countries in the number of net additional jobs created over two decades is highlighted by comparing the United States and Japan. Over 31 million additional jobs were added to the U.S. economy between 1960 and 1980, whereas Japan added almost 11 million in the same period. Even when allowance is made for an average population ratio (15 years and over) of almost 2:1, the U.S. employment performance greatly outstripped the Japanese. A calculation based on changes in total hours worked would, however, considerably reduce the American advantage.

Table 2.1   Employment Growth, Employment-to-Population Ratios, and Unemployment Rates, 15 Years and Over, Both Sexes, Six Countries, 1960-1980

	Australia	Germany	Great Britain	Japan	Sweden	United States
Total employment[a]						
1960 (000)	4,823.8[b]	26,086.5	22,220.0	44,600.0	3,658.7[c]	68,292.0
1980 (000)	6,246.7	25,548.0[d]	21,906.0	55,360.0	4,232.3	99,373.0
Annual growth rate[e]	1.8	-0.3	*	1.0	0.9	1.9
Country rank	2	6	5	3	4	1
Youth[f] share						
1960	26.8[b]	26.0	22.2	23.3	18.5[c]	17.0
1980	25.1	20.6[d]	21.6[g]	12.2	15.9	22.5
E/P ratios[a]						
1960	.59[b]	.60	.57	.68	.66[c]	.57
1980	.58	.51[d]	.55[g]	.62	.70	.60
Unemployment rates[a,h]						
1960	1.6[b]	1.1	2.1	1.7	1.7[c]	5.5
1980	6.1	3.0[d]	7.4	2.0	2.0	7.1
Country rank[i]	2	3	1	5.5	5.5	4

*Less than 0.05 percent. Discontinuous series 1960-72 and 1973-80.
[a]15 years and over, except 16-74 in Sweden, 16 and over in the United States and, in 1980, in Great Britain. [b]1966. [c]1963. [d]1979. [e]Computed from the least squares trend of the logarithms of annual employment data. [f]Less than 25 years old. [g]1972. [h]Adjusted to U.S. concepts by Bureau of Labor Statistics. [i]Percentage point change 1960 to 1980.

Note: Employment data are annual averages of monthly data, except Sweden (quarterly before 1970), Australia (August data) and Great Britain (mid-year estimates). Employment includes paid employees, employers, self-employed, unpaid family workers, apprentices, part-time workers, and the armed forces. Great Britain excludes employers, self-employed, family workers, and armed forces. Australia excludes armed forces. Sweden excludes military conscripts not previously employed. Temporarily laid-off excluded, except in United States. Great Britain includes some unemployed with recent jobs. Population data include the armed forces, except Australia, and institutionalized persons, except United States. Germany includes West Berlin. Japan excludes Okinawa in 1960.

Source: Australia 1974-82; Germany 1978-82; unpublished data; Germany 1963-82; Great Britain 1960-1982a; unpublished data; Great Britain 1960-82b; Japan 1960-82; Sweden 1963-82; United States 1978b, 1981a; Moy and Sorrentino 1981; unpublished data on international unemployment rates adjusted to U.S. concepts by BLS.

Overall employment growth owed much to the expansion in female employment. The excess of female over male positive employment growth rates was greatest in Sweden, the U.S., and Australia, where the differential was 2.0 percentage points or more (Tables 2.2, 2.3; Japan 1981b). Positive growth for British females offset a decline in the male rate, while in Germany the decline for females was smaller than for males. In Japan, the rate of female employment expansion was lower than the male, but the latter was higher than the male growth rate in the other countries. The number of net new female jobs conveys dramatically the contribution of women's employment to the total. For example, in the United States, for the period 1960-80, the number of female jobs increased by more than 19.5 million, against a male rise of over 11.5 million. Similarly, as Swedish women showed over 550,000

Table 2.2   Employment Growth, Males, by Age, Six Countries, 1960-1980

	Australia	Germany	Great Britain	Japan	Sweden	United States
Total employment[a]						
1960 (000)	3,365.6[b]	16,412.6	14,370.0	26,480.0	2,315.6[c]	46,386.0
1980 (000)	3,970.9	16,024.0[d]	14,060.0[e]	33,940.0	2,326.8	57,931.0
Annual growth rate[f]	1.1	-0.3	-0.3	1.3	*	1.2
Country rank	3	5.5	5.5	1	4	2
Teenage employment[g]						
1960 (000)	337.8[b]	1,494.5	1,281.0	2,310.0	160.2[c]	2,758.0
1980 (000)	350.1	1,275.5[d]	1,078.0[e]	690.0	118.2	4,294.0
Annual growth rate[f]	0.3	-0.8	-2.1	-7.0	-1.7	2.6
Country rank	2	3	5	6	4	1
Young adult employment[h]						
1960 (000)	398.7[b]	2,125.6	1,334.0	3,200.0	210.6[c]	4,720.0
1980 (000)	516.0	1,655.3[d]	1,569.0[e]	2,690.0	231.6	7,989.0
Annual growth rate[f]	1.3	-0.8	2.1	-1.2	-0.2	2.9
Country rank	3	5	2	6	4	1
Adult employment[i]						
1960 (000)	2,629.2[b]	12,792.5	11,755.0	20,970.0	1,944.8[c]	38,908.0
1980 (000)	3,104.8	13,093.2[d]	11,413.0[e]	30,560.0	1,977.0	45,648.0
Annual growth rate[f]	1.1	-0.2	-0.4	2.0	0.1	0.8
Country rank	2	5	6	1	4	3

*Less than 0.05 percent.
[a]15 years and over, except 16-74 in Sweden, 16 and over in the United States.   [b]1966.
[c]1963.   [d]1979.   [e]1972.   [f]Computed from the least squares trend of the logarithms of annual employment data.   [g]15-19, except 16-19 in Sweden and the United States.   [h]20-24.
[i]25 and over, except 25-74 in Sweden.

Note: German age group data 1960-1974 were developed from estimates by IAB.

Source: See sources and notes to Table 2.1.

new jobs, many of them part-time, men registered a net gain of only 11,000.

Employment/population ratios (E/P) that establish the proportions of the population employed at the beginning and the end of the period indicate that the strong employment growth of the U.S. and Australia is less impressive and that of Sweden and Japan becomes more significant. E/P ratios, considered one of the most accurate indicators of labor market conditions (Leon 1981a), show that in 1960 or another initial year, E/P ratios in the six countries for both sexes 15 years and over had a narrow range of .57 to .68, where 1.00 would represent employment of all in an age-sex group. Japan and Sweden had the highest E/P ratios, chiefly due to the elevated E/P ratios of their females, although Japanese and Swedish male E/P ratios also somewhat exceeded those in the other countries (Table 2.4). Thus, at the outset, total employment levels in Japan and Sweden were higher in relation to population than in the other countries, including the U.S. and Australia, the leaders in total employment growth 1960–80 whose 1960 E/P ratios were among the lowest.

Table 2.3   Employment Growth, Females, by Age, Six Countries, 1960-1980

	Australia	Germany	Great Britain	Japan	Sweden	United States
Total employment[a]						
1960 (000)	1,458.2[b]	9,673.9	7,850.0	18,120.0	1,343.1[c]	21,906.0
1980 (000)	2,275.8	9,524.0[d]	8,553.0[e]	21,420.0	1,905.5	41,442.0
Annual growth rate[f]	3.1	-0.2	0.8	0.7	2.3	3.3
Country rank	2	6	4	5	3	1
Teenage employment[g]						
1960 (000)	313.7[b]	1,383.7	1,266.0	2,150.0	143.4[c]	1,776.0
1980 (000)	300.9	1,025.7[d]	1,051.0[e]	720.0	110.9	3,615.0
Annual growth rate[f]	-0.4	-1.9	-2.0	-6.5	-1.5	4.2
Country rank	2	4	5	6	3	1
Young adult employment[h]						
1960 (000)	241.1[b]	1,771.4	1,050.0	2,730.0	161.4[c]	2,376.0
1980 (000)	398.2	1,303.8[d]	1,181.0[e]	2,640.0	213.1	6,437.0
Annual growth rate[f]	2.8	-1.3	2.0	-0.5	1.0	5.5
Country rank	2	6	3	5	4	1
Adult employment[i]						
1960 (000)	903.4[b]	6,518.8	5,534.0	13,240.0	1,038.3[c]	17,754.0
1980 (000)	1,576.7	7,194.4[d]	6,321.0[e]	18,060.0	1,581.5	31,390.0
Annual growth rate[f]	4.1	0.3	1.1	1.6	2.8	2.8
Country rank	1	6	5	4	2.5	2.5

[a]15 years and over, except 16-74 in Sweden, 16 and over in the United States.   [b]1966.   [c]1963.   [d]1979.   [e]1972.   [f]Computed from the least squares trend of the logarithms of annual employment data.   [g]15-19, except 16-19 in Sweden and the United States.   [h]20-24.   [i]25 and over, except 25-74 in Sweden.

Source: See sources and notes to Tables 2.1, 2.2.

Compared to 1960, 1980 E/P ratios for both sexes 15 years and over had declined in four countries (Germany, Japan, Great Britain, and Australia), and had increased in Sweden (to .70) and the U.S. (to .60). Sweden and Japan continued in leading positions, while the U.S. had moved from last to third place and Australia remained in fourth place (Table 2.1). Germany, which slipped from third to last place, and Britain, in fifth place after having tied for last in 1960, clearly accounted for the widened inter-country range of E/P ratios in 1980; 19 percentage points now separated the countries, instead of the 11 shown in 1960. The increased proportion of women at work in Sweden and the U.S. offset the decline in male E/P ratios (15 and over) that all six countries experienced due to prolonged education and earlier retirement. While E/P ratios for females (15 years and over) also rose in Australia and Great Britain in connection with the growth of employment in the service sector, the increase was insufficient to counteract the male E/P decrease. In Germany and Japan, each sex showed a drop in E/P ratios; the female decrease was attributable to the decline of employment on family farms and in small businesses without offsetting shifts into industrial and service employment. Despite the decreased male E/P ratios in Japan, in 1980 Japan and Sweden still led in this category due to a slower reduction in retirement age, while for females,

Table 2.4 Employment-to-Population Ratios, by Age and Sex, Six Countries,
          1960–1980

	15 years and over[a]		25 years and over[b]		20–24 years		15–19 years[c]	
	1960	1980	1960	1980	1960	1980	1960	1980
	(ratio)							
Males								
Australia	.83[d]	.74	.85[d]	.76	.93[d]	.83	.65[d]	.54
Germany	.82	.69[e]	.82	.71[e]	.87[e]	.72[e]	.72	.49[e]
Great Britain	.78	.71[f]	.77	.72[f]	.84	.80[f]	.74	.56[f]
Japan	.84	.78	.90	.87	.86	.67	.52	.16
Sweden	.84[g]	.77	.87[g]	.79	.80[g]	.82	.61[g]	.52
United States	.80	.73	.83	.75	.84	.77	.51	.51
Females								
Australia	.35[d]	.41	.28[d]	.37	.57[d]	.65	.61[d]	.48
Germany	.41	.36[e]	.34	.33[e]	.76	.60[e]	.69	.41[e]
Great Britain	.38	.40[f]	.32	.36[f]	.64	.61[f]	.75	.57[f]
Japan	.54	.47	.52	.48	.70	.68	.48	.18
Sweden	.48[g]	.63	.46[g]	.63	.63[g]	.78	.57[g]	.51
United States	.36	.48	.35	.46	.42	.62	.34	.44

[a]16–74 in Sweden; 16 and over in the United States. [b]25–74 in Sweden.
[c]16–19 in Sweden and the United States. [d]1966. [e]1979. [f]1972. [g]1963.

Source: See sources and notes to Tables 2.1, 2.2.

Sweden's primacy was unchallenged due to the influx of women and the growth of part-time work to 45 percent of female employment.

By the measure of overall unemployment rates also, Japanese and Swedish employment growth 1960–80 appeared to be more adequate to the needs of the labor force than American and Australian. Japan and Sweden had the lowest total unemployment rates and the U.S. and Australia among the highest in 1979, using rates made more comparable by adjustment to U.S. concepts (Table 2.1). For special reasons, visible unemployment tended to remain relatively low in Sweden and Japan. In Sweden, widespread labor market measures provided employment status for a large proportion of potentially unemployed persons (Rehnberg 1981; Björklund et al. 1979, Table 1). The tendency of Japanese companies to retain or transfer employees within and among their companies when work is slack limited the reduction in employment levels (Shimada 1980). Germany also kept its unemployment rate artificially low by deliberate efforts to reduce labor force participation and send foreign workers home (Schmid 1981). Thus, trends over two decades in the employment climate in the six countries, judged by E/P ratios and unemployment rates, revealed the U.S. and Australia in a less favorable position and Japan and Sweden in a more favorable light than was indicated by employment growth rates alone.

A full exploration of the explanatory factors in cross-national differences in total employment growth lies beyond our present purposes, even if an agreed upon conceptual framework and all of the necessary data were available. A few obvious variables can be tested, however, using Spearman rank correlation coefficients. Thus, a close and significant association was found for the six countries between rank in growth of total employment and in growth of population (15 years and over both sexes) 1960–80 ($r_s = +.77$).* This result demonstrates the importance of the size of the potential labor supply for employment growth in industrialized countries; in such countries the demographic factor may also serve as a proxy for growth in aggregate demand. Country ranks for employment and population growth did not differ by more than one rank. Australia, Britain, and Japan displayed annual population growth rates (15 years and over) exceeding those for total employment, while the reverse was true in Sweden and the U.S., and is explained by the rapid rise of female employment in those countries. Germany, on the other hand, had population growth accompanied by a decline in employment.

Country ranks in growth in Gross Domestic Product (GDP) performed poorly as an explanation of the country ranks in employment growth ($r_s = +.20$).† Based on 1975 prices, GDP rose in all six countries (OECD 1981c) and in each case far more rapidly than employment 1960–79. It is likely that the variety, complexity, and changeability of the factors entering into actual GDP growth tend to complicate the relationship between medium-term GDP and employment growth. If such factors as technology, sectoral distribution of employment, and labor intensity of output were held constant, the expected positive and proportionate impact on employment growth rates might be visible.

Finally, country ranks for the percentage point advance in unemployment rates failed to show the expected inverse relation to ranks based on employment growth ($r_s = -.26$). Unemployment rates of prime-age males, often used as an indicator of labor market tightness and general economic conditions, might have been a superior variable, but comparable data for the six countries were not available for the required time period.

---

*Indicates that rank correlation is significant at the .05 level. The Spearman rank rather than the Pearson product-moment correlation method of analysis was used because hypothesis testing with small sample sizes is subject to less restrictive assumptions of normality in rank correlation procedures than in Pearson-type correlations. Rank correlation allows analysis of data where absolutes refer to countries of disparate size, and where slight definitional or coverage variations may reduce the cross-national comparability of the data. The two methods, however, should yield quite similar results, since they ask basically the same questions of the data. For example, the Pearson correlation of growth of population (15 years and over) and growth of total employment in the six countries was $r = +.82$ compared to the Spearman $r_s - +.77$, cited above.

†Indicates that rank correlation is not significant at the .05 or .10 levels.

In summary, with recognition of the limitations of data on total employment, our examination of the trends in the numbers employed in six countries has shown:

• Greatest employment growth over the period 1960–80 occurred in Australia and the U.S., the non-European countries, which had consistent annual increases.
• Least employment growth occurred in Germany and Britain, where alternating periods of increase and decline prevailed.
• Most of the growth in employment or failure to decline more was attributable to the surge in female employment, much of it part-time.
• Employment/Population (E/P) ratios displayed divergent trends and a widening range over the period. Male E/P ratios declined in all countries, whereas female E/P ratios fell only in two countries.
• Sweden and Japan displayed the highest E/P ratios over the period and the smallest rise in visible unemployment, suggesting a favorable relative labor market position. Australia and the United States compared less favorably by the E/P ratio and unemployment measures.
• While a close association between employment growth and population growth was found in a rank correlation, both the positive relationship between employment growth and GDP growth and the inverse relationship with increased unemployment rates were weak.

Youth Employment Trends

While a deeper understanding of the causes of divergent trends in total employment would assist in the analysis of cross-national differences in the employment growth rates for the youth groups, it would not provide all of the required explanations, because the direction and/or magnitude of employment changes in the individual youth groups in the six countries tended to differ from those for total employment (Tables 2.1, 2.2, 2.3). The usual pattern for youth was either lower positive growth rates than for adults or the total, or negative rates for the youth group while the relevant adults and the total showed positive growth or smaller negative rates. Although such divergence from adult patterns was more pronounced for teenagers than for young adults, it was present for both age groups; similarities between the sexes in youth employment trends reinforced the observed age variations. The American pattern, in which each age-sex group experienced positive employment growth, and all youth growth rates exceeded those of both adults and the total of the same sex, was distinctly atypical. Even in Australia, only the rate of young adult males exceeded the rates of both male adults and the male total. In sum, cross-national patterns of employment growth in total and by age-sex groups lacked uniformity.

TEENAGE MALES

Great disparity among the six countries was displayed in the teenage male employment record 1960–80, ranging from impressive annual growth of 2.6 percent in the U.S. down to the enormous annual decline in Japan of −7.0 percent. Adult males (25 years and over) exhibited less variability, but still spread from 2.0 percent growth per year in Japan to −0.4 percent in Great Britain (to 1972). Teenage male employment declined in every country except the U.S. and Australia, while adult male employment rose in every country except Germany and Britain (Table 2.2). Therefore, four countries, the U.S., Australia, Germany and Britain, had the same direction of change for both adult and teenage males, and two, Japan and Sweden, displayed opposite directions. Among the two latter countries, Japan clearly offered the most dramatic contrast, with almost 10 million adult male jobs gained while more than 1.5 million teenage male jobs were lost.

Even where the direction of employment change was the same for the two age groups, the magnitude of the rate of change varied considerably (Table 2.2). The teenage male rate of increase in Australia was much smaller than that of adult males, while in Germany and especially in Britain the teenage male rate of decline was substantially greater than that of adult males. In the U.S., on the other hand, the annual percent increase for adult males was considerably exceeded by the rise for teenage males. Positive growth of teenage male employment in the U.S. and Australia was in considerable measure due to a rising ratio of part-time to full-time employment, representing both choice by a relatively larger student component of the age group in 1980 than in 1960, and, especially in Australia, a reduced availability of full-time jobs for economic reasons in the latter year.

Year-to-year direction of employment changes revealed two groups of countries in regard to conformity between teenage and adult males, although the magnitude of rates of change was substantially different for the two age groups in each of the countries. Three countries showed a correspondence between teenage and adult males in the direction of annual change, if only for part of the period. Annual movements in U.S. teenage male employment, mostly in an upward direction, closely resembled those of adult males throughout the period. In Sweden, the parallels were visible from 1972, but annual fluctuations were small and moved in both directions. In the short period covered by British data, a marked similarity of downward movement was shown 1965–72, allowing a year's lag in the teenage trend. In the other three countries, a resemblance between the annual movements of teenage and adult males either was not present (Australia and Germany) or the two groups' annual movements were in opposite directions (Japan). In 1965–66, all of the countries, except the U.S. and Australia, began a period of annual declines in male teenage employment, lasting seven to twelve years.

Disparate teenage male employment growth rates in the six countries only partially convey differences in the state of the labor market for this age-sex group. Tables 2.4 and 2.5 show the changes in male teenage E/P ratios and teenage shares of total employment, both of which are heavily influenced by demographic trends, trends in educational enrollment rates, and cyclical changes in demand. The range of male teenage E/P ratios in 1960 was quite wide, from .51 to .74; in 1980, excluding Japan's extraordinary .16, the countries were grouped from .49 to .54. Only the U.S. displayed no decline over the two decades (Table 2.4). Shares of total male employment dropped in each country except the U.S., but decreased markedly in Japan (Table 2.5).

Taking these employment indicators together, it can be said that negative teenage male employment growth rates, declining E/P ratios, and a decrease in a group's share of total employment might be acceptable and even viewed favorably, if unemployment rates for the group remained low and educational enrollment rates rose. By this criterion, the astounding drop in Japan's teenage male employment growth rate, in excess of the drop in teenage male population, can be viewed as consistent with an adequate teenage employment situation, indeed a more favorable one than in the other countries. Though the Japanese teenage male E/P ratio and share of total male employment also plunged, the low unemployment rates for the age group, the large number of reported vacancies for each junior high and senior high school graduate over most of the period, and employers' complaints of shortages of young workers confirm that the decline in employment was not induced by reduced demand (see Chapter 7). Ranking of the other countries is difficult, in terms of the adequacy of the teenage male employment situation, but perhaps Germany, Sweden, the U.S., Australia and Great Britain would follow Japan, in that order.

Placement of the employment growth rates for male teenagers 1960–80 in the context of other developments affecting the labor market position of the age-sex group, such as demographic pressure, unemployment trends and general economic conditions, has led to a different ranking of countries. Instead of the ranks for teenage male employment growth rates shown in Table 2.2, in which the U.S., Australia, Germany, Sweden, Great Britain, and Japan followed in sequence, Japan would move to first place, followed by Germany, Sweden, the U.S. and Australia, with Great Britain in last.

TEENAGE FEMALES

Similarity in the employment trends of teenage females and teenage males would be expected on the basis of shared demographic and educational enrollment trends. Country ranks for teenage employment

Table 2.5 Shares of Total Employment, by Age and Sex, Six Countries, 1960-1980

	Proportion of total male employment[a] held by		Proportion of total female employment[a] held by		Proportion of total both sexes employment[a] held by	
	Male teenagers[b]	Male young adults[c]	Female teenagers[b]	Female young adults[c]	Male adults[d]	Female adults[d]
			(percentage)			
Australia						
1966	10.0	11.8	21.5	16.5	54.5	18.7
1970	8.9	13.3	17.1	18.8	52.6	20.8
1975	8.5	12.8	14.4	17.4	51.5	23.6
1980	8.8	13.0	13.2	17.5	49.7	25.2
Germany						
1960	9.1	13.0	14.3	18.3	49.0	25.0
1965	7.8	8.3	12.8	13.1	53.3	27.0
1970	6.8	7.9	10.7	13.1	54.7	27.4
1975	7.8	9.3	10.8	13.4	52.3	28.1
1979	8.0	10.3	10.8	13.7	51.2	28.2
Great Britain						
1960	8.9	9.3	16.1	13.4	52.9	24.9
1965	9.8	10.4	17.4	12.9	50.8	25.3
1970	7.9	12.0	13.4	14.7	49.9	27.1
Japan						
1960	8.7	12.1	11.9	15.1	47.0	29.7
1965	6.9	13.9	10.0	17.0	47.8	28.9
1970	4.7	13.8	7.5	18.3	49.5	29.2
1975	2.4	10.4	4.2	15.0	54.6	30.2
1980	2.0	7.9	3.4	12.3	55.2	32.6
Sweden						
1965	6.8	10.2	10.1	13.2	52.6	28.1
1970	5.0	10.8	7.0	13.5	51.0	31.3
1975	5.3	10.0	6.4	11.5	48.8	34.8
1980	5.1	10.0	5.8	11.2	46.7	37.4
United States						
1960	5.9	10.2	8.1	10.8	57.0	26.0
1965	6.8	11.5	8.6	12.6	54.3	26.5
1970	7.3	13.2	9.2	15.2	50.6	27.4
1975	7.8	13.4	9.7	15.9	48.3	28.8
1980	7.4	13.8	8.7	15.5	45.9	31.6

[a]15 years and over, except 16-74 in Sweden, 16 and over in the United States. [b]15-19; 16-19 in Sweden and the United States. [c]20-24. [d]25 and over, except 25-74 in Sweden.

Source: See sources and notes to Tables 2.1, 2.2.

growth indeed were almost identical for the two sexes; only Germany and Sweden reversed third and fourth places in the case of teenage females (Table 2.3). The range in female teenage growth rates among the countries was even wider than for male teenagers, from 4.2 percent annual growth in the U.S. to 6.5 percent per year change in Japan. Teenage female growth was greater, or the decline was smaller, than that of teenage males in the U.S., Great Britain, Japan, and Sweden, while the opposite situation obtained in Germany and Australia. Teenage female E/P ratios followed the same path as those of teenage males 1960–80, except for the American female rise (Table 2.4). Likewise, shares of total employment of the same sex 1960–80 followed the same course for teenagers of each sex in the six countries, although starting levels and magnitudes of change differed (Table 2.5).

Given the resemblance between the sexes, it also is not surprising that teenage female employment showed negative change in five countries; the contrast with adult female growth was sharp because the latter was positive in all six countries (Table 2.3). Only U.S. teenage females departed from a pattern in which teenage females were more removed from adult female employment trends than teenage males were in regard to adult males. Changes in the absolute numbers of jobs are striking. Japan's loss of almost 1.5 million teenage female jobs contrasts with a growth of almost 5 million new jobs for adult females, while the addition of nearly 2 million jobs for American teenage females, remarkable as it is against decline in the other countries, paled beside the addition of over 13.6 million jobs for American adult women. In the six countries, the direction of annual fluctuations in the levels of teenage female employment corresponded more closely to trends for male teenagers than for adult females; only in the United States were teenage female and adult female year-to-year trends similar in direction.

The quantitative adequacy of employment provision cannot be tested by employment growth rates alone. According to national data, teenage females generally tended to have higher unemployment rates than comparable males, except in Britain before 1976 and Japan from 1966 to 1979. Underrecording of female employment is common in Britain and elsewhere. In addition, there was more concealed teenage female than male unemployment, partly because of the social acceptability of young women remaining at home upon the completion of compulsory education. Nevertheless, a revised ranking of countries, based on factors in addition to employment growth rates, probably also holds for teenage females, since movements in their unemployment rates, E/P ratios, and employment shares tended to resemble those of teenage males.

YOUNG ADULT MALES

Young adult males constituted a higher proportion of male employment than of the male population throughout the period, except in Japan in the later years, signifying the importance of this age-sex group to the labor force. The direction of change of male young adult employment more closely resembled teenagers than male adults (Table 2.2). In fact, the only deviation in direction between the two male youth groups occurred in Britain, where a 2.1 percent annual rate of expansion for young adults was matched by an equal rate of contraction for teenagers. In relationship to adults, on the other hand, only in Australia and the U.S. (positive growth) and in Germany (negative growth) did the direction of young adult employment change coincide with that for adult males. Even when the direction was the same, the magnitude of rates of change for young adult males tended to depart from that of adult males. Australia and the U.S. showed more growth for young adult than for adult males, while the German male young adult rate decreased more than that of male adults (Table 2.2).

Country ranks in employment growth rates varied somewhat more between young adult and adult males than between young adult and teenage males; in the latter comparison, three countries had identical ranks and ranks were close in a fourth country. The range of employment growth rates for young adults was from 2.9 percent growth per year in the U.S. down to −1.2 percent in Japan. These were the same first and last country ranks, but a narrower range than shown by male teenagers; country ranks were different and the spread was wider for young adult than for male adults. In all six countries, the direction of year-to-year employment changes of young adult males conformed more to adult male patterns than to those of male teenagers. Except in the U.S., and to a lesser extent in Sweden, young adult and teenage male year-to-year employment levels tended to move in an uncoordinated fashion. Among the six countries, the closest correspondence between annual employment oscillations of young adult and adult males was in the U.S., followed by Sweden and Germany (after 1967); least similarity between the two age groups was shown by Japan.

E/P ratios of young adult males were much higher than those of teenage males because of the latter's greater school attendance rates. Indeed, young adult male E/P ratios exceeded those of adult males in 1960 and 1980, except in Japan in both years and in Sweden in the initial year (Table 2.4). A finer breakdown of the adult male group would have revealed the low and declining E/P ratios of the older age groups, close to retirement age, and in most countries higher E/P ratios for prime age than young adult males. Australia had the highest young adult male E/P ratio in both 1960 and 1980. Sweden was lowest in 1960, replaced by Japan in 1980. The cross-national range of young adult E/P ratios was narrower than for teenagers, especially in 1980. A downward direction of young adult ratios over the period 1960–80 was displayed except in Sweden. Such a decrease accorded with the movement observed among male teenagers and was attributable to the combined effects of a rise in young adult educational enrollment rates and a surge in unemployment rates; the latter especially affected Australia, Germany and Great Britain (Table 2.5).

Young adult male shares of total male employment rose in Australia, Great Britain, and the United States and drifted up and down in the other three countries from 1960 to 1980 (Table 2.5). In 1960, shares were very close in the six countries, ranging from 9.3 (Britain) to 13.0 percent (Germany), but by 1980 they spread from 7.9 (Japan) to 13.8 percent (U.S.), about the same range as for teenage males, but narrower than for adult males.

Unemployment rates for young adults in 1960, standardized to U.S. concepts but covering both sexes, were low in all countries (not exceeding 2 percent), except in the United States (Sorrentino 1981). The increase in unemployment rates 1960 to 1979, using both the standardized rate and national rates for young adult males only, was most severe in Australia, Great Britain, and Germany. The U.S. remained with the highest unemployment rate in 1979, despite a small rise over 1960. As a result, country ranks in the adequacy of employment provision for young adult males over the period do not coincide with their ranks in employment growth shown in Table 2.2. On a revised ranking according to adequacy, Japan again would appear in first place, followed by Germany and Sweden. Britain, Australia and the U.S., probably in that order, bring up the rear.

YOUNG ADULT FEMALES

Young adult females in four countries (except for Germany and Japan) had positive employment growth, over 1 percent a year in each case. In only two countries, Britain and the U.S., did young adult females have higher employment growth rates than did adult females, all of whom showed positive growth over the period 1960–80. But in all countries, young adult females experienced higher growth rates, or less of a decline, than did female teenagers, and in four countries young adult females had a more favorable employment trend than young adult males (Table 2.3). The direction of employment change for young adult females was the same as for young adult males in all countries except Sweden, and the same as for adult females in all but Germany and Japan.

American young adult females, with a 5.5 percent per year growth rate, and over 4 million new jobs created from 1960 to 1980, had the highest growth of all the age-sex groups presented; as in the case of U.S. males, student jobs played a role in the growth. American teenagers and Australian adult women were next in order, displaying annual growth rates of over 4 percent. Among the males, no group exceeded American young adults whose 2.9 percent growth rate still fell below that of several female age-sex groups. German young adult females were unusual in having a greater drop than young adult males.

With a few exceptions, yearly fluctuations in the employment levels of young adult females more closely resembled those of young adult males than those of adult women or female teenagers. American young adult and adult females, however, both had constant upward year-to-year movement of employment throughout. For briefer periods, the annual employment levels of Swedish and Australian young adult and teenage females moved up and down together, with some differences of timing in Australia.

Young adult female E/P ratios exceeded those of adult women in 1960 and 1980 in all six countries, and also were greater than those of teenage females, except for Britain in 1960 and Australia in 1966 (Table 2.4). A finer age breakdown of adult women probably would have removed young adult women from first place in several countries. From 1960 to 1980, young adult female E/P ratios rose in Australia, Sweden, and the U.S., and fell in the other countries. Ranging from .60 to .78, 1980 E/P ratios were closer together than in 1960 when the spread was from .42 in the U.S. to .76 in Germany. The U.S. rise of 20 percentage points over the period was the largest growth in E/P ratio for any age-sex group presented.

Changes in E/P ratios of young adult females from 1960 to 1980 resulted from varying combinations of changes in population and employment. Thus, the rise in Australia and the U.S. was attributable to a greater growth of employment than population, while in Sweden it was due to the decline of population combined with an expansion in employment. Britain experienced a drop in the E/P ratio because the young adult female population advanced more than their employment level, but in Germany and Japan employment contracted more than population. Young adult females reflected in their E/P ratios some trends affecting all of the youth groups—demographic factors, rising educational enrollment rates, a propensity to work while attending school, and mounting unemployment rates. In addition, this age-sex group had some special factors tending toward higher ratios—later age of marriage and child-bearing, fewer children, and higher labor force participation rates of wives and mothers, the latter appearing only in recent years in Germany and Japan (Reubens et al. 1981, ch.4). There also were special features in Germany and Japan promoting lower E/P ratios for young adult females, mainly the displacement of females from family farms and family businesses without rapid entrance to other types of employment.

As in the case of young adult males, young adult females had a higher share of total female employment than of the female population, 15 years and over. The direction of growth in population and employment among young adults also was identical for the two sexes in four countries. Further, in each country, the change in the young adult female share of total female employment during 1960-80 was in the same direction as for young adult males (Table 2.5). The 1960 range of young adult female shares was from 10.8 percent in the U.S. up to 18.3 percent in Germany. By 1980, Sweden with 11.2 percent was in last place, while Australia's 17.5 percent qualified for first place.

It is more difficult to determine whether country ranks in employment adequacy coincide with ranks in employment growth in the case of young adult females than for the other three youth groups. Published unemployment rates must be given less weight than for the other youth groups because the hidden reserve of young women who would seek employment under favorable circumstances is likely to be larger than in the other youth groups and might outnumber those listed as unemployed, and because the dimensions of this group cannot be compared across nations. Probably Sweden would be in first place, followed by the U.S. and Australia; in all three, but especially in Sweden, the availability of part-time jobs would contribute to the favorable adequacy rank. Britain might come next. Japan and Germany would be last, since social constraints as well as business practices are likely to have restricted the employment of this age group to a greater extent than in the other countries.

The foregoing review of youth employment trends in the six countries has indicated:

- A lack of correspondence between youth and adult or total trends in employment.
- Differences in employment trends between the two youth groups within and across countries.
- Similarities in employment trends between the sexes in each youth age group.
- An absence of uniformity in country patterns of total employment change and its relation to change in the various age-sex groups.

Explanatory Factors

Cross-national differences in medium-term trends in the number of employed youth are analyzed through Spearman rank correlations. Multiple regression analysis was not used with this set of independent variables because of the extent of multicollinearity and autocorrelation. The first of the six variables chosen as explanatory factors was the population growth rate of each youth group. For comparison purposes, the second variable used was population growth rates for those 15 years and over. Changes in educational enrollment rates was the third variable and changes in unemployment rates of the individual youth groups was the fourth. As a fifth variable, the growth of adult female employment was chosen as a likely influence. For the sixth, and final, variable we took overall employment growth. As a measure of overall economic performance and tightness in the labor market, changes in the unemployment rate of male prime-age workers would be a useful variable, but fully comparable data were not available. In addition, factors that cannot be quantified at present for comparative purposes, such as

Table 2.6   Spearman Rank Correlations Between Youth Employment Growth
             Rates and Selected Variables, by Age and Sex, Six Countries,
             1960–1980

	15–19 years[a]		20–24 years	
	Males	Females	Males	Females
	(rank correlation)			
Population growth rate:				
own age-sex group	+.93[b]	+.71[b]	+.77[b]	+.77[b]
15 years and over, both sexes	+.60[c]	+.54	+.09	+.43
Change in own group educational				
enrollment rate	−1.00[b]	−.60[c]	−.26	+.09
Change in unemployment rate,				
own age group, both sexes	−.03	+.09	+.03	−.03
Employment growth rate:				
adult females	+.46	+.67[c]	+.35	+.70
15 years and over, both sexes	+.49	+.60[c]	+.43	+.77[b]

[a]16–19 in Sweden and the United States.
[b]Significant at the .05 level.
[c]Significant at the .10 level.

Source: Tables 2.1, 2.2, 2.3; Population data: see sources to Table 2.1;
Educational enrollment rates: Reubens et al. 1981, Table A3.2; Unemployment
rates: Sorrentino 1981, Table 1.

changes in the wages of young workers or the relative earnings of young
and adult workers, also are considered.

It is hypothesized that country ranks for population growth rates in
each youth group will show a positive, significant correlation with
country ranks in employment growth for the same age-sex group, while
country ranks in population growth 15 years and over, both sexes, will
produce insignificant rank correlations. Table 2.6 indicates that these
hypotheses are supported; in industrialized countries there is a close
but not precise response of employment to population change in the
youth groups. No fixed relationship is suggested; the change within
countries in E/P ratios over time and differences among countries in
the amount of change in the E/P ratios of youth, shown in Table 2.3,
establish the point. Nor is it maintained that every increase in population
is matched by an increase in employment. Our evidence only shows
that country ranks in the two variables are closely correlated, as they
were for a larger number of countries when population and labor force
change were measured (Reubens et al. 1981, ch.4).

As a major activity of the youth groups, especially teenagers, enrollment in educational institutions might be expected to correlate
closely but inversely with employment levels, to the extent that students
do not simultaneously hold jobs, and educational enrollments are not

drawn from those who otherwise would be out of the labor force. Educational enrollment rates (EER) generally rose in all of the youth age-sex groups in all of the countries. Changes in EER had a major impact on E/P ratios of teenagers as well as on their shares of total employment of the same sex, although the rise in the proportion of student workers was notable in the United States. Therefore, it comes as no surprise that an inverse, significant correlation between country ranks in EER change and employment growth rates is sustained for teenagers, especially males. Young adult males, although showing the inverse relation, had a low, nonsignificant rank correlation, perhaps because of the tendency of university students, especially American, Swedish, and German, to hold jobs. Ranks for Australia, Japan, and Britain were as hypothesized. As expected, young adult females failed to show the relationship because the large reserve of women in the age group who were out of the labor force at the outset provided a source for increased rates of educational enrollments that were not a substitute for rising proportions in employment.

For each age-sex group, the countries with the least increase in youth unemployment rates over the period might be expected to show the greatest expansion of employment, if unemployment and employment are reciprocal. Either because other forces predominated or because we chose youth unemployment data that the U.S. Bureau of Labor Statistics had conformed to U.S. definitions and these data referred to both sexes, this variable was not significant in any of the four cases. It is also possible that in some countries a separation according to full-time or part-time status would have improved the results.

Many analysts have considered employment growth for adult females competitive with employment growth for the youth groups. The hypothesis, therefore, would be that country ranks in growth rates of adult female employment would correlate inversely and significantly with country ranks in employment growth of each youth group. Not only does Table 2.6 show no inverse correlation, but the ranks for the female youth groups correlated positively and significantly with those of adult females, suggesting complementarity rather than substitutability. The smaller and insignificant rank correlations of the two male youth groups imply that sharp sex distinctions should be made in the analysis. The rank correlation between total employment growth rates and the growth rates of the youth groups also did not find a significant relation for young males, presumably because of the dominance of female growth in the total. In the case of young females, the increase in part-time work and service sector jobs, factors that also influenced total and adult female employment growth, probably contribute to the high, significant correlations in both tests.

Among the variables that were quantifiable, only ranks in own group population growth performed well in all four youth groups. Together with changes in educational enrollment rates, population growth provided strong evidence that for teenagers supply-side factors were key. Additional variables, especially on the demand side, should be investigated. For example, country ranks in the relative cost to employers of hiring a young person rather than an adult would be a useful variable, but truly comparable data have not been produced despite substantial contributions to this subject in the later country chapters. An inverse relation would be postulated between a relative earnings rise and employment growth for youth. Postwar changes in relative earnings may, however, have been an effect as well as, or more than, a cause of change in employment levels, as Chapter 7 asserts for Japan where the rise in the relative earnings of male youth probably was directly caused by the decrease in the number seeking employment due to demographic and educational enrollment changes that reduced the number of available youth at the same time that the demand for such workers surged. Thus, the supply side seemed to be the dominant explanation of the rise in relative earnings. The same explanation was not, however, given in other country chapters in which this phenomenon was observed.

Summary

Some of the more important findings of this chapter about levels of employment are:

- A wide range of aggregate employment growth rates 1960–80, ranging from 1.9 percent annually in the U.S. to −0.3 percent in Germany (Table 2.1).
- Higher employment growth rates, or smaller declines, for females than males in most cases (Tables 2.2, 2.3).
- Declines in teenage employment, except for both American groups and Australian males (Tables 2.2, 2.3).
- Positive young adult male employment growth in three countries, and in four countries for young adult females (Tables 2.2, 2.3).
- Consistent directions of change in population and employment for male teenagers in four countries, for female teenagers in two countries, and for young adults of both sexes in five countries.
- Declining teenage E/P ratios 1960–80 except for U.S. females, and decreasing E/P ratios 1960–80 for young male adults, except in Sweden. Increased young adult female E/P ratios in Australia, Sweden, and the U.S. (Table 2.4).
- Declining teenage shares of same sex total employment, except in the U.S. 1960–80. Decreasing young adult shares except in Australia, Britain, and the U.S. (Table 2.5).
- Altered country ranks for the adequacy of the youth employment situation upon consideration of changes in population, educational enrollments, part-time work, and unemployment rates.

• Few acceptable explanatory factors in cross-national differences between total and youth employment growth rates, except for obvious
  connection with population growth rates (Table 2.6).

Cross-national differences in the composition and characteristics of
youth employment in the six countries, the subject of country chapters,
may be related to the varying medium-term trends in the number of
persons employed, both total and in the youth groups, as reported in
this chapter.

3

Occupational Dissimilarity by Age and Sex

Beatrice G. Reubens and
John A.C. Harrisson

If significant and consistent differences between the jobs of youth and other age groups can be established in a cross-national analysis, the case for the existence of a distinct youth labor market would be strengthened and the process of job allocation in industrialized economies might be better understood.

Study of the types of employment held by various age-sex groups can be undertaken through analysis of the detailed occupational information in population censuses. Admittedly, the occupational classifications devised for census purposes are not ideal to describe a complex employment structure; moreover, these categories are altered from census to census and vary from country to country. Nor is self-reporting of occupations an entirely satisfactory source of data, though other sources are not superior. As a recent German study points out, occupational data obtained from employers, which differ fairly widely from census data, tend to err on the side of being overly specific, reporting departmental assignment rather than occupation (Troll 1981). Thus, in most countries the detailed data from recent censuses represent the best occupational data currently available, although changes in the 1980 U.S. census and the 1981 British census, for example, will improve the occupational data for further studies (Bregger 1982; GB 1981a).

Four of the six countries in this book—Great Britain, Japan, Sweden and the United States—have been selected for the comparison; time and other constraints caused the omission of Australia and West Germany, but the author of Chapter 5 on Germany has conducted a similar analysis, using a less detailed occupational breakdown than the one used in this chapter. Some might question the inclusion of Japan on the grounds that occupational distinctions are not much used or understood in Japan, people identify themselves with their firm, and many companies do not make fixed occupational assignments, but rather rotate personnel. These valid observations notwithstanding, discussions with officials in Japan's Bureau of Statistics of the Prime Minister's Office convinced us that Japanese census data on occupations are sufficiently reliable and comparable with the other three countries. Japanese census forms call for a full description of job tasks, providing the 600 census staff responsible for occupational classification with the information for assigning all respondents to occupational categories, including those who state that their jobs involved the "general affairs of the company."

Census data for Japan and Sweden are for 1975, while those for the United States and Great Britain are for 1970 and 1971, respectively. Because of differences between the two sets of countries in the level and rate of decline of primary sector employment, the time gap in data serves to increase the similarity of occupational distributions. The number of detailed occupations in each census was 441 for the United States, 286 for Japan, 282 for Sweden, and 223 for Great Britain (Table A3.1). The Appendix to this chapter lists the significant differences among the countries that may affect the conclusions. At appropriate points in the text, reference is made to data differences that may influence the results.

In this chapter, five main measures are used. First, the most common occupations of the youth groups in the four countries are compared. Second, youth-intensive occupations, those employing a larger than average proportion of young people, are identified and discussed comparatively. Third, comparisons of the most common occupations are made among age-sex groups and across countries. Fourth, occupational concentration and the sex-intensity of occupational distributions are discussed by age and sex cross-nationally. Last, indexes of occupational dissimilarity (IOD) between various age-sex groups are analyzed cross-nationally.

Most Common Occupations of Youth

If youth labor markets are clearly defined, we would expect to find the same type of occupations among young people in each of the countries, possibly with sex differences. We would also expect differences between teenagers and young adults and still sharper divergence between youth as a whole and adults. A review of the limited number of detailed occupations that account for a large share of the total employment of each youth group facilitates comparisons within and across countries (Tables 3.1–3.6). Compiled from 396 detailed census occupations in the U.S., 285 in Japan, 281 in Sweden and 221 in Great Britain, our lists of most common occupations are affected by the total number of detailed occupations analyzed, the method of disaggregating occupations,

the consistency of the classification system, and the degree of adherence
to an occupational hierarchy in the titles (see Appendix to Chapter 3).
The most common occupations are also considered in terms of the top
5 percent of occupations, in order to compensate for the varying number
of occupations in each country's census. Occupational information
presented here pertains to the 1970s and may not depict the current
position.

The division into age groups also influences the cross-national findings;
we use 15–19 (or 16–19) and 20–24 as the youth groups. Each youth
group includes both new labor force entrants and those with work
experience, but variations in educational patterns create inter-country
divergence in the average age and proportion in employment. The full
range of teenage years is relevant only in Britain because in 1971 the
vast majority of the age group left school at 15. Japan is at the other
extreme, since very few teenagers under 18 were employed in 1975.
Sweden (1975) and the U.S. (1970) occupy middle positions, with the
higher proportion of American teenagers enrolled in school offset by
the higher proportion of American students holding jobs. In both
countries, however, employed teenagers under 18 tend to be somewhat
different from the remainder of the teen group. Since the Swedish data
cover only those who worked 20 hours or more a week, the discussion
below slights Swedish youth who worked fewer hours, and should be
borne in mind in cross-national comparisons. In each of the countries,
most employed out-of-school teenagers had completed a given level of
education—lower secondary in Britain and upper secondary in the other
three countries, although Sweden's upper secondary course is shorter
and more vocationally oriented than those of the U.S. and Japan.

Compared to teenagers, young adults display greater contrast between
those with substantial work experience and those who have just entered
employment, in this case from some form of tertiary education that
often leads directly to a higher occupational status than the rest of the
age cohort has achieved. The proportion of young adult males who
enter work from tertiary education would be highest in Japan, followed
closely by the U.S., with Sweden and Great Britain next (Reubens et
al. 1981). Young adult females present a more complex picture in which
a number of trends are visible for the age group—higher educational
enrollment and completion rates, a greater propensity of more highly
educated females to seek and retain employment, declining marriage
rates and fewer children, and an increased tendency of married females
and young mothers to hold jobs.

Examination of the most common occupations of youth in the four
countries focuses on inter-country differences between youth of the same
age and sex as well as cross-sex and age variations. Tables 3.1–3.4
present the occupational titles of the 20 most common occupations for
each youth age-sex group in the four countries, the percentage of total
employment for each age-sex group attributable to each listed occupation,

Table 3.1   Most Common Occupations of Female Teenagers, Four Countries, Recent Census Year

Great Britain 1971: 15-19 years		Japan 1975: 15-19 years	
(percentage distribution)		(percentage distribution)	
26.9	Clerical workers[a]	23.1	Clerical workers
12.9	Retail salespersons and assistants	15.0	Bookkeepers
12.1	Typists and secretaries	10.6	Salespersons
5.4	Hand and machine sewers and embroiderers	4.2	Waitresses[b]
4.8	Hairdressers, barbers, beauticians	3.9	Spinners
4.0	Nurses	3.8	Nurses
3.4	Office machine operators	3.7	Medical and public health technicians (n.e.c.)
2.8	Packers and wrappers	3.6	Sewing machine operators
1.4	Telephone operators	2.7	Hairdressers, beauticians[c]
1.3	Personal service workers	2.4	Textile workers (n.e.c.)
1.0	Laboratory technicians and assistants	2.2	Electrical machinery assemblers and repairers
(76.0)	Top 5 percent of most common occupations	1.4	Farmers and silk growers
0.9	Waitresses	1.3	Weavers
0.8	Printing workers (n.e.c.)	1.1	Package wrappers (small articles)
0.8	Electrical product assemblers	(79.0)	Top 5 percent of most common occupations
0.8	Agricultural workers (n.e.c.)	0.9	Key punch operators
0.8	Leather workers (footwear)	0.8	Cooks
0.7	Warehouse and stores laborers	0.8	Telephone operators
0.7	Food processing workers (n.e.c.)	0.7	Bakery and confectionery workers
0.7	Knitters	0.7	Conductors (transport)
0.6	Laundry and clothing cleaners	0.7	Service workers (n.e.c.)
(82.8)	Total of twenty most common occupations	(83.6)	Total of twenty most common occupations
100.0	Total all occupations	100.0	Total all occupations

Sweden 1975: 16-19 years		United States 1970: 16-19 years	
12.7	Nursing and midwife assistants	10.5	Retail salespersons
11.3	Typists, secretaries, office clerks	8.5	Waitresses
10.4	Child care personnel	7.7	Secretaries
10.1	Retail salespersons and assistants	6.6	Cashiers
4.4	Household helpers	6.0	Typists
3.4	Kindergarten teachers	4.0	Clerical workers (n.e.c.)
2.9	Household and office cleaners	2.8	Nursing assistants, orderlies
2.5	Waitresses	2.8	File clerks
2.5	Cashiers (shops, restaurants)	2.7	Child care personnel (private household)
2.3	Hairdressers, barbers, beauticians	2.4	Telephone operators
2.2	Packers and wrappers	2.4	Bookkeepers
2.1	Tailors and dressmakers	1.7	Office machine operators
2.0	Dental assistants	1.6	Office receptionists
1.8	Telephone, radio and TV repairers	1.6	Operatives (n.e.c.)
(70.6)	Top 5 percent of most common occupations	1.5	Sewers and stitchers
1.4	Housekeeping service workers (n.e.c.)	1.4	Food service workers (n.e.c.)[d]
1.3	Psychiatric care personnel	1.3	Food counter and fountain workers
1.2	Warehouse and stores laborers	1.1	Hairdressers, beauticians[c]
1.2	Machine tool makers and operators	1.0	Cooks[d]
1.0	Telephone operators	1.0	Library assistants
1.0	Farmworkers	(68.6)	Top 5 percent of most common occupations
(77.7)	Total of twenty most common occupations	(68.6)	Total of twenty most common occupations
100.0	Total all occupations	100.0	Total all occupations

[a]Includes cashiers. [b]Excludes bars. [c]Excludes barbers. [d]Excludes private household.

Note: n.e.c. means "not elsewhere classified". In United States, excludes "allocated" component of occupational title.

Source: Same as Table 3.7.

and the total share for the top 5 percent of occupations and the 20 most common for each age-sex group.

Young females display greater occupational similarity cross-nationally than young males. Teenage females in all four countries show few occupations that are not low level and few that hold promise of much upward career mobility (Table 3.1). Sales and clerical occupations are high among the most common occupations; in many cases such jobs involve an assistant position with little responsibility. Personal service occupations, such as nurse's assistant, waitress, and hairdresser, also are prevalent for this age group in all of the countries, as are jobs in labor-intensive, low paid manufacturing (textiles, clothing), and packing and wrapping in factories and shops. Farm work appears, except in the U.S., but in Britain and Sweden it usually is a paid laborer's job, while in Japan unpaid family work predominates. German results confirm this description, although they cover 15–24 year-old females and thus are not directly comparable (Table 5.6).

Differences among the countries in the most common teenage female occupations probably are partially attributable to variations in the occupational classification systems. While the U.S. list contains a heavy representation of service and clerical occupations, the Swedish list, based on those who worked 20 hours or more, includes relatively more technical occupations than in the other countries. Japan has the most diversified list and the British list seems most highly industrial. Medical and public health technician and transportation conductor appear only on Japan's list, while Great Britain alone shows laboratory technician and assistant.

Several occupations concerned with child care and domestic service are listed in Sweden, reflecting both the high labor force participation rates of Swedish mothers and limited job opportunities for teenagers who have not completed upper secondary school. In addition, dental assistant, kindergarten teacher, and telephone, radio and television repairer appeared on the Swedish teenage female list, indicating access to some higher status or better paid jobs not shown to the same extent in the other countries or in the 1960 Swedish census (Sweden 1964a). Among Swedish females aged 16–24 working fewer than 20 hours, household and office cleaner and retail salesperson and assistant were the top occupations in 1975, accounting for almost one-third of the total. Division of the U.S. list of occupations by school status, separately for 16–17 and 18–19 year-olds, also reveals substantial divergence by school enrollment status as well as by age (see Chapter 9).

Although the occupational distribution of employed young adult females should reflect added years of work experience compared to teenagers as well as an influx of females with tertiary education, the most common occupations of young adult females do not depart markedly from those of teenage females (Table 3.2). Moreover, the four countries display similarity in the few occupations shown by young adult females but not by teenagers; for example, nurse and schoolteacher are important occupations for young adult females. It is possible that young adult females would have shown a more favorable occupational situation vis-à-vis teenagers if additional occupations employing smaller shares of each age group had been included. Some support for this view is found in the census occupational distribution by major groups, comparing the proportions in the two age groups employed in the combined professional and technical, and managerial and administrative occupational categories.

Teenage males, compared to their female counterparts, appear to have a better paid, wider range of occupations, although still predominantly low level, in keeping with their age, educational attainment, and work experience (Table 3.3). Among teenagers, males generally had superior opportunities for training and advancement in their occupations, with less difference between the sexes in the U.S. than in the other countries. Most common occupations of teenage males vary among the four nations. Clearly reflecting a potential for substantial training for skilled crafts occupations, the British list suggests that a majority of male teenagers in at least 10 of the 20 most common occupations were apprentices or trainees; other most common occupations also included such training (Great Britain 1975a, Table 10). From the mid-1970s the proportion of employed British teenage males in craft training shrank, due in part to the slump in the economy and in part to underlying changes in occupational and skill composition. The German data on young males also indicate the overwhelming impact of apprenticeship (Table 5.5).

Single year of age 1971 census data for British youth show that certain occupations rise in share of employment with each year of age. Among these are clerical workers, assemblers, armed forces, and construction laborers. Conversely, occupations such as shop assistant, apprentice, agricultural worker n.e.c., and butcher decline in relative importance as teenagers grow older (GB 1975a). The British list contains no occupation identifiable as "youth job," although such jobs have long been a creature of British youth employment (Casson 1979). A "youth job" in Britain may be identified as a low paid, usually dead-end job that is not open to those 18 and over, mainly because higher wages must be paid.

Japanese teenage males had a fairly wide range of occupations, including traveling salesman and bookkeeper, usually found among older persons. Delivery worker, seventh most common, would count as a "youth job." Opportunities for training in Japan are more a function of size of firm than of occupation (see Chapter 7). Manual work, some of it with training, characterizes the first six occupations on the Swedish teenage male list and employed over 35 percent of those who worked 20 hours or more. In 1960, delivery workers and shop salespersons had been included in the top six occupations (Sweden 1964a). Unlike the other countries, the unskilled laborer category did not appear in Sweden. Nor were white collar occupations as important as in Britain and Japan.

Table 3.2 Most Common Occupations of Female Young Adults, Four Countries, Recent Census Year

Great Britain 1971: 20-24 years		Japan 1975: 20-24 years	
(percentage distribution)		(percentage distribution)	
24.1	Clerical workers[a]	29.1	Clerical workers
17.6	Typists and secretaries	15.7	Bookkeepers
6.5	Retail salespersons and assistants	10.1	Salespersons
6.2	Nurses	4.0	Nurses
5.3	Primary and secondary school teachers	3.1	Waitresses[b]
3.9	Office machine operators	2.8	Farmers and silk growers
2.6	Hand and machine sewers and embroiderers	2.3	Sewing machine operators
2.4	Hairdressers, barbers, beauticians	2.2	Kindergarten assistants
1.6	Packers and wrappers	1.9	Electrical machinery assemblers and repairers
1.6	Personal service workers	1.5	Hairdressers, beauticians[c]
1.5	Telephone operators	1.4	Telephone operators
(73.3)	Top 5 percent of most common occupations	1.3	Medical and public health technicians (n.e.c.)
1.3	Laboratory technicians and assistants	1.3	Primary school teachers
0.8	Electrical product assemblers	1.3	Kindergarten teachers
0.7	Machine tool operators	(78.0)	Top 5 percent of most common occupations
0.7	Household and office cleaners	0.9	Cooks
0.7	Waitresses	0.9	Typists
0.6	Engineering and related workers (n.e.c.)	0.8	Key punch operators
0.6	Technicians and assistants (n.e.c.)	0.7	Bar and cabaret waitresses
0.6	Printing workers (n.e.c.)	0.7	Dressmakers
0.6	Retail shop managers	0.6	Barbers
(79.9)	Total of twenty most common occupations	(82.6)	Total of twenty most common occupations
100.0	Total all occupations	100.0	Total all occupations

Sweden 1975: 20-24 years		United States 1970: 20-24 years	
19.0	Typists, secretaries, office clerks	14.0	Secretaries
13.8	Nursing and midwife assistants	5.4	Typists
6.3	Retail salespersons and assistants	4.7	Primary school teachers
4.4	Child care personnel	3.9	Clerical workers (n.e.c.)
2.6	Nurses	3.8	Bookkeepers
2.6	Primary school teachers	3.4	Retail salespersons
2.2	Household helpers	2.9	Waitresses
2.2	Kindergarten teachers	2.7	Nurses
2.1	Household and office cleaners	2.6	Office machine operators
2.1	Clerical workers^d	2.5	Hairdressers, beauticians^c
2.0	Dental assistants	2.3	Cashiers
1.8	Laboratory technicians and assistants	2.2	Secondary school teachers
1.6	Hairdressers, barbers, beauticians	2.0	Nursing assistants, orderlies
1.5	Psychiatric care personnel	2.0	Operatives (n.e.c.)
(64.6)	Top 5 percent of most common occupations	2.0	Sewers and stitchers
1.4	Cashiers (shops, restaurants)	1.9	Telephone operators
1.4	Tailors and dressmakers	1.6	File clerks
1.4	Machine tool makers and operators	1.6	Office receptionists
1.3	Telephone, radio and TV repairers	1.5	Assemblers
1.2	Waitresses	1.5	Bank tellers
1.2	Office machine operators	(64.2)	Top 5 percent of most common occupations
(72.7)	Total of twenty most common occupations	(64.2)	Total of twenty most common occupations
100.0	Total all occupations	100.0	Total all occupations

aIncludes cashiers. bExcludes bars. cExcludes barbers. dIncludes cashiers (n.e.c.).

Note: n.e.c. means "not elsewhere classified." In United States, excludes "allocated" component of occupational title.

Source: Same as Table 3.7.

Table 3.3 Most Common Occupations of Male Teenagers, Four Countries, Recent Census Year

Great Britain 1971: 15-19 years		Japan 1975: 15-19 years	
(percentage distribution)		(percentage distribution)	
7.8	Clerical workers[a]	6.5	Salespersons
4.1	Retail salespersons and assistants	5.7	Clerical workers
4.0	Electricians	5.2	Carpenters
3.9	Motor vehicle repairers	4.2	Motor vehicle repairers
3.8	Apprentices and crafts trainees (engineering and related)	4.1	Cooks
		3.6	Farmers and silk growers
3.7	Laborers and unskilled workers (n.e.c.)	2.8	Delivery workers
3.5	Armed forces	2.7	Metal processing workers (n.e.c.)
3.4	Machine fitters and assemblers	2.5	Armed forces
3.1	Warehouse and stores laborers	2.5	Welders
2.8	Carpenters	2.4	Electrical machinery assemblers and repairers
2.7	Agricultural workers (n.e.c.)	2.4	Metal cutting machine operators
(42.8)	Top 5 percent of most common occupations	2.0	Bookkeepers
1.8	Construction laborers	2.0	Plasterers
1.8	Plumbers, gas fitters	(48.6)	Top 5 percent of most common occupations
1.8	Butchers and meat cutters	1.8	Laborers and unskilled workers (n.e.c.)
1.5	Machine tool operators	1.8	Electrical equipment fitters
1.5	Painters and decorators (n.e.c.)	1.7	Motor vehicle drivers
1.5	Machine repairers and maintenance fitters	1.6	Machine assemblers
1.4	Craft workers (n.e.c.)	1.6	Traveling salespersons[b]
1.3	Engineering and related laborers	1.5	Construction laborers
1.2	Welders	(58.8)	Total of twenty most common occupations
(56.6)	Total of twenty most common occupations	100.0	Total all occupations
100.0	Total all occupations		

Sweden 1975: 16-19 years

9.3	Machine tool makers and operators
8.7	Machine assemblers and repairers
5.5	Warehouse and stores laborers
4.3	Farmworkers
4.0	Welders
4.0	Electricians and electrical workers
3.8	Retail salespersons and assistants
2.9	Metalworkers
2.9	Furniture makers and woodworkers
2.5	Carpenters
2.2	Painters and finishers (construction)
2.1	Laborers and unskilled workers
1.7	Operators of material handling equipment
1.6	Telephone, radio and TV repairers
(55.5)	Top 5 percent of most common occupations
1.6	Loggers and related forestry workers
1.6	Concrete and construction workers
1.5	Mail clerks and office messengers
1.3	Typists, secretaries, office clerks
1.3	Sailors (merchant marine)
1.2	Plumbers, pipe fitters
(64.0)	Total of twenty most common occupations
100.0	Total all occupations

United States 1970: 16-19 years

9.1	Warehouse and stores laborers
5.8	Garage and gas station workers
5.2	Retail salespersons
4.2	Janitors
4.1	Operatives (n.e.c.)
3.9	Farm laborers[c]
3.8	Laborers (n.e.c.)
2.9	Cooks[d]
2.2	Delivery workers
2.1	Freight handlers and related laborers
2.0	Waiters' assistants (busboys)
1.9	Dishwashers
1.8	Construction laborers[e]
1.7	Stock clerks, storekeepers
1.6	Cashiers
1.5	Motor vehicle repairers
1.4	Gardening and related laborers[f]
1.2	Newspaper delivery workers (newsboys)
1.1	Food service workers (n.e.c.)[d]
1.1	Truck drivers
(58.6)	Top 5 percent of most common occupations
(58.6)	Total of twenty most common occupations
100.0	Total all occupations

[a]Includes cashiers. [b]Excludes insurance. [c]Excludes unpaid family workers. [d]Excludes private household. [e]Excludes carpenters' assistants. [f]Excludes farm.

Note: n.e.c. means "not elsewhere classified". In United States, excludes "allocated" component of occupational title.

Source: Same as Table 3.7.

However, over one-quarter of Swedish males aged 16–24 who worked fewer than 20 hours were mail delivery workers or retail salespersons and assistants.

American teenage males display a larger share of low level, low paid, high turnover service occupations, fewer manual occupations incorporating skill training, and more "youth jobs" than in the other countries. This applies both to 16–17 and 18–19 year-olds and to in and out-of-school youth, but less so to out-of-school older teenage males. Among the low level service occupations appearing in the U.S. are janitor, dishwasher, office cleaner, short order cook, and vehicle washer, while "youth jobs" include gas station attendant, busboy, newsboy, fast-food establishment employee and delivery worker (see Cohen and Schwartz 1980; Plewes 1982). Industrial and construction work involved about 10 percent of American teenagers and warehouse and freight handling occupied another 11 percent.

Differences between the U.S. and other countries for teenage males are attributable to the more rapid growth and higher share of service occupations in U.S. employment totals, the suitability of many of these occupations to part-time work, the high proportion of the age group in school and the large fraction of high school and college students with jobs, in part because their academic programs are less demanding than those in other countries. Moreover, older workers in other countries perform some of the jobs American teenagers hold. It is possible that the type of employment available to U.S. teenagers is related to higher rates of job turnover and more persistent elevation of unemployment rates than in the other three countries.

Cross-national differences in the most common occupations are less marked among young adult males than teenagers (Table 3.4). Many occupations were the same for young adult males and teenagers, but had somewhat different ranks on the lists. For example, armed forces was second most important for British young adults and seventh for teenagers, while motor vehicle repairer ranked eighth for young adults and fourth for teenagers. American young adults listed truck drivers in third place, but for teenagers it was last on the list of twenty. Young adult male occupations differing from those of teenagers reflected the former group's acquisition of work experience and/or maturity, on the one hand, and increased educational qualifications, on the other. While the minimum age for such occupations as motor vehicle driving or assembly line work vary among the countries, there is some uniformity in regard to occupations requiring advanced education, substantial experience, or demonstrated responsibility.

Despite the advances registered by young adult males compared to teenage males, the distribution of occupations by major occupational groups indicates that the professional-technical and managerial-administrative categories combined account for minor shares of the employment of young adult males in each country. The U.S. leads with 19.4 percent, followed by 15.7 percent in Britain, 10.9 percent in Sweden, and 5.6 percent in Japan. Review of the most common occupations of the youth groups in the four countries confirms the occupational advantages of young males over females and the small advance made by young adult males compared to teenagers; nevertheless, this exceeds the progress with age shown by young adult females. The inferiority of the American male teenage occupational distribution probably would not disappear even if the teenage employed consisted of fewer student workers.

Youth-Intensive Occupations

Identification of "youth jobs" or a "youth labor market" can be made more precise by limiting the selection to those most common occupations that also preponderantly employ young people. An occupation in which a large proportion of all youth are employed may be one in which the youth share of total occupational employment is average or below average, disqualifying it from consideration. However, if the detailed occupations in which a large proportion of young people work also are occupations that consist largely or primarily of young people (youth-intensive occupations), a stronger case can be made for the existence of a separate youth labor market. If employment in the youth-intensive occupations accounts for a relatively small share of the total employment of the youth group, a distinct youth labor market cannot be assumed, although the concept of "youth jobs" remains intact. Identification of the youth-intensive occupations also may foster an understanding of earnings differentials among youth, in keeping with a recent research finding that in nearly all countries the proportion of young workers employed in an industry is "the main source of differentiation in pay between industries" (Marsden 1980, p.57).

In order to establish the most youth-intensive occupations for each youth age-sex group in the four countries, we computed the share of each youth age-sex group in the total employment of the sex, as reported in the census. These shares range from 2.6 percent for Japanese teenage males to 15.1 percent for American young adult females; half of the 16 entries fall between 10.4 and 15.1 percent and the proportions are consistent with the shares shown in Chapter 2. In each country, the young female shares are higher than the young male, although the differences are small in most cases. We count as youth-intensive only occupations with an above average share of the youth age-sex group, and exclude occupations whose total employment for one sex does not equal or exceed 0.05 percent of the total employment in all occupations for that sex. We give lesser attention to the combined share of all four youth groups in occupations, although some calculations along these lines are presented, omitting the occupations in which youth-intensity for individual age-sex groups is small.

The selection of the 20 most youth-intensive occupations results in the identification of some occupations whose youth share is not much

Table 3.4 Most Common Occupations of Male Young Adults, Four Countries, Recent Census Year

Great Britain 1971: 20-24 years		Japan 1975: 20-24 years	
(percentage distribution)		(percentage distribution)	
8.6	Clerical workers[a]	9.7	Clerical workers
3.6	Armed forces	8.6	Salespersons
3.2	Truck drivers	4.7	Motor vehicle drivers
3.1	Machine fitters and assemblers	4.5	Traveling salespersons[b]
2.8	Electricians	3.4	Carpenters
2.5	Laborers and unskilled workers (n.e.c.)	3.2	Farmers and silk growers
2.2	Warehouse and stores laborers	3.2	Cooks
2.1	Motor vehicle workers	3.0	Bookkeepers
2.1	Technicians and assistants (n.e.c.)	2.6	Motor vehicle repairers
2.1	Carpenters	2.3	Electrical machinery assemblers and repairers
1.9	Construction laborers	2.0	Armed forces
(34.2)	Top 5 percent of most common occupations	1.9	Draftsmen
1.8	Draftsmen	1.7	Welders
1.7	Retail salespersons and assistants	1.7	Metal processing workers (n.e.c.)
1.5	Machine tool operators	(52.5)	Top 5 percent of most common occupations
1.5	Agricultural workers (n.e.c.)	1.6	Electrical equipment fitters
1.5	Machine repairers and maintenance fitters	1.5	Construction workers (n.e.c.)
1.4	Traveling salespersons and agents	1.4	Delivery workers
1.3	Retail shop managers	1.4	Construction laborers
1.3	Plumbers, gas fitters	1.3	Metal cutting machine operators
1.3	Primary and secondary school teachers	1.2	Machine repairers
(47.5)	Total of twenty most common occupations	(60.9)	Total of twenty most common occupations
100.0	Total all occupations	100.0	Total all occupations

Sweden 1975: 20-24 years		United States 1970: 20-24 years	
8.0	Machine assemblers and repairers	5.2	Operatives (n.e.c.)
6.3	Machine tool makers and operators	3.2	Retail salespersons
5.0	Motor vehicle drivers	2.5	Truck drivers
4.2	Electricians and electrical workers	2.1	Managers and administrators (salaried n.e.c.)
3.6	Warehouse and stores laborers	2.1	Motor vehicle repairers
3.1	Welders	1.8	Freight handlers and related laborers
3.1	Carpenters	1.8	Assemblers
2.7	Retail salespersons and assistants	1.7	Janitors
2.1	Typists, secretaries, office clerks	1.7	Delivery workers
2.0	Farmworkers	1.7	Farm laborers^d
2.0	Operators of material handling equipment	1.6	Laborers (n.e.c.)
1.9	Furniture makers and woodworkers	1.6	Construction laborers^e
1.9	Painters and finishers (construction)	1.5	Warehouse and stores laborers
1.8	Traveling salespersons and agents	1.5	Secondary school teachers
(47.7)	Top 5 percent of most common occupations	1.5	Carpenters
1.7	Metalworkers	1.4	Garage and gas station workers
1.6	Armed forces^c	1.3	Traveling salespersons^b
1.6	Concrete and construction workers	1.3	Welders
1.5	Loggers and related forestry workers	1.2	Draftsmen
1.5	Telephone, radio and TV repairers	1.2	Clerical workers (n.e.c.)
1.4	Mechanical engineers and technicians	(37.9)	Top 5 percent of most common occupations
(55.9)	Total of twenty most common occupations	(37.9)	Total of twenty most common occupations
100.0	Total all occupations	100.0	Total all occupations

^{a}Includes cashiers. ^{b}Excludes insurance. ^{c}Excludes conscripts. ^{d}Excludes unpaid family workers. ^{e}Excludes carpenters' assistants.

Note: n.e.c. means "not elsewhere classified." In United States, excludes "allocated" component of occupational title.

Source: Same as Table 3.7.

higher than the average youth share of all occupations. Youth-intensity in occupations is not marked when each age-sex group is considered separately. In the four countries, a youth group held half or more of an occupation's employment in only a few youth-intensive occupations. In fact, in 11 of the 16 youth groups, including all four in Sweden, the highest youth share in any occupation is under 50 percent. Japanese teenage males display a youth-intensive range of only 5.0 to 14.0 percent.

Moreover, in each youth group fewer than half of the youth-intensive occupations also are most common occupations; young adult males show fewer such occupations than the other youth age-sex groups. Occupations that are simultaneously youth-intensive and most common account for relatively little of the total employment of each youth group. With the exception of Japanese young adult females and British and American female teenagers, the youth age-sex groups show a higher share of their employment in the 20 most common occupations that are *not* youth-intensive than in those that are. These relationships weaken the case for a discrete youth labor market.

If identical occupations in all four countries can be shown to be youth-intensive, whether or not they are also most common, even if only for one age-sex group, the designation "youth jobs" gains validity. Similarly, the appearance of the same youth-intensive occupations in three or four age-sex groups would provide evidence of youth jobs. To begin with, few occupations are youth-intensive in all of the countries. The armed forces would have qualified for the two male groups in all four countries, if U.S. data did not exclude the armed forces and Sweden did not exclude military conscripts. In addition, hairdressers and beauticians (in some cases including barbers), office machine operators, clerical workers, laboratory technicians (including a part of Japanese medical and public health technicians n.e.c.), teachers, cooks, and telephone line and cable workers or repairers are youth-intensive for at least one age-sex group in all four countries, although the degree of youth-intensity of these occupations varies considerably among the countries.

In each country, relatively few youth-intensive occupations appear in as many as three or four of the youth-age groups. Four youth-intensive occupations in Britain are found in all four youth age-sex groups; these are hairdresser (including beautician and barber); office machine operator; armed forces; and laboratory technician and assistant. The combined youth shares of total (male plus female) employment in these occupations range from 75 to 43 percent. Sweden shows one such occupation, telephone, radio, and television repairer, but all four youth groups account for only 30.5 percent of total employment in that occupation. Japan and the U.S. have five and six occupations, respectively, that are youth-intensive for three of the four age-sex groups, while in this category Britain has three and Sweden four occupations. Both the proportion of all employment attributable to the three or four youth groups combined and the nature of these occupations argues against the concept of a distinct youth labor market.

However, the youth-intensive lists for each country do confirm the existence of "youth jobs," allowing for differences among countries in their type and number. Our earlier characterization of some of the most common occupations of young people as "youth jobs" is consistent with the evidence on youth-intensive occupations that are also most common occupations. The youth-intensive lists yield no new "youth jobs" in Britain, Japan or Sweden. In the U.S., most of the identified "youth jobs" are sustained, but a few are not youth-intensive; examples are gardeners and related workers, listed for teenage males, and food service workers n.e.c., listed for teenage females. In some cases, greater specificity in the occupational designations is required to segregate the "youth job" component.

The remaining 20 most youth-intensive occupations which are not among the 20 most common youth occupations account for relatively little youth employment, but include several occupations that could be called "youth jobs." For British teenage males there is truck and van boy, while in Sweden, gas station attendant (teenage males), chimney sweep (young adult males), and mail clerk and office messenger (teenage females) qualify. Several "youth jobs" can be added for U.S. teenage males: food counter and fountain worker; recreation and entertainment attendant; library assistant; office messenger; parking attendant; and office mail clerk. Young adult American males also show two of the above occupations. For American teenage females, recreation and entertainment attendant; office mail clerk; and counter clerk (excluding food) can be added. No new "youth jobs" appear in the Japanese lists.

Thus, the full inventory of the 20 most youth-intensive jobs confirms that "youth jobs" are particularly a feature of the employment of American teenagers, as has been recorded by American analysts (Barton 1975; Folk 1968; Osterman 1980). While "youth jobs" undoubtedly exist in the other countries, they are less numerous and involve a smaller porportion of youth employment, especially among teenagers.

Apart from youth jobs, other distinct types of youth-intensive occupations are revealed by the inventory. Trainee positions, restricted to young persons by law or custom and thus constituting a form of non-competing labor, are a major category, best exemplified by teenage apprentices in Britain. As Chapter 5 indicates, teenagers in Germany fall heavily in this category. Another type of youth-intensive occupation is largely confined to youth by virtue of the requirements of the job, for example, fashion model, athlete, cabaret waitress, the armed forces. Among young adults in particular, some technical and sub-professional occupations exhibit a high degree of youth-intensity. Examples are draftsman, technician, dental assistant, and computer programmer. In addition, there are low level jobs in which youth are an important, but not necessarily predominant element, sharing employment with older workers, immigrants, or other disadvantaged groups (Mayhew and Rosewell 1978; Osterman 1980; Willauer 1974).

Comparison of Adult and Youth Occupations

If there are serious barriers against entry by young people into the occupations held by adults, there should be wide and consistent differences in the groups' most common occupations, with a minimum of overlap. Patterns should repeat from country to country, so that clear distinctions emerge in the prestige, rewards, responsibilities and tasks of the occupations held by youth and adults. Our assessment of the social status and relative earnings of the most common occupations by age group is based on the work of many authorities (e.g., Blau and Duncan 1967; Buchele 1976; Duncan 1961; Goldthorpe and Hope 1974; Hodge and Siegal 1966; Lydall 1968; Marsden 1980, 1981; Mayhew and Rosewell 1979; Osterman 1980; Phelps Brown 1977; Routh 1980; Saunders and Marsden 1981; Sommers 1974; Willauer 1974).

The 20 most common occupations of adult males in each country (Table 3.5) converge closely with those of young males, especially with young adults who held 14 (15 in Japan) of the same occupations (Table 3.4). Teenage males (Table 3.3) duplicate adult males in 16 occupations in Japan, 12 in Sweden, 10 in Great Britain, and 9 in the United States. The extent of overlapping in Japan is partly attributable to special features of the occupational designations. The Japanese classification "farmer," the single most important occupation for adult males in 1975, is somewhat misleading. Currently, only 15 percent of farm household heads in Japan are exclusively engaged in farming; the rest simultaneously have jobs in local industry, construction, or other activities. Of this latter group, about 70 percent actually follow farming as a secondary activity while working mainly at another job; other family members do the main farm work (Japan 1979a; *New York Times* 1981a). Yet all such males would have been called farmers in the census because they owned farms. Furthermore, Chapter 7 indicates that the occupational classification system used in the Japanese census tends to overstate the number employed as clerical workers relative to other countries because of the occupational titles assigned to new college graduates in the firms.

American teenage males show least overlap with the most common occupations of adult males, in part due to the relatively high employment rate of students and their special occupational distribution. Thus, 16–17 year-old employed American males, among whom 85 percent were students (US 1973b, Table 217), had only 6 of the same occupations as male adults, compared to 10 in the case of 18–19 year-old males, among whom students comprised 50 percent of the employed. The small number of identical occupations for male teenagers in Britain, compared to Sweden and Japan, is attributable to the youth of employed British teenagers as a result of early school-leaving.

The four countries show few similarities in the specific most common occupations that are the same for male adults and young males. No occupation appears in all four countries for all three groups—adult, teenage, and young adult males. Truck or vehicle driver, and traveling salesman (except Great Britain) are common to four countries for young adult and adult males. Assembler in manufacturing industries, welder, carpenter, warehouse laborer, retail salesperson, and clerical worker are other occupations that appear in two or more countries for three age groups.

Is is apparent that low to medium level occupations predominate among the adult male occupations that are also held by young males. A few occupations have a potential for considerable earnings by mature workers, for example, traveling salesman or carpenter; differences in status within an occupation, such as an assistant or learner position that would be relevant to young people, are revealed in only a few of the occupational titles. On the whole, a large core of these most common occupations, employing a substantial proportion of each male age group in each of the countries, contains no career ladders.

Important occupations of adult males that do not appear on the most common list for younger males consist of two main types—higher paid, prestigious occupations and low level, mainly industrial, occupations. In turn, the most common occupations of male teenagers that are not on the adult male list can be characterized either as "youth jobs" or trainee positions set aside for youth. The lower levels of some technical/professional occupations, appearing on some of the lists for young adult males, are not on the adult male lists. In terms of the share of total employment of the youth groups accounted for by most common occupations that were identical to those of adult males, proportions are very similar for the two youth groups in each country. Japan shows just over 50 percent, Sweden 46 percent, Great Britain around one-third, and the U.S. close to 30 percent.

In each list of most common occupations, those in first and second place command special attention. Two groups of countries can be distinguished as regards the top occupations of males—Britain and Japan, on the one hand, and Sweden and the U.S., on the other. In Britain, clerical work is first for all male age groups, while in Japan it is first or second. In 1966, the British census also showed clerical work as the leading occupation for the male age groups. The foremost male occupations are moderately female intensive in Britain and sex-neutral in Japan.

In Sweden and the United States, manual occupations predominate on the male lists. Farmworker has been top occupation for Swedish male teenagers and farmer for male adults in 1960, but by 1975 these occupations had declined in rank; otherwise, little had changed in occupational ranks. The leading occupations of young males in the United States are warehouse and stores laborer (teenagers) and operative n.e.c. (young adults). A division within the teenage male group is

Table 3.5 Most Common Occupations of Male Adults, Four Countries, Recent Census Year

Great Britain 1971: 25 years and over

(percentage distribution)

6.2	Clerical workers[a]
4.3	Truck drivers
3.1	Warehouse and stores laborers
2.9	Laborers and unskilled workers (n.e.c.)
2.5	Machine fitters and assemblers
2.2	Managers (n.e.c.)
1.9	Retail shop managers
1.6	Laborers and unskilled workers (engineering and related)
1.6	Traveling salespersons and agents
1.6	Coal miners (underground)
1.5	Construction workers (n.e.c.)
(29.4)	Top 5 percent of most common occupations
1.5	Machine repairers and maintenance fitters
1.5	Machine tool operators
1.5	Electricians
1.5	Carpenters
1.5	Primary and secondary school teachers
1.4	Construction laborers
1.3	Agricultural workers (n.e.c.)
1.3	Machine tool setters
1.3	Engineering and related workers (n.e.c.)
(42.2)	Total of twenty most common occupations
100.0	Total all occupations

Japan 1975: 25 years and over

(percentage distribution)

9.8	Farmers and silk growers
9.7	Clerical workers
5.4	Motor vehicle drivers
4.4	Salespersons
3.5	Managers and administrators (n.e.c.)
3.2	Company directors and managers
3.1	Traveling salespersons[b]
2.9	Retail shop owners and dealers
2.5	Bookkeepers
2.4	Carpenters
2.0	Construction laborers
1.6	Cooks
1.4	Metal processing workers (n.e.c.)
1.2	Welders
(53.1)	Top 5 percent of most common occupations
1.0	Metal cutting machine operators
0.9	Construction workers (n.e.c.)
0.9	Laborers and unskilled workers (n.e.c.)
0.8	Electrical equipment fitters
0.8	Machine assemblers
0.8	Motor vehicle repairers
(58.3)	Total of twenty most common occupations
100.0	Total all occupations

Sweden 1975: 25 years and over		United States 1970: 25 years and over	
15.9	Typists, secretaries, office clerks	8.3	Secretaries
7.9	Retail salespersons and assistants	5.0	Retail salespersons
7.3	Nursing and midwife assistants	4.7	Bookkeepers
5.4	Household and office cleaners	4.4	Elementary school teachers
3.0	Child care personnel	3.1	Sewers and stitchers
2.9	Nurses	3.1	Nurses
2.8	Primary school teachers	3.0	Clerical workers (n.e.c.)
2.8	Clerical workers[e]	2.7	Household service workers
2.7	Household helpers	2.7	Operatives (n.e.c.)
2.5	Private household service workers	2.6	Waitresses
2.1	Farmworkers	2.4	Typists
1.8	Waitresses	2.1	Cooks[g]
1.6	Tailors and dressmakers	2.1	Nursing assistants, orderlies
1.4	Secondary school teachers (theoretical subjects)	2.0	Cashiers
(60.1)	Top 5 percent of most common occupations	1.7	Secondary school teachers
1.3	Cashiers (shops, restaurants)	1.7	Assemblers
1.2	Social workers	1.3	Hairdressers, beauticians[d]
1.2	Telephone operators	1.3	Manufacturing inspectors
1.1	Farmers and foresters[f]	1.2	Office machine operators
1.0	Kindergarten teachers	1.2	Packers and wrappers[h]
1.0	Retail shop owners	(56.6)	Top 5 percent of most common occupations
(66.9)	Total of twenty most common occupations	(56.6)	Total of twenty most common occupations
100.0	Total all occupations	100.0	Total all occupations

[a]Includes cashiers. [b]Excludes public institutions. [c]Excludes bars. [d]Excludes barbers. [e]Includes cashiers (n.e.c.).
[f]Excludes loggers. [g]Excludes private household. [h]Excludes meat.

Note: n.e.c. means "not elsewhere classified." In United States, excludes "allocated" component of occupational title.

Source: Same as Table 3.7.

reflected by the 18–19 year-olds having the same foremost occupation as young adults, while 16–17 year-olds record the same first occupation as the whole teenage male group. American adult males, unlike those in the other countries, displayed a high status and high earnings occupation in first place—salaried managers and administrators n.e.c. The proportion in this occupation would have been even larger if the U.S. had used the less detailed classification of the other countries. In further contrast to Britain and Japan, the foremost male occupations in Sweden were highly male-intensive, and highly or moderately male-intensive in the U.S.

Using the adult female lists of 20 most common occupations as the benchmark (Table 3.6), we find that young adult females show a somewhat smaller correspondence than do their male counterparts, except in the U.S. where 16 occupations are identical; Great Britain and Japan have 12 and Sweden 13 occupations. Teenage females have the same number of identical occupations as teenage males in Great Britain and Sweden, three fewer in Japan and four more in the U.S. In all four countries, important occupations of adult females also are found on the most common lists of teenage and young adult females and apply equally to Swedish females aged 16–24 working fewer than 20 hours. Similarities not only in the degree of female occupational segregation but also in its specific components are clearly demonstrated. Thus, lists for the three female age groups in all four countries show salesperson and nurse or nurse assistant. Typist, secretary, sewers (hand and machine), waitress, and teacher also are common occupations in several countries.

Adult female most common occupations that are not identical to those of younger females tend to be low level, including household and office cleaner in Britain, unskilled worker in Japan, and household service worker in Sweden and the United States. In contrast to the situation for males, the nonidentical female occupations, on balance, reveal very little occupational superiority for adult over younger females. Adult women show a marked bifurcation between a small proportion in mid-level occupations and a much larger share in low level occupations, while younger females display a narrow continuum of occupations, rather than a cleavage.

Because of the concentration of all female employment in relatively few occupations, an extraordinarily high share of the total employment of female youth is found in the occupations identical to those of adult females, ranging from 55–58 percent in the U.S. upward to 72–73 percent in Japan. The percentages were slightly higher for young adults than teenage females, except in Sweden. These results imply high substitutability among females of all ages—higher than for males, but greater specificity of jobs is required for firm conclusions.

The top one or two occupations of females, unlike the mixed cross-national pattern for males, show white collar occupations, and especially office work, at the head of the list for all age groups in each country, except for Japanese female adults. Moreover, all are moderately or highly female-intensive, except in Japan (sex-neutral). In Britain, clerical worker is the top occupation for all age groups of females in 1971 as it was in 1966; female and male top occupations are identical. Office work also predominates for young adult and adult females in Sweden and the United States, with typist, secretary, office clerk first in the former, and secretary in the latter. Nursing and midwife assistant are at the top for Swedish teenage females, having been seventh in 1960 when retail salesperson and assistant was first; these changes reflect the rapid growth of public services in Sweden 1960–75. The other two Swedish female age groups showed less change in occupational ranks 1960–75, although farm work declined in importance for all age groups. Retail salesperson leads the American teenage list. Within the American female teenage group, different foremost occupations appeared—retail salesperson for 16–17 year-olds and secretary for 18–19 year-olds.

Some findings arise from the examination of the top occupations. First, in regard to age differences within the same sex, the nomenclature and nature of each group's top occupations made it difficult to distinguish occupational levels. Second, the countries showed divergent patterns in regard to sex differences in top occupations. Finally, the nature of the divergence in top occupations suggests significant differences in the staffing and employment practices of firms and industries between the two groups of countries, Britain and Japan, on the one hand, and Sweden and the U.S., on the other.

The high degree of occupational correspondence observed among the age groups of the same sex is subject to varied interpretations. One view is that the census occupational titles do not sufficiently reveal differences in levels of responsibility and productivity within occupations. Another view is that the cross-sectional data accurately reflect longitudinal histories, controlling for underlying changes in the occupational structure; a majority of the employed population experience only a relatively small upward or downward movement in the occupational hierarchy over their work lives. Such advances in earnings, work conditions, and status that most individuals achieve as they mature and the advantages such persons exhibit over younger persons in the identical occupations are primarily the result of length of service in the occupation, and often in the job. Such relationships have been established in the Japanese employment system (see Chapter 7) and recently have been found in the U.S. (Medoff and Abraham 1980).

Comparisons between most common occupations of adults and youth of the opposite sex compound the age difference with more powerful sex differences. If it is true that adult males have the most favorable occupational distribution, it is important to make the comparison. As expected, the two female youth groups have far fewer identical occupations to adult males than their male counterparts. Moreover, adult females have no more identical occupations that young adult females, except in Japan. Among the countries, Japanese females have the highest rate of agreement with adult male most common occupations, reflecting

Table 3.6 Most Common Occupations of Female Adults, Four Countries, Recent Census Year

Great Britain 1971: 25 years and over		Japan 1975: 25 years and over	
(percentage distribution)		(percentage distribution)	
15.7	Clerical workers[a]	20.5	Farmers and silk growers
9.1	Retail salespersons and assistants	10.1	Clerical workers
7.0	Typists and secretaries	9.9	Salespersons
6.6	Household and office cleaners	6.6	Bookkeepers
6.3	Personal service workers	4.2	Cooks
4.5	Nurses	2.7	Waitresses[c]
4.4	Food counter and fountain workers[b]	2.4	Sewing machine operators
4.0	Primary and secondary school teachers	2.4	Laborers and unskilled workers (n.e.c.)
2.6	Packers and wrappers	2.0	Retail shop owners and dealers
2.2	Hand and machine sewers and embroiderers	1.6	Nurses
1.7	Cooks	1.3	Electrical machinery assemblers and repairers
(64.1)	Top 5 percent of most common occupations	1.2	Primary school teachers
1.6	Kitchen assistants, dishwashers	1.1	Package wrappers (small articles)
1.3	Retail shop managers	1.0	Insurance agents
1.2	Laborers and unskilled workers (n.e.c.)	(67.0)	Top 5 percent of most common occupations
1.1	Office machine operators	1.0	Hairdressers, beauticians[d]
1.1	Bartenders	1.0	Metal processing workers (n.e.c.)
1.0	Warehouse and stores laborers	1.0	Sanitation laborers
1.0	Waitresses	0.9	Weavers
1.0	Telephone operators	0.8	Textile workers (n.e.c.)
0.9	Service workers (n.e.c.)	0.8	Dressmakers
(74.3)	Total of twenty most common occupations	(72.5)	Total of twenty most common occupations
100.0	Total all occupations	100.0	Total all occupations

	Sweden 1975: 25 years and over		United States 1970: 25 years and over
4.9	Motor vehicle drivers	5.5	Managers and administrators (salaried n.e.c.)
4.6	Machine assemblers and repairers	3.6	Operatives (n.e.c.)
4.4	Farmers and foresters^c	3.5	Foremen (n.e.c.)
4.1	Traveling salespersons and agents	3.0	Truck drivers
4.1	Mechanical engineers and technicians	3.0	Farmers
3.7	Machine tool makers and operators	2.3	Traveling salespersons^b
2.7	Architects, civil engineers and construction technicians	2.2	Retail salespersons
2.6	Carpenters	2.1	Janitors
2.2	Warehouse and stores laborers	1.9	Managers and administrators (self-employed n.e.c.)
2.1	Electricians and electrical workers	1.9	Carpenters
2.0	Electrical and electronics engineers and technicians	1.6	Motor vehicle repairers
1.9	Concrete and construction workers	1.3	Heavy equipment repairers
1.7	Welders	1.2	Professional accountants
1.6	Loggers and related forestry workers	1.1	Farm laborers^d
(42.6)	Top 5 percent of most common occupations	1.1	Delivery workers
1.5	Typists, secretaries, office clerks	1.1	Welders
1.5	Painters and finishers (construction)	1.1	Secondary school teachers
1.4	Furniture makers and woodworkers	1.0	Electricians
1.3	Managers and administrators (n.e.c.)	1.0	Construction laborers^e
1.3	Public administrators and officials	1.0	Laborers (n.e.c.)
1.3	Laborers and unskilled workers	(40.5)	Top 5 percent of most common occupations
(50.9)	Total of twenty most common occupations	(40.5)	Total of twenty most common occupations
100.0	Total all occupations	100.0	Total all occupations

^aIncludes cashiers. ^bExcludes insurance. ^cExcludes loggers. ^dExcludes unpaid family workers. ^eExcludes carpenters' assistants.

Note: n.e.c. means "not elsewhere classified." In United States, excludes "allocated" component of occupational title.

Source: Same as Table 3.7.

the size and character of employment in traditional Japanese occupations and the importance of self-employment and unpaid family employment, as well as a weakly developed concept of occupations. Sweden manifests the smallest overlap between adult males and females.

The share of employment in occupations held in common with adult males is much smaller for females than for young males, except in Great Britain for young adult females and in Japan where the adult male list also contains the three leading female occupations. The specific occupations held in common by adult males and females show little cross-national uniformity. A wider cross-national range appears in the proportion of employment in occupations held both by adult males and the female groups than in a similar comparison of adult males with young males.

A comparison between adult female most common occupations and those of young males can throw light on the potential substitutability between the two groups, an issue that has arisen in recent discussions of youth unemployment. Although young men correspond more closely to adult women in the number of identical occupations than young women do with respect to adult men, the number of such occupations is not large. Japanese young males exhibit the largest and Swedish young males the smallest number of identical occupations; the range is from seven to three for young adults and eight to three for teenagers.

Young men have slightly lower proportions of their total employment in occupations identical to those of adult women than young females have in relation to adult males, except in Sweden and the United States. In the most common occupations, which account for a substantial share of the total employment of male youth, there is only a limited scope for substitution, except in Japan. Among the four countries, the overlap in the most common occupations, measured by the shares of employment found in identical occupations for young males and adult females, was smallest in Sweden, followed by Great Britain, the U.S., and Japan. Another measure, the percentage point difference between shares, also confirms that in each country the occupations of young males that are nonidentical, and hence potentially nonsubstitutable for those of adult females, constitute an important part of the employment of young males within the most common occupations.

The degree of sex segregation in occupations has more influence on nonidentical occupations between adult females and young males than the hierarchy of occupations. Thus, young males were in different rather than lower level occupations from those held by adult females. In comparisons among males alone, adult males' nonidentical occupations among the most common reveal enough higher level occupations to establish age and experience as valid differentiators between the age groups. At the same time, a residual of adult males remain in low level jobs.

Occupational Concentration by Age and Sex

If the youth groups are represented in fewer occupations than adults or if a higher proportion of youth than adult employment is concentrated in a few occupations, youth may suffer from "crowding" which undermines their bargaining position on wages and working conditions (cf. Bergmann 1971). The same situation may occur between the sexes, holding age constant. In each of the four countries, female youth show a higher proportion of their total employment than adult women do in the top 5 percent or the 20 most common occupations (Tables 3.1, 3.2, 3.6). The disparity among the age groups in each country, however, was not great. The spread in concentration rates in the top 5 percent of occupations between teenage and adult females was 12 percentage points in Great Britain, Japan, and the U.S. and 10 points in Sweden. Young adult females had somewhat lower differentials.

British and Swedish male youth show the same age progression as females in occupational concentration, each having a gap of 13 percentage points between teenage and adult male employment proportions in the top 5 percent of occupations (Tables 3.3, 3.4, 3.5). In the U.S., however, young adult males have a slightly lower rate than adult males and the spread between teenagers and young adults is over 20 percentage points. In Japan, adult males show greatest concentration and teenage males least, probably because of the special occupational role of farming and the prevalence of older men as farmers. The gap, however, is less than 5 percentage points.

Differences among countries in the level of concentration rates for each age-sex group were fairly consistent and marked, suggesting that cross-national variations in the structure and content of the census occupational classifications may have influenced the levels. Within countries, the variations were fairly orderly and predictable and do not support the view that occupational concentration by age is a major cause of disparity in the occupational distributions of youth and adults.

When attention turns to differences between the sexes in occupational concentration, it is clear that in each country females are far more concentrated occupationally than are males (Tables 3.1–3.6). Allowance must be made, of course, for the prevailing style of detailed occupational classifications which tend to subdivide male occupations, such as engineer, by type of industry and tend to aggregate female occupations, such as typist or clerical, without regard to industry or other subdivisions (Bregger 1982; Miller et al. 1980; Jonung 1983). Nevertheless, the extent of female concentration in the top 5 percent of occupations is striking. Among adult women, the range is from 57 to 67 percent, while for adult males it is 29 to 53 percent. Female teenagers with a spread of 67 to 79 percent far exceed male teenagers' range of 43 to 59 percent, and young adult females, falling between 64 and 78 percent, contrast with the 34 to 53 percent shown by young adult males. Similar results are shown for Germany in Chapter 5.

The share of total employment accounted for by the most important occupation was far greater for females in all countries than for males. In 11 of the 12 female age-sex groups, 10 percent or more of total employment was covered by the foremost occupation, and in four groups the share exceeded 20 percent. For males, in none of the 12 age-sex groups did the top occupation reach a 10 percent share; the shares in the 12 groups ranged from 9.8 percent down to 4.9 percent.

Relative sex crowding is strongest in Britain, while the smallest differentials in sex concentration rates occur in Sweden and the U.S., based on both the top 5 percent and 20 most common occupations. Among the three age groups, young adults, on average, have the largest sex differentials, followed by teenagers and adults. To the extent that *relative* occupational concentration is in itself a disadvantage, British and Japanese females are in a less favorable position than American and Swedish women. The nature of the specific occupations is, however, crucial to a final judgment.

Sex Intensity of Occupations

Not only are females concentrated in a smaller number of occupations than males, but many of these occupations are disproportionately composed of female employees, leading to concern about occupational segregation of the sexes. If the sexes were distributed in the detailed occupations exactly as they are in total employment, the female share would be about 35–40 percent and among the youth groups would be half or slightly over, depending on the country. In fact, most occupations are more male intensive or female intensive than the average sex share of total employment indicates. Using five designations of sex-intensity, ranging from highly same-sex-intensive (85 percent or more of total employment) to highly opposite-sex-intensive (15 percent or less of total employment), we found none of the top 5 percent of occupations of any age-sex group highly opposite-sex intensive, save for one occupation of Swedish young adult males and one of British young adult females. Except among Japanese adult females and American teenage females, the largest number of occupations among the top 5 percent is highly same-sex-intensive.

While in each country more male than female occupations in the top 5 percent are highly same-sex-intensive, differences between the sexes are greater and more pervasive in Sweden and the U.S. than in Japan and Great Britain. Sweden shows the largest proportion of highly same-sex-intensive occupations among the top 5 percent and Japan the lowest proportion. Sex-neutral occupations (either sex having 40 to 59 percent of total employment) are important only in Japan where they usually outnumber the moderately same-sex-intensive or moderately opposite-sex-intensive categories. The explanation probably lies in Japan's small-scale family farming, and diverse clerical positions that occupy both sexes.

Other cross-national studies support our general findings, insofar as they deal with the same countries (Hakim 1979; Jonung 1983). Analysts are concerned about the causes of persistent and widespread sex segregation in occupations and the consequences for female access to the more attractive jobs and career ladders (Rytina 1982). Whether occupational segregation by itself establishes the disparities between the sexes or is part of a broader system of inequality remains to be explored (Jonung 1983). The pre-labor market situation and labor market choices of each sex as well as employer choices are the key issues (Beller 1982; England 1982).

Occupational Dissimilarity Indexes

The foregoing analysis of the most common detailed occupations suggests that the concept of a distinct youth market has been overplayed. We find that the lines between youth and adult labor markets are quite blurred. But what our research clearly shows is a sharp delineation between male and female markets. Furthermore, the lines are sharply drawn between the sexes in the youth market. While some generalizations can be made about "typical" youth jobs, typicality varies by country. To substantiate our claim that youth markets are not well defined, and to summarize the earlier comparisons, we have computed Indexes of Occupational Similarity (IOD) based on the complete distribution of detailed occupations for each age-sex group in four countries.

The IOD is a well-known and easily interpreted measure (Duncan and Duncan 1955; Sakoda 1981). To obtain the IOD, two comparison groups are chosen and their occupational distributions are established for an identical list of occupations. The differences between the two age-sex groups in the proportion in each occupation are recorded and summed. The sum is divided by two and multiplied by 100. The resulting index can range from 0, which means there is no dissimilarity in the occupational distributions of the two comparison groups, to 100, which means complete dissimilarity. IODs express the degree to which the occupational distribution of one subgroup would have to change in order to make it identical to the distribution of the subgroup to which it is being compared. IODs value all occupations equally; as much weight is given, for example, to the occupational distance between a bank president and bank teller as to that between a bank teller and a bank clerk. IODs do not assume that any occupational distribution is superior to any other; they merely measure differences. IODs are influenced by the level of disaggregation of occupations used in the comparisons; compression of occupational categories results in a cancellation of occupational disparities and reduction in the IODs.

Table 3.7   Indexes of Occupational Dissimilarity, Detailed Occupational
            Classification, by Age and Sex, Four Countries, Recent Census Year

Comparison Groups	Great Britain 1971	Japan 1975	Sweden 1975	United States 1970
	Indexes of Occupational Dissimilarity (IOD)*			
Same Sex, Different Age				
15–19 M / 20–24 M	23.7	20.5	22.5[a]	38.4[a]
15–19 M / 25+ M	36.3	39.3	45.6[a]	53.4[a]
20–24 M / 25+ M	21.6	28.7	29.0	25.5
15–19 F / 20–24 F	20.6	18.7	26.1[a]	32.3[a]
15–19 F / 25+ F	35.3	46.0	34.3[a]	36.8[a]
20–24 F / 25+ F	32.1	42.7	21.7	21.8
Same Age, Different Sex				
15–19 M / 15–19 F	67.9	67.2	71.0[a]	65.7[a]
20–24 M / 20–24 F	67.0	60.2	70.4	63.6
25+ M / 25+ F	66.1	48.6	70.7	65.1
Different Age and Sex				
15–19 M / 20–24 F	68.4	70.4	73.1[a]	69.9[a]
15–19 M / 25+ F	65.4	58.2	73.3[a]	60.9[a]
20–24 M / 25+ F	64.5	51.6	69.5	62.0
15–19 F / 20–24 M	71.1	61.6	69.0[a]	70.0[a]
15–19 F / 25+ M	76.3	68.8	78.3[a]	77.6[a]
20–24 F / 25+ M	62.2	65.9	76.8	72.2

*An IOD expresses the degree to which the occupational distribution of one sub-
group would have to change in order to make it identical to the distribution of
the subgroup to which it is being compared.
[a] 16–19.

Note: Occupational data include employees, family workers, apprentices, employers
(except Great Britain), self-employed (except Great Britain), armed forces
(except United States), and students with jobs (except Great Britain). Swedish
data refer only to those who worked 20 hours or more in the reference week. Data
include 221 occupations in Great Britain, 285 in Japan, 281 in Sweden, and 426 in
the United States.

Source: Calculated from: GB 1975, Part II, Table 13; Japan 1978, Vol. 5, Part 1,
Division 1, Table 9; Sweden 1979, Vol. 6:2, Table 13; US 1973, Vol. PC(2)-7A,
Tables 38 and 40.

The IODs in Table 3.7 have been computed from recent censuses
for Great Britain, Japan, Sweden, and the U.S. They cover 15 age-sex
comparison groups, subdivided into three main categories—different
age groups of the same sex, same age groups of different sex, and
different age and sex groups. We have used the most detailed occupations
in each national census, numbering 221, 285, 281, and 426 respectively.
Similar information on West Germany is available in Chapter 5, but
it is based on 87 occupations, the intermediate classification, and results
in lower IODs than would have been achieved with the more detailed
list.

As Table 3.7 indicates, the IODs in the four countries exhibit common patterns and levels in regard to the 15 main comparison groups. National variations in census occupational classifications and data, such as are highlighted in the Appendix to Chapter 3, appear to have little effect on IODs, since only slight cross-national divergence is visible and other causes can be adduced. Overall, these cross-national results support our findings from the earlier review of most common occupations and suggest some uniformities among industrialized countries.

IODs for different age groups of the same sex are expected to be fairly low, indicating occupational similarity, because the detailed occupations in none of the four country censuses fully capture the fine distinctions in job tasks and responsibilities that distinguish younger from mature workers (Bregger 1982; Miller et al. 1980). Since the most common detailed occupations of the various age groups were shown previously to be similar for the same sex, the IOD results in Table 3.7 arc not surprising and give little support to the hypothesis of a separate youth labor market. The IODs for the different age groups of the same sex do, however, establish that young adults differ from teenagers; only the latter possibly depart enough from adult occupational distributions to be considered distinct.

Most of the IODs comparing young adults to adults are under 30 percent, while those of teenagers/adults range upward from 34 percent (Table 3.7). Unusually high IODs for Japanese females in both youth groups reflect the relative unimportance of agriculture for young women and its significance for adult women, many of whom work on family farms. The U.S. IOD for male teenagers is high in comparison to other countries; the IOD for U.S. 16–17 year-olds/adult males is 65.1 and for 18–19 year-olds/adult males 47.7. However, the IOD of American female teenagers compared to adults is in line with those in the other countries. Employed American teenagers are heavily enrolled in school, especially among 16–17 year-olds.

The generally low IODs in comparisons of same sex but different age suggest a fairly high degrcc of labor substitutability or complementarity of teenage and young adult for adult workers. This finding agrees with econometric studies of males, mostly American, that find workers of various ages fairly easily substitutable (Hamermesh and Grant 1979, p.533 table 4; Grant and Hamermesh 1980; Anderson 1977; Freeman 1979; Welch and Cunningham 1978; Johnson and Blakemore 1979). Widespread substitutability and complementarity among age groups are contraindicative of separate youth labor markets, or youth jobs as a predominant feature of employment of the age group.

We expected lower and a narrower range of IODs for females than males in the age comparisons because of the concentration (or crowding) of females into relatively few occupations. With few exceptions, comparison groups of males have slightly higher IODs than corresponding females, but the range of male IODs in Great Britain and Japan is no larger or smaller than that for females. In Sweden and the U.S. our expectation was borne out (Table 3.7).

Youth groups demonstrate a high degree of occupational similarity; IOD differences between teenagers and young adults of the same sex are small, given the disparities between the two age groups in educational qualifications, length of work experience, skill levels, family responsibilities, availability for full-time work, ability to move geographically, age barriers to recruitment for certain occupations, and employers' adverse attitudes toward hiring some teenagers (OECD 1978a, 1981c; Jolly et al. 1980; Jolly and Mingay 1978). All eight IODs that compared teenagers to young adults fall between 18 and 27 percent, except for the U.S. where a larger number of detailed occupations, more attention to the occupational hierarchy than in other countries, and the weight of in-school youth's occupations tend to raise the IODs of the younger group. Within the teenage group, younger, out-of-school teenagers exhibit occupational dissimilarity from older teenagers in, for example, comparisons between the occupations of British 15 year-olds and all teenagers, and between the initial occupations of those leaving Japanese junior high school, mostly at 15, and those leaving senior high school, mostly at 18 (Great Britain 1975a, Table 13; Chapter 7).

In all four countries, age proves to be a less important determinant of occupational dissimilarity than sex. Sex differences in occupations are pervasive and well entrenched. While comparisons in the four countries of age groups of the same sex produce IODs of under 40 percent in the majority of cases, comparisons between the two sexes, either with the same age or different age groups, produce IODs in excess of 60 percent in all but three of the 36 comparisons, and a substantial number are over 70 percent (Table 3.7). Strikingly high IODs are registered in all comparisons of occupational distributions of males with females, whether or not age differences are present. In addition, among the four countries, IODs have a narrower range in cross-sex comparisons than in comparisons between age groups of the same sex. Commonly, two-thirds or more of females would have had to change their occupations in order to achieve an occupational distribution akin to that of the male comparison group. The primary factors are the segregation of males and females in occupations in which there are few persons of the other sex and the crowding of women into relatively few occupations compared to the male distribution.

These factors have been documented in all industrialized countries (OECD 1980c; Barrett 1973; Bergmann 1971; Blau and Hendricks 1979; Cook and Hayashi 1980; Hakim 1979, 1981; Jonung 1978, 1983; Kuwahara 1979; *Le Monde* 1979; Livraghi 1981; Reubens and Reubens 1977; Selby Smith 1981; Sullerot 1971; Willms 1980). So pronounced has been the occupational crowding of women that a British study of occupational differences between racial groups, which found considerable occupational crowding among males of the less favored racial groups, concluded that female-male dissimilarities were "much more striking than any differences between women of different origins" (Mayhew and Rosewell 1978, p.244).

There is some evidence in recent detailed studies of individual countries that occupational segregation has declined slightly over time (Hakim 1981; Jonung 1983; Kuwahara 1979; Beller 1982). In part, this is due to movement by females into occupations that males have been leaving (Jonung 1983; Reubens and Reubens 1977). Moreover, Hakim (1981) established for Great Britain that decreased horizontal segregation (by type of occupation), with which our data deal, has been accompanied by increased vertical segregation, that is, the type of work done by the two sexes within occupational categories; males were found to do the more skilled, responsible or better paid work nationally and even more in subnational data and company records.

In Table 3.7, Sweden shows the highest level of occupational dissimilarity between the sexes (IODs of 78.3–69.0), followed by the U.S. (77.6–60.9), Great Britain (76.3–62.2), and Japan (70.4–48.6). Exhibiting less sex segregation in occupations than the other three countries, Japanese IODs are lowest in six of nine male/female comparisons and highest in none. In addition to the previously mentioned aspects of Japanese occupational classifications which tend to reduce IODs, another possible explanation is that, even within the same detailed occupational classification, Japanese traditions and specific employer practices make sharp differentiations between males and females in all of the other relevant aspects of employment (Cook and Hayashi 1980). Japan's low IODs between the sexes mask the real differences between men and women within a given occupation in access to the "good" jobs, usually defined as jobs in large private firms, government, and public agencies (Koshiro 1981, pp. 7–8). Moreover, in spite of having the smallest degree of sex dissimilarity, Japanese IODs are still high enough to permit substantial occupational divergence between the sexes, as well as relatively low shares of females in the more prestigious and highly paid occupations, compared to the other three countries.

It is more surprising that Sweden, one of the leaders in women's rights, somewhat exceeds the other countries in occupational separation of the sexes. Swedish IODs are highest in eight of the nine sex comparison groups; only in comparisons of teenage females with young adult males are the U.S. and Great Britain slightly above Sweden. Swedish IODs presumably would have been even higher if their data, like that of the other countries, had included those who worked less than 20 hours; such workers are disproportionately female and work in female dominated occupations. The elevated labor force participation rates of Swedish females, based on the rapid growth of the public sector and its service jobs, probably contribute to sex segregation in Sweden. Moreover, although Swedish females have larger proportions in professional and technical occupations than women in other countries, such women have tended to be in different occupations than men.

It should be borne in mind that, by itself, the level of IODs does not reveal whether the employment situation of females relative to males was better in one country than another. Many other aspects of employment that are not covered by IODs or cross-sectional census occupational data influence such a determination. Swedish male-female earnings differentials probably are smaller than in the other three countries because of the wage policy of the strong trade unions and the mode of collective bargaining in Sweden. For example, females in manufacturing earned 91.5 percent of the male level in 1979. Jonung (1983) posits that higher occupational segregation rates may accompany smaller earnings differentials between the sexes, as employers who are barred from expressing discrimination through wage rates resort to exclusionary policies on admission to occupations.

It would be expected that occupational dissimilarity between the sexes would be less marked among youth than adults because attained education (level and type), work experience, and on-the-job training would be more similar for youth than adults and changing attitudes also would seem to favor youth. Contrary to expectations, in the four countries, sex dissimilarity in the same age group is greatest for teenagers, but not by much, except in Japan where IODs for male/female comparisons decline with advancing age; in Sweden and the U.S. there is a slight drop and then a small rise. The very low IOD for Japanese male/female adults, which still exceeds other Japanese IODs comparing the same sex, is attributable to the importance of agricultural and clerical work for adults of both sexes and their fairly even shares of total employment in these two fields. Jonung (1983) found only slight differences in Sweden by detailed age groups and the same trend among all ages toward less segregation over time. German dissimilarity for young people exceeds that for adults and is attributed to the influence of the sex-biased apprenticeship training occupations on early employment (Chapter 5).

The high IODs shown when detailed occupations are compared across the sexes imply fairly limited occupational substitutability between males and females. Least substitutability seems to exist between young females and adult males. Even when age is the same, substitutability between the sexes appears to be restricted. In discussing substitutability or competition for jobs between young people and adult females, the group whose employment has increased most rapidly, some analysts have combined the data for youth of both sexes (Grant and Hamermesh 1980; Osterman 1980; Australia 1979a, p.23; OECD 1978a; Great Britain 1978a; see also, Reubens 1980, pp.121–122). This procedure seems unwise, since youth to adult IODs for the same sex are reasonably low, but rise considerably when sex is different. Therefore, substitutability, complementarity, and competition in jobs between young males and adult females appears to be potentially more limited than similar relationships between adult and young females.

Summary

Detailed, three-digit, occupational data from the latest available population censuses of Great Britain (1971), Japan (1975), Sweden (1975), and the United States (1970) were analyzed in order to determine the extent and nature of age and sex occupational differences within and across countries. Addition of data on other dimensions of employment, such as earnings, hours worked, years of work experience, and educational attainment facilitates cross-national comparisons. Longitudinal data, collected on a comparable basis in a large number of countries, would provide the most desirable data base.

Within the limitations imposed by the cross-sectional census data, we constructed several measures—the most common occupations of youth, the most youth-intensive occupations, comparisons of most common occupations by age and sex, occupational concentration, the sex intensity of occupations, and indexes of occupational dissimilarity. Three age groups were utilized—teenagers (15–19 or 16–19), young adults (20–24) and adults (25 and over); each sex was treated separately at all times.

The main conclusions were consistent across the measures and may be summarized as follows:

- Differences in occupational distributions by age for the same sex were not great, but the large number of detailed occupations that were identical for adults and youth of the same sex probably conceal age differences within occupations in rank, responsibility, and earnings.
- No firm evidence of a separate youth labor market could be found in any of the countries, but "youth jobs" were identifiable in the detailed occupations and would have been even more visible with additional information on job tasks, size of firm, and other employment information.
- Age differences in occupations between teenagers and young adults, on the one hand, and between the two youth groups and adults, on the other, were more pronounced in the United States than in the other three countries. American teenagers displayed an adverse occupational distribution with a large number of "youth jobs" that may be related to observed high job turnover and persistently elevated unemployment rates.
- Potential substitutability of youth groups for adults of the same sex seemed reasonably high, on the basis of occupational similarity, but cross-sex substitutability appeared to be limited.
- Japan and Great Britain registered a smaller degree of disparity than Sweden and the United States in virtually every measure of age and sex occupational differences. There appeared to be two groups of countries at many points in the analysis.

- In all countries, differences in occupations between the sexes greatly exceeded those between age groups of the same sex, reflecting the pervasive and strong separation between male and female occupations and the crowding of females into relatively few occupations.

Appendix
National Census Occupational Data

Occupational data have been drawn from the 1971 and 1966 censuses of Great Britain, the 1975 census of Japan, the 1975 and 1960 censuses of Sweden, and the 1970 census of the United States (GB 1975a, 1968a; Japan 1978b; Sweden 1979a, 1964a; US 1973a). Chart B3.1 shows the relevant points of difference among the censuses. The avoidance of census enumerations in winter or summer, as well as adoption of a standard reference week for the occupational data minimize differences among the countries. Swedish data for 1975 exclude those working under 20 hours a week, disproportionately affecting women and youth. The omission of British employers and the self-employed in the census table we analyzed tends to understate slightly the differences between adult males and other age-sex groups in Britain, on the one hand, and between British and other adult males, on the other.

Students who work during the census reference period are included in Japan, Sweden, and the United States; in each case the census reference period was a time when schools, colleges and universities were in session. In Britain, whose census does not count the small number of employed students, the 1971 results slightly understate the amount of youth employment and somewhat alter its character compared to the other countries. Unpaid family workers are included in occupational data in all four countries, but in Britain and Japan, no minimum number of hours worked was imposed; in Sweden only those who worked 20 hours or more were included in the relevant table; and in the United States, a minimum of 15 hours of work in the reference week was stipulated. The main effect of these definitions was to augment Japanese data relatively, since unpaid family work was of considerable numerical significance, particularly for females. Finally, male youth employment in the United States was understated compared to the other countries because the U.S. detailed occupational tables, unlike the other countries, referred only to civilian employment.

Cross-national comparisons also are affected by variations among the censuses in their occupational classification systems, both in terms of the numbers of major (1-digit), intermediate (2-digit) and detailed (3-digit) level occupations identified and in the manner of separating and combining categories. The degree of disaggregation at the 3-digit level and the consistency of its application affect both the national and cross-national computations for the Indexes of Occupational Dissimilarity, the most common occupations, and the youth-intensive occupations. Sweden's census identified nine 1-digit categories, the fewest, while both Japan and the United States listed 12 major level groups. Great Britain's census listed the largest number of occupations at the 1-digit level, 27, but this also constituted the British 2-digit level. At the 2-digit level, which may be regarded as a subdivision of major occupation groups or as a combination of detailed level groups, Sweden's 45 intermediate groupings and Japan's 52 compared with 129 in the United States. At the detailed level, the 441 occupations identified in the U.S. census compared with 223 in Britain, 282 in Sweden and 286 in Japan (Table A3.1).

The larger number of detailed occupations in the U.S. census permitted finer breakdowns in many cases. Some 2-digit level occupations in the U.S. were similar to 3-digit level occupations in other countries. For example, the American 2-digit level occupation of "office machine operator" appeared in other countries at the 3-digit level; the Japanese census specified both key puncher and office machine operator. In the U.S., office machine operator was subdivided at the 3-digit level into operators of bookkeeping and billing machines; calculating machines; computers and peripheral equipment; duplicating machines; keypunch machines; tabulating machines; and office machines n.e.c. However,

Table A3.1 Occupational Data in Censuses, Four Countries

	Great Britain		Japan	Sweden		United States
	Apr.	Apr.	Oct.	Nov.	Nov.	Apr.
Enumeration date	1971	1966	1975	1975	1960	1970
Sample base (percentage)	10	10	20[a]	100	100	5
Coverage						
Employers	No	No	Yes	Yes	Yes[b]	Yes
Self-employed	No	No	Yes	Yes	Yes[b]	Yes
Employees	Yes	Yes	Yes	Yes	Yes[b]	Yes
Unpaid family workers	Yes	Yes	Yes	Yes[c]	Yes[c]	Yes[d]
Temporarily absent from work[e]	Yes	Yes	Yes[f]	Yes[g]	Yes[g]	Yes
Students with jobs	No	No	Yes	Yes	Yes	Yes
Unemployed	No	No	No	No	No	No
Armed forces	Yes	Yes	Yes	Yes[h]	Yes[h]	No
Detailed occupations						
Identified in census	223	211	286	282	291	441
Used for IOD[i]	223	*	286	282	*	426
Used for MCO/YIO[k]	221	209	285	281	290	396
Intermediate occupations	27	27	52	45	59	129
Major occupations			12	9	9	12

*Not calculated

[a]100 percent sample used for institutionalized population and self-defense forces.
[b]Minimum of at least half of normal hours worked in reference week required.
[c]Minimum of 16 hours work required in agriculture, forestry and fishing. [d]Minimum of 15 hours work required. [e]Due to holiday, sickness, injury, industrial dispute, temporary layoff, bad weather etc., with job awaiting on return. [f]Provided absent for no more than 30 days, or if paid. [g]Provided absent for no more than 4 months. [h]Excluding conscripts in first period of military service. [i]Indexes of Occupational Dissimilarity. [j]Most Common Occupations/Youth Intensive Occupations.

Source: GB 1975a, 1968a; Japan 1978b; Sweden 1979a, 1964a; US 1973a.

for purposes of consistency across countries, we consolidated the American office machine operator group to form a single detailed occupation.

Greatest disaggregation was not necessarily shown by the American census in every case, however. The Swedish 1975 census listed 19 agricultural, forestry and fishing detailed occupations, compared with 13 in Japan, where the sector was of greater importance proportionately, 9 in the U.S. and 6 in Britain. Disaggregation of manufacturing assemblers also varied across countries. The United States census contained a single category for assemblers, at both the 2 and 3-digit level. Britain and Sweden divided the category between electrical and electronic, and general machine assemblers at the 3-digit level, while Japan identified at least 9 assembly occupations, subdividing both the electrical and general machine groups by type of assembly (vehicle, aircraft, ship, general machine, etc.), though including persons who repaired machines in some assembly occupations; in other countries, the repairers were a separate occupation.

Countries vary in the degree to which the occupations identified by the census were classified along truly occupational, rather than industrial lines. Occupational categories identify the type of work and imply the tasks performed and human behaviors associated with the job, while industrial categories classify work by the type of product produced (Sommers 1979, p.3). The later development of occupational concepts leads to an industrial bias in most occupational classifications devised for statistical purposes. On the whole, the United States census has made greater distinctions between the occupational and industrial concepts than the other three countries. All four countries categorize professional and technical, managers and administrators, clerical, sales and service workers in occupational rather than industrial groupings at major, minor and detailed levels.

Industry classifications appear at different levels in the occupational lists of the four countries. In the British census many of the 1-digit or major-level groups were organized by industry, especially for manual occupations (engineering worker, textile worker, printing worker, construction worker). The other countries introduced industry-based classifications at the intermediate or 2-digit level. The U.S. displays least industrial classification of occupations at the intermediate level, in part because the larger number of 2-digit categories allows more specific functional identification of occupations, introducing some industrial-based classifications to the 3-digit level. The U.S. census utilized industrial titles mainly at the 4-digit level which no other country had.

The national censuses also varied as to distinctions among occupational ranks. At the 1-digit level, only the U.S. census specifically separated skill levels into three major occupations: craft workers (including foremen), operatives, and laborers; the British census presented "laborers" as a separate 1-digit group. In the U.S., at the 1-digit level, farmer and farm manager were one group and farm laborer and farm foreman another. Britain, Japan, and Sweden differentiated skill levels in agricultural occupations at the 3-digit level, however. In all three countries, farmers were distinguished from operatives (such as machinery driver) and agricultural laborers (such as gardener and timber feller).

The U.S. census, unlike the others, further subdivided skills at the 2-digit level. At the 3-digit level, skill levels were separately identified in the U.S. detailed occupations, but usually were not specified in the other countries. For example, at the 3-digit level the U.S. distinguished between metal crafts workers, such as boilermaker, millwright and molder; metal operatives, such as furnaceman, plater and welder; and metal industry laborer. In Britain, Japan, and Sweden, some 3-digit occupation titles included "operative" in the appellation, while others clearly combined skill levels, such as Sweden's machine toolmaker and operator, a single detailed occupation. Among the professional occupations, the level of school in which teachers were employed (nursery, kindergarten, elementary, or secondary school) or the rank held in colleges and universities were part of the 3-digit classification in all four countries. Similarly, within the food service occupations, most countries differentiated at the 3-digit level between cook, kitchen assistant or dishwasher, and waiter, but only the U.S. census separately listed waiters' assistant (busboy).

Apprentices, as part of a formal apprenticeship training system, were a significant occupation only in Great Britain (1971) and the United States. In Britain only one apprentice classification, engineering and related, was recorded as a detailed occupation. However, information on apprentices and trainees by industry and/or occupation was provided in another census table. In the United States census, apprentices were separately listed as subdivisions of the 3-digit level. Therefore, U.S. apprentices were included in their relevant occupations in the data used to construct the IODs (Indexes of Occupational Dissimilarity); this accounts for the difference of 15 between the 441 occupations officially identified in the census and the 426 used in our IOD calculations.

Some of the censuses contained detailed occupations peculiar to that country. As expected, the Japanese census had the most; some examples were seaweed and shell gatherer; *kimono* maker; bean-curd, paste of arum root, and other allied products maker; *tatami* installer; Japanese umbrella, lantern and fan maker; and *geisha-girl*. Sweden listed *ombudsman* and reindeer herder.

In order to construct comparable occupational distribution tables at the 1-digit level, we regrouped occupational categories at all three levels. We used eight 1-digit or major classifications for all countries: professional and technical; managers and administrators; clerical; sales; manual (including transport and mining); service (including military); farmers, forestry and fishing; and unclassified. The U.S. was reduced to seven 1-digit groups since it lacked the unclassified group. This procedure did not cause major reallocations, but mainly led to the compression of existing major groups, especially in the manual and service categories and generally in Great Britain, whose 1-digit level categories were quite detailed. There was sufficient agreement among the four countries on such categories as professional and technical, managers and administrators, clerical, and sales, so that they remained virtually untouched.

In assembling the data to construct the IODs (Indexes of Occupational Dissimilarity), all detailed occupations were used, including those designated as unclassified (in the U.S. called "allocated"). A number of modifications were made to the census data for the calculation of the most common occupations for youth and the youth-intensive occupations. First, the total number of 3-digit, detailed occupations used was smaller than the total identified by each census. In Britain, Japan, and Sweden, the difference was slight. The unclassified were not counted as an occupation, although the number was included in total employment for the age-sex group. The remaining adjustment in Britain was the exclusion of the relatively small category of commonwealth and foreign armed forces, which improved consistency among the four countries. In the U.S., we omitted twelve detailed occupations in the seven major groups. These were called "allocated" and referred to unclassifiable persons; the numbers involved were added into the total employment of the age-sex groups. In addition, some U.S. detailed sales occupations were amended slightly and consolidated, for greater consistency with the other countries. In total, 396 occupations were used instead of 441 for the U.S.

Occupational titles have been standardized where possible across countries and adapted to eliminate sex-specific appellations. For example, our occupation "motor vehicle repairer" covers "motor mechanic, auto engineer" in Britain, "automobile repairman" in Japan, and "automobile mechanic" in the United States. Truck driver, the U.S. census category, also has been used to cover the British occupation "driver of road goods vehicle," while "motor vehicle driver" covers "automobile driver" (Japan) and "motor vehicle and tram driver" (Sweden). The standardized category of "hairdresser, barber and beautician" covers the British title "hairdresser, manicurist and beautician," and the Swedish title "hairdresser and beautician"; in these countries, barber was included without specification. In Japan and the U.S. where barbers were separated, "hairdresser, beautician" covers the Japanese census category "beautician," while in the United States, it covers "hairdresser and cosmetologists."

Certain minor adjustments were made to data collected from the British 1966 and Swedish 1960 censuses in order to use them for MCO comparisons. For example, the teenage coverage in Sweden changed from 14–19 years in 1960 to 16–19 years in 1975, reflecting the advance in the compulsory school-leaving age.

References to Chapters 1, 2, and 3

Aigner, D.J., and Cain, G.G. 1977. "Statistical Theories of Discrimination in Labor Markets." *Industrial and Labor Relations Review,* January.

Anderson, J. 1977. "Labor Force Age Structure Changes and Relative Wages." Unpublished paper, Harvard University.

AUSTRALIA
1974–82. *The Labour Force.* Australian Bureau of Statistics. Canberra: ABS, monthly.

1979a. *Employment of Demographic Groups in Australian Industry.* Research Reports 3. Bureau of Industry Economics. Canberra: AGPS (Australian Government Publishing Service).

1979b. *Job Markets. Economic and Statistical Aspects of the Australian Market for Labour.* Treasury Economic Papers no.4. Canberra: AGPS.

Barrett, N.S. 1973. "Have Swedish Women Achieved Equality?" *Challenge,* November-December.

Barton, P.E. 1975. "Youth Employment and Career Entry." In Wolfbein, S.L., ed. *Labor Market Information for Youths.* Philadelphia: Temple University.

Beck, E.M.; Horan, P.M.; and Tolbert II, C.M. 1978. "Stratification in a Dual Economy: A Sectoral Model of Earnings Determination." *American Sociological Review,* October.

Becker, G.S. 1964. *Human Capital. A Theoretical and Empirical Analysis.* New York: National Bureau of Economic Research.

Beller, A.H. 1982. "Occupational Segregation by Sex: Determinants and Changes." *Journal of Human Resources,* Summer.

Bergmann, B.R. 1971. "The Effect on White Incomes of Discrimination in Employment." *Journal of Political Economy,* March–April.

Bibb, R., and Form, W.H. 1977. "The Effects of Industrial, Occupational, and Sex Stratification on Wages in Blue-Collar Markets." *Social Forces,* June.

Björklund, A.; Johannesson, J.; and Persson-Tanimura, I. 1979. *Labour Market Policy and Labour Market Development in Sweden during the 1960's and 1970's.* IIM/79–14. Berlin: International Institute of Management.

Blau, F.D., and Hendricks, W.D. 1979. "Occupational Segregation by Sex: Trends and Prospects." *Journal of Human Resources,* Spring.

Blau, P.M., and Duncan, O.D. 1967. *The American Occupational Structure.* New York: John Wiley.

Bose, C.E. 1973. *Jobs and Gender: Sex and Occupational Prestige.* Baltimore, Md.: Center for Metropolitan Planning and Research, Johns Hopkins University.

Bowers, N. 1981. "The Dynamics of Youth Labor Force Flows: An Empirical Examination of Data from the Current Population Survey." Unpublished paper, Bureau of Labor Statistics.

Bregger, H.E. 1982. "Labor Force Data from the CPS to Undergo Revision in January 1983." *Monthly Labor Review,* November.

Brown, C. 1982. "Dead-end Jobs and Youth Unemployment." In Freeman, R.B. and Wise, D.A., eds. *The Youth Labor Market Problem: Its Nature, Causes, and Consequences.* Chicago, Ill.: University of Chicago Press.

Buchele, R.K. 1976. *Jobs and Workers: A Labor Market Segmentation Perspective on the Work Experience of Young Men.* PB-273809. National Technical Information Service, Department of Commerce. Springfield, Va.: NTIS.

————. 1980. *Sex Differences in Employment and Earnings: A Labor Market Segmentation Perspective.* International Working Party on Labour Market Segmentation. Berlin: Forschungsstelle Sozialökonomik der Arbeit, Freie Universität Berlin.

Cain, G.G. 1976. "The Challenge of Segmented Labor Market Theories to Orthodox Theory: A Survey." *Journal of Economic Literature,* December.

————. 1977. *A Reanalysis of the International Relationship Between Income and Labor Supply.* Discussion Paper 440-77. Madison, Wis.: Institute for Research on Poverty, University of Wisconsin-Madison.

Cain, G.G.; Hansen, W.L.; and Weisbrod, B.A. 1969. "Classification of Occupations: Some Problems of Economic Interpretation." *Proceedings,* American Statistical Association.

Carnoy, M. 1978. *Segmented Labor Markets: A Review of the Theoretical and Empirical Literature and Its Implications for Educational Planning.* Paris: International Institute for Educational Planning.

Casson, M. 1979. *Youth Unemployment.* London: Macmillan.

Clark, K., and Summers, L. 1982. "The Dynamics of Youth Unemployment." In Freeman, R.B. and Wise, A.D., eds. *The Youth Labor Market Problem: Its Nature, Causes, and Consequences.* Chicago: University of Chicago Press.

Cohen, M.S., and Schwartz, A.R. 1980. "U.S. Labor Turnover: Analysis of a New Measure." *Monthly Labor Review,* November.

Collier, P. 1978. *Crisis in Youth Unemployment?* Research Paper 33. Coventry, England: Manpower Research Group, Centre for Industrial Economic and Business Research, University of Warwick.

Cook, A.H., and Hayashi, H. 1980. *Working Women in Japan.* Cornell International Industrial and Labor Relations Report no.10. Ithaca, N.Y.: New York State School of Labor and Industrial Relations, Cornell University.

Denton, F.T.; Robb, A.L.; and Spencer, B.G. 1980. *Unemployment and Labour Force Behaviour of Young People: Evidence from Canada and Ontario.* Ontario Economic Council Research Studies. Toronto: University of Toronto Press.

Doeringer, P., and Piore, M. 1971. *Internal Labor Markets and Manpower Analysis.* Lexington, Mass.: D.C. Heath.

Duncan, O.D. 1961. "A Socio-economic Index for All Occupations." In Reiss, A.J., ed., *Occupations and Social Status.* New York: Free Press of Glencoe.

Duncan, O.D., and Duncan, B. 1955. "A Methodological Analysis of Segregation Indexes." *American Sociological Review,* April.

Duncan, O.D., and Featherman, D.L. 1973. "Psychological and Cultural Factors in the Process of Occupational Achievement." In Goldberger, A.S. and Duncan, O.D., eds. *Structural Models in the Social Sciences.* New York: Seminar Press.

Duncan, O.D.; Featherman, D.L.; and Duncan, B. 1972. *Socioeconomic Background and Achievement.* New York: Academic Press.

Edwards, R.C. 1979. *Contested Terrain.* New York: Basic Books.

Edwards, R.C.; Reich, M.; and Gordon, D.M., eds. 1975. *Labor Market Segmentation.* Lexington, Mass.: D.C. Heath.

England, P. 1982. "The Failure of Human Capital Theory to Explain Occupational Sex Segregation." *Journal of Human Resources,* Summer.

Falkenburg, F., and Vissers, A. 1978. *Theorie van de dubbele Arbeidsmarkt (Theories of the Dual Labor Market).* Tilburg, Netherlands: IVA.

Featherman, D.L.; Hauser, R.M.; and Sewell, W.H. 1974. "Towards Comparable Data on Inequality and Stratification: Pespectives on the Second Generation of National Mobility Studies." *The American Sociologist,* February.

Fine, S.A. 1968. "The Use of the Dictionary of Occupational Titles as a Source of Estimates of Education and Training Requirements." *Journal of Human Resources,* Summer.

Folk, H. 1968. "The Problem of Youth Unemployment." In *The Transition from School to Work.* Report Series no.111. Princeton, N.J.: Industrial Relations Section, Princeton University.

Form, W.H., and Huber, J. 1976. "Occupational Power." In Dubin, R., ed. *Handbook of Work, Organization and Society.* Chicago, Ill.: Rand McNally.

Freedman, M.K. 1976. *Labor Markets: Segments and Shelters.* Montclair, N.J.: Allanheld, Osmun.

Freeman, R.B. 1979. "The Effect of Demographic Factors on Age-Earnings Profiles." *Journal of Human Resources,* Summer.

Freiburghaus, D. 1976. "Zentrale Kontroversen der neueren Arbeitsmarktpolitik" ("Central Controversies in the Newer Labor Market Policy"). In Bolle, M., ed. *Arbeitsmarkttheorie und Arbeitsmarktpolitik (Labor Market Theory and Labor Market Policy).* Opladen, West Germany: Leske/Budrich.

Fuchs, V.R. 1980. *Economic Growth and the Rise of Service Employment.* Working Paper no.486. Cambridge, Mass.: National Bureau of Economic Research.

GERMANY

1963–82. *Stand und Entwicklung der Bevölkerung (Status and Development of the Population).* Fachserie 1, Reihe 1.1. Wiesbaden: Statistisches Bundesamt, annual.

1978–82. *Arbeits-und Sozialstatistik, Hauptergebnisse (Work and Social Statistics, Main Results).* Bingen: Robert Schulz, annual.

1980a. *Employment Policy in Germany—Challenges and Concepts for the 1980s.* Nürnberg: Federal Employment Institute.

Glass, D. 1954. *Social Mobility in Britain.* London: Routledge and Keegan Paul.

Goldstein, H. 1980. "Recent Structural Changes in Employment in the United States." Paper for Conservation of Human Resources, Columbia University, New York.

Goldthorpe, J.H., and Hope, K. 1974. *The Social Grading of Occupations: A New Approach and Scale.* Oxford: Clarendon Press.

Grant, J.H., and Hamermesh, D.S. 1980. *Labor Market Competition Among Youths, White Women and Others.* Working Paper no.519. Cambridge, Mass.: National Bureau of Economic Research.

GREAT BRITAIN

1960–82a. Department of Employment *Gazette.* "Employment in Great Britain; Analysis by Age, Sex, Region and Industry," various issues. London: HMSO (Her Majesty's Stationery Office).

1960–82b. *Annual Abstract of Statistics.* Central Statistical Office, various issues. London: HMSO.

1968a. General Register Office. *Sample Census 1966, Great Britain.* Economic Activity Tables, Part I. London: HMSO.

1975a. Office of Population Censuses and Surveys. *Census 1971, Great Britain.* Economic Activity, Part II (10% Sample). London: HMSO.

1978a. *Young People and Work.* Manpower Studies no. 19781. Manpower Services Commission. London: HMSO.

1981a. *Relationship Between the 1970 and 1980 Occupational Classifications.* Unpublished tables. London: Office of Population Censuses and Surveys.

Gregory, R.G., and Foster, W. 1981. *The Contribution of Employment Separation to Teenage Unemployment.* Discussion Paper no.31. Canberra: Centre for Economic Policy Research, The Australian National University.

Hakim, C. 1979. *Occupational Segregation.* Research Paper no.9. London: Department of Employment.

————. 1981. "Job Segregation: Trends in the 1970s." Department of Employment *Gazette,* December.

Hall, R.E. 1970. "Why is the Unemployment Rate So High at Full Employment?" *Brookings Papers on Economic Activity,* no.3.

Hamermesh, D.S., and Grant, J.H. 1979. "Econometric Studies of Labor-Labor Substitution and their Implications for Policy." *Journal of Human Resources,* Fall.

Harrison, B., and Sum, A. 1979. *Labor Market Data Needs from the Perspective of 'Dual' or 'Segmented' Labor Market Research.* Background Paper no.29. National Commission on Employment and Unemployment Statistics. Washington: GPO.

Hodge, R.W., and Siegal, P.M. 1966. "The Classification of Occupations: Some Problems of Sociological Interpretation." *Proceedings,* American Statistical Association.

Hönekopp, E., and Ullmann, H. 1980. "Auf dem Weg zur Dienstleistungsökonomie? Wirschafts-und Beschaftigungsstrukturen ausgewählter industriestaaten im Vergleich" ("Towards a Service Economy? A Comparison of Economic and Employment Structures of Selected Industrial Countries"). *Mitteilungen aus er Arbeitsmarkt-und Berufsforschung,* no.2. Stuttgart: W. Kohlhammer.

Jackson, J.A., ed. 1970. *Professions and Professionalization.* London: Cambridge University Press.

JAPAN

1960–82. *Annual Report of the Labor Force Survey.* Tokyo: Office of the Prime Minister. Bureau of Statistics.

1978a. *Japan Statistical Yearbook 1978.* Tokyo: Office of the Prime Minister, Bureau of Statistics.

1978b. *1975 Population Census of Japan. Results of Detailed Tabulation.* (Twenty Percent Sample Tabulation). Whole Japan. Volume 5, Part 1, Division 1. Tokyo: Office of the Prime Minister, Bureau of Statistics.

1979a. *Towards Improving the Foundations of Living and Expanding Opportunities.* Annual Reports on National Life. Tokyo: Economic Planning Agency.

1980a. "The 1979 Labor White Paper." *Japan Labor Bulletin,* October.

1981a. "Junior and Senior High School Graduate Job Seekers to Decline Next Year." *Japan Labor Bulletin,* January.

1981b. "The 1980 Labor White Paper: International Comparison of Labor Productivity and Female Employment Problems." *Japan Labor Bulletin,* September.

Johnson, G.E., and Blakemore, A. 1979. "The Potential Impact of Employment Policy on the Unemployment Rate Consistent with Non-Accelerating Inflation." Proceedings, American Economic Association. *American Economic Review,* May.

Jolly, J.; Creigh, S.; and Mingay, A. 1980. *Age as a Factor in Employment.* Research Paper no.11. Unit for Manpower Studies. London: Department of Employment.

Jolly, J., and Mingay, A. 1978. "Age Qualifications for Entry to Occupations." Department of Employment *Gazette,* June. London: HMSO.

Jonung, C. 1978. "Sexual Equality in the Swedish Labor Market." *Monthly Labor Review,* October.

_____. 1983. *Patterns of Occupational Segregation by Sex in the Labor Market,* forthcoming.

Kalachek, E. 1969a. "Determinants of Teenage Employment." *Journal of Human Resources,* Winter.

_____. 1969b. *The Youth Labor Market.* Policy Papers in Human Resources and Industrial Relations no.12. Ann Arbor, Mich.: The Institute of Labor and Industrial Relations, University of Michigan and Wayne State University.

Kalleberg, A.L., and Sorensen, A.B. 1979. "The Sociology of Labor Markets." *Annual Review of Sociology,* vol.5.

King, A.G. 1979. *Comments* on Harrison, B. and Sum, A. *Labor Market Data Needs from the Perspective of 'Dual' or 'Segmented' Labor Market Research.* Background Paper no.29. National Commission on Employment and Unemployment Statistics. Washington: GPO (Government Printing Office).

Koshiro, K. 1981. "Problematic Changes in the Labor Market (II)." *Japan Labor Bulletin,* June.

Kuwahara, Y. 1979. "Occupational Structure by Age and Sex in Japan." *Japan Labor Bulletin,* October.

_____. 1981. "Growing Service Employment in the Japanese Manufacturing Sector." *Japan Labor Bulletin,* July.

Le Monde. 1979. "Women's Jobs: Crumbling Cliches." Translation in *Manchester Guardian Weekly,* August 12.

Ledrut, R. 1966. *Sociologie du chômage (Sociology of Unemployment).* Paris: Presse Universitaire de France.

Leon, C.B. 1981a. "The Employment-Population Ratio: Its Value in Labor Force Analysis." *Monthly Labor Review,* February.

_____. 1981b. "Employed but Not at Work: Unpaid and Paid Absence." *Monthly Labor Review,* November.

Lipset, S., and Bendix, R. 1959. *Social Mobility in Industrial Society.* Berkeley, Cal.: University of California Press.

Livraghi, R. 1981. "La discriminazione tra le donne: l'istruzione" ("Discrimination Against Women: Education"). *Notizario CERES di Economia de Lavoro,* September. Rome: Centro Richerche Economiche e Sociali.

Loveridge, R., and Mok, A.L. 1979. *Theories of Labour Market Segmentation.* Leiden, Netherlands: Martinus Nijhoff.

Lucas, R.E.B. 1974. "The Distribution of Job Characteristics." *Review of Economics and Statistics,* November.

Lutz, B. 1969. "Produktionsprozess und Berufqualifikation" ("Production Processes and Occupational Qualifications"). In Adorno, T.W., ed. *Spatkapitalismus öder Industriegesellschaft?* Stuttgart: Enke.

_____. 1976. "Bildungssystem und Beschäftigungsstruktur in Deutschland und Frankreich. Zum Einfluss des Bildungssystems auf die Gestaltung betrieblicher Arbeitskräftestrukturen" ("Educational Systems and Employment Structures in Germany and France. On the Influence of Educational Systems on Manpower Structures of Firms"). In Mendius, H.G. et al., eds. *Betreib-Arbeitsmarkt-Qualifikation I.* Frankfurt: Aspekte.

Lydall, H. 1968. *The Structure of Earnings.* Oxford: Oxford University Press.

Maneval, K.; Schröer, J.; and Herbrich, K. 1976. *Wirtschafts-,Berufs- und Sozialstructurentwicklung in einigen Industriestaaten (Industrial, Occupational and Social Structure Developments in Industrialized Countries).* BeitrAB 9. Nürnberg: Federal Employment Institute, Institute for Labor Market Research.

Marsden, D. 1980. *Study of Changes in the Wage Structure of Manual Workers in Industry in Six Community Countries since 1966, and Proposals for the Development of Future Community Surveys.* Eurostat/C2/80032. Luxembourg: Eurostat. Statistical Office of the European Communities.

_____. 1981. "Vive la Différence: Pay Differentials in Britain, West Germany, France, and Italy." Department of Employment *Gazette,* July. London: HMSO.

Marshall, R. 1974. "The Economics of Racial Discrimination: A Survey." *Journal of Economic Literature,* September.

Maurice, M.; Sorge, A.; and Warner, M. 1980. "Societal Differences in Organizing Manufacturing Units: A Comparison of France, West Germany and Great Britain." *Organization Studies,* no.1.

Mayhew, K., and Rosewell, B. 1978. "Immigrants and Occupational Crowding in Great Britain." *Oxford Bulletin of Economics and Statistics,* August.

_____. 1979. "Labour Market Segmentation in Britain." *Oxford Bulletin of Economics and Statistics,* May.

Medoff, J.L., and Abraham, K.G. 1980. "Experience, Performance, and Earnings." *Quarterly Journal of Economics,* December.

Merrilees, W.J., and Wilson, R.A. 1979. *Disequilibrium in the Labour Market for Young People in Great Britain.* Discussion Paper. Coventry, England: Manpower Research Group, Centre for Industrial Economic and Business Research, University of Warwick.

Metcalf, D. 1980. *Low Pay, Occupational Mobility and Minimum Wage Policy in Britain.* Discussion Paper no.80. London: Centre for Labour Economics, London School of Economics.

Miller, A.R.; Treiman, D.J.; Cain, P.S.; and Roos, P.A. 1980. *Work, Jobs, and Occupations: A Critical Review of the Dictionary of Occupational Titles.* Washington: National Academy Press.

Mincer, J. 1970. "The Distribution of Labor Incomes: A Survey with Special References to the Human Capital Approach." *Journal of Economic Literature,* March.

_____. 1974. *Schooling, Experience and Earnings.* New York: National Bureau of Economic Research.

Mincer, J., and Leighton, L. 1982. "Labor Turnover and Youth Unemployment." In Freeman, R.B. and Wise, D.A., eds. *The Youth Labor Market Problem: Its Nature, Causes, and Consequences.* Chicago, Ill.: University of Chicago Press.

Moy, J. 1979. "Recent Labor Market Trends in Nine Industrial Nations." *Monthly Labor Review,* May.

Moy, J., and Sorrentino, C. 1981. "Unemployment, Labor Force Trends, and Layoff Practices in 10 Countries." *Monthly Labor Review,* December.

New York Times. 1981a. "Japan Farmers Left Out of Economic Miracle." September 10.

OECD (Organization for Economic Cooperation and Development)

1978a. *Youth Unemployment.* A Report on the High Level Conference on Youth Unemployment. 2 vols. Paris: OECD.

1980a. *Labour Force Statistics 1967–78.* Paris: OECD.

1980b. *Women and Employment.* Paris: OECD.

1980c. *National Accounts Statistics, 1950–1978.* Paris: OECD.

1981a. *Main Economic Indicators. Historical Statistics, 1960–1980.* Paris: OECD.

1981b. *National Accounts of OECD Countries,* vol.1. Paris: OECD.

1981c. *Youth Unemployment: The Causes and Consequences.* Paris: OECD.

1982a. *The Challenge of Unemployment.* Paris: OECD.

Okun, A.M. 1973. "Upward Mobility in a High Pressure Economy." *Brookings Papers on Economic Activity,* no.1.

Osterman, P. 1980. *Getting Started: The Youth Labor Market.* Cambridge, Mass.: MIT Press.

Phelps Brown, E. 1977. *The Inequality of Pay.* Oxford: Oxford University Press.

Piore, M. 1978. "Unemployment and Inflation: An Alternative View." *Challenge,* May-June.

Plewes, T.J. 1982. "Better Measures of Service Employment Goal of Bureau Survey Redesign." *Monthly Labor Review,* November.

Pollard, T.K. 1982. "Changes over the 1970s in the Employment Patterns of Black and White Young Men." In Borus, M.E., ed. *Pathways to the Future, Vol.2: A Final Report on the National Longitudinal Survey of Youth Labor Market Experience, 1980.* Columbus, Ohio: Center for Human Resource Research, The Ohio State University.

Psacharopoulos, G. 1978. "Labour Market Duality and Income Distribution: The Case of the U.K." In Shorrocks, A. and Krelle, W., eds. *The Economics of Income Distribution.* Amsterdam: North–Holland.

Rehnberg, B. 1981. "Swedish Labour Market Policy in a New Economic Climate. Paper prepared for a Conference on European and American Labor Market Policies, Reston, Virginia, November.

Reubens, B.G. 1980. "Review of Foreign Experience." In Anderson, B.E. and Sawhill, I.V., eds. *Youth Employment and Public Policy.* Englewood Cliffs, N.J.: Prentice-Hall.

Reubens, B.G.; Harrisson, J.A.C.; and Rupp, K. 1981. *The Youth Labor Force 1945-1995: A Cross-National Analysis.* Totowa, N.J.: Allanheld, Osmun.

Reubens, B.G., and Reubens, E.P. 1977. "Women Workers, Nontraditional Occupations, and Full Employment." In Cahn, A., ed. *American Women Workers in a Full Employment Economy.* New York: Praeger.

Rosenberg, S. 1975. *The Dual Labor Market: Its Existence and Consequences.* PB-244320. National Technical Information Service, Department of Commerce. Springfield, Va.: NTIS.

Routh, G. 1980. *Occupation and Pay in Great Britain 1966-1979.* 2nd ed. London: Macmillan.

Rubery, J. 1978. "Structured Labour Markets, Worker Organization and Low Pay." *Cambridge Journal of Economics,* March.

Rubery, J., and Wilkinson, F. 1980. "Outwork and Segmented Labour Markets." Paper prepared for a conference of the International Working Party on Labour Market Segmentation, Cambridge, England, September.

Rumberger, R.W. 1981. "The Changing Skill Requirements of Jobs in the U.S. Economy." *Industrial and Labor Relations Review,* July.

Rutter, M., and Madge, N. 1976. *Cycles of Disadvantage—A Review of Research.* London: Heinemann.

Ryan, P. 1980. *The Empirical Analysis of Labour Market Segmentation.* International Working Party on Labour Market Segmentation. Berlin: Forschungsstelle Sozialökonomie der Arbeit, Freie Universität Berlin.

Rytina, N.F. 1982. "Earnings of Men and Women: A Look at Specific Occupations." *Monthly Labor Review,* April.

Sakoda, J.M. 1981. "A Generalized Index of Dissimilarity." *Demography,* May.

Saunders, C., and Marsden, D. 1981. *Pay Inequalities in the European Community.* London: Butterworth.

Sawyer, M. 1976. *Income Distribution in OECD Countries.* Paris: OECD.

Schiller, B.R. 1973. *The Economics of Poverty and Discrimination.* Englewood Cliffs, N.J.: Prentice-Hall.

Schmid, G. 1981. "Employment Policy in the Federal Republic of Germany: Lessons to be Learned." Paper prepared for Conference on European and American Labor Market Policies, Reston, Virginia, November.

Scoville, J.G. 1966. "Education and Training Requirements for Occupations." *Review of Economics and Statistics,* November.

――――. 1969. *The Job Content of the U.S. Economy.* New York: McGraw-Hill.

――――. 1972. *Manpower and Occupational Analysis: Concepts and Measurement.* Lexington, Mass.: D.C. Heath.

Selby Smith, J. 1981. "The Concentration of Female Employment in the Australian Labor Market: 1972-1980." Unpublished paper. Prepared for OECD, Paris.

Sewell, W., and Hauser, R. 1975. *Education, Occupation, and Earnings: Achievement in the Early Career.* New York: Academic Press.

Shimada, H. 1980. *The Japanese Employment System.* Tokyo: The Japan Institute of Labor.

Sleeper, R.D. 1975. "Labour Mobility over the Life Cycle." *British Journal of Industrial Relations,* June.

Sommers, D. 1974. "Occupational Rankings for Men and Women by Earnings." *Monthly Labor Review,* August.

Occupational Dissimilarity by Age and Sex

_____ . 1979. *Empirical Evidence on Occupational Mobility*. Information Series no.193. Columbus, Ohio: The National Center for Research in Vocational Education, The Ohio State University.

Sorensen, A.B. 1974. "A Model for Occupational Careers." *American Journal of Sociology*, March.

Sorge, A., and Warner, M. 1980. "Manpower Training, Manufacturing Organization and Workplace Relations in Great Britain and West Germany." *British Journal of Industrial Relations*, November.

Sorrentino, C. 1981. "Youth Unemployment: An International Perspective." *Monthly Labor Review*, July.

Spilerman, S. 1977. "Careers, Labor Market Structure, and Socioeconomic Achievement." *American Journal of Sociology*, November.

Stewart, A.; Prandy, K., and Blackburn, R.M. 1980. *Social Stratification and Occupations*. London: Macmillan.

Stiglitz, J.E. 1973. "Approaches to the Economics of Discrimination." *American Economic Review*, Papers and Proceedings, May.

Sullerot, E. 1971. *Women, Society and Change*. London: Wiedenfeld and Nicolson.

SWEDEN

1963–82. *Arbetskraftsundersökningen*, Årsmedeltal (*Labor Force Survey*, Annual Averages). Stockholm: SCB (Statistiska Centralbyrån).

1964a. *Folkräkningen den 1 November 1960* (*Census of the Population in 1960*). Del IX. Näringsgren, yrke, pendling, hushåll och utbildning i hela riket, länsvis m.m. (Part 9. Industry, Occupation, Commuting, Households and Education in the Whole Country, by County etc.). Stockholm: SCB (Statistiska Centralbyrån).

1979a. *Folk- och Bostadsräkningen 1975* (*Population and Housing Census 1975*). Del 6:2. Förvärvsarbetande nattbefolkning i hela riket och länen m.m. (Part 6:2. Economically active resident population in the whole country and in the counties etc.). Stockholm: SCB (Statistiska Centralbyrån).

Thurow, L.C. 1969. *Poverty and Discrimination*. Washington: Brookings Institution.

_____ . 1975. *Generating Inequality: Mechanisms of Distribution in the U.S. Economy*. New York: Basic Books.

Thurow, L.C., and Lucas, R.E.B. 1972. "The American Distribution of Income: A Structural Problem." Prepared for the Joint Economic Committee of Congress. 92nd Congress, 2nd session. Washington: GPO.

Troll, L. 1981. "Unschärfen bei der Erfassung des ausgeubten Berufs und Ansätze zur Verbesserung statistischer Nachweise" ("Difficulties in Assessing the Job Held and Approaches to Improve Statistical Data"). *Mitteilungen aus der Arbeitsmarkt-und Berufsforschung*, no.2. Stuttgart: W. Kohlhammer.

UNITED STATES

1973a. *1970 Census of Population*. Occupational Characteristics, Vol PC(2)–7A. Department of Commerce. Bureau of the Census. Washington: GPO (Government Printing Office).

1973b. *1970 Census of Population*. Detailed Characteristics, Vol. PC(1)–D1. Department of Commerce. Bureau of the Census. Washington: GPO.

1978a. *International Comparisons of Unemployment*. Bulletin 1979. Bureau of Labor Statistics, Department of Labor. Washington: GPO.

1978b. *Employment and Training Report of the President, 1978*. Department of Labor. Washington: GPO.

1981a. *Employment and Training Report of the President, 1981*. Department of Labor. Washington: GPO.

1981b. *The National Industry-Occupation Employment Matrix, 1970, 1978 and Projected 1990*. Bulletin 2086. Department of Labor, Bureau of Labor Statistics. Washington: GPO.

Vroman, W. 1977. "Worker Upgrading and the Business Cycle." *Brookings Papers on Economic Activity*, no.1.

Wachter, M.L. 1974. "Primary and Secondary Labor Markets: A Critique of the Dual Approach." *Brookings Papers on Economic Activity*, no.3.

Welch, F., and Cunningham, J. 1978. "Effects of Minimum Wages on the Level and Compensation of Youth Employment." *Review of Economics and Statistics,* February.

Willauer, E.T., Jr. 1974. *The Demand for Youth Labor: A Cross-Sectional Approach.* CAC Document no.132. Center for Advanced Computation, University of Illinois at Urbana-Champaign.

Willms, A. 1980. *Die Entwicklung der Frauenerwerbstätigkeit im Deutschen Reich—Eine historisch-soziologische Studie. (The Development of Female Labor Force Participation in the German Republic—A Historical-sociological Study).* BeitrAB 50. Nürnberg: Federal Employment Institute, Institute for Labor Market Research.

4

Youth Employment in Australia

Paul Paterson and Keith Mackay

There have been some major changes in the employment situation of Australian youth (15–24 year-olds) over the past 15 years, both in an absolute sense and relative to adults.* Between 1966 and 1981 total youth employment increased by 24 percent, but this resulted from very different changes for the various subgroups. There was no change over the period in the total number of teenagers (15–19 year-olds) employed, although a 6 percent employment growth of male teenagers was offset by decreased employment of female teenagers. Young adults (20–24 year-olds) had an increase in employment of almost 50 percent, with females having an employment growth of 70 percent, double that of males. The youth situation contrasts with the situation for adults (25 years and over), with males in the latter age group experiencing a growth in employment over this period of 20 percent and females 80 percent.

A notable aspect of youth employment has been the rapid growth in part-time work. Over the past ten years alone, part-time youth workers increased from 7 percent of total youth employment to 16 percent, with the rise somewhat greater for females than males. While the number in part-time employment increased rapidly to bring about this situation, the total number in full-time employment remained constant over the past decade. Almost all the growth in part-time youth employment over the past decade is attributable to the increased participation in the labor force of school pupils and students at post-school educational institutions, groups which in earlier times did not participate in the labor force.

While variations in total employment have been matched fairly closely by variations in the size of the labor force for adults, this has

---

*The authors are grateful to Norman Fisher, Garth Lampe, Beatrice Reubens, and Laurie Kupkee for advice and comments. Nevertheless, the usual caveats apply.

not been so for youth. For both teenagers and young adults, relatively slow growth in employment (24 percent as a whole over the 1966–81 period) has been outrun by more rapid growth in the labor force, this labor force growth resulting largely from population growth. In the case of young males there was also a decline in education participation rates. As a result, youth unemployment has increased dramatically over the period. The large pool of unemployed youth since the mid-1970s suggests that aggregate employment has been largely demand-determined in recent years. In addition to the effects of the recession on youth unemployment, it is possible that there has been a noncyclical divergence in the relationship between youth and adult unemployment rates. This could have serious implications for youth.

Before proceeding to the detailed analysis, we note that most of the analysis in this chapter utilizes cross-sectional data from the regular labor force survey conducted by the Australian Bureau of Statistics (ABS). The lack of well-developed longitudinal data for Australia has constrained to some extent the range and depth of issues dealt with, but considerable ground is covered nonetheless.

Education and Training Systems and Outputs

Current schooling systems in Australia have the opportunity to reflect the academically-oriented philosophy that all pupils should receive a general education suitable to carry them on to tertiary education if desired. Vocational education has increasingly been seen as a later phase, after age 16 or 18. Formal schooling is generally compulsory up to the age of 15 years. Other important points are Year 10 (when most pupils would be 16 years old) and Year 12 (18 years), which are designed as terminating stages of schooling for different types of students; the more academically-oriented students tend to leave in Year 12, the final year of formal schooling. In 1981, over 90 percent of both males and females remained at school until at least Year 10, while 32 percent of males and almost 38 percent of females remained until Year 12 (ABS unpublished estimates). While the proportion remaining till Year 10 increased for both males and females between 1971 and 1981 (from about 80 percent in 1971 for both groups), the increase in the proportion remaining till Year 12 was confined to females (from 27 percent in 1971).

School participation rates are an alternative way of expressing the schooling behavior of young people. In August 1981, 87 percent of 15 year-olds were in school, 57 percent of 16 year-olds, 30 percent of 17 year-olds and 5 percent of 18 year-olds (ABS unpublished estimates). These are generally greater than 1971 rates (ABS VI, 1971). In 1981, females displayed a greater tendency to participate in schooling than males, the reverse of the situation in 1971.

Three main types of institution offer formal post-school training in Australia: colleges of technical and further education, universities, and colleges of advanced education. Technical and further education colleges offer a variety of courses for all age groups and are classified into six streams: professional; para-professional; trades; other skilled; preparatory; and adult education. These courses have varying educational prerequisites, ranging from no specified level to completion of Year 10 or 11 of secondary schooling. Included in these courses are the classroom training components of apprenticeship schemes and many education-based government manpower training programs. More than 11 percent of the teenage population and 5 percent of 20–25 year-olds were enrolled at colleges of technical and further education in 1981 (ABS 1981c, Table 8). Most people were enrolled part-time, with the higher part-time participation of males than females reflecting the former's greater involvment in apprenticeships.

Australian universities provide professional tertiary training in the usual fields, including the social sciences and the physical sciences. Entrance is restricted to those who meet educational prerequisites which generally involve completion of Year 12 at a specified standard. The university participation rate in 1981 was 3.5 percent for 15–19 year-olds and 4.7 percent for 20–25 year-olds, with these rates slightly higher for female than male teenagers, but substantially higher for male than female 20–25 year-olds (ABS 1981c, Table 8). Most young university students were enrolled full-time, with this tendency strongest for the teenage group.

Colleges of advanced education were designed to provide "a broad comprehensive system of tertiary education, with an emphasis different from but complementary to, tertiary education provided by the universities" (HR 1965). Slightly fewer people enroll in advanced education courses than in university courses, although for teenagers the reverse is true. The participation rate in advanced education college for both teenagers and 20–25 year-olds was about 4 percent in 1981 (ABS 1981c, Table 8). Most advanced education students enroll full-time, particularly in the teenage group.

Some structured post-school education and training takes place outside the three elements of the education system identified above. For example, the major responsibility for the development of skilled workers rests with industry under the apprenticeship system, and much of nurse education is provided within hospitals. The apprenticeship system provides the main means of entry into certain important skilled trades; the full extent of other training of young people in industry is not known. In certain occupations formal training is restricted to those able to obtain employment as an apprentice.

Apprenticeships are formal legal contracts between the apprentice or trainee and the parent or guardian, on the one hand, and the employer, on the other. Entry into apprentice training is generally restricted to young people, although adult apprenticeships have been encouraged in some areas in recent years, but with minimal success. It is estimated that approximately 40 percent of male school-leavers enter apprenticeships each year (BLMR estimate). However, relatively few females enter apprenticeships. Some apprenticeships require formal schooling up to Year 10, while others require only "a reasonable level of education" (Williams Committee 1979, p.343). Most apprenticeships are four years in duration. There are 70 principal trade areas to which apprentices are commonly indentured, forming seven "trade groups": metal; electrical; building; printing; vehicle; food; and other trades. The metal trades group is the most important single group and accounts for more than one-third of all new indentures registered annually; the metal, electrical and building trade groups together account for around 70 percent of all new indentures (Williams Committee 1979, p.343). Hairdressing is the main apprenticeable trade for females.

Training consists of both on-the-job learning and formal courses. Qualified tradesman status is obtained by satisfactorily completing the formal courses and the on-the-job training period; no specific examination of skills takes place. Apprentices are paid a specific incremental proportion of adult wages, depending on their year of training, rising to 85–90 percent in the last year in many cases. It has been suggested that although the costs of employing an apprentice in the early years of training may outweigh the returns in terms of work output, this is balanced in the later years of training when productivity outruns the costs of employment (Merrilees 1980a).

Between 1973–74 and 1978–79 there was a 50 percent increase in the proportion of full-time employed young males and females who had post-school qualifications, with some increase occurring for nearly all types of qualifications (ABS II; ABS IV). Part of this increase may be attributable to changing educational participation rates, changes in the age structure of the youth group, and to the possibility that decreases in employment are borne disproportionately by the least qualified. Nevertheless, it is clear that general levels of educational attainment have increased substantially in recent years. Little information exists on changes in the quality of education; a recent study found evidence of a slight improvement in Australian school students' literacy and numeracy between 1975 and 1980 (Bourke et al. 1981).

Educational participation may be viewed by some individuals as an alternative to competing in the labor market. Thus in a recession, when employment opportunities for youth are depressed and the opportunity cost of full-time education (income foregone) is lower, there might be an increased tendency to participate in schooling and tertiary education. On the other hand, recession may lower the expected return to education, with this tending to reduce education participation. The available econometric evidence suggests that the current recession in Australia has on balance induced only a very small proportion of school students to remain at school rather than enter the labor force. Merrilees (1981) has estimated that the school participation rate of teenagers would have been 1.1 percentage points lower in 1979 in the absence of the recession, with females constituting 70 percent of these "reluctant students." Data on the number of school students actively looking for full-time work suggest a similar number (ABS III, September 1979, Table 8; ABS 1979b, Table 8). University and college of advanced education participation rates have decreased for all young males and for teenage females since the mid-1970s, with these falls more or less paralleling the deepening of the recession. The increase in university and college of advanced education participation rates of young adult females parallels the increase in their labor force participation rates.

It has been suggested that increases in unemployment benefit payments in 1973 and 1974 may have induced a decrease in school retention rates by increasing the opportunity cost of being at school (e.g., Karmel 1979). There is, however, no strong evidence of a significant effect (King 1980; Merrilees 1981). Finally, it has been claimed that the decline since the mid-1970s in the availability of financial assistance for full-time study has increased the cost to young people of higher education, and as a result has reduced their level of participation (TEC 1981). At the same time, the rapid increase in the availability of part-time employment may have acted as a subsidy and therefore an inducement to educational participation; these effects have not been quantified.

Institutional Background

Guidance and Placement of Youth. School counselors provide career guidance to young people at school. Vocational guidance is also available from the Commonwealth Employment Service, the job placement agency of the Federal Government. Another dimension of preparation for work is the "work experience" program for school students, involving short-term or on-the-job work experience (usually unpaid), job observation, and community service projects. A survey of schools in 1977 indicated that over half of secondary schools in Australia have work experience programs (Cole 1979). In recent years government Transition from School to Work programs have also provided preparation for work. These schemes are aimed at increasing employability through improving basic literacy, numeracy, and job skills; participants are paid an allowance while attending courses at technical and further education colleges. Preapprenticeship courses are also aimed at helping young people move from school to work. However, the numbers involved in these schemes have not been large. In 1980–81, young people commencing Transition and preapprenticeship courses represented only about 2.5 percent of youth placed in Federal manpower training programs (BLMR 1982a; DEYA 1982a).

Assistance in job placement is undertaken by the Commonwealth Employment Service, through a network of local offices throughout the country. It is estimated that about 20 percent of all job vacancies, as defined by the ABS, are currently filled by the Commonwealth Employment Service, with about 30 percent of all vacancies being notified to the Service and 75 percent of these being filled (DEYA 1982a, p.iii; ABS 1981b, Table 4). Separate estimates cannot be made for youth and adults.

Wage Setting and Other Working Conditions. Most jobs in Australia (90 percent of all employees, including youth) are covered by industrial "awards" prescribing minimum wages, normal hours of work, training provisions, health and safety standards and other conditions of employment (DT 1979, p.39). These awards are set by Federal and State tribunals under the authority of particular legislative provisions. Employment of young people is in some cases covered by special provisions within the awards, but in other cases they are employed under the same conditions as adults. In addition, legislation relating directly to the employment of child labor also exists. Such legislation in general restricts employment to those over the legal school-leaving age, specifies certain dangerous conditions under which youth no more than 16 years-old cannot be employed, and requires that such youth not work at night or work excessively long hours.

Wages actually paid for most jobs consist of the award rate for the particular classification of work plus any over-award payments. Award rates are regularly increased across-the-board in line with "national wage case" decisions made by the Australian Conciliation and Arbitration Commission, the Federal award-setting body. Rates of pay under individual awards are also adjusted to reflect changes in productivity and other conditions in specific industries and occupations. Since 1972 award rates have been set without regard to sex, with women receiving "equal pay for work of equal value" (DT 1979, p.48). Over-award payments reflect the outcome of negotiations between trade unions and employers outside the award system, and in May 1981 they were estimated to represent 2.5 percent of average weekly earnings for all male employees and 1.5 percent for females (ABS 1981a, Table 15). This is considered to be a conservative estimate.

The majority of awards distinguish between "juniors," persons less than 21 years of age, and "adults," persons aged 21 years or over. In most of the more important awards, minimum junior wages are set as a percentage of minimum wages payable to adults, with an incremental scale based on age. In other cases, award wages for both juniors and adults are specified as monetary amounts. In still other cases, no distinction is drawn between juniors and adults, requiring that juniors be paid adult rates.

Trade Union Membership. It is estimated that just over 50 percent of all employees in Australia were members of a trade union in 1976 (ABS 1976, Table 6). Teenagers were less highly unionized than other age groups, with 34 percent of teenage male employees and 41 percent of teenage females being members of unions. The unionization rate for young adults, very similar to that for adults, was 56 percent for males and 44 percent for females. Overall, youth (15–24 years) constituted some 23 percent of all trade union members in 1976, while making up 28 percent of all employees.

Government Manpower Programs and Financial Assistance to Youth. A wide range of government manpower training programs is directed toward youth to ease the transition from school and to encourage skill training (DEYA 1981). There is some emphasis on wage subsidy programs aimed at assisting disadvantaged, unemployed youth; around 30 percent of youth placements were in wage subsidy schemes in 1980–81 (BLMR 1982a; DEYA 1982a). In recent years, however, there has been an increasing emphasis on improving basic employability through special vocational education courses. It is currently estimated that the Federal Government annually assists about one out of every ten in the youth labor force (15–24 years-old), with program assistance being disproportionately concentrated among 16 and 17 year-olds (BLMR 1982a).

A range of financial assistance for youth is available to young people or their parents, including unemployment benefit payments, payments under government manpower programs, benefits for tertiary education students, and family allowances. Unemployment benefit payments, varying from $A36 per week for single 16- and 17 year-olds to $A58.10 per week for persons aged 18 years or over, have no prerequisite of previous employment and no limit on duration of benefits, suggesting that they are a welfare payment rather than unemployment insurance. This particular form of benefit payment is important because of the number of young people who receive it and its potential impact on young people's labor market behavior. In recent years, 75 percent of unemployed youth and 74 percent of unemployed adults have drawn benefits; it is estimated that 10 percent of the entire youth labor force received benefits.

Student Workers

One of the most notable aspects of the Australian youth labor market in the 1970s has been the growing overlap between educational participation and employment. Almost one-third of 20–25 year-olds, and just under one-quarter of teenage full-time students held jobs in May 1981 (Table 4.1). At this time, full-time teenage students held almost 75 percent of teenage part-time employment, part-time students accounted for another 5 percent, while nonstudent teenagers captured only about 20 percent. It is believed that the large majority of teenage part-time students are apprentices, almost all of whom, in turn, are male. Full-time teenage students gained almost 90 percent of the growth in teenage part-time employment between 1971 and 1981 (BLMR 1982b). Among 20–25 year-olds, however, nonstudents held almost 70 percent

Table 4.1   Youth Employment, by Age, Hours of Work, and Student Status, Both
Sexes, Australia, May 1981

	Proportion employed		
	Part-time	Full-time	Total
		(percentage)	
15-19 years[a]			
Full-time students	19.4	3.1	22.5
Part-time students[b]	5.4	90.2	95.6
Nonstudents	5.7	72.0	77.7
Total	11.8	43.3	55.1
20-25 years[a]			
Full-time students	26.8	6.0	32.8
Part-time students[c]	6.6	84.0	90.6
Nonstudents	6.3	70.2	76.5
Total	7.8	66.8	74.6
	Type of employment		
	Part-time	Full-time	Total
		(percentage distribution)	
15-19 years[a]			
Full-time students	73.2	3.2	18.2
Part-time students[b]	5.1	23.5	19.7
Nonstudents	21.6	73.3	62.2
Total	100.0	100.0	100.0
20-25 years[a]			
Full-time students	24.4	0.6	3.1
Part-time students[c]	7.5	11.3	10.9
Nonstudents	68.0	88.1	86.0
Total	100.0	100.0	100.0

[a]No sex division of the data is available. [b]Part-time teenage students
constituted 20.2 percent of all teenage students. [c]Part-time 20-25 year-old
students constituted 55.6 percent of all 20-25 year-old students.

Source: ABS 1981c, Table 6.

of part-time employment, and nonstudents and part-time students were
more likely to be employed on a full-time than a part-time basis.

There are a number of possible causes of the strong trend toward
student employment. It has been argued that in the current recession,
with unemployment relatively high for all groups, some school students
may attempt to supplement a lowered level of total family income by
entering the labor force and finding a job while remaining at school
(Stricker and Sheehan 1981). Such persons could be viewed as being
additional to the "normal" workforce. A recent survey of employed
14–19 year-old school students in South Australia found that 10 percent

of them gave this as one of their reasons for working (Bentley and O'Neil 1982). This evidence provides only weak support for the additional worker hypothesis. In addition, it is notable that the number of part-time jobs held by school students grew by 19 percent per annum in both the 1971–76 and 1976–81 periods. This fairly steady growth of school student part-time employment in each period occurred despite the sharp deepening of the current recession in 1974. This in turn suggests that the phenomenon of school attendance and concurrent employment was not primarily recession-induced.

An alternative explanation is that there has been a reduction in the number of nonstudent teenagers wanting part-time work due to a change in the unemployment benefit payments system. Gregory and Duncan (1980) have argued that the terms and conditions which applied to this system in the early and mid-1970s caused an increase in teenage labor supply. They believe that the relatively high level of unemployment benefits in comparison with average weekly earnings, and the dollar-for-dollar reduction in unemployment benefits for other income in excess of $A3 per week acted as a disincentive to unemployed teenagers to accept part-time work. This, they argue, allowed school students to capture a large proportion of the increasing number of part-time jobs available to teenagers, and this resulted in an increase in teenage labor supply.

Additional labor supply influences include the wish of young students to gain part-time work experience to facilitate their entry into the full-time workforce; this reason was given by 54 percent of employed school students in the South Australian survey (Bentley and O'Neil 1982). In addition, student part-time employment might be seen as a response to declining real levels of government financial assistance. It has also been suggested that social changes, such as the greater desire for financial and social independence on the part of young people, were responsible for the increase in the supply of student labor (Merrilees 1980b).

The role of demand factors in the expansion of part-time youth employment has also been stressed. Sweet (1980, 1981) has argued that structural factors have resulted in extensive changes in the organization of work by retail and service industries, and that this has resulted in a demand for a less skilled workforce which is prepared to work shorter and more flexible hours. The available data confirm that over 70 percent of male and female employed school students worked in the wholesale and retail trade industry in 1978 (ABS 1978, Table 6). It is also possible that these changes in the nature of some types of part-time work reflect to some extent a response by employers to changing educational participation rates. Female, but not male, school enrollment rates have risen over the past decade and it is reasonable to suppose that on average the more able students stay on at school (ABS VI; Williams 1980). To avail themselves of these more able people, employers may have restructured full-time jobs into part-time jobs.

The part-time jobs of school students involve on average about 7 hours per week, whereas the part-time jobs of nonstudents average 20 hours, and all jobs of teenage nonstudents involve an average of 36 hours per week (ABS 1978, Table 10; ABS IV 1978, Table 13). This suggests that some of the lost full-time youth jobs were offset by a considerably larger number of new part-time youth jobs. Thus, school students constituted about 12 percent of all employed teenagers in August 1978, but they contributed only 2.6 percent of the total weekly hours worked by all teenagers; their total labor input was therefore relatively insignificant.

Each of these explanations for the growing trend toward educational participation and concurrent employment could be at least partially correct. What is clear is that there are a number of complex, interacting demand and supply factors which underlie the phenomenon.

The growing phenomenon of student workers may have important labor market consequences. The Commonwealth Department of Education (CDE 1976) has argued that most student part-time jobs are viewed by young people as being simply a source of income, although sometimes a sympathetic link with an employer or workplace influences their vocational choice and may even hasten the date of leaving school. On the other hand, unattractive working conditions may stimulate a new interest in study and attainment of qualifications. Sweet (1981) has argued that the participation of school students in the labor market provides only a most general type of work experience, particularly as the jobs which they obtain tend to be seasonal, casual, or temporary in nature. It will be possible to examine the consequences of such labor force experience as Australian longitudinal data become available over the next few years.

The student worker phenomenon may also affect nonstudent youth. For instance, nonstudent youth may have difficulties in competing with student youth in the labor force, given that students of any particular age tend to be more able and to have a higher educational attainment than nonstudents of the same age. Data on the occupation and industry mix of student and nonstudent employment suggest, however, that the extent of competition may not be great. Employed teenage school students are concentrated in sales occupations (44 percent), and in the skilled worker, production process, and laborer occupations (20 percent) (ABS 1978, Table 8). In contrast, employed teenagers not attending school are concentrated in the skilled worker, etc. occupations (39 percent) and in clerical occupations (25 percent). Since teenage students and nonstudents are concentrated in different types of occupations, this suggests that competition between the two groups may be limited. In terms of industry structure, employed school students are overwhelmingly concentrated in the wholesale and retail trade (72 percent), while other employed teenagers are more evenly spread across industries— 32 percent in the wholesale and retail trade, 21 percent in manufacturing, 10 percent in finance, insurance, etc. (ABS 1978, Table 7). Again, this suggests that competition between students and teenage nonstudents may be limited.

Trade union membership among employed school students is lower than among comparable nonstudents. In South Australia it has been estimated at 17 percent (Bentley and O'Neil 1982), compared to 37 percent in the case of all employed teenagers (ABS 1976, Table 6). Employed school students also appear to be disproportionately concentrated in areas of employment in which the largest numbers of complaints concerning breaches of award-wage conditions have been made—cafes and restaurants, delicatessens, shops, offices, hotels and clubs, and hairdressers (Bentley and O'Neil 1982). This suggests that employed full-time students are concentrated in the secondary labor market.

Jobs of Out-of-School Youth

This section examines the job characteristics of nonstudents. A key aspect of youth employment is the transition from full-time education to the full-time labor force. The limited data available on this issue relate to youth who ceased full-time attendance at an educational institution in the previous year. In 1981, the unemployment rates of these recent leavers were several percentage points higher than those of other nonstudent youth in the labor force, both for teenagers and for 20–25 year-olds (ABS 1981c, Table 6). In 1978, the unemployment rates of recent school-leavers were almost identical for males and females (ABS 1978, Table 5). For each sex, there appears to be a negative relationship between the unemployment rate and the age of leaving school (ABS 1978, Table 5). This could reflect the influence of those characteristics of individuals which tend to be correlated with age: educational attainment, maturity, motivation, and the possession of part-time work experience.

Only 60 percent of a sample of 17 year-olds who had been early school-leavers between 1975 and 1978 were at least reasonably satisfied with their first jobs (Williams 1980, p.75). Since young Australians appear to have a strong commitment to the work ethic (King 1981; Earley 1981), this suggests that the relatively high rate of dissatisfaction (40 percent) with first jobs relates mainly to the nature of the work which is accepted by early school-leavers. It is not known whether this reflects young people's lack of knowledge about different types of jobs, or whether early school-leavers may be largely restricted to jobs which require low levels of skill and/or little prior work experience, and thus which may have inherently low levels of job satisfaction.

The occupations and industries of employed nonstudents are now examined, and in particular the youth-intensity of these jobs is considered. An important issue here is whether or not youth are concentrated in declining or growth industries; data constraints prevent examination

Table 4.2   Youth-Intensity of Employment, by Industry and Sex, Australia, 1981

	Relative youth intensity[a]	
	Male youth	Female youth
	(ratio)	
Agriculture, forestry, fishing, hunting	1.55	0.95
Mining	0.72	*
Food, beverages, tobacco	0.95	0.74
Textiles, clothing, footwear	0.78	0.74
Wood, wood products, furniture	1.71	*
Paper products, printing, publishing	0.99	0.99
Basic metal products	1.10	*
Fabricated metal products	1.18	0.82
Transport equipment	1.00	*
Other industrial machinery, household appliances	1.10	0.56
Leather, rubber, plastic, etc.	1.00	0.84
Other manufacturing	0.70	*
Electricity, gas, water	0.68	1.02
General construction	1.02	1.21
Special-trade construction	1.68	*
Wholesale trade	0.96	0.97
Retail trade	1.74	1.47
Road transport	0.62	*
Rail transport	0.83	*
Other transport, storage	0.55	1.03
Communications	0.64	0.81
Finance, investment	1.30	1.75
Insurance	0.89	1.34
Property, business services	0.86	1.20
Public administration, defense	0.63	0.98
Community services	0.51	0.76
Entertainment, recreation, personal services, etc.	1.20	1.01
All industries	1.00	1.00

*Relative standard error greater than 20 percent.
[a]Youth-intensive industries show ratios above 1.00 for under 25 year-olds. Employment relates to full-time wage and salary earners.

Source: Unpublished data from ABS Labour Force Survey, August 1981.

of the issues of secondary labor markets. Occupation and industry data are not collected on a student/nonstudent basis. Nonetheless, a reasonable approximation to the nonstudent situation is given by data on full-time youth employment, since Table 4.1 shows that nonstudents account for an overwhelming share of teenage and young adult full-time employment. Moreover, the bulk of students who are in full-time employment are studying part-time, the great majority of whom are apprentices whose educational attendance is directly related to their current employment.

Using the method developed in Chapter 6 for Great Britain, Table 4.2 shows the male and female youth-intensity of industries in 1981, measured at the one or two-digit industry level. Teenagers and young adults of the same sex have been added together because the sex-segregation of employment has resulted in essentially similar industry distributions of employment by age (Power 1975; Selby Smith 1978; BLMR 1982b). The ratio of youth-intensity for each industry is calculated by dividing the share of youth full-time employment in that industry by the share of total full-time same-sex employment in the industry. For example, almost 3.47 percent of male youth and 3.14 percent of all males worked in the basic metal products industry; the youth-intensity ratio is therefore 1.10 and the industry ranks as mildly youth-intensive. Youth-intensity is more significant for male than for female youth, measured by the number of industries with ratios above 1.0, the amount of the excess, and the proportion of total youth employment in those industries. Thus for male youth, ten of the 27 industries had ratios greater than 1.0, and these accounted for 54 percent of male youth employment; five industries had male youth ratios greater than 1.25. In the case of female youth, eight industries had ratios over 1.0, accounting for 47 percent of female youth employment; three industries had a female youth ratio greater than 1.25. The industries in which male youth were disproportionately concentrated were often not the same as those of female youth. Two notable exceptions were retail trade, and finance and investment; these two industries employed 19 percent of male and 30 percent of female youth.

The changes over the past decade in youth and total employment indicate that five of the ten industries in which young males were disproportionately concentrated experienced a decline in total employment over the decade; however, young males themselves experienced a decline in employment in only two of these industries (Table 4.3). In contrast, young females experienced a reduction in employment in two of the three female youth-intensive industries in which total employment also fell. Female youth employment in particular industries tended to change in the same direction as total employment. However, a similar relationship did not hold for male youth. In eight of the ten male youth-intensive industries, young males had a larger percentage increase (or a smaller percentage decrease) than all persons. The same is true of female youth in only two of the eight female youth-intensive industries; in five of the remaining industries female youth had a larger percentage decrease (or a smaller percentage increase) than all persons. It appears that female youth employment is more closely tied to changes in total employment in individual industries than is male youth employment. This could have resulted from the sex-segregation of employment, as females are relatively concentrated in a small range of jobs (Power 1975; Selby Smith 1978).

Youth and Adult Employment Compared

Employers in different industries tend to have particular requirements for certain types of labor with particular skills, abilities, and experience.

Table 4.3 Employment Change in Youth-Intensive Industries, by Age and Sex, Australia, 1971-1981

	Employment change[a]		
	Male youth[b]	Female youth[b]	All ages, both sexes
	(percentage)		
Agriculture, forestry, fishing, hunting	-25	*	-15
Wood, wood products, furniture	+34	*	+ 4
Basic metal products	+12	*	0
Fabricated metal products	+ 3	*	- 7
Other industrial machinery, household appliances	+ 6	*	-16
Electricity, gas, water	*	+ 7	+18
General construction	-38	**	-39
Special-trade construction	+14	*	+13
Retail trade	+14	- 3	- 5
Other transport, storage	*	+25	+14
Finance, investment	- 7	+34	+37
Insurance	*	-24	-13
Property, business services	*	+ 5	+27
Entertainment, recreation, personal services, etc.	+65	- 7	0
All industries	- 1	- 4	+ 5

*Youth-intensity ratio less than 1.0. **Relative standard error greater than 20 percent.
[a]Full-time wage and salary earners. [b]Under 25 years old.

Source: Unpublished data from ABS Labour Force Surveys, August 1971 and August 1981.

Young people who compete in the labor market often do not have the skills and experience comparable to those of adult workers, although this competitive disadvantage can sometimes be overcome by relatively lower wages. Many employers have criticized youth attitudes to work, and anecdotal evidence suggests these criticisms have become more widespread in recent years. Evidence of the belief by employers that the aspirations of many young people are set too high, with the consequence that they reject work of a monotonous and repetitive nature, has been found in surveys of employers by Williams and Priest (1978) in Western Australia, and by the Sydney Chamber of Commerce (SCC 1981). On the other hand, some employers believe that many young people do not really want to work. These employer perceptions are important, even if they are not correct, insofar as they affect employer recruitment practices.

It is possible that the requirements of employers in individual industries might explain the concentration of certain demographic groups, including youth, in particular industries. Table 4.4 shows the industrial

Table 4.4 Employment, by Industry, Age, Sex, and Hours of Work, Australia, 1981

	Male youth[a]		Female youth[a]		Adult males[a]		Adult females[a]	
	Full-time	Part-time	Full-time	Part-time	Full-time	Part-time	Full-time	Part-time
			(percentage distribution)					
Agriculture, forestry, fishing, hunting	5.1	*	1.0	*	2.7	*	1.1	1.9
Mining	1.9	*	*	*	2.9	*	*	*
Manufacturing	29.1	9.0	13.5	3.5	27.0	12.0	21.6	7.6
Electricity, gas, water	2.4	*	0.9	*	3.8	*	0.8	*
Construction	11.0	5.8	1.3	*	7.7	*	1.1	1.9
Wholesale, retail trade	22.7	49.8	25.2	48.1	14.9	12.1	15.1	20.8
Transport, storage	5.0	*	2.6	*	8.2	6.8	2.5	1.5
Communications	1.9	*	1.5	*	3.3	*	2.1	1.4
Finance, etc.[b]	7.5	*	19.6	3.2	7.2	9.5	9.3	8.7
Public administration, defense	3.9	*	5.9	*	6.9	*	6.1	2.9
Community services	5.4	6.8	22.6	16.8	12.1	30.6	34.2	38.1
Entertainment, etc.[c]	4.0	16.3	5.6	22.7	3.1	13.5	5.5	14.7
Total	100.0	100.0	100.0	100.0	100.0	100.0	100.0	100.0

*Relative standard error greater than 20 percent.
[a]Employed wage and salary earners. Youth are under 25 years old and adults are 25 years and over. [b]Finance, insurance, real estate and business services. [c]Entertainment, recreation, restaurants, hotels and personal services.

Source: Unpublished data from ABS Labour Force Survey, August 1981.

structure of youth and adult employment in 1981, divided according to sex and full-time/part-time employment status. A majority of employed full-time male youth (52 percent) was concentrated in just two industries: manufacturing, and wholesale and retail trade. Adult males were more evenly spread across industries, although manufacturing and wholesale and retail trade accounted for 42 percent of full-time male adults. Over 80 percent of employed full-time young females were located in four industries: wholesale and retail trade, finance, community services and manufacturing. A similar proportion of adult females was also employed in these four industries. It can be concluded that the major industry distribution of youth and adult employment is broadly similar for each sex.

The industry structures of full-time and part-time employment were markedly different for both age groups and each sex. As we saw in a previous section of this chapter, a large proportion of youth part-time employees were full-time students. The wholesale and retail trade industry accounted for almost half of youth part-time employment of each sex. The next largest employer of part-time youth labor was the entertainment, recreation, restaurants, hotels and personal services industry: it employed 16 percent of males and 23 percent of females. Adult part-time employment was somewhat more evenly spread across industries. The largest single employer was community services, which accounted for 31 percent of adult male part-time employment, and 38 percent of adult females.

Public sector employment increased by 29 percent between 1971 and 1981, and it currently accounts for 30 percent of total employment (BLMR 1982b). Private sector employment increased by only 8 percent over the same period. It is estimated that male and female 15–20 year-olds were the only groups to experience large decreases (14 percent) in the public sector proportion of their total employment over the decade. In contrast, adults and 21–24 year-old females experienced large increases in this proportion over the period. If the employment of 15–20 year-olds in the public sector had grown at the same rate as did total public sector employment, their public sector employment in 1981 would have been about 70,000 higher than it actually was. It is interesting to juxtapose this figure with the 127,000 unemployed 15–20 year-olds in 1981 (ABS III, August 1981, Tables 6 and 7). On the surface at least, the failure of 15–20 year-olds to share in the growth of government employment has been a significant influence on their labor market position.

An important aspect of a comparison between youth and adult employment is the relative extent of mobility between jobs. Job mobility involves a change of employer and/or job location. Table 4.5 shows the extent of job mobility, by age and sex, in 1972 and 1979. It appears that 20–24 year-olds have the highest propensity to change jobs over a year. In 1979, 23 percent of employed young adults changed jobs, compared with 18 percent of teenagers, and 11 percent of adults. There

Table 4.5   Employed Persons Who Changed Jobs, by Age and Sex, Australia, 1972
            and 1979

Age	Year	Males[a]	Females[a]
		(percentage)	
15–19	1979	16.8	18.9
	1972	26.4	28.0
20–24	1979	24.4	20.0
	1972	30.1	27.0
25 and over	1979	11.8	9.0
	1972	14.4	12.3

[a]Employed persons who changed jobs once or more in the previous year. A
change of job involves a change of employer and/or a change of job location.

Source: ABS III, December 1979, Table 10; ABS 1972, Table 16; ABS V, 1972,
Table 20 and 1980, Table 25.

was a markedly lower incidence of job-changing for each of the six
demographic groups in 1979 than in 1972, probably reflecting the
deterrence to voluntary separations in the current recessionary period
(DEYA I, November 1972 and November 1979). The paucity of unfilled
vacancies has made it more difficult to find another job, and has
increased the risk of unemployment, with consequent foregone earnings.
This hypothesis is given added support when it is noted that the
reduction in job-changing was greatest for those age groups which had
the largest increase in unemployment rates. Females were generally
estimated to have had a slightly lower propensity to change jobs than
males, and this could be related to their generally higher unemployment
rates. The exception to this was teenagers: here differences between
males and females were statistically insignificant at the 95 percent
confidence level.

The importance of the relatively high job turnover of youth has been
highlighted by the work of Gregory and Stricker (1981) and Gregory
and Foster (1981). They have found that unemployed teenage males
as a group have the same probability of finding a job as do unemployed
mature adult males. Thus the relatively high teenage unemployment
rates are partly attributable to their higher job turnover.

There are a number of reasons why individuals change their job
voluntarily or involuntarily. These include layoffs, the attraction of
higher wages or better working conditions elsewhere, health or medical
reasons, and personal or family reasons. It has often been suggested
that young people tend to change jobs more frequently than older
workers in their search for more suitable employment, as a corollary
to gaining knowledge of different types of jobs (Casson 1979). This

hypothesis would seem to imply a relatively high level of job dissatisfaction among youth as compared to adults. The available data confirms
that higher proportions of youth were dissatisfied or very dissatisfied
than were adults. In 1979, for example, about 11 percent of all teenagers
and 13 percent of young adults fell into this category, compared with
8 percent of adults (ABS 1979a, Table 2). It is interesting that there
are no consistent differences between males and females in terms of
their job dissatisfaction, despite the narrower occupational opportunities
facing females, and their lower average earnings (BLMR 1982b).

Youth change occupations more often when changing jobs than older
workers (ABS V 1980, Table 25), and this is also consistent with the
hypothesis that youth change jobs more often than older workers because
of a greater lack of knowledge about the nature of different types of
jobs and their own long-term aspirations and goals. Relatively high
levels of youth job-changing may also be associated with high involuntary
separations. Youth may be the first to be retrenched when an employer
decides to reduce the number of his employees (the "last-in-first-out"
principle), and/or they may be concentrated in unstable employment
of a temporary or seasonal nature because of their lower skills and
work experience.

The available data relating to reasons for job-changing appear to be
consistent with two complementary hypotheses. First, young people are
searching for better jobs: an hypothesis that emphasizes the role of
labor supply in job-changing. Second, young people change jobs involuntarily, because they are the first to be retrenched by employers,
and/or they are concentrated in unstable employment of a temporary
or seasonal nature. The relative importance of these two hypotheses,
one based on labor supply and the other on labor demand factors, has
yet to be established in Australia.

Hours of Work and Other Working Conditions

A notable aspect of employment in Australia since the early 1970s has
been the rapid rise in the number and share of part-time jobs (under
35 hours a week). This increase was proportionately largest in the case
of youth. The net result has been a substantial increase in the proportion
of total employment which is part-time; between 1970 and 1981, the
proportion rose from 8 percent to 22 percent in the case of teenagers,
from 6 percent to 11 percent in the case of young adults, and from
12 percent to 17 percent in the case of adults. The trends in part-time
and full-time employment are also reflected in the trends of average
weekly hours worked. Unpublished ABS data show that teenagers worked
an average of 31.5 hours per week in August 1981 (down 14 percent
from the 1970 figure), young adults worked an average of 35.5 hours
per week (down 7 percent), while adults worked 37 hours per week
(down 5 percent). Females on average worked a smaller number of

hours per week than males; in August 1981 the difference varied between 3 hours in the case of teenagers to 12 hours in the case of adults.

The trends in part-time employment have a number of implications for youth. There appears to be a segmentation of the labor market into full-time and part-time components. Thus in August 1981, only 22 percent of part-time youth workers would have preferred to work more hours per week, and 10 percent were actively looking for full-time work (ABS III, August 1981, Table 21). While no information is available on the proportion of full-time youth workers who would prefer to work part-time, it is known that in 1979, 16 percent of young employees (full-time plus part-time) would have preferred to work fewer hours per week (ABS 1979a, Table 37). In addition, some writers (e.g., Sweet 1980) have argued that a higher proportion of part-time than full-time work is insecure, is not part of a long-term career ladder, and intrinsically lacks job satisfaction. This kind of work conforms to the stereotype of a secondary labor market (Cain 1976). A notable aspect of recent years is the general predominance of females in the part-time labor market. Thus in 1981, young females held 62 percent of part-time, but only 41 percent of full-time youth employment (ABS III, August 1981, Table 6).

Most of the data on the working conditions of youth in comparison with adults relate to the subjective perceptions individuals have of their working environments. This section concerns employees, both sexes combined, who worked at least 20 hours per week at the time of the 1979 opinion survey (ABS 1979a). About 30 percent of youth and adults would have liked more responsibility in their jobs. While there was only a small difference between young and adult males in the proportion who would have liked more responsibility, there was a considerable difference in the proportions of young and adult females, 28 and 19 percent, respectively. This difference could reflect the differing nature of the jobs in which female youth and female adults are employed, but it is also possible that they reflect a slightly greater willingness of female adults to be satisfied with jobs which do not require considerable responsibility.

A greater proportion of youth than of adults would have preferred their jobs to be "more worthwhile," 17 percent as compared to 12 percent, and to have "more variety," 24 percent and 14 percent. This suggests that a higher proportion of youth than of adults viewed their jobs as being boring or monotonous. It is interesting that identical proportions of youth and adults, 18 percent, would have liked their jobs to have better physical working conditions and 16 percent wished for improved health or safety standards.

Similar proportions of youth and adults, just over 20 percent, were dissatisfied or very dissatisfied with the level of their gross pay. In terms of the number and types of employee fringe benefits such as low-interest loans, company pensions, free or discounted goods and services, housing subsidies or provision, young males received less than male adults, but young females received more than female adults. Thus, 62 percent of male teenagers received one or more benefits, compared with 78 percent of male adults; the corresponding figures for female employees were 65 percent and 75 percent. The difference between the proportions of male and female youth receiving one or more benefits was statistically insignificant at the 95 percent confidence level. The similarity in the number of benefits received by male and female youth suggests, in turn, that the large difference between male and female adults may be due to the relative failure of females to gain senior positions of employment and thus be eligible for employee benefits.

Relative Earnings

In recent years much of the discussion of the youth labor market has centered around the effects of increases in youth earnings relative to those of adults. Changes in relative earnings have resulted from changes in the institutionally determined awards described above, which set the minimum rates of pay for juniors (under age 21) in specific occupations, and from changes in wage payments above the awards. As wages are dominated by the award component, it is likely that changes in youth and adult wage relativities are mainly driven by award changes. Trends in the ratio of apprentice to skilled worker award rates of pay for several occupations are shown in Table 4.6. It is clear that there was a compression in award wage relativities between apprentices and skilled workers in the early to mid-1970s. For example, the ratio of award rates for apprentices in relation to toolmakers in the metal and vehicle industries was reduced by over 7 percentage points, or 17 percent, between 1972 and 1973. This compression of relative award wages may be partly attributable to the growing trend toward payment of adult wage rates at earlier ages, as well as to the flat-rate money wage increases awarded to both juniors and adults by the Australian Conciliation and Arbitration Commission in national wage case decisions (NILS 1974).

These trends are also apparent when the ratios of junior to adult hourly earnings of full-time workers are examined (Table 4.7). Here adults are defined by ABS to be both persons aged 21 years or over and persons under 21 who are receiving "adult" rates of pay. A difficulty in interpreting this table is that in circumstances where an increasing proportion of persons 20 years old or less is receiving adult earnings, rises in the ratio of junior to adult earnings will be systematically and increasingly understated. For males, junior full-time earnings relative to adults rose steadily from 1971 to 1977 before declining slightly. For females, relative junior full-time earnings moved downward from 1966 to 1974, rose to a peak in 1976 above the 1966 level and then fell away fairly sharply. For part-time employees, junior male earnings relative to those of male adults rose strongly from 1970 to 1975 before leveling off. Relative part-time earnings for junior females fluctuated

Table 4.6 Award Wage Rates, Apprentices Relative to Skilled Workers, Both Sexes, Australia, 1971-1979

	1971	1972	1973	1974	1975	1976	1977	1978	1979
				(percentage)					
Apprentice to toolmaker[a]									
metal industry	43.3	43.8	51.2	52.0	52.2	52.2	52.4	n.a.	n.a.
vehicle industry	43.3	43.8	51.2	52.0	52.2	52.2	52.4	n.a.	n.a.
Apprentice to tradesman[b]									
metal industry	47.3	47.3	55.0	55.0	55.0	55.0	55.0	55.0	55.0
Apprentice to head cook[c]	46.8	46.8	47.7	48.8	51.2	64.4	64.6	n.a.	n.a.
Apprentice to carpenter (tradesman)[d]	27.2	29.8	28.0	27.5	30.2	40.6	40.5	40.1	41.8

[a]Based on Commonwealth award wages operative in South Australia. Apprentice rates relate to second year apprentices serving four-year term. [b]Relates to Commonwealth awards in New South Wales, and second year apprentices. [c]Relates to State awards operative in South Australia. Apprentice rates relate to 18-19 year-olds. [d]Relates to Commonwealth awards in Victoria, and first year apprentices.

Source: NILS 1977; estimates by Bureau of Labour Market Research.

Table 4.7   Hourly Earnings of Juniors Relative to Adults,
            Full-time Employees, by Sex, Australia, 1966-1980

	Males[a]	Females[a]
	(ratio)	
1966	.51	.67
1967	.51	.67
1968	.52	.66
1969	.52	.66
1970	.52	.67
1971	.51	.66
1972	.52	.65
1973	.53	.66
1974	.54	.65
1975	.55	.67
1976	.55	.68
1977	.55	.67
1978	.55	.67
1979	.54	.66
1980	.54	.65

[a]Non-managerial employees in the private sector who work
30 hours or more per week.

Note: Juniors are under 21 years old.
Source: ABS I.

markedly over the period, ending up lower in 1980 than in 1966. Overall, the evidence suggests that earnings of male juniors rose relative to male adults over the first half of the 1970s, finishing up a little higher in 1980 than 1966. This trend was not evident for females.

With the move to equal pay for women over the 1970s, earnings for junior females increased relative to earnings for junior males (ABS I). Therefore, while junior males suffered a reversal in competitiveness in relation to adult males, they improved relative to females of their own age. At the same time junior males also improved their competitiveness relative to adult females, this being of interest in the light of the view that young males may compete for the same jobs as married females. These changes in male/female relativities have occurred for both full-time and part-time workers.

An examination of employment trends reveals no simple relationship between relative earnings and relative employment levels. For example, the part-time employment of adult males and females grew at similar rates over the 1970s; however, adult females enjoyed a considerably faster increase in their earnings. It is apparent that a number of complex factors influence relative employment levels. An offsetting influence to the disadvantageous relative wages of male youth in relation to adults has been the wage subsidies in a range of government manpower training programs. This could help to explain why the available econometric evidence suggests that the compression in wage relativities in the 1970s has not had a significant influence on the demand for youth labor (Gregory and Stricker 1981; Stricker and Sheehan 1978). However, it has been argued that apprentices have suffered a larger compression of wage relativities than other junior males, and that this "would have operated to make apprentice training distinctly less attractive to employers" (NILS 1977, p.19). Notwithstanding this disincentive effect on apprentice training, the number of apprentices in training grew by 26 percent between 1972 and 1981 (DEYA 1982b, Table 4), perhaps reflecting in part the government's support for apprenticeship training over the latter half of the period.

Summary and Conclusions

The 1970s have seen a sharp increase in youth part-time employment and in the proportion of these jobs held by full-time students. The growth in such jobs appears to be largely unrelated to the recession. The apparent segmentation between youth part-time and full-time workers indicates a lack of direct competition between student and nonstudent youth on the supply side, although some competition may exist on the demand side if employers deliberately convert some full-time jobs into part-time jobs in order to recruit students, whom they may consider more attractive workers.

The work of teenage students appears to provide them with only a most general type of work experience, not least because they appear to be concentrated in the secondary labor market. Evidence is not available on whether or not this work experience significantly influences their entry and establishment in the labor force.

While some employers have expressed the belief that educational standards have declined in recent years, the available evidence provides no support for this belief. Thus it appears that high youth unemployment in Australia cannot be attributed to declining educational standards. Employers have also criticized youth attitudes to work, and they have asserted that many young people do not want to work or have work aspirations which are set too high.

These employer attitudes are partially refuted by evidence which shows that young Australians as a whole have a strong commitment to the work ethic, although a large proportion of early school-leavers are dissatisfied with their first jobs after leaving school. This dissatisfaction could reflect a lack of knowledge about different types of work, or the restriction of early school-leavers to jobs which have inherently low levels of job satisfaction. Higher proportions of youth than adults appear to view their jobs as boring or monotonous. Similar factors could explain the relatively high job mobility and job dissatisfaction of young people as a whole. It is interesting to note that there is no consistent difference between males and females in terms of their job dissatisfaction, despite the narrower occupational opportunities and lower average earnings of females. School-leavers appear to be more successful in gaining employment the older they are when they leave school, although this need not reflect a causal relationship. Rather, it is likely that success in finding a job is related to an individual's educational attainment, personal motivation and maturity, and that these personal characteristics also happen to be related to age.

The employment of female youth appears to have been more closely tied to changes to total employment in individual industries than has been the employment of male youth. At the same time, 15–20 year-olds of both sexes have failed to share in the substantial growth in public sector employment over the past decade.

There was a compression of male (but not female) junior : adult wage relativities in the early and mid-1970s. Junior female wages have also risen in relation to junior male wages as a result of the move toward equal pay for women. An offsetting influence on the disadvantageous relative wages of male youth in relation to adults has been the wage subsidies in a range of Government manpower training programs. This could help explain why the available econometric evidence suggests that the compression in wage relativities has not had a significant influence on the demand for youth labor. The Federal Government has also placed an increasing emphasis on improving basic employability and providing vocational education. Programs directed to unemployed youth provide basic or specific training for the transition from school to work, with assisted periods of work experience and training at the workplace. The effectiveness of this government assistance is unknown.

The study of youth employment in this chapter yields interesting insights into the problem of youth unemployment, particularly in the light of the important possibility that there has been a noncyclical divergence in the relationship between youth and adult unemployment rates. Most of the evidence presented in this chapter, however, is consistent with the belief that the historically high youth unemployment rates in Australia could be largely eliminated by a return to conditions of full employment. Nonetheless, the disturbing possibility exists that, even when an economic recovery takes place, the unemployment rates of youth may fall to some extent but remain historically high. It is possible that there have been changes in youth attitudes to work and employer attitudes to youth in recent years, resulting in a competitive disadvantage for youth in the labor market. Any such disadvantage could in principle be offset by changes in other youth attributes, such as relative wages or continuing improvements in educational attainment. Whether or not such improvements will actually take place remains to be seen. In addition, the severity and sustained nature of the current recession have increased the number of young people who have been unemployed for lengthy periods of time, and this could have long-term "scarring" effects on their subsequent patterns of employment and earnings.

A final issue relates to whether or not the types and characteristics of jobs held by youth make them particularly vulnerable to long run, noncyclical changes in the structure of the economy, such as those resulting from technological change. The available evidence on this is limited, although we noted earlier that the level of female youth employment is more closely related to changes in the industrial structure of employment than is the level of male youth employment. Thus the employment of young females may tend to be disproportionately influenced by, and therefore vulnerable to, the fortunes of the industries in which they are traditionally employed.

References: Australia

ABS (Australian Bureau of Statistics). I. *Earnings and Hours of Employees, Australia.* cat.no.6304.0. Canberra: AGPS (Australian Government Publishing Service).
_____. II. *Income Distribution, Australia.* Part I. cat.no.6502.0. Canberra: AGPS.
_____. III. *The Labour Force, Australia.* cat.no.6203.0. Canberra: AGPS.
_____. IV. *The Labour Force, Australia.* cat.no.6204.0. Canberra: AGPS.
_____. V. *Labour Mobility, Australia.* cat.no.6209.0. Canberra: AGPS.
_____. VI. *Schools, Australia.* cat.no.4202.0. Canberra: AGPS.
_____. 1972. *The Labour Force.* cat.no.6.22. Canberra: AGPS.
_____. 1976. *Trade Union Members, Australia.* cat.no.6325.0. Canberra: AGPS.
_____. 1978. *Employment Status of Teenagers, Australia.* cat.no.6234.0. Canberra: AGPS.
_____. 1979a. *Working Conditions, Australia.* cat.no.6335.0. Canberra: AGPS.
_____. 1979b. *Persons Not in the Labour Force (Including Discouraged Jobseekers), Australia.* cat.no.6220.0, September. Canberra: AGPS.
_____. 1981a. *Earnings and Hours of Employees, Distribution and Composition, Australia.* cat.no.6306.0. Canberra: AGPS.
_____. 1981b. *Job Vacancies, Australia.* cat.no.6321.0, May. Canberra: AGPS.
_____. 1981c. *Transition from Education to Work, Australia.* cat.no.6227.0. Canberra: AGPS.
Bentley, P., and O'Neill, M. 1982. "School Participation and Labour Force Participation of Teenagers." In *Proceedings of the Bureau of Labour Market Research Workshop on Labour Force Participation.* Canberra: AGPS.
BLMR (Bureau of Labour Market Research). 1982a. *The Personal and Labour Market Characteristics of Young People Placed in National Manpower Programs.* Canberra: forthcoming.
_____. 1982b. *Youth Employment Patterns.* Canberra: forthcoming.
Bourke, S.F., et al. 1981. *Performance in Literacy and Numeracy: 1980.* Australian Educational Council. Canberra: AGPS.
Cain, G.G. 1976. "The Challenge of Segmented Labor Market Theories to Orthodox Theory: A Survey." *Journal of Economic Literature,* December.
Casson, M. 1979. *Youth Unemployment.* London: Macmillan Press.
CDE (Commonwealth Department of Education). 1976. *Report of the Working Party on the Transition from Secondary Education to Employment.* Canberra: AGPS.
Cole, P. 1979. *Work Experience: An Australian Perspective.* Melbourne: Victorian Department of Education.

DEYA (Department of Employment and Youth Affairs). I. *Monthly Review of the Employment Situation.* Canberra: AGPS.
————. 1981. *Employment and Manpower Services Guide.* Canberra: AGPS.
————. 1982a. *Annual Report 1980–81.* Canberra: AGPS.
————. 1982b. *Apprenticeship Statistics 1971–72 to 1980–81.* Canberra: AGPS.
DT (Department of the Treasury). 1979. *Job Markets—Economic and Statistical Aspects of the Australian Market for Labour.* Canberra: AGPS.
Earley, P.D. 1981. "Girls Need Jobs Too You Know!: Unemployment, Sex Roles and Female Identity." *Australian Journal of Social Issues,* August.
Gregory, R.G., and Duncan, R.C. 1980. "High Teenage Unemployment: The Role of Atypical Labour Supply Behaviour." *Economic Record,* December.
Gregory, R.G., and Foster, W. 1981. *The Contribution of Employment Separation to Teenage Unemployment.* Australian National University, Centre for Economic Policy Research, Discussion Paper no.31, July.
Gregory, R.G., and Stricker, P. 1981. "Teenage Employment and Unemployment in the 1970s." In *Youth Employment, Education and Training Conference Papers.* Canberra: Centre for Economic Policy Research, Australian National University.
HR (House of Representatives). 1965. *Debates,* 24 March, p.268. Statement by the Rt. Hon. Sir Robert Menzies. Canberra: AGPS.
Karmel, P. 1979. "Youth, Education and Employment." Radford Memorial Lecture, delivered to the Australian Association for Research in Education, Melbourne.
King, S.E. 1980. "Some Reactions to Professor Karmel's 1979 Radford Memorial Lecture on Youth, Education and Employment." *Education Research and Perspectives,* December.
————. 1981. "Attitudes of Australian Youth to Work, School and Unemployment: A Review of Some Recent Australian Research." *Unicorn,* February.
Merrilees, W. 1980a. "Alternative Models of Apprentice Recruitment With Special Reference to the British Engineering Industry." Paper delivered to the Ninth Conference of Economists, Brisbane, August.
————. 1980b. "An Economic Framework for Explaining Teenage Unemployment." *Australian Bulletin of Labour,* December.
————. 1981. "The Effects of Labour Market Conditions on School Enrollment Rates." *Australian Economic Review,* Third Quarter.
NILS (National Institute for Labour Studies). 1974. "The Australian Labour Market." *Australian Bulletin of Labour,* September.
————. 1977. "The Australian Labour Market." *Australian Bulletin of Labour,* September.
Power, M. 1975. "Women's Work is Never Done—by Men: A Socio-economic Model of Sex-typing in Occupations." *Journal of Industrial Relations,* September.
SCC (Sydney Chamber of Commerce). 1981. *Educational Survey.* Sydney: SCC.
Selby Smith, J.M. 1978. "Changes in Employment by Occupation: 1974 to 1977." *Journal of Industrial Relations,* September.
Stricker, P., and Sheehan, P. 1978. "Youth Unemployment in Australia: A Survey." *Australian Economic Review,* First Quarter.
————. 1981. *Hidden Unemployment: The Australian Experience.* Institute for Applied Economic and Social Research, University of Melbourne. Melbourne: IAESR.
Sweet, R. 1980. *The New Marginal Workers: Teenage Part-time Employment in Australia in the 1970s.* Research Report, Department of Technical and Further Education, New South Wales.
————. 1981. "The Teenage Labour Market: Trends and Prospects." Paper delivered at a public seminar sponsored by the Victorian Institute of Secondary Education, Melbourne, October.
TEC (Tertiary Education Commission). 1981. *Report for 1982-83 Triennium.* Vol.1, Part 1. Recommendations and Guidelines. Canberra: AGPS.
Williams Committee. 1979. *Education, Training and Employment.* Report of the Committee of Inquiry into Education and Training. Vol.1. Canberra: AGPS.

Williams, T., et al. 1980. *School Work and Career. Seventeen-Year-Olds in Australia.* Australian Council for Educational Research. Monograph no.6. Hawthorn, Victoria: ACER.

Williams, J., and Priest, T.A. 1978. *Attitudes of Employers to School Leavers in Western Australia.* Education Department of Western Australia. Cooperative Research Series Report no.2.

5

Youth Employment in West Germany

Karen Schober

For about two decades after World War II, the labor market situation of young people seemed rather similar to that of other age groups in West Germany. Due to a rapidly growing economy, low birth rates during and after World War II, and increasing educational enrollment rates, young people had excellent employment opportunities no matter what level of education or training they had completed. Although mobility and advancement chances and working conditions varied among educational levels, even unskilled and less qualified young people found more than enough well-paid jobs (MAGS 1979).

This situation changed rapidly as the number of apprenticeships offered in both private firms and the public sector decreased from 1970 to 1975 and a deep economic recession began in 1974–75, reducing the number of jobs available to skilled as well as unskilled youth. At the same time an increased number of teenagers were entering the labor market, the result of high births in the early 1960s. All of this caused a rise in teenage and young adult unemployment rates to levels unknown in West Germany since the early 1950s. The adverse general and youth unemployment situation has persisted and the prospects for youth employment in the first half of the 1980s seem unfavorable despite a peaking of the number of school-leavers in 1981 and a subsequent decline to 1987 as well as higher levels of apprenticeship intake than in 1970–75 (BMBW 1981a). In addition, unemployment among university graduates, formerly unknown in Germany, began to rise, reflecting the persistent shortage of jobs on all educational levels (Tessaring 1977, 1981). A growing number of university graduates have had to take jobs below their customary level. These jobs were then no longer available to young people from lower educational levels. This "displacement-competition" reinforces the employment problems of disadvantaged youth—those who do not obtain a leaver's certificate from compulsory education, often because they are physically, mentally, or socially hand-icapped; some may even be multiply disadvantaged. An increasing proportion are the children of foreign workers. In recent years, evidence has accumulated of labor market segmentation that might affect the opportunities of some young people, especially the disadvantaged groups. Still another factor whose effects on the employment situation of youth have yet to be identified are observed attitudinal changes among young people over the past ten years concerning their general perspectives on life as well as their future working lives; these changing values seem to be closely linked to uncertain employment prospects (Jugendwerk der Deutschen Shell 1981).

Educational and Training Systems and Their Outputs

Since 1969 most of the 11 states in West Germany have set compulsory full-time education at nine years; a few have added a tenth year recently. Over 60 percent of young people voluntarily attend full-time school for at least ten years, or until age 16, so that the most common age of leaving school is 15 or 16. In addition, the states, which have jurisdiction over education, all have legislation compelling youth under 18 who are not in full-time education to attend a part-time vocational school for one to two days a week. This provision, covering over 1.7 million young people in 1981, equally affects apprentices, unskilled workers, and youth out of the labor force. Because apprentices need the theoretical instruction in schools to pass their examinations, they attend willingly. But unskilled youth and those at home, mostly girls, are not pleased with the part-time schools where they receive some general and vocational instruction, usually not directly related to their jobs. There is considerable non-registration, absenteeism, and boredom, especially among second generation foreign youth of whom only half attend (Schober 1981). Moreover, some employers reject the under-18s because the school requirement disrupts work schedules and increases labor costs. School authorities in certain areas have excused some youth from school attendance if their job depends on being able to work full-time. In states providing a tenth full-time school year with vocational content, completion of the year may satisfy the entire part-time school requirement.

The structure of the school system in West Germany largely dictates the opportunities for additional education, initial vocational training, and first employment as well as later career advancement. After a comprehensive four-year primary school education, pupils are divided up at age 10–11 among different types of schools; a small proportion attend comprehensive schools. Children with behavioral problems and the physically or mentally handicapped who are unable to keep up with normal standards are sent to special schools (*Sonderschule*). The main upper primary school (*Hauptschule*) leads to the basic school-leaving certificate (*Haupschulabschluss*), usually at age 15. The intermediate school (*Realschule*) goes through tenth grade and offers a certificate, usually at age 16, permitting entrance to technical schools as well as some forms of higher education. Finally, the senior school (*Gymnasium*) runs through 13th grade, usually completed at age 19, and provides a certificate (*Abitur*) permitting university entrance; it is also possible to obtain a lower certificate on successful completion of the tenth grade.

There are few transfers among these school types. Although government subsidies are available to low-income families so that children can continue past tenth grade, pupils at the senior school are disproportionately drawn from families of higher socioeconomic status and income (BMBW 1982b). In 1980, 47 percent of all school-leavers had gone no further than the compulsory level, a notable change from 1960 when three-fourths were in this category. Those with intermediate certificates constituted 36 percent of the total in 1980, up from 16 percent in 1960. Holders of the *Abitur* almost doubled their share over the two decades, rising from 9 to 17 percent (BMBW 1981b).

The educational attainment of employed 15–19 year-olds, which excludes teenagers still at school, showed an advance in 1978 over 1970. In 1978 about 72 percent had gone no further than compulsory school, 26 percent had the intermediate certificate and, as might be expected, almost none had the *Abitur* or similar certificates (Table 5.1). A fifth of a cohort of leavers from *Gymnasium* in 1970 still were enrolled at universities eight years later; the male employment rate, 88 percent, was considerably higher than the female, 75 percent (Kaiser et al. 1980b). German university studies are so prolonged (and for males are interrupted by 15 months of military service) that educational data for the 20–24 year-old group do not capture the proportion completing a university degree, nor do employment data for the age group reflect many of the jobs that university graduates customarily fill. Thus, the usual generational gap in education between adults and young adults does not appear, and, in fact, adults show a higher proportion with completed university education than young adults (SB 1980). In 1978, only 7 percent of employed 20–24 year-olds had the *Abitur* or similar certificate and the proportion with a university degree was miniscule (Table 5.1).

There are large differences in educational attainment by sex, nationality, social background, and regions. Especially in rural districts the opportunity to attend school beyond compulsory level is very limited; for many young people the intermediate or senior school is too distant for daily travel and public boarding schools are rare. The proportion of teenagers holding the intermediate certificate or the *Abitur* is much higher in the larger cities than in the smaller towns and rural districts (*Arbeitsgruppe am MPI* 1979). The educational attainment of young women has risen since 1970 and now almost exceeds that of young males. Females have higher enrollment rates at intermediate schools and about the same rates as males at senior schools (Saterdag and

Table 5.1   General and Vocational Educational Attainment of Employed Population,
            by Age and Sex, West Germany, 1978

	15-19 years		20-24 years		15 years and over	
General education	Male	Female	Male	Female	Male	Female
Total number[a] (000)	1,239	976	1,641	1,333	16,326	9,695
		(percentage distribution)				
Compulsory school	78.4	63.7	69.6	57.2	74.2	70.1
Intermediate school	19.4	34.3	21.1	33.4	15.1	22.4
Qualification for higher technical school	0.6	0.8	2.6	2.2	2.3	1.2
Qualification for university	1.6	1.2	6.7	7.2	8.4	6.3
Vocational education						
Total number[b] (000)	558	547	1,519	1,250	15,184	8,946
		(percentage distribution)				
No vocational training	35.2	34.9	21.9	20.5	20.7	38.2
Vocational training[c]	62.1	60.0	71.1	68.5	58.7	50.0
Technical school	0.7	0.8	3.0	3.5	9.3	3.0
Higher technical school	*	*	1.1	1.3	3.2	1.2
University	0.1	0.6	0.9	2.7	6.2	5.0
Other vocational training	1.9	3.7	2.0	3.5	1.9	2.6

*Less than 0.05 percent.
[a]Includes apprentices, regular military, and foreign employed.   [b]Excludes
apprentices; includes regular military and foreign employed.   [c]Apprenticeship or
full-time vocational school.

Source: SB 1980; tables from Federal Statistical Office (SB).

Stegmann 1980). Boys also attend the special schools (*Sonderschule*)
more frequently than girls, a fact that does not necessarily indicate
different intellectual capacities but rather, different treatment of boys
and girls who show poor school performance. Only about 10 percent
of teenagers leaving the special schools obtain a basic leaving certificate,
restricting their chances for vocational training and limiting their later
employment (SB 1981a).

The compulsory school attendance rate of the children of foreign
workers rose from about 70 percent in the mid-1970s to about 85
percent in 1980. Attendance at primary school approaches 100 percent,
but the rate is considerably lower in the upper primary school (Schober
1981). Because of language problems, cultural differences, ghetto-like
housing concentrations, and a low socioeconomic status which puts
pressure on youth to work at the earliest age, most young foreigners
have low school grades and poor attendance. Only about half of them
achieve the basic school-leaving certificate, in part because many have
come to West Germany at age ten or later and have had only a few
years in German schools. Those attending the German schools from

the beginning are more successful, and about 85 percent, a lower proportion than of German pupils, earn a basic certificate (Mehrländer et al. 1981).

Initial vocational training or education is highly developed for those who leave the upper-primary and intermediate schools, as well for *Gymnasium* leavers who do not immediately enter universities. Apprenticeship, regulated by the Vocational Training Act of 1969 (*Berufsbildungsgesetz*), is the main type and the only legal form of initial on-the-job training for young people under 18 in some 450 designated occupations, spanning a wide variety and level of economic activities and including agriculture and the public sector. Each training occupation has a curriculum specifying the content, organization and duration of training (2 to 3½ years) and the related theoretical instruction in a part-time vocational school for one or two days a week, as well as the final, qualifying examinations. Training in the firm is to be given by qualified instructors who have passed examinations; often instructors are the senior craftsmen or the qualified owners of smaller shops.

Apprentices are workers, trainees, and pupils. They contribute to output and are part of the workforce, belonging to trade unions. They have a training contract with a private firm or a public authority, are counted as full-time employees, are fully covered by all social insurance programs, and are paid for attending part-time school or off-the-job training centers. Special protection against dismissal under the Vocational Training Act provides that, after the initial probationary three-month period, apprentices may not be dismissed during the training years, and must be given six-weeks notice before the end of their training if they are not offered posts as regular employees. Apprentice allowances are set by collective bargaining as fractions of the skilled rate for the occupation; the law provides an increase with each successive year of training. Their allowances generally are higher than those of comparable students.

A new form, the basic vocational training year (*Berufsgrundbildungsjahr BGJ*), was introduced in the early 1970s. It was to substitute for the first year of apprenticeship training, providing knowledge of a broad occupational field and aiding youth to choose their specific apprenticeship training occupation. Since many employers have refused to recognize the basic vocational training year as the first year of apprenticeship, the number of young people attending the BGJ did not grow as rapidly as was planned. In 1980, 13 percent of all school-leavers aiming for apprenticeship were enrolled in BGJ (BiBB 1982), most because they failed to obtain an apprenticeship place with a firm. Under persistent high youth unemployment, the BGJ has become a "waiting room" for school-leavers without an apprenticeship contract. After leaving the BGJ, only half of the young people have found an apprenticeship place (Westhoff and Mahnke 1980). In addition, many who obtain a place conceal their BGJ from the employer or do not receive credit for it as the first year of apprenticeship (Lemke and Schmidt-Hackenberg 1980).

Besides the BGJ a variety of full-time vocational schools exist at different levels, ranging from simple work preparatory courses for those without the basic leaver's certificate (*Berufsvorbereitungsjahr*) to full-time, multi-year vocational or technical school offering recognized vocational credentials, some almost at university level (*Berufsfachschule, Fachschule, Fachhochschule*). The majority of full-time vocational or technical courses are in occupational fields and levels where apprenticeship training is absent or scarce. Examples are health occupations, kindergarten and nursery teachers, business administration, and clerical occupations. In some of these schools or courses, practical experience or even a completed apprenticeship is a prerequisite, while others have integrated periods of practical work in their curricula. Girls and young women attend full-time vocational and technical schools to a greater extent than males (Stegmann and Kraft 1982).

About three-fourths of young people who have left school with and without a certificate from compulsory school and about two-thirds of those with the intermediate school certificate take up an apprenticeship. In 1980, three years after leaving the upper primary school, intermediate school, or first part of *Gymnasium,* 46 percent of the 1977 cohort, then aged 18–19, were still in full-time general or vocational education or apprenticeship. Another 4 percent were in military service, 44 percent were employed with a work contract, and 5 percent were unemployed or out of the labor force (Stegmann and Kraft 1982).

Some four-fifths of those with an *Abitur* currently continue at a higher technical school (*Fachhochschule*) or a university (Stegmann and Kraft 1982). The proportion of teenagers enrolled in full-time vocational schools and technical and higher technical schools has increased considerably within the last twenty years, especially from the intermediate schools where over 20 percent of leavers currently enter vocational-technical schools. In addition, some who have completed an apprenticeship continue in full-time vocational or technical schools immediately or after some years of work experience (BiBB and IAB 1981). In 1980, 13 percent of the 1977 cohort of school-leavers 15–16 years old had both started an apprenticeship and, before or afterward, entered a vocational or technical school. Despite their greater general education, the vocational education level of young females is far behind that of young males (Stegmann and Kraft 1982).

The proportion of 15–18 year-olds not receiving initial vocational training of any kind is now very small, having declined from around 18 percent in 1960 to about 6 percent in 1980 (MAGS 1979; BMBW 1981b). Formerly about two-thirds of youth without any vocational education were girls who had completed compulsory school or even more. The remainder were males from the special schools or from upper primary schools without a leaver's certificate (MAGS 1979). But now children of foreign workers are increasingly found in this group; only 20 percent of the 15–18 year-old foreigners are enrolled in an apprenticeship or a full-time vocational school. Over one-third of them do not receive any kind of vocational education or training. Their share of this group will increase in the future because they constitute a growing fraction of the youth population (Schober 1981).

There are large differences by regions and economic sectors in the distribution of apprenticeships and full-time vocational schools, so that the educational opportunities for school-leavers vary significantly between regions as well as occupational fields (BiBB 1981; IAB 1977). Rural districts usually offer few and distant full-time schools, leading most school-leavers to request an apprenticeship. But these too are few in rural areas and exist only in special occupational fields such as artisan, agriculture, and trade; there are hardly any industrial training opportunities. While the large cities offer a variety of full-time schools as well as apprenticeships in the industrial and the service sectors, even there opportunities may be limited if the city has an economic mono-structure, e.g., mining or iron and steel. Such cities offer industrial training places mainly in these economic sectors and mostly for boys; usually girls have fewer industrial training opportunities than boys. Varying with the overall level of employment, the vocational education situation usually is better in South-west Germany than in Northrhine-Westphalia, Saarland, and Rhineland-Pfalz. In order to equalize these regional and sectoral differences, the Training Places Promotion Act of 1976, subsequently declared unconstitutional, stated that the number of apprenticeships offered by employers should at least be 12.5 percent above the demand by youth. However, this ratio has not been achieved. In 1981 the number of apprenticeships offered was about 2.5 percent higher than the demand, and in 1982 the situation was worse (BMBW 1982a).

Since levels of general and vocational educational attainment are inextricably intertwined in West Germany, people are usually classified by the highest level achieved among four levels: no vocational education; apprenticeship; full-time vocational school or middle-level technical schools; and university diploma or, since 1973, diploma from higher technical schools. Using this classification for the age group 15–30, and making some estimates beyond the official data, it is clear that apprenticeship is the dominant form of initial training, accounting for 60 percent of the total in 1978, a reduction from 75 percent in 1960. By 1978 those with a university diploma were in second place with 18 percent, 10 percentage points over 1960. Following closely, technical and other full-time vocational schools showed 14 percent, a large rise from 2 percent in 1960. The residual group, those with no vocational education, came to only 8 percent in 1978, having dropped from 15 percent in 1960 (BMBW 1981b).

Higher levels of both general and vocational education are related to the shift toward service and white collar occupations in many industries. Germany entered the 1960s with the lowest proportion of academically educated manpower among the Western European countries (Tessaring and Werner 1981). But then there was a strong demand for university graduates, especially in engineering and teaching, as well as for skilled and highly qualified manpower at other levels. During the late 1970s young people modified their educational enrollment patterns in reaction to the slack labor market. For example, the proportion of young people with *Abitur* definitely planning on a university education fell from almost 90 percent in the early 1970s to 67 percent in 1979. The growing awareness among young people and their parents that a university degree did not guarantee stable employment and higher income led a rising proportion of graduates from the *Gymnasium* and Intermediate School to enter apprenticeships, competing with young people having no more than compulsory school at a time when the demand for places outstripped the supply offered by employers (Stegmann and Kraft 1982; BMBW 1981a).

Institutional Background

Legislative regulation of job search, working conditions and other aspects of the workplace is highly developed in West Germany; several provisions relate only to youth. Nonetheless, legislation also provides that wage-setting and collective bargaining shall be free from government intervention, so that no legal minimum wage exists.

Preparation for Working Life, Occupational Guidance and Job Placement. Some preparation for working life (*Arbeitslehre*) occurs during the last two years of school. It is supposed to be a combination of polytechnical training and career education. The Federal Employment Office (BA) also is developing curricula to improve career education in schools (Dibbern 1974). Although many efforts have been made, *Arbeitslehre* is not yet fully developed. Critics say that the bad preparation in school for working life causes difficulty with occupational choice for many school-leavers (Biermann-Berlin 1979). Occupational guidance is organized and controlled by the Federal Employment Office and its local employment offices, which are the only legal dispensers of these services and of placements in apprenticeships and other jobs (Meisel 1978). In the year prior to the end of school, counselors, visiting the schools, give a whole class information on the general labor market situation, discuss problems of occupational choice, and outline training opportunities. Prospective school-leavers are invited to the employment office for individual counseling and about 60 percent came in the 1981–82 school year, a smaller percentage than in earlier years. Since employers are not required to notify their apprenticeship vacancies to public employment offices, only about two-thirds of all apprenticeship places were filled by the public employment service in 1981–82 (BMBW 1981b). Nevertheless, because of advance planning on all sides, apprentices are likely to enter the labor market with less intervening unemployment than other youth of the same age who also are served by the local employment service, but in different sections than serve youth seeking apprenticeships.

Young Workers Protection Act (Jugendarbeitsschutzgesetz) 1976. It covers all 15–18 year-olds, including apprentices, and limits work of 13–15 year-olds to a few industries (farms, hotels, restaurants), and for no more than four hours a day. An 8-hour day (including rest periods in special rooms), and 40 hours a week are the maximum for 15–18 year-olds; this is more restrictive than the general hours legislation (*Arbeitszeitordnung*). Paid release from work is provided for those attending part-time school, as described above. Minimum paid annual leave declines from 30 weekdays per year for under 16 year-olds to 25 days for those 17 but not 18, with other workers assured of 18 days per year under another act (*Mindesturlaubsgesetz*). Work at nights, on Sundays and holidays is forbidden to 15–18 year-olds, as are piece-work, assembly line and other jobs with a fixed pace. A medical examination, repeated at intervals, must be conducted before work or apprenticeship starts. Industrial inspection officers are in charge of enforcement, but they are not able to police small shops adequately. The main trade union federation (DGB) estimates that only 4 percent of all violations are reported and that only a small fraction of these cases lead to sanctions against the offending employers (Stark von der Haar 1977, p.117).

Maternity Protection Act (Mutterschutzgesetz) 1968, amended 1979. Protection from dismissal is given from beginning of pregnancy to four months after birth. Paid leave is payable for six weeks before and six months after child-bearing. Maternity allowance is payable from health insurance. Workplace must provide rest periods and other suitable conditions for pregnant women.

Workplace Constitution Act (Betriebsverfassungs- und Personalvertretungsgesetz) 1977. All establishments with five or more employees must elect a Works Council, and a special youth representative on the Council is required if there are five or more employees under 18. Special interests of young workers are the only matters on which the youth representatives may vote, and only the whole Council may act on issues concerning youth. All members of the Council have special protection from dismissal.

Dismisssal Protection Act (Kündigungsschutzgesetz) 1969, amended 1978. Young workers share with all other workers in the procedures required before dismissal can take place. Each dismissal has to be justified by the employer either on economic grounds or because of the behavior of the employee. If economic reasons lead to a dismissal, the employer has to select among his employees according to social criteria that favor age and family obligations. This stipulation quite often leads to the dismissal of young people who have no family responsibilities. Each dismissal has to be agreed to by the Works Council, composed of elected representatives of the employees.

Government Labor Market Programs and Financial Aid to Youth. Since unemployment began to rise in 1974–75, the government has offered the private sector subsidies to stimulate additional training and employment of youth, especially disadvantaged or handicapped youth who were unable to find an ordinary apprenticeship (Schober and Hochgürtel 1980). Job creation programs to provide community services not regularly offered also hire unemployed youth.

Allowances are payable to tenth-year and above full-time vocational school pupils and to eleventh year and above general education pupils whose families' incomes are below limits set under the 1971 Federal Education Promotion Act (*Bundesausbildungsförderungsgesetz*). Students in higher education who do not live with their parents are judged by their own incomes and receive the largest amounts, while pupils living at home receive less than half as much. Apprentices from low income families can obtain a supplement to their allowance from the Federal Employment Office out of unemployment insurance funds. Certain vocational training courses offer a stipend to those attending them. While school-leavers and new entrants are not eligible for unemployment benefits, they can receive social welfare benefits. In 1977, 72 percent of all registered teenagers, 80 percent of young adults and 84 percent of adults drew unemployment benefits, which paid 68 percent of the last net income per week for a maximum of one year (Cramer 1981). Unemployment assistance at a 58 percent rate is paid to youth who continue to be unemployed and cannot be maintained by their families.

Trade Unions. A trade union membership rate of 20 percent for apprentices and young workers, 15–19 years old, compares to 30 percent for 20–24 year-olds and 33 percent of all ages (INFRATEST 1978). The age disparity is attributed to disproportionate concentration of teenagers in small firms or artisan shops in which trade union organization tends to be weak. It is the policy of the trade unions to abolish prevailing wage-rate differentials for each year of age under 19 years (blue collar) and under 21 years (white collar). The trade unions support the present practice of setting apprentices' allowances through collective bargaining, insisting that apprentices should have a work contract as well as a training contract, since they do productive work from which employers gain.

Trade unions have sponsored collective agreements with industry branches to offer a minimum occupational training and income (90 percent of the apprentice allowance) to youth who are low academic achievers, handicapped, unskilled, or foreigners. The employer and young person make a one year "caring contract" in addition to a work contract. If such youth later enter the firm's apprenticeship ranks or get an unlimited work contract, the firms can receive a subsidy from public labor market programs.

Educational Attainment and Employment Paths

In any given age cohort, the higher the level of general and vocational education, the higher the likelihood of labor force participation and, among labor force participants, the higher the likelihood of being employed rather than unemployed. Educational attainment levels also directly influence the initial jobs held by young people and lead to lifelong career differences within a cohort, possibly as great as the employment differences between young people and adults at any given time. Information for a recent year suggests six major divisions in the working population that directly relate to level of educational attainment.

- Youth and adults with no vocational education mainly work as blue collar workers in all age and sex groups.
- With rising educational levels, white collar work gains importance in all age and sex groups and general education may substitute to a certain extent for vocational education.
- A large majority of females with completed apprenticeship or technical school education hold white collar jobs in all age groups.
- The percentage of employers and self-employed is highest among males and females with technical school education and increases with age due to legislation on the artisan sector that prescribes further education for a craftsman who wants to establish his own firm (*Meisterausbildung*).
- The percentage who are civil service officials increases with level of education. Almost 60 percent of female university graduates between 25 and 30 years are in this group, due to the large share of school-teachers in the total. University graduates work in the public sector to a large extent (Tessaring and Werner 1981; Kaiser et al. 1980a). Among university graduates of all ages in 1978, 64 percent had a job in the public sector, compared to 36 percent for higher technical school graduates, and 20 percent for the whole labor force (Tessaring and Werner 1981). Employment in the public sector offers great job security and benefits, but entrance is restricted in times of economic recession.
- The high proportion in the public sector among 25 to 30 year-old males and females also arises because many university graduates remain at the university as research or teaching assistants with no more than a five year work contract. In this period they can do postgraduate work toward a doctorate. For a number of university graduates, this activity, included in the public sector, is part of their career planning.

Other factors lead to job hierarchies based on educational levels. Laws prescribe certain educational levels for entrance to many professions and custom or practice dictates that entrants to most of the clerical or administration jobs should have an intermediate school certificate or *Abitur*. Other occupations specify a minimum age, automatically leading to higher qualifications because prospective employees choose education or training rather than the scarce and stigmatized unskilled jobs.

Also, rising educational levels in the manpower supply push up the standards required by employers. Over the period 1960–80, the employed in all age groups showed rising general and vocational educational levels without an equivalent change in the occupational structure. The reduced disparity between the sexes in vocational education levels among employed young people was not fully reflected in their employment patterns. A corresponding rise in the educational attainment of apprentices appeared from 1970 to 1978; male apprentices with more than compulsory education went from over 20 percent to 40 percent of the total, and for females the increase was from 22 percent to 52 percent (BMBW 1981a). However, the rise was not equal in all apprenticeship trades, since those most sought by young people showed the competitive increase first. Thus, in most of the clerical and sales occupations the proportion of apprentices having more than compulsory education has been far above average, whereas in a number of traditional artisan occupations the educational level of apprentices is below average (BA 1981).

Jobs of Young People

The main employment divisions among young people (15–18) are between apprentices and unskilled workers. In 1979–80 there were over 1.6 million apprentices, over 100,000 young unskilled blue collar workers, over 6,500 young unskilled white collar workers, and 4,000 unpaid family workers (BMBW 1981b). As apprenticeships are completed, these youth move mainly into jobs leading to full skilled status. Older teenage entrants who have completed a two-year full-time vocational school are able to move into the same jobs as youth who have completed a white collar apprenticeship; some may qualify for higher posts. Graduates of the universities and higher technical schools have an occupational distribution based on their field of concentration in studies. Neither the West German educational system nor the employment structure favor job-holding by enrolled youth during the academic term. As a consequence, student-workers do not influence the occupational structure of youth employment. Many students take jobs in the vacation periods, but these are likely to be unrelated to the positions they take when they have completed their studies.

School-leavers who do not enter an apprenticeship at age 15 or 16 can find only a limited selection of unskilled jobs; in these no training is offered, no special skills are developed, and little responsibility is given over equipment, tools, products, or persons (IAB 1980; Höhn 1974; Schlaffke 1976). Such "marginal jobs" tend to be dead-end paths in career development. As newcomers to the firm, these youth have a relatively low social status, being inferior to every older worker, whether skilled or unskilled. Some large firms assign a senior worker to look after these young workers.

These unskilled jobs also are filled by older workers, mainly those who were displaced from their former occupations by age, disability or other factors, those who have moved downward during their working lives, and those who never advanced. There is a high concentration of young and older workers (over 55) and some competition between the two for such unskilled jobs as office and delivery workers, door-to-door salesperson, home and office cleaners, warehouse and storage workers, and doorman. Within the past 20 years, the availability of these unskilled jobs has decreased since many firms reserve such jobs for their own older and handicapped workers.

Sex differences in the occupational patterns of unskilled youth show almost the same differences as between general male and female employment. Teenage girls have high percentages in the textile and leather industry as well as in the food and beverage industry, where they mostly work at automatic packing and filling of machines. Many of them do simple assembly work in the electronic branch or control the final product. A considerable proportion also work in private households. Teenage boys, however, are more often engaged in unskilled or semi-skilled manual work within the metal and construction industries (Schober-Gottwald 1976; Höhn 1974; Braun and Gravalas 1980). The children of foreign workers who hold jobs are concentrated much more than German youth in the category "unskilled laborer n.e.c."; they work more often as assemblers, storage and transportation workers, in cleaning jobs and in food services (Schober 1982).

A cross-sectional analysis of first jobs shows that toward the beginning of the period 1949–79 young people without vocational education entered work relatively frequently in agriculture, industry and the artisan trades. Since the 1960s the proportion of young people starting in these branches has declined and increasing shares of unskilled teenagers start in wholesale and retail trade and other service sectors (BiBB and IAB 1981). The relative decline of agricultural employment, the development of more capital-intensive and less labor-intensive manufacturing, as well as the enforced rationalization process in production and administration, have eliminated many of the marginal jobs that in earlier years enabled unskilled teenagers to gain experience and some qualifications by watching and imitating senior workers. Moreover, highly mechanized and numerically-controlled manufacturing or administrative processes do not permit the watching and imitating of others (von Henninges 1975). Thus the hypothesis seems plausible that an increasing segmentation has appeared and is likely to be intensified between the jobs of unskilled teenagers and the jobs of other youth.

Youth entering and remaining in unskilled jobs exhibit a greater vulnerability to unemployment than those who complete an apprenticeship or vocational education. Almost three-fourths of unemployed teenagers have no vocational training or education and one-third lack even the compulsory school certificate (IAB 1980). Half of the unemployed unskilled teenagers under 18 who had never held a job were seeking an apprenticeship but could not find a place (IAB 1980). In the past few years the absolute and relative number of unemployed youth under 18 has been sharply reduced by the addition of a compulsory or voluntary tenth year of education, a deliberate expansion of apprenticeship places in firms and other training institutions, and special training and job creation measures for this age group (Schober and Hochgürtel 1980). Another factor tending to hold down teenage unemployment numbers and rates is the failure of the official statistics to count as unemployed those youth who are seeking an apprenticeship place but who have not registered at the employment service for an ordinary job. Within the low unemployment rate for the under-18s, female teenagers account for a disproportionate share.

In comparison to the residual and unfavored position of unskilled youth, apprentices are insulated and protected. Recruited in a manner that minimizes unemployment between leaving school and taking the first job, apprentices are safe from dismissal during the training period except for cause or the firm's failure or extreme economic distress. Apprentices completing their period also are given advance notice if they will not be retained by their firm. Customarily, well over half of apprentices remain with the training firm for one year.

The proportion declined somewhat as the number in apprenticeship was expanded at the government's request. Of the school-leavers of 1977 who completed their apprenticeship by October 1980, over half remained in the training firm; only 5 percent had been dismissed after their examination, 10 percent wanted to continue their education, and 30 percent preferred to work in another firm (Stegmann and Kraft 1982). As a result, relatively few were unemployed. In 1978, for example, apprentices with a recently completed training comprised only 19 percent of teenage unemployment (IAB 1980).

Because of the age limits and special characteristics of apprenticeship, apprentices are not in competition with other age groups. The employment security enjoyed by established workers does not discourage the recruitment of apprentices, since no permanent commitment to an apprentice is made by the employer. While the number of apprenticeship places does fluctuate with business conditions, in a recession there is more flexibility and greater opportunity to maintain or expand the number of apprenticeship places than in ordinary jobs. During their training, apprentices are protected by special health and safety regulations. They are set apart from other workers in the daily life of the firm and in the social and hierarchical relations within the firm; there is considerable variation in this according to the size of the firm and the nature of its productive processes.

The jobs held by teenagers show the clear advantage of those who have completed an apprenticeship, especially for males and in blue collar jobs. While in 1970 about one-third of male teenagers without apprenticeship held unskilled jobs in such fields as metal processing, construction, electrical machinery production, and warehousing and materials handling, less than 5 percent of those with a completed apprenticeship, or comparable vocational education, were in these jobs. About 30 percent of young females without an apprenticeship or other vocational education, but only 10 percent with it, held unskilled jobs (Schober-Gottwald 1976). To some extent females can substitute additional general education for vocational education to enter white collar jobs. Most apprentices are able to utilize the skills acquired during training in the jobs obtained after apprenticeship, although the proportion is currently lower than it was for those completing an apprenticeship earlier (Stegmann and Kraft 1982; BiBB and IAB 1981).

As is shown later, the wages of unskilled teenagers are likely to exceed the allowances paid to comparable apprentices, allowing for the variations among industries and regions. The differential between the two, representing apprentices' investment to increase their future earnings and status, is difficult to translate into more favorable labor costs to the employer because there are extra costs for apprentices that do not appear for unskilled youth.

Because of the size and diversity of the apprenticeship system, all apprentices do not enter equally promising occupations or receive equal training. Outcomes for the individual apprentice depend on the particular training occupation, the length of training specified, the size of firm, the economic sector, the net costs of training, the degree of substitutability among occupations, the region, the sex of the apprentice, and whether the occupation is blue collar or white collar (Hofbauer and Stooss 1975; Alex 1980).

Apprentice allowances also vary by occupation, industry, and region. Since employers finance apprenticeship, they offer a disproportionate number of places in the sectors, industries and occupations in which training costs are relatively low and the productive process permits apprentices to contribute to the output of goods and services during training (Lenhardt and Schober 1980; Baethge et al. 1980; Edding 1980). Such firms and shops tend to be small and are located in the artisan or handicraft sector. For example, the repair shop attached to the sales showroom of an automobile company would be classified in the artisan sector, while the sales and automobile manufacturing operations would be in the industry and commerce sector. The industry and commerce sector and the public sector tend to train only as many, or even fewer, apprentices than they require, hiring the rest from the artisan sector's surplus.

Small artisan firms trained 40 percent of all apprentices in 1980, but employed only 17 percent of the working population (BMBW 1981b; BiBB and IAB 1981). While more than 60 percent of apprentices were trained in enterprises with fewer than 50 workers and almost 35 percent trained in places with less than 10 employees in 1970–79, a much smaller percent of the whole working population was employed in such firms in 1979 (BMBW 1980; BiBB and IAB 1981). The majority of apprentices in the industry sector receive their training in firms with over 1,000 employees. In such firms a separate training department usually supervises the apprentices and offers structured training, often fully in a separate institution or workshop in the first year. Some of the largest firms provide their own theoretical education, freeing the apprentices from attendance at the public part-time school.

The discrepancy between the composition of apprenticeship places and the employment system has been intensified during the period of government pressure on firms to expand the number of apprenticeship places, since the artisan sector responded to a greater extent than others. In times of strong labor demand, the discrepancy does not create much downgrading or unemployment among those completing apprenticeships, although there always is greater occupational transferability and substitutability in some apprenticeship occupations than others (Schober-Gottwald 1976; Hofbauer 1977). In times of recession, however, those who train in occupations for which the subsequent demand is not strong are more likely to be unemployed. Among male teenagers the oversupplied apprenticeship occupations are auto mechanics, bakers, painters, and carpenters, and among female teenagers, salespersons, hairdressers, and personal service occupations (IAB 1980).

In many cases, the artisan sector offers an excellent social environment for the integration of teenagers into working life and the teaching of good work habits. Personal relationships are close in the small firms and socioeconomic and other hierarchical distinctions tend to be overlooked, making it easier for young people to become accustomed to the requirements of work. But, on the other hand, especially in the small shops, often there is no regular training curriculum or special instructor with both occupational and pedagogical skills. Many things that are taught may be of no use in subsequent jobs because production methods and processes are different in large industrial firms or because the jobs are in entirely new industries and occupations (Lenhardt and Schober 1980; Hofbauer 1977; Baethge et al. 1980). Thus, for many teenagers, the advantage of apprenticeship in small firms is largely in the preparation for and socialization into working life, rather than in acquisition of specific occupational skills. A young person who leaves a small artisan firm after apprenticeship to transfer to a large industrial firm may have the status of an unskilled worker.

While the internal training differences among apprentices are of great importance and should not be glossed over in an uncritical approval of the whole institution of apprenticeship, it remains true that apprenticeship of any kind is superior to the alternative of entering the teenage labor market as an unskilled worker. The large proportion of teenagers in apprenticeship kept their unemployment rates equal to those of young adults up to 1975. Thereafter, assisted by special measures for the youngest teenagers, the 15-19 rate declined more rapidly to 1979 and rose less after 1979 than the young adult rate (IAB 1980; ANBA 1982, no.2). The impact of unemployment on teenagers seems to be both light and delayed, while an equal or greater burden falls on young adults, whose situation has also been affected by a rise in unemployment among those with higher educational attainment (Tessaring 1981).

Foreign youth are very heavily affected by unemployment, although this does not show up in the official registered unemployment figures. In September 1981, 24,000 teenage foreigners were registered as unemployed, giving them an unemployment rate of 19 percent compared with almost 6 percent for all youth under 20 years (Schober 1982). But since many young foreigners who remain in the Federal Republic of Germany for less than two years do not obtain a working permit, they are not registered as unemployed. Taking these into account, about one-third of all 15-18 year-old foreigners neither have jobs nor are enrolled in school or vocational training (Schober 1981). This is a challenge to the West German society; measures against foreign youth unemployment seem very urgent.

High youth unemployment generally goes together with high total unemployment and there are no regional differences in the ratio of youth to adult unemployment. Unemployment usually is extremely high in the large cities of the coal mining and steel district in Northrhine-Westphalia and Saarland, and in rural districts in the east that border on communist nations. Lower unemployment rates are found in Southwest Germany (Baden-Württemberg) where there is a mixed economy (industrial and rural, with large companies, and many small firms) (IAB 1980).

Youth and Adult Employment Compared

A division between youth and adult jobs, both cross-sectionally and longitudinally, seems quite natural, based mainly on the influence of age on the level of educational and occupational qualifications and the amount of work experience acquired. In this context, the entry jobs of most teenagers and young adults serve to give a broad initial vocational training in an occupational field, opening a variety of employment opportunities as well as chances for further education and upward mobility with passing years.

Youth and adult employment can be compared in regard to employment status. In West Germany all of the differences between white collar and blue collar jobs favor the former, especially in regard to the environment of the job itself, amount and method of salary payment,

Table 5.2 Working Population, by Age, Sex, and Employment Status, West Germany, 1961 and 1980

Age	Sex	Year	Total number[a]	Self-employed	Family workers	Civil service official[b]	White collar	Blue collar	Apprentice
			(000)			(percentage distribution)			
15-19	Male	1980	1,259	0.3	1.1	6.0	5.1	27.5	60.0
		1961	1,669	0.0	4.3	1.4	5.1	39.9	49.3
15-19	Female	1980	992	0.3	1.0	1.1	28.0	21.0	48.6
		1961	1,550	0.0	6.6	0.1	28.8	31.0	33.4
20-24	Male	1980	1,787	2.0	1.2	14.6	20.1	56.7	5.4
		1961	2,009	1.4	5.4	3.3	15.1	71.8	3.0
20-24	Female	1980	1,430	1.0	1.5	3.3	65.4	23.9	4.9
		1961	1,669	0,7	10.1	1.0	46.4	40.4	1.4
25 and over	Male	1980	13,736	13.1	0.7	9.7	30.4	46.1	0.0
		1961	12,918	19.2	2.3	7.8	20.2	50.5	0.0
25 and over	Female	1980	7,671	6.1	10.0	4.5	47.6	31.8	0.0
		1961	6,713	10.7	28.6	2.0	24.5	34.2	0.0

[a]Includes apprentices, regular military in 1980, and employed foreign workers; excludes those in compulsory national service. [b]Includes teachers, police, local government employees, regular military, etc.

Source: SB 1968; SB 1981c; tables from Federal Statistical Office (SB).

social status, social security benefits, and protection from dismissal. Even where the skill content is higher in a blue collar job, the other aspects of white collar work tend to be superior. In addition, whether one works for government or the private sector or is an employer or an employee is an important indicator of status in which significant age group differences are found.

Apprenticeship, which was the most important status for teenagers in 1980, played almost no role for young adults or adults (Table 5.2). About 55 percent of employed teenagers were apprentices in 1980, a rise of over 13 percentage points from 1961. Among male teenagers, apprentices accounted for 60 percent in 1980, up 11 percentage points from 1961. Female teenagers showed close to half of the age group in apprenticeship in 1980, a growth from one-third in 1961. As would be expected, relatively few employers and self-employed or civil service officials were shown among teenagers, as well as a smaller proportion of white collar and family workers than among young adults or adults. However, 15 year-olds of each sex had a higher proportion of family workers than any other age group, corresponding to the relatively large percentage of 15 year-olds in agriculture.

Among young adult males, blue collar jobs have dominated throughout the postwar period, but displayed a declining share since 1961 (Table

5.2). Young adult females, on the other hand, exhibited a large and rising share in white collar occupations. Over three-fourths of male and female adults were blue collar and white collar workers, respectively. Compared to adults, young adults had lower proportions in the employer/ self-employed, civil service official, and unpaid family worker categories. While girls and young women tend to be employed in white collar occupations to a greater extent than boys and young men, the civil service category, which includes public administration at various levels, the police, the regular military (excluding compulsory national service), and all kinds of teachers, is comprised of significantly more males than females.

A comparison of the industrial distribution of apprentices and trainees, on the one hand, and that of all other wage and salary earners, on the other, also reveals the differences between youth and adult employment (Table 5.3). Almost 40 percent of apprentices were in trade and services, but under 30 percent of all other workers were in these industry groups. Manufacturing industries accounted for 36 percent of apprentices and 42 percent of all others. As indicated earlier, these differences between apprentices and other employed persons partially result from the forces influencing the industrial and occupational distribution of apprenticeships.

It is also possible to compare the employment of young workers and adults, using the two-digit census classifications of occupations (87 categories) and computing Indexes of Occupational Dissimilarity (IOD) according to the method described in Chapter 3. Partly because of the high level of aggregation of the occupational data, the IODs show relatively little same-sex occupational dissimilarity between adult males and young males (under 25) or between male apprentices and employed males under 25 in 1961, 1970, or 1980 (Table 5.4). The highest IOD was 34.6 and the lowest 27.5. Among females, the range was from 45.2 to 25.8. Comparisons among males and females revealed, as had earlier comparisons in Chapter 3 for other countries, that occupational differences between the sexes far exceeded any within a sex (Table 5.5). In each census year the cross-sex comparison in the younger group (under 25) showed a considerably higher IOD than that of the adults. A final comparison of the amount of dissimilarity in occupational structure from one census period to another indicated that for each age-sex group, relatively little change occurred over the two ten-year periods, but it tended to be cumulative 1961–80. Younger males and adult females had the higher IODs in a same-sex comparison.

Detailed information on the occupations of young males (under 25), drawn from the two-digit occupational classification of the census, indicates that the 450 recognized training occupations of the apprenticeship system have a permanent influence on the most common occupations of all males, but especially of those under 25. In 1980, the five most important occupations of young males, accounting for 38.5 percent of their total employment, as well as the top 20 occupations,

Table 5.3   Industry of Apprentices and Trainees Compared to Other Wage and
            Salary Employees, Both Sexes, West Germany, 1979

	Apprentices and trainees	Wage and salary earners[a]
	(percentage distribution)	
Agriculture, forestry, fishing	2.5	0.9
Energy, water, mining, quarrying	1.5	2.4
Manufacturing, total	36.2	42.0
Chemicals	1.5	3.1
Synthetic products	0.6	1.8
Pottery, china, earthenware	0.8	1.9
Iron and steel	2.6	3.6
Steel products, mechanical engineering, vehicles	13.4	11.9
Electrical engineering, precision instruments	5.7	8.4
Wood, furniture	2.7	2.1
Paper	0.3	0.9
Printing	0.7	1.1
Leather, footwear	0.3	0.5
Textiles	0.7	1.7
Clothing	1.6	1.5
Food, beverages, tobacco	5.3	3.4
Building, construction, total	9.5	8.0
Construction	4.0	6.1
Equipment	5.5	1.9
Wholesale and retail trade	17.7	13.6
Transportation, communications	2.6	4.9
Finance, insurance	3.4	3.6
Services, total	22.0	16.0
Restaurants, hotels, catering	2.5	1.9
Cleaning, hygiene, hairdressing	3.9	1.2
Sciences, arts, journalism	2.9	3.9
Public health	8.0	4.3
Legal and economic consultancy	2.3	0.9
Other services	2.4	3.8
Nonprofit organizations, private households	1.4	1.7
Public sector, social insurance	3.1	6.8
Not stated	0.1	0.1
Total	100.0	100.0
Total number	1,623,395	18,949,513

[a]Includes employed foreign workers; excludes apprentices and trainees, regular military and those in compulsory national service.

Source: BMBW 1981a, p.128.

Table 5.4   Indexes of Occupational Dissimilarity, by Age and Sex, West
Germany, 1961, 1970, and 1980

	Indexes of occupational dissimilarity[a]		
Comparison groups	1980	1970	1961
Same sex groups, different age groups			
Under 25[b] / 25+ (male)	33.9	34.6	27.5
Apprentices / employed under 25 (male)·	33.1	28.6	31.9
Under 25[b] / 25+ (female)	25.8	30.0	34.6
Apprentices / employed under 25 (female)	29.3	29.4	45.2
Same age groups, different sex groups			
Under 25[b] (male) / under 25[b] (female)	64.0	62.4	61.2
25+ (male) / 25+ (female)	54.7	56.6	54.2

	Males		Females	
Same age/sex groups, different years	Under 25[b]	25 and over	Under 25[b]	25 and over
1980 / 1970	12.6	11.0	14.7	12.1
1970 / 1961	20.9	13.5	18.5	22.7
1980 / 1961	23.1	20.6	27.4	32.5

[a]See Chapter 3 for method. The indexes represent comparisons of 87 occupations for
each age-sex group. [b]Includes apprentices, employed foreign workers, and regular
military; excludes compulsory national service.

Source: Computed from SB 1968; SB 1974; SB 1981c, and tables from the Federal
Statistical Office (SB).

accounting for 73.0 percent of their total employment, corresponded,
with a few exceptions, to the numerically important apprenticeship
occupations (SB 1981b). Adult male workers are more dispersed throughout the occupational structure than young adult males because professional and civil service employment follow after the lengthy educational
and qualification process. In 1980, however, 58.1 percent of the total
employment of adult males was in the twenty most common male
youth occupations. This was a smaller share than for the youth, but
not inconsiderable.

Security forces, with the regular military added, were in first place
in 1980 with 8.5 percent of male youth employment. In addition to
various types of metal processing and building and construction occupations, the 20 most common occupations in 1980 included clerical,
sales, and bank and insurance occupations, all of which were apprenticeship training occupations (Table 5.5). Less than 10 percent of the
employment in the 20 most common occupations was accounted for
by such occupations as laborer n.e.c., warehouse and materials handling
worker, and car or truck driver. There was considerable stability in the
leading youth occupations in 1961, 1970, and 1980; only four occupations
were not on the 1980 list of the 20 most common occupations but
appeared on either the 1970 or the 1961 list. Increased shares of total
male youth employment were registered 1961–80 by mechanics, clerical
workers, electricians, and unskilled laborers n.e.c., while decreases were

Table 5.5   Most Common Occupations of Males Under 25 Years Old,
            West Germany, 1980

Young males in occupation as percentage of total employment of young males	Most common occupations[a]
8.5	Armed forces, protective service workers
7.9	Machine fitters, assemblers and repairers
7.8	Typists, secretaries, office clerks
7.2	Smiths and forge operators
7.1	Electricians
(38.5)	Top 5 percent of most common occupations
4.8	Laborers and unskilled workers (n.e.c.)
3.7	Salespersons
3.0	Motor vehicle and transport operators
2.9	Plumbers, gas fitters
2.8	Bricklayers and masons
2.7	Carpenters
2.4	Painters
1.8	Clerical workers (banking, insurance)
1.8	Warehouse and stores laborers
1.7	Machine tool makers
1.5	Metalworkers
1.5	Bakery and confectionery workers
1.3	Agricultural workers[b]
1.3	Technicians
1.3	Butchers and meat cutters
(73.0)	Total of twenty most common occupations
100.0	Total all occupations

[a]Includes regular military, apprentices and employed foreign
 workers; excludes those in compulsory national service.
[b]Includes paid and unpaid family workers.

Note: n.e.c. means "not elsewhere classified".

Source: Computed from SB 1981c and tables from the Federal
Statistical Office (SB).

shown by farm workers, machinists and fitters, salespersons, bricklayers, stores, and transportation workers. The general trend in male occupations has been toward processing operations and away from traditional materials, tools, or product-oriented occupations, resulting in increases in the proportions of both highly qualified personnel and unskilled workers (Chaberny and Gottwald 1976). Decreases in employment in certain occupations, such as wholesale and retail trade and the textile and leather industries, follow from structural changes in production methods and consumer demand.

As might be expected, the most common occupations of male youth were, with few exceptions, highly male intensive. The 20 most common occupations coincided with 11 of the most youth-intensive occupations, that is, occupations having a high proportion of males under 25. Security services, with 44.9 percent of total male employment accounted for by males under 25, was the most youth-intensive; only seven of the 20 most common male youth occupations had a youth share of less than 18 percent, the average share of youth in all occupations.

In 1980, the vast majority of young females (under 25) worked in clerical, sales, personal service, or social service occupations (Table 5.6). Among the 20 most common occupations, only a few were technical or production occupations, such as textile workers, assembly workers, technical assistants or laborers n.e.c. Females are concentrated in a few occupational fields compared to males; the top five occupations of young females accounted for 61 percent and the top 20 occupations accounted for 88 percent of total employment of young females (under 25). Almost as high a concentration rate (83.7 percent) in the same five occupations was shown by employed females 25 and over. Female concentration appears to be greater than male in part because the occupational classification system divides the production sphere, which is largely male, into a greater number of subdivisions than it does in the service occupations, which are mostly female.

From 1961 to 1980, the occupational structure of young females did not change much; only six occupations on the 1961 and 1970 lists of the 20 most common occupations were not on the 1980 list. A large absolute and relative increase in employment occurred in health service occupations below physician level and in social services, as well as in bank and insurance occupations. Among unskilled jobs, a relative rise appeared in female laborers n.e.c. and a sharp decline in share occurred in textiles, domestic service, and agricultural work (including family workers). The changing occupational pattern of young females, to a greater extent than that of young males, reflects the trend toward a service society and the structural decline of such industries as textiles. The top 20 occupations of young females were far less female-intensive than those of young males; only one of the young female top 20 had a female intensity over 90 percent and seven had a rate of under 50 percent. The 20 most common female youth occupations also contained 10 of the 20 most youth-intensive occupations, that is, occupations in which the young female share of female employment most exceeded the young female average share of all occupations (24 percent).

Within the past ten years there had been a trend, reinforced by governmental support and public opinion, that young women should enter male occupations in order to improve their training and employment chances. Although this development has not yet produced major structural changes in male and female employment patterns, the

Table 5.6   Most Common Occupations of Females Under 25 Years Old,
            West Germany, 1980

Young females in occupation as percentage of total employment of young females	Most common occupations[a]
25.6	Typists, secretaries, office clerks
15.1	Salespersons
12.2	Health service assistants
4.2	Hairdressers, barbers, beauticians
3.9	Laborers and unskilled workers (n.e.c.)
(61.0)	Top 5 percent of most common occupations
3.8	Textile workers
3.5	Social workers
3.3	Clerical workers (banking, insurance)
2.3	Expediters and production controllers
1.9	Technical assistants
1.8	Private household workers
1.6	Bookkeepers, cashiers and computer operators
1.5	Waitresses
1.3	Household and office cleaners
1.2	Assemblers, metalworkers (n.e.c.)
1.2	Cooks and kitchen workers
1.0	Agricultural workers[b]
0.9	Managers
0.9	Teachers
0.8	Gardening and related laborers (excl. farm)
(88.0)	Total of twenty most common occupations
100.0	Total all occupations

[a]Includes apprentices and employed foreign workers.   [b]Includes
paid and unpaid family workers.

Note: n.e.c. means "not elsewhere classified".

Source: Computed from SB 1981c and tables from the Federal
Statistical Office (SB).

data show some progress among the participants (IAB 1982). It cannot
be said whether the enlarged training and employment of young women
in male occupations will continue through the life of these cohorts or
whether there will be a later switch to the same female occupations as
their mothers held.

Youth-adult unemployment rates have tended to be quite close, with
female rates higher in every age group (Cramer 1981). The proportion
experiencing some unemployment during a year was considerably higher
for the two youth groups than for adult age groups and the incidence

rate was higher for females than males. Average duration of a spell of unemployment showed the reverse pattern by age, being longer with increasing age and, except for the two oldest groups, longer on average for females than males. The number of spells of unemployment per year varied little over the age groups and two sexes (Cramer 1981).

Relative Earnings

The earnings of youth relative to adults are a misleading indicator in Germany because apprentices are excluded and the youth group therefore is both reduced and untypical of the whole teenage population. Inclusion of apprentices would depress the relative earnings ratios shown in Table 5.7, but more in the earlier years than the later, since the ratio of apprentices' allowances to the basic weekly wages of young unskilled workers has become more favorable over the past 20 years (Stark von der Haar 1977).

Despite the limitations of the data, several interesting points emerge in Table 5.7. The level of relative earnings ratios was much the same for male and female highly qualified youth in both the blue collar and white collar categories, although blue collar youth earned a higher proportion of adult wages than did white collar youth, indicating that the latter had greater opportunities for later earnings growth. Among the low qualified, however, female youth had higher relative earnings than male youth in blue and white collar jobs alike, an indication that the gap between male and female earnings widens with age. The highest relative earnings were shown by white collar females (under 21) with minimal qualifications and the lowest relative earnings were found among the same white collar age group with the greatest qualifications, again indicating varying prospects with age (Table 5.7).

Blue collar youth (under 18) of each sex with the lowest qualifications exhibited an advancing earnings ratio relative to adults of the same qualification level, but blue collar youth with the highest qualifications mostly suffered a decline in relative earnings over the period 1962–78 (Table 5.7). Similarly, the relative earnings of highly qualified blue collar youth declined vis-à-vis youth with lowest qualifications, probably because of the effects of trade union policies favoring the equalization of wage differentials between age and qualification groups and a greatly reduced number of youth under 18 with the highest qualifications.

The push of youth into white collar occupations was offset by stable or declining relative earnings for all groups 1962–78, except for highly qualified male youth (Table 5.7). For both sexes, young white collar workers of low qualifications maintained a strong relative earnings advantage over their counterparts with high qualifications, mostly because highly qualified adult white collar workers display greater earnings gains than adults with low qualifications.

At every age, educational level, and occupational type, females earn less than males. Only a single exception appears in Table 5.7 where

Table 5.7   Weekly or Monthly Earnings of Youth Relative to Adults, by Age, Sex, Vocational Qualification, and Type of Work, West Germany, 1962-1978

	1962	1966	1972	1978
Males		(ratio)		
Under 18 / 18 and over, lowest qualification[a,b]	.54	.52	.57	.60
Under 18 / 18 and over, highest qualification[a,c]	.66	.63	.69	.58
Under 21 / 21 and over, lowest qualification[b,d]	.64	.60	n.a.	.64
Under 21 / 21 and over, highest qualification[c,d]	.50	n.a.	n.a.	.55
Females				
Under 18 / 18 and over, lowest qualification[a,b]	.63	.63	.66	.66
Under 18 / 18 and over, highest qualification[a,c]	.66	.68	.66	.59
Under 21 / 21 and over, lowest qualification[b,d]	.79	.76	n.a.	.78
Under 21 / 21 and over, highest qualification[c,d]	.49	.60	n.a.	.44
Females/Males				
Under 18, lowest qualification[a,b]	.82	.88	.84	.86
Under 18, highest qualification[a,c]	.67	.73	.65	.75
Under 21, lowest qualification[b,d]	.92	.93	n.a.	1.04
Under 21, highest qualification[c,d]	.73	n.a.	n.a.	.80
18 and over, lowest qualification[a,b]	.71	.72	.72	.77
18 and over, highest qualification[a,c]	.68	.68	.67	.73
21 and over, lowest qualification[b,d]	.75	.73	n.a.	.86
21 and over, highest qualification[c,d]	.75	.76	n.a.	.99

[a]Blue collar full-time workers, excluding apprentices.   [b]Lowest qualification means persons doing simple work that requires no formal vocational training.   [c]Highest qualification means persons with responsible, skilled jobs requiring long experience and training.   [d]White collar full-time workers, excluding apprentices.

Source: SB 1966-82, and tables from the Federal Statistical Office (SB).

female/male ratios are shown. Among youth with the lowest qualifications, females earned almost as much as males. The sex ratios generally were closer to parity for youth than adults. Some narrowing of the sex gap in earnings appeared over the 1962–78 period, especially in comparing the first and last years (Table 5.7). Within each sex, white collar workers usually have higher earnings than blue collar, even when the jobs are comparable in responsibility and education of the incumbents is equal (Clement et al. 1980; SB 1981d).

Data on net incomes, rather than earnings, include apprentices. The important differences in earnings of apprentices and young workers and the impact on youth/adult relative income can be seen. In 1981, only 1.4 percent of employed males and 16.7 percent of females 25 years and over had net incomes under DM 1,000 a month. The corresponding proportion for all employed 15–24 year-old males (including apprentices) was 45.9, dropping to 25.4 percent when apprentices were excluded; for females, the two figures were 49.0 and 38.1 (SB 1982). By contrast, apprentices, mostly under 18 years old, showed almost 90 percent of males and females with under DM 600 per month income and virtually all were below DM 1,000 (SB 1982, p.55). Relative to the agreed wages of skilled workers, first year apprentice allowances come to only 28 to 35 percent, rising to 40–50 percent in the last year, except in construction where 56 percent is paid in the third year.

There is no doubt that young unskilled workers of the same age cost employers more than apprentices in direct wage payments, although the earnings and incomes data exaggerate the differences because young workers' gross earnings can be swollen by longer hours of work and bonuses that are not available to apprentices. This difference in wage cost is considered essential to the maintenance of the apprenticeship system, inasmuch as employers incur other direct and indirect costs as a result of the training element of apprenticeship. In fact, many employers wish to hold steady or reduce apprentice allowances because of the rising costs of training, while other persons argue that apprentices should be treated like students and be paid by the government. In that case, the entire status and relation of apprentices to the firm would be altered and much closer government supervision would be required, a development opposed by employers. As stated earlier, the trade unions reject both approaches, favoring continued determination by collective bargaining, a position endorsed in November 1981 at a tripartite conference of European Community nations on the material and social standing of young people during the transition from school to work (CEDEFOP 1982).

Within the apprentice group, allowances vary not only by year of training but also by age, occupation, region, and other factors; all allowances are set by collective bargaining agreements. Because of the sex segregation in apprenticeships, males tend to have slightly higher monthly incomes than females, although the difference is not large (SB 1982). White collar apprentices of each sex also have slightly higher incomes than blue collar, but again the difference is not substantial and is much the same for males and females (SB 1982). Data for the typically male and female apprenticeship occupations would lead to different expectations. Apprenticeships filled mostly by males had considerably higher allowances than typically female apprenticeships (Münch and Jung 1980). Thus, among blue collar trades, first year construction apprentices received DM 534 in 1979, while apprentice hairdressers started at DM 195–200 and apprentices in women's clothing handwork began at DM 145 a month. Apprentices in industry tend to receive higher allowances than those in artisan work, and exceptionally high allowances are paid by such firms as Volkswagen which have their own schedules.

Hours of Work and Other Conditions

Smaller shares of young people (15–24) of each sex than of adults worked less than 40 hours in 1981. Only 1.4 percent of male youth and 7.0 percent of female youth were in this category, compared to 2.2 percent and 31.6 percent, respectively, among all employed (SB 1982). An unmet need exists in all age groups for additional part-time jobs; 11 percent of males under 25 and a fourth of such females expressed this desire in a recent survey (EMNID 1980). Overtime work is slightly less prevalent among youth than others; about one-fourth of youth customarily work over 40 hours a week (INFRATEST 1978, table 14.1; ENMID 1980). Even youth under 18 do overtime work, although it is forbidden by law. A 1970 survey showed that over 50 percent of apprentices and two-thirds of young workers put in over 8 hours a day or 40 hours a week (Stark von der Haar 1977).

Young workers (under 25) also have lower proportions than adults in shift work, night work, and work on Sundays and holidays (EUROSTAT 1977, Tables IV/V, V/5, VI/5; INFRATEST 1978, Table 15.1; EMNID 1980; Münstermann and Preiser 1978). Among young shift workers (under 25), 26 percent had already been on shift work for over three years but under five years, and 14 percent had been on for 5–10 years (Münstermann and Preiser 1978).

Some workers under 25 receive a few less days of paid leave than older age groups. Industries vary both on the number of leave days and age differentials, but grant more days than the Young Workers Protection Act provides (Clasen 1981). In 1981, the range for 18 year-olds in 15 major industry groups was from 18 days, the legal minimum, to 29.

Attitude surveys have revealed that relatively fewer young than adult workers report strain from such job characteristics as noise, unhygienic environment, heavy work, high work speed, and bad weather, but teenagers were more likely than the total to report monotonous, uninteresting work or physically demanding work (INFRATEST 1978, Table 15.1; FAG 1979; EUROSTAT 1977). Work accidents have been more frequent for younger workers. While in 1975 the average was 6 per 100 for total employment, it was 8 for 17 year-olds, 12 for 18 year-olds, 14 for 20 year-olds, and 7 for 23 year-olds (Stark von der Haar 1977). The rise for 20 year-olds reflects exposure to a greater variety of machinery and processes than younger persons had, while the decline in the accident rate by age 23 indicates the benefit of longer work experience.

Longitudinal Surveys

Although a considerable part of lifetime occupational mobility takes place within the first ten years of working life, only a few special studies have investigated the job changes of young people. The entrance into working life after finishing general and vocational education is not a single step, but involves a process of occupational mobility lasting several years. A study of occupational changes 1970 to 1979, based on those who had entered working life after completing an apprenticeship and excluding military personnel, provides information by age groups, including those who were 15–24 years old in 1970 (BiBB and IAB 1981).

About 52 percent of those who were 15–24 in 1970 showed occupational change by 1979, compared to only 26 percent for the 25–34 age group and even lower rates beyond that age. A crucial time for occupational change is immediately after completion of vocational training. Two-fifths of all young people with a completed blue collar apprenticeship, for instance, changed occupations within one year after their apprenticeship examinations (BiBB and IAB 1981). Of the young people who changed occupations, 65 percent experienced other changes at the same time, including 35 percent with upward mobility and 7 percent with downward movement. On the other hand, older persons' occupational changes were mostly associated with no change in status, though 18 percent involved downward mobility (BiBB and IAB 1981). Compared to older persons, the under 25 group more frequently moved from unskilled to skilled blue collar worker, from simple white collar to higher white collar occupations, and from blue to white collar jobs (Hofbauer 1981).

A comparison by sex over the life span indicates that males make a regular movement from blue to white collar occupations with increasing age, reflecting both development within the individual career and structural changes in economic and occupational patterns. On the other hand, young females, starting with a high proportion in white collar occupations, show a decreasing proportion in these occupations with increasing age. A rising proportion of adult females appears among family workers, the self-employed, and blue collar workers. This sex difference, revealed in cross-sectional and longitudinal data, is partly due to inter-generational changes, resulting from the higher educational levels of the younger women, as shown in cross-sectional data, and partly to women's interruption of work during the years of rearing children. The latter often leads to an inability to return to their initial occupations and acceptance of unskilled factory jobs.

Occupational change among young persons 19–30 years old has been relatively more frequent among those with the minimal school-leaving certificate or apprenticeship in a blue collar occupation than among those with a vocational or technical school education or an apprenticeship in a white collar occupation (BMBW 1981c). Among those who changed occupations, 44 percent sought higher earnings, 20 percent sought to improve the type of work or working conditions, and 14 percent changed because of poor present and future prospects in the occupation. Unsatisfactory conditions in the job were relatively more important to those with more education, while financial motivation and job security influenced the less qualified youth (BMBW 1981c).

There is much evidence that occupational and status mobility are closely connected to the type of industry and the size of firm. It was already mentioned in the section on youth jobs that almost half of a cohort of apprentices left their training establishments immediately or within the first year after examination—mostly those coming from small firms or retail shops with either low earnings or poor future prospects for stable employment. A longitudinal survey conducted retrospectively in 1970 shows similar results for males (Hofbauer et al. 1974). The length of employment in the firm increases with the size of firm. Over three-fifths of all male employees who were employed in large firms in 1955 remained with the firm for 15 years or more, compared to only 24 percent who worked in firms with fewer than ten employees. There are no differences in this regard between younger and older employees, but there are large differences according to level of qualification or occupational status. Unskilled laborers and low level white collar employees remain for a shorter time in a given firm than do highly qualified blue or white collar workers. This of course also reflects the less secure position of less qualified workers who are the first to be discharged when economic adversity strikes the firm.

Summary

Up to the mid-seventies West Germany had not experienced the problems of youth unemployment and difficulties in the transition from school to work. The well-established apprenticeship system of vocational training, the main path of vocational education for about 60 percent of West German youth, guarantees a smooth transition from school to work. Although apprentices are paid much less than unskilled young workers of the same age, there has been an increasing trend toward apprenticeship training in the past 20 years among young people who leave general education at age 15 or 16.

There also had been an increasing trend toward more years and higher levels of general education, mostly voluntary, but recently compulsory for the tenth year, mainly as a measure against youth unemployment. While in the 1960s West Germany had the smallest proportion of youth with higher education in Western Europe, by 1980 one-fourth of the relevant age group were university students.

The jobs held by young people are strongly determined by the apprenticeship system of vocational education which still is greatly influenced by the artisan sector of production. More than 40 percent of apprentices are trained in small firms. Among the 20 most common occupations of young people, there is a predominance of the most common apprenticeship training fields, such as machine fitters, electricians, office clerks, sales persons, and health service occupations.

Much evidence is present of a highly segmented labor market between young males and females, duplicating the adult labor market. Only about 5 percent of female apprentices obtain training in male dominated occupations and even fewer male apprentices train in female dominated occupations. Young females mostly enter white collar training occupations, while young males are chiefly in blue collar apprenticeships. In an effort to change the situation, government financial support has been offered to employers who accept girls into male apprenticeship trades, but the long-run success of this program remains to be seen.

Young workers who enter working life without vocational training have unskilled jobs, unfavorable working conditions, and high risk of unemployment, whereas apprentices are protected by law against dismissal and bad working conditions. Foreign youth suffer more than other groups from slack labor demand as well as from the shortages of apprenticeship training places in firms. Coming from an impoverished social background and lacking command of the German language, many foreign youth acquire little education and only a few are able to get apprenticeship places.

The most striking difference between youth and adult jobs is that between apprenticeship and later jobs. There are about 450 training occupations open to youth which lead to a variety of adult jobs via occupational mobility and further education or on-the-job training. Among youth entering the labor market there is a rising trend toward white collar occupations, while adults currently tend to move from blue collar to white collar jobs, self-employment, employer, or civil service status.

The youth earnings situation reflects the strong efforts of trade union policy to eliminate wage differences. Usually, young people (under 21) earn between 50 and 80 percent of the adult level, but there are large differences by level of qualification, industry, and size of firm.

Occupational mobility to a large extent takes place within the first years of working life. More than half of all young people under 25 have changed their occupation at least once, in many cases improving their occupational status and income. But ever since labor market demand has weakened, a number of young people, even those with a completed apprenticeship, have had to accept unskilled jobs.

Future prospects are that youth labor market problems will persist throughout the 1980s because the large cohorts born in the 1960s will be entering the labor market and because the economic recession shows no signs of ending soon. The demand for unskilled youth is likely to decrease steadily and many well-educated young people will have growing difficulties in entering the labor market and especially in obtaining jobs commensurate with their education and training.

References: West Germany

Alex, L. 1980. "Berufsausbildung: Struktur und Entwicklungstendenzen" ("Vocational Training: Patterns and Trends"). *Berufsbildung in Wissenschaft und Praxis*. Berlin: Beuth, December.

ANBA. 1982. *Amtliche Nachrichten der Bundesanstalt für Arbeit* (*Monthly Reports from the Federal Employment Office*). Nürnberg, monthly.

Arbeitsgruppe am MPI. 1979. (Max-Planck-Institute for Educational Research). *Das Bildungswesen in der Bundesrepublik Deutschland* (*Educational System in the Federal Republic of Germany*). Reinbeck: Rowolt.

BA (Federal Employment Office). 1981. *Berufsberatung 1979/80—Ergebnisse der Berufsberatungsstatistik* (*Vocational Counseling 1979-80—Results of Vocational Counseling Statistics*). Nürnberg: BA.

Baethge, M., et al. 1980. *Ausbildungs- und Berufsstartprobleme von Jugendlichen* (*Difficulties of Vocational Training and Initial Employment of Young People*). Göttingen: Soziologisches Forschungsinstitut (SOFI).

BiBB (Federal Institute for Vocational Training Research). 1981. *Berufsbildung in der Bundesrepublik Deutschland* (*Vocational Training in the Federal Republic of Germany*). Berlin: BiBB.

————. 1982. *Das Berufsgrundbildungsjahr im Schuljahr 1980/81* (*The Basic Vocational Training Year in 1980-81*). Berlin: BiBB.

BiBB and IAB (Institute for Employment Research). 1981. *Qualifikation und Berufsverlauf* (*Qualification and Occupational Career*). Berlin and Nürnberg: BiBB and IAB.

Biermann-Berlin. 1979. *Zur Problematik von Jugendlichen ohne Hauptschulabschluss und ohne Berufsausbildung* (*The Problems of Youth Without an Elementary School Certificate and Without Vocational Training*). Beiträge zur Arbeitsmarkt- und Berufsforschung, vol.38. Nürnberg: IAB.

BMBW (Federal Minister for Education and Science). 1980. *Berufsbildungsbericht 1980* (*Vocational Training Report 1980*). Bonn: BMBW.

————. 1981a. *Berufsbildungsbericht 1981* (*Vocational Training Report 1981*). Bonn: BMBW.

————. 1981b. *Grund- und Strukturdaten 1981/82* (*Basic and Structural Data 1981-82*). Bonn: BMBW.

————. 1981c. *Berichtssystem Bildung-Beschäftigung (BSBB).* Repräsentative Erhebung 1979 bei 19–30 jährigen Bundesbürgern (*Reporting System on Education and Employment. Representative Survey on 19 to 30 Year-old Citizens*). Bonn: BMBW.

————. 1982a. *Berufsbildungsbericht 1982* (*Vocational Training Report 1982*). Bonn: BMBW.

————. 1982b. *Arbeiterkinder im Bildungssystem* (*Children of Blue Collar Workers in the Educational System*). Bonn: BMBW.

Braun, F., and Gravalas, B. 1980. *Die Benachteilung junger frauen in Ausbildung und Erwerbstätigkeit* (*Disadvantages of Young Women in Education and Employment*). Munich: Deutsches Jugendinstitut.

CEDEFOP (*European Centre for the Development of Vocational Training*). 1982. *Soziales und materieller Status der Jugendlichen in der Europäischen Gemeinschaft* (*The Social and Material Status of Youth in the European Community*). Berlin: CEDEFOP.

Chaberny, A., and Gottwald, K. 1976. "Strukturelle Entwicklungstendenzen im Beschäftigungssystem der Bundesrepublik Deutschland ab 1960 unter besonderer Berücksichtigung der Änderung von Tätigkeits- und Anforderungsprofilen" ("Structural Development in Employment Patterns in the Federal Republic of Germany Since 1960 with Regard to Changing Patterns of Job Characteristics and Requirements"). In Deutscher Bildungsrat, ed. *Gutachten und Studien der Bildungskommission*, vol.57. Stuttgart: Klett.

Clasen, L. 1981. "40 Stunden fün fast alle" ("40 Hours for Almost Everybody"). *Bundesarbeitsblatt*, no.3.

Clement, W., et al. 1980. "Zur Entwicklung der qualifikationsspezifischen Einkommensrelationen in der Bundesrepublik Deutschland" ("On the Development of Income Differentials by Qualification Levels in the Federal Republic of Germany"). *Mitteilungen aus der Arbeitsmarkt- und Berufsforschung*, no.2. Stuttgart: Kohlhammer.

Cramer, U., 1981. "Bewegungsanalyse der Arbeitslosigkeit von Jugendlichen" ("Flow Analysis of Youth Unemployment"). *Mitteilungen aus der Arbeitsmarkt- und Berufsforschung,* no.2. Stuttgart: Kohlhammer.

Dibbern, et al. 1974. *Berufswahl unterricht in der vorberuflichen Bildung (Career Education in Prevocational Education).* Bad Heilbrunn: Klinkhardt.

Edding, F. 1980. "Das duale System in Übergang zur Pluralität der Lernorte" ("The Dual System in Transition to Multiple Learning Places"). *Berufsbildung in Wissenschaft und Praxis.* Berlin: Beuth, December.

EMNID (Institute GmbH & Co.). 1980. *Lage, Dauer, Tatsachen, Entwicklungen, Erwartungen und Verteilung der Arbeitszeit—Tabellenband A (Placement, Duration, Facts, Trends, Expectations and Distribution of Working Hours. Tables, vol.A).* Bielefeld: EMNID.

EUROSTAT (Statistical Office of the European Community). 1977. *Arbeitsbedingungen in den Mitgliedstaaten der Europäischen Gemeinschaft 1975 (Working Conditions in the Member States of the European Community 1975).* Brussels: EUROSTAT.

FAG (Research Group Work and Health). 1979. *Erhebung über das Arbeitsleben 1978. Hauptergebnisse einer vergleichenden Untersuchung zu subjektiven Sozialindikatoren in den Ländern der Europäischen Gemeinschaft (Survey on Working Life 1978. Main Results of a Cross-national Study on Subjective Social Indicators in the Countries of the European Community).* Dortmund: FAG.

von Henninges, H. 1975. "Bestimmungsgründe für die Veränderung des Umfangs der Facharbeiternachwuchsausbildung in der Industrie" (Determinant Factors for the Change in the Scope of Industrial Training for Skilled Occupations"). *Mitteilungen aus der Arbeitsmarkt- und Berufsforschung,* no.4. Stuttgart: Kohlhammer.

Hofbauer, H. 1977. "Strukturdiskrepanzen zwischen Bildungs- und Beschäftigungssystem im Bereich der betrieblichen Berufsausbildung für Facharbeiterberufe" ("Structural Discrepancies Between the Educational and Employment System in the Field of Industrial Training for Skilled Occupations"). *Mitteilungen aus der Arbeitsmarkt- und Berufsforschung,* no.2. Stuttgart: Kohlhammer.

————. 1980. "Statusmobilität in den 70er Jahren" ("Status Mobility in the Seventies"). *Mitteilungen aus der Arbeitsmarkt-und Berufsforschung,* no.4. Stuttgart: Kohlhammer.

————. 1981. "Berufswege von Erwerbstätigen mit Facharbeiterausbildung" ("Occupational Career of Employed Persons with Training for the Blue Collar Skilled Trades"). *Mitteilungen aus der Arbeitsmarkt- und Berufsforschung,* no.2. Stuttgart: Kohlhammer.

Hofbauer, H.; König, P:, and Nagel, E. 1974. "Betriebszugehörigkeitsdauer bei männlichen deutschen Arbeitnehmern" ("Duration of Employment in a Firm for German Male Workers"). *Mitteilungen aus der Arbeitsmarkt- und Berufsforschung,* no.3. Stuttgart: Kohlhammer.

Hofbauer H., and Stooss, F. 1975. "Defizite und Überschusse an betrieblichen Ausbildungsplätzen nach Wirtschafts- und Berufsgruppen" ("Shortage and Surplus of Industrial Training Possibilities by Industry and Occupational Group"). *Mitteilungen aus der Arbeitsmarkt- und Berufsforschung,* no.2. Stuttgart: Kohlhammer.

Höhn, E., ed. 1974. *Ungelernte in der Bundesrepublik Deutschland. Soziale Situation, Begabungsstruktur und Bildungsmotivation (Unskilled Youth in the Federal Republic of Germany. Social Situation, Intellectual Structure and Achievement Motivation).* Kaiserslautern: Pfaff Gedächtnisstiftung.

IAB (Institute for Employment Research). 1977. *Berufsbildung und Arbeitsmarkt (Vocational Training and Labor Market).* Nürnberg: IAB.

————. 1980. *Jugendlichen beim Übergang in Ausbildung und Beruf (Youth in Transition to Training and Employment).* Beiträge zur Arbeitsmarkt- und Berufsforschung, vol.43. Nürnberg: IAB

————. 1982. *Mädchen in Männerberufen (Girls in Male Occupations).* Summary Report, February 24. Nürnberg: IAB.

INFRATEST. 1978. Sozialforschung. *Repräsentativbefragung zur Fortbildungs- und Mobilitätsbereitschaft beschäftigter Arbeitnehmer (Representative Survey on Potential*

Mobility and Further Education Among Employed Persons). Material- und Tabellenband 5. Munich: INFRATEST.

Jugendwerk der Deutschen Shell. 1981. *Jugend '81. Lebensentwürfe, Alltagskulturen, Zukunftsbilder* (*Youth '81. Life Perspectives, Culture, Views of the Future*), vol.1. Hamburg: Jugendwerk der Deutschen Shell.

Kaiser, M., et al. 1980a. "Berufliche Integration von Fachhoch-schulabsolventen" ("Occupational Integration of Graduates of Higher Technical Schools"). *Mitteilungen aus der Arbeitsmarkt- und Berufsforschung*, no.1. Stuttgart: Kohlhammer.

_____. 1980b. "Arbiturienten des Jahrgungs 1970 in Studium und Beruf—eine Verbleibsanalyse" ("The Transition of Secondary School Graduates of 1970 to Higher Education and Employment"). *Mitteilungen aus der Arbeitsmarkt- und Berufsforschung*, no.20. Stuttgart: Kohlhammer.

Lemke, I., and Schmidt-Hackenberg, B. 1980. "Zum Ausbau des Berufsgrundbildungsjahrs als verbindlichem ersten Ausbildungsjahr" ("The Vocational Basic Training Year as a Compulsory First Year of Apprenticeship"). *Berufsbildung in Wissenschaft und Praxis*, no.4. Berlin: Beuth.

Lenhardt, G., and Schober, K. 1980. "Der schwierige Berufsstart: Jugendarbeitslosigkeit und Lehrstellenmarkt" ("The Difficult Entrance to Working Life"). In MPI, ed. *Bildung in der Bundesrepublik Deutschland* (*Education in the Federal Republic of Germany*), vol.2. Stuttgart: Klett-Cotta.

MAGS (Minister for Labor and Social Affairs of Northrhine-Westphalia). 1979. *Jugendliche ohne Ausbilungsvertrag. Bericht der Wissenschaftlichen Kommission* (*Youth Without a Vocational Training Contract. Report of the Scientific Commission*). Düsseldorf: MAGS.

Mehrländer, U., et al. 1981. *Situation der ausländischen Arbeitnehmer und ihrer Familienangehörigen in der Bundesrepublik Deutschland*. Repräsentativuntersuchung '80. Forschungsbericht im Auftrag des Bundesministeriums für Arbeit und Sozialordnung (*The Situation of Foreign Workers and their Families in the Federal Republic of Germany*. Survey '80. Research Report for the Federal Minister for Labor and Social Affairs). Bonn: Bundesministerium für Arbeit und Sozialordnung.

Meisel, H. 1978. *Die deutsche Berufsberatung* (*Vocational Guidance in Germany*). Stuttgart: Kohlhammer.

Münch, J., and Jung, E. 1980. *Sozialer und materieller Status von Jugendlichen in der Bundesrepublik Deutschland. Studie im Auftrag des Europäischen Zentrums zur Förderung der Berufsausbildung (CEDEFOP)* (*Social and Economic Status of Youth in the Federal Republic of Germany. A Study for the European Center for the Development of Vocational Training (CEDEFOP)*). Berlin: CEDEFOP.

Münstermann, J., and Preiser, K. 1978. *Schichtarbeit in der Bundesrepublik Deutschland*. Sozialwissenschaftliche Bilanzierung des Forschungsstandes, statistische Trends und Massnahmeempfehlungen. Bericht über ein Forschungsvorhaben im Auftrag des bundesministeriums für Arbeit und Sozialordnung (BMAS) (*Shift-work in the Federal Republic of Germany*. Summary of Research, Statistical Trends and Recommendations. Report on a Research Project Carried Out for BMAS). Bonn: BMAS.

Saterdag, H., and Stegmann, H. 1980. *Jugendliche beim Übergang vom Bildungs-in das Beschäftigungssystem* (*Youth in the Transition from Education to Employment System*). Beiträge zur Arbeitsmarkt- und Berufsforschung, vol.41. Nürnberg: IAB.

SB (Federal Statistical Office). 1966–82. *Gehalts- und Lohnstrukturerhebungen, I. Gewerbliche Wirtschaft und Dienstleistungsbereich. Arbeiter verdienste. Gehalts- und Lohnstrukturerhebungen, I. Gewerbliche Wirtschaft und Dienstleistungsbereich. Angestellten verdienste* (*Surveys on the Structure of Wages and Salaries in Manufacturing and Service Industries for Blue Collar and White Collar Workers*). Stuttgart: Kohlhammer.

_____. 1968. *Ergebnisse der Volks- und Berufszählung 1961* (*Results of the Population Census 1961*). Stuttgart: Kohlhammer.

_____. 1974. *Volks- und Berufszählung vom 27. Mai 1970. Bevölkerung nach dem Ausbildungsstand, demographischen Merkmalen und Beteiligung am Erwerbsleben* (*Population and Occupational Census, May 27, 1970. Population by Educational Status,*

Demographic Characteristics and Labor Force Participation), vol.13. Stuttgart: Kohlhammer.

──────. 1980. *Beruf, Ausbildung und Arbeitsbedingungen der Erwerbstätigen. Ergebnisse des Mikrozensus 1978 (Occupation, Education and Working Conditions of Employed. Results of Mikrozensus 1978*). Fachserie 1, Reihe 4.1.2. Stuttgart: Kohlhammer.

──────. 1981a. *Bildung im Zahlenspiegel (Statistics on Education)*. Stuttgart: Kohlhammer.

──────. 1981b. *Berufliche Bildung 1980 (Vocational Training 1980)*. Fachserie 11, Reihe 3. Stuttgart: Kohlhammer.

──────. 1981c. *Stand und Entwicklung der Erwerbstätigkeit 1980. Ergebnisse des Mikrozensus 1980 (State and Development of Gainful Employment 1980. Results of the Labor Force Sample Survey 1980)*. Fachserie 1, Reihe 4.1.1. Stuttgart: Kohlhammer.

──────. 1981d. *Statistisches Jahrbuch 1981 für die Bundesrepublik Deutschland (Statistical Yearbook 1981 for the Federal Republic of Germany)*. Stuttgart: Kohlhammer.

──────. 1982. *Stand und Entwicklung der Erwerbstätigkeit 1981. Ergebnisse des Mikrozensus 1981* (State and Development of Gainful Employment 1981. Results of the Labor Force Sample Survey 1981). Fachserie 1, Reihe 4.1.1. Stuttgart: Kohlhammer.

Schlaffke, W., ed. 1976. *Jugendarbeitslosigkeit. Unlösbare Aufgabe für das Bildungs- und Beschäftigungssystem? (Youth Unemployment. An Insoluble Problem for the Educational and Employment Systems?)*. Cologne: Deutscher Instituts Verlag.

Schober-Gottwald, K. 1976. "Jugendliche ohne Berufsausbildung. Eine Literaturstudie unter besonderer Berücksichtigung der vorgeschlagenen Lösungsansätze und Massnahmen" ("Youth Without Vocational Training. A Literature Survey with Special Attention to Efforts and Measures to Solve the Problem"). *Mitteilungen aus der Arbeitsmarkt- und Berufsforschung*, no.2. Stuttgart: Kohlhammer.

Schober, K. 1981. "Zur Ausbildungs- und Arbeitsmarktsituation ausländischer Jugendlicher in der Bundesrepublik Deutschland—gegenwärtige Lage und künftige Perspektiven" ("The Educational and Employment Situation of Foreign Youth in the Federal Republic of Germany—Current Situation and Future Prospects"). *Mitteilungen aus der Arbeitsmarkt- und Berufsforschung*, no.1. Stuttgart: Kohlhammer.

──────. 1982. "Die 'wachsende Minorität'—Ausbildungs- und Arbeitsmarktprobleme der zweiten Generation" ("The Growing Minority—Educational and Labor Market Problems of the Second Generation"). *Gewerkschaftliche Monatshefte*, no.7. Cologne: Bund.

Schober, K., and Hochgürtel, G. 1980. *Bewältigung der Krise oder Verwaltung des Mangels? Die Staatliche Massnahmen zur Bekämpfung der Jugendarbeitslosigkeit 1974–1979 (Overcoming the Crisis or Administering a Shortage? Government Programs Against Youth Unemployment 1974–1979)*. Bonn: Verlag Neue Gesellschaft.

Stark von der Haar, E. 1977. *Arbeiterjungend- heute. Jugend ohne Zukunft? (Working Youth Today. Youth Without a Future?)*. Neuwied: Luchterhand.

Stegmann, H., and Kraft, H. 1982. "Jugendliche an der Schwelle von der Berufsausbildung in die Erwerbstätigkeit: Methode und erste Ergebnisse der Wiederholungserhebung Ende 1980" ("Young People at the Point of Moving from Vocational Training to Employment: Methods and Initial Results of a Repeated Sampling at the End of 1980"). *Mitteilungen aus der Arbeitsmarkt-und Berufsforschung*, no.1. Stuttgart: Kohlhammer.

Tessaring, M. 1977. "Qualifikationsspezifische Arbeitslosigkeit in der Bundesrepublik Deutschland" ("The Relationship Between Qualifications and Unemployment in the Federal Republic of Germany"). *Mitteilungen aus der Arbeitsmarkt-und Berufsforschung*, no.2. Stuttgart: Kohlhammer.

──────. 1981. "Arbeitslosigkeit, Verbleib und Beschäftigungsmöglichkeiten der Hochschulabsolventen" ("Unemployment, Career Patterns and Employment Opportunities of University Graduates"). *Mitteilungen aus der Arbeitsmarkt- und Berufsforschung*, no.4. Stuttgart: Kohlhammer.

Tessaring, M., and Werner, H. 1981. *Beschäftigung und Arbeitsmarkt für Hochschulabsolventen in den Ländern der Europäischen Gemeinschaft (Employment and Labor Market for*

University Graduates in the Countries of the European Community). Beiträge zur Arbeitsmarkt- und Berufsforschung, vol.46. Nürnberg: IAB.

Westhoff, G. 1981. "Erste Ergebnisse aus der Erhebung bei Absolventen der Berufsvorbereitung 1980" ("Initial Results from the Survey on Youth in Work Preparatory Course 1980"). *Berufsbildung in Wissenschaft und Praxis,* no.1. Berlin: Beuth.

Westhoff, G., and Mahnke, H. 1980. *Ausbildungs- und Berufswege von Absolventen beruflicher Vollzeitschulen. Ergebnisse einer Repräsentativbefragung in October 1979 (Educational and Employment Paths of Young People Leaving Full-time Vocational Schools. Results of a Sample Survey, October 1979*). Berlin: BiBB.

6

Youth Employment in Great Britain

David Metcalf and John Richards

About eight million 16–24 year-olds live in Great Britain. The number of teenagers and young adults has increased substantially since World War II, rising by over 20 percent from 1951 to 1981. A much smaller fraction of the teenage population participates in the labor force now than in 1951, due mainly to the increased probability of teenagers remaining in education. Young adult males also had a small decline in participation rates. As an offset there was a large rise in the proportion of economically active females aged 20–24 in the 1970s, reflecting a later age of marriage, a falling birth rate (until 1977), and the trend increase in participation rates among married women which itself is partly explained by the expansion of female-intensive occupations in the 1970s.

Another way of looking at trends in youth employment is to study employment:population (E/P) ratios. It was shown in Chapter 2 that between 1960 and 1972 teenage E/P ratios fell from .74 to .56 for males and from .75 to .57 for females. These falls were far less marked for young adults (Table 2.3). Over this period the share of 15–24 year-old employment in total employment fell modestly from 22.2 percent to 21.6 percent (Table 2.1).

The state secondary education system has changed greatly since World War II. The compulsory leaving age has been raised twice and the previous selective system has largely been replaced with a nonselective comprehensive education system. Associated with this switch from selective to nonselective schooling has been a substantial rise in the average qualification level possessed by school-leavers (15 or 16 to 18). School-leavers wishing to acquire a particular craft or professional skill go to colleges of further education or enter apprenticeships. Attempts are being made to improve vocational education and the apprenticeship system.

There has been considerable stability in the post-war period in the types of first job entered by school-leavers. For example, around two-fifths of boys entered apprenticeships and a similar proportion of girls have gone into clerical jobs. Recently the employment prospects of school-leavers have become bleaker so particular problems have come to the fore. These include the occupational composition of young black and brown workers compared with their white counterparts and the relationship between industrial and occupational mix in a particular area and young peoples' job prospects. These and other dimensions of youth employment are examined below.

In 1949 among manual males, those aged under 21 earned well under half the adult rate, but now they earn over three-fifths of adult pay. However, school-leaver and youth unemployment only became a major problem in the mid-1970s and the pay of teenagers relative to adults has not changed since then.

Education and Examination System

Public nontertiary education is administered by Local Authorities with control and guidance from the Department of Education and Science on matters like the nature of the school system (selective or nonselective), curriculum, and examinations. There is a small but prominent private sector in both primary (5–11 year-olds) and secondary education (11–18 year-olds). Tertiary education is undertaken from age 18 in universities, colleges, and polytechnics. Only about 13–14 percent of 18 year-olds go on to higher education. Degree courses last three years and very few students pursue postgraduate qualifications.

In the late 1960s and in the 1970s, a fundamental change took place in the structure of state schools. Previously all 10 or 11 year-olds took an exam which essentially labeled them for life (the iniquitous 11 plus exam). Those who passed, approximately a quarter of each cohort, went on to more academic grammar schools, while those who failed went on to secondary modern schools. The patent inequity of this system and the belief that it may have contributed to poor economic performance resulted in grammar and secondary modern schools being replaced by comprehensive schools which aim to have a nonselective intake of pupils. The minimum school leaving age has been raised twice since World War II. In 1947 it was raised from 14 to 15 and in 1972–73 it was raised to 16. This means that compulsory education in Britain now is one of the longest in the world—from 5 to 16 years of age.

The examination system in schools is quite complex; there is no overall diploma in secondary education. Around age 16, pupils sit for subject matter exams of either the Certificate of Secondary Education (CSE) or the General Certificate of Education Ordinary Level (GCE "O" Level). The CSE is less demanding academically than the GCE. Those who remain in school beyond age 16 may take some additional

CSE or GCE "O" Level exams; most will take GCE Advanced ("A") Levels at age 18. The GCE system was historically used predominantly by grammar and private schools and was essentially determined by the exam-oriented university entrance. The CSE was grafted on to the system in the 1970s largely to ensure that nearly all children aimed at school qualifications rather than just the minority which took GCEs. These GCE and CSE exams are administered externally by a number of examining boards, each setting their own exams. The boards frequently operate from leading universities. Typically a school would offer around 20 GCE examination subjects and pupils aiming for higher education would take 5 to 8 "O" Levels and 3 "A" Levels. Changes in the exam system are under discussion.

School-leavers are now massively better qualified, in terms of formal qualifications, than they were 20 years ago. In 1930, over 90 percent of leavers had no qualifications. In 1961–62, three-quarters left school with no qualifications and only 8 percent had any "A" Levels. By 1978–79 only one in seven left school unqualified and 15 percent had one or more "A" Levels. Although the main reason for the reduction in unqualified leavers is the introduction of the Certificate of Secondary Education, it is noticeable that there has been a steady increase in the proportions at each qualification level. Each successive school leaving cohort now apprears to be better formally qualified than its predecessor. Among the 1961–62 school-leavers, only one in four had any GCE "O" or "A" Level qualifications, but this proportion had risen to one in two for 1978–79 school leavers (DES 1962–82). Regional and area differences are marked. The racial minorities, especially blacks and brown females, tend to have fewer qualifications than comparable white British (Smith 1977, p.323).

Since 1961–62, the annual number of school-leavers in England and Wales has been U-shaped. Currently about 800,000 16–18 year-olds leave school each year, and most depart at 16. During the 1960s, there was a substantial rise in the number of 16–18 year-old school-leavers going on to Further Education or Higher Education. In 1961–62, only 13 percent of school-leavers remained in full-time education, yet a decade later this proportion had risen by over half to 22 percent. However, in the 1970s the proportion has remained virtually constant, with just over one in five school-leavers staying in the education system. There are large regional and area differences in staying-on rates (DES 1980a). Black and brown youth tend to have higher staying-on rates than white British, but these frequently reflect an effort to catch up on examinations not taken at the usual time.

In 1976–77, the activities of 16–18 year-olds were as follows: 62 percent were employed (14 percent in apprenticeship and other employment with day release for further education and 48 percent in jobs with evening or no further education); 8 percent were unemployed or out of the labor force; 30 percent were studying in schools and further education colleges, over half to study for "A" Levels and the rest to take "O" Level or CSE exams or to do six-month vocational courses (Booth 1980). Since 1976–77, the proportion in unemployment and full-time education has risen as the share in jobs has fallen (DES 1980a). In 1979, a little over 45 percent of 16 year-olds had entered their first employment by December of that year (more boys than girls), some 50 percent continued in full-time education or training, and the rest were unemployed or out of the labor force (DE 1982a).

The decision on whether to remain in the education system beyond the statutory school-leaving age has been analyzed by Pissarides (1979), and Dolphin (1981) has undertaken a similar analysis of the demand for higher education. Pissarides found a trend increase of 5.4 percent a year 1955–69 in the staying-on rate of 16 year-olds, but by 1976 the actual rate was below the trend rate by 11 percentage points for boys and 6 percentage points for girls. Attempting to explain the "unexpected" decrease in the staying-on rate, Pissarides viewed post-compulsory education as both a consumer good and an investment good. The investment good component of the demand for education is analyzed by relating the staying-on rate to earnings, unemployment, and employment opportunities; the series on earnings are combined into the present value of earnings associated with staying-on in education compared with the present value if the individual leaves at 16.

The findings, confirming that education is both a consumer good and investment good, suggest that economic considerations play a very strong part in the decision to remain in the education system. While it is a "luxury" in the strict economic sense in that a given increase in income induces a more than proportionate increase in the demand for education, the investment good nature of the demand for education dominates the results. The decision to stay or leave is very sensitive to the present value of earnings (at age 16) from leaving school at 16 and from staying-on. Before 1970 the present value of lifetime earnings for the stayer was one-and-a-half times as large as that for the leaver. This clearly encouraged a growing proportion to remain in school. But in the 1970s this changed. The maintenance grant paid to students and, most importantly, the starting pay of qualified labor both fell relative to youths' earnings and this was not offset by the higher pay of stayers later in life.

This decline in the relative starting pay of the stayers is almost certainly not due to factors operating from the demand side. Employment in education-intensive sectors grew faster in the 1970s than in the 1960s and 1950s and this would have tended to raise (not lower) the pay of stayers. Supply side factors are more likely to explain the decline. The high birth rate of the later 1940s and the exceptionally fast expansion of further and higher education in the 1960s probably put so much pressure on the market for newly qualified manpower that their relative pay collapsed despite the favorable demand conditions.

Dolphin (1981) obtained similar results in analyzing the demand for higher education between 1966–67 and 1979–80, also using a cost-benefit framework (cf. Freeman 1981). Pissarides and Dolphin clearly show that the demand for post-16 education is largely a matter of costs and benefits. Any policy maker wishing to improve the quality of the labor force via the school and college system will have to influence either or both of the costs and returns to increments of education.

Vocational Education and Initial Training System

Two-thirds of British workers have no vocational qualifications at all, by far the worst figure of any country in Western Europe (Prais 1981). Not surprisingly this had led to considerable heart-searching about craft and related training. In addition, rising levels of youth unemployment have brought forth successive programs for youth which cover over half the school-leaving cohort and incorporate successively greater elements of training.

For those who leave school at 16–17 and want specific occupational skill training, there are two options: full-time one or two-year courses at colleges of further education (CFE) or apprenticeship or other struc-tured on-the-job training. Those leaving at 18 or 19 have available CFE courses and structured training in industry leading to professional qualifications, such as accountant. They also can enter tertiary education specializing in occupational preparation, usually at professional-technical level. CFEs made provision in 1976–77 for about 7 percent of the 16–18 year-olds (Booth 1980). They offered courses leading to City and Guilds craft certificates, diplomas of the Technician Education Council (TEC) and the Business Education Council (BEC), ordinary national diplomas (OND), and courses leading to professional qualifications or college awards (DES 1980a).

Apprenticeship is not regulated by any legislation and it is regarded as a form of employment subject to collective bargaining. While day or block release for theoretical training is well-established, it is not a statutory requirement. The training period generally lasts four years, but some occupations take longer. Apprenticeships are not easily entered after age 16. In 1979, 89.5 percent of male apprentices were 16 and the rest were 17; almost none were older. Among girls, however, 17 year-olds constituted over one-fifth (DE 1982a). Black and brown youth have fared poorly in obtaining apprenticeships, especially since the recession.

Males are much more likely to undertake apprenticeship training than females; in 1979, the ratio was 8:1 (DE 1982a). This is not explained simply by the different types of jobs taken by males and females since, in almost every industry and occupation, apprentices form a higher proportion of male entrants than of female entrants. Apprenticeships tend to be concentrated in a few craft occupations. Manufacturing has by far the largest number of apprentices, almost half of all males. Within the manufacturing sector itself, there is a marked concentration toward engineering which has two-thirds of male apprentices but under half of male manufacturing employment. Girls in their first jobs are heavily concentrated in the service industries (nearly 90 percent). Hairdressing and beauticians account for over two-thirds of female apprenticeships (DE 1980b, 1982a).

Opportunities to enter apprenticeship are strongly influenced by cyclical trends and the production requirements of the firm. The numbers undergoing formal training in all manufacturing industries increased from around 390,000 in 1964 to a peak of under 450,000 in 1968. By 1980 this figure had fallen back to 240,000. Since the drop in employment since 1968 has been relatively smaller than the decline in the number of trainees, the proportion of all employees receiving formal training also has declined, from 5.6 percent to 3.6 percent 1968–80 (DE 1980a).

Considerable criticism has surrounded the apprenticeship system in Britain. The principal criticisms concern the antiquated nature of a system based on serving time rather than achieving proficiency, and the applicability of a narrow and obsolete training content to the new industrial technology which does not conform to the traditional lines of demarcation rigorously laid down by the craft unions. Therefore in the development of public policy on industrial training, successive attempts have been made to reform the system.

One major initiative came in 1964 with the passage of the Industrial Training Act which created an Industrial Training Board (ITB) for each industry. The ITBs were charged with the responsibility of overseeing training policy, stimulating the quantity and quality of training, and sharing the costs more evenly between firms via a levy-grant system (Pliatzky 1980). The influence of the ITBs is shortly to be severely curtailed, since only seven are to be retained—in Clothing, Construction, Engineering, Hotel and Catering, Road Transport, Rubber/Plastics Processing, and Petroleum. The responsibility for training in industries where the Boards are to be dismantled will be passed to voluntary industry bodies. The effect of these measures will be to reduce to one-third the proportion of the country's employees in sectors covered by the Boards.

A discussion document (MSC 1975) which highlighted the annual entry of up to 300,000 young people into occupations with little or no systematic training resulted in two initiatives. First, more training by industry at the craft and technical apprenticeship level was to be directed at young people, including unemployed school-leavers. Second, Unified Vocational Preparation (UVP), a pilot program run by the Training Services Division of the Manpower Services Commission, was introduced for employed youth who normally receive no training. There are two main strands in the most recent training proposals for employed youngsters (MSC 1981d). First, the UVP Scheme is to be expanded fivefold by 1984–85 to provide 50,000 places. Under UVP the government provides grants to employers who cooperate in providing integrated training, further education, and work experience. Second, there is to be yet another attempt to reform apprenticeship training. By 1985, the government intends that the traditional age-restricted apprenticeship should be replaced by a system of training to recognized standards.

As a result of the major youth unemployment program, discussed below, and dissatisfaction with some aspects of it, the Manpower Services Commission (1981d) made training proposals which were broadly endorsed by the government in a White Paper (DE 1981). The centerpiece of the new proposals is the transition from the current YOP to a far more training-intensive Youth Training Scheme (YTS). It is to be run by the MSC and still will concentrate on unemployed school-leavers. When all of these new initiatives are on stream by 1984–85 public expenditure on training, outside the education system, will total £1500m a year, of which £1000m will be accounted for by the YTS.

The YTS is to be fully operational by September 1983 when it will provide places for 300,000 young people at any one time. From September 1983 the government intends to guarantee an early offer of a year-long place on the YTS to any unemployed minimum-age school-leaver. Although the training program will be adapted to the individual's ability, it should contain four main elements:

– *induction and assessment* of existing skills and attainments.
– acquisition of *basic skills* like numeracy and literacy; and the development of practical competence in tools, office machinery and communication.
– *occupationally relevant education and training by work* experience with a minimum of 3 months off-the-job training.
– *guidance and counseling throughout the program.*

A record of the progress made will be given to the young person on leaving the YTS.

The YTS raises two important issues. First, it amounts essentially to a "pre-vocational" training year for many unemployed school-leavers. Given that Britain already has a relatively long duration of compulsory schooling, it is an open question whether this pre-vocational year would not make more sense as the last year in school rather than the first year out of it.

Second, will the YTS in effect kill off the regular youth labor market for 16 and 17 year-olds? If employers are getting such labor at no wage cost they may have little incentive to hire teenagers through the normal channels. It may well prove necessary to subsidize the regular employment of perhaps 300,000 youth to encourage employers not to rely solely on YTS as the source of teenage recruitment (Layard 1982b).

Institutional Background

Careers Information and Guidance. The development of government assistance to young people in choosing employment started in 1909.

In the postwar period, two pieces of legislation stand out as being responsible for shaping the current public employment and training services. The Employment and Training Act of 1948 established a Central Youth Employment Executive and National Youth Employment Council. It also gave local education authorities (LEA) the opportunity to operate a Careers Service (formerly Youth Employment Service) for those under 18 with finance coming from a 75 percent specific grant from the government. This opportunity had been seized by some 143 LEAs out of a possible 198, and the remaining 55 LEAs came under the aegis of the Department of Employment. This local division of responsibility had changed, however, with the passage of the 1973 Employment and Training Act which required, for the first time, careers services to be provided as a mandatory duty by LEAs.

The Careers Service is charged with the responsibility of providing all youth up to the age of 18, whether in school, further education, or employment, with appropriate vocational information, help and guidance, as well as assistance in job placement. Inevitably, a large proportion of staff time is devoted to counseling those sixteen year-olds who form the large majority of first time school-leavers. As a basic minimum it attempts to give advice on how to choose a job or career followed by a personal interview which takes place during the latter part of the final year at school. The system of career counseling within the schools themselves is a flexible, varied, and informal one. Headmasters take it upon themselves to offer careers advice in the smaller schools, but at the larger comprehensives this is delegated to two or more teachers. Similarly, there are differences in emphasis on the form of advice offered ranging from film shows and work visits to speakers from business and industry, the Armed Forces, and the Police.

Welfare in Employment. Once in employment, there are various pieces of legislation to protect the welfare of youth. Currently, those below school-leaving age must not be employed in mines, factories, or industrial undertakings. With certain exceptions, youth more than two years below school-leaving age must not be employed at all. In the final two years before school-leaving age, they can only be employed for a total of two hours on any school day between 6 a.m. and 8 p.m. Exceptions are made for licensed entertainment and street trading. The Education Act of 1944, however, gives a local authority the right to prohibit the employment of children wherever it appears that the work may adversely affect the child's health, fitness, or educational attainment.

The maximum hours of work, earliest start and latest finish times, and maximum lengths of continuous working without a break for youths above school-leaving age are controlled by the Factories Act of 1961. The maximum number of working hours per week is 48 with no more than 9 or 10 working hours per day or 6 days per week, spread over an 11 or 12 hour period between 7 a.m. and 8 p.m. The maximum continuous spell of work without a break of at least half-an-hour is 4½ hours, which may be increased to 5 hours if an intermediate 10 minute break is allowed. If the hours of work are extended beyond those set out above, this is classified as "overtime," which is permissible providing the District Inspector of Factories is notified, although overtime is limited to no more than 100 hours in a 25 week period and 6 hours in any week.

The provisions of the 1961 Act also have the general effect of precluding young persons on shift systems. The Secretary of State for Employment may authorize employment of young persons on a double-day shift system, provided the shifts do not begin before 6 a.m. nor end after 10 p.m. (2 p.m. on Saturdays) and the hours of each shift do not exceed an average of eight hours a day. This is limited to an overall maximum of 48 in any week and 88 in any two consecutive weeks. Furthermore, each shift must include a meal-break of at least half-an-hour. Before authorization is granted, a secret ballot of the workforce, in accordance with The Shift System in Factories and Workshops Order of 1936, must provide a consenting majority. The Secretary of State has the power to revoke an authorization if there is evidence of any abuse or if the legally stipulated minimum conditions have not been met.

The prohibition of nightwork for young people dates back to the Employment of Women, Young Persons and Children Act of 1920. The Secretary of State for Employment may grant an exemption lifting the above restrictions if "it is desirable in the public interest to do so for the purposes of maintaining or increasing the efficiency of industry or transport." General exemptions extend to a whole industry, or to a section of industry. They are made by ministerial regulation and have no time limit. An example of a general exemption is where youth are allowed to be employed on "round the clock" shift systems in certain continuous process industries. Where such exemptions apply, however, young people may not do more than six turns in any week; the interval between successive turns may not be less than 14 hours and they cannot be employed between midnight and 6 a.m. in two successive weeks. The total hours worked cannot be more than 56 in any week, or 144 in any period of three weeks. Special exemptions apply to individual factories and must be reviewed every year. Specific details giving reasons, hours, and length of time must be submitted by the employer to the Factory Inspector. While such legislation relates to factories, there are jobs outside manufacturing, for example, in offices, hospitals, and agriculture where the working hours of young persons are free of legal restrictions.

Wage Regulation. The rules and regulations governing the pay of youth are fixed from two sources, collective bargaining, and Wages Councils. Collectively bargained rates of pay are laid down as minimum rates and vary by both age and industry. In April 1980 for example, 16 year-old apprentices in newspaper printing earned 30 percent of the craftsman's rate while in match manufacture the corresponding figure was 80 percent. In most cases, the full rate for males does not become payable before the age of 21, which used to mark the end of an apprenticeship, but this has changed with the fall in the age of majority; females reach full rates at 18. State intervention to fix minimum pay for adults and teenagers has a seventy year history. In 1909, the first Trade Board's Act was passed which established four boards—in the so-called "sweated trades"—to set minimum wages. They were rechristened Wages Councils in 1945, and in 1979 they numbered 41, covering industries where no adequate machinery exists for the regulation of wages. Not surprisingly, it is youth in the agricultural, textile, clothing, and retail sectors who are covered by such bodies.

Employment Security. Very little employment protection legislation exists specifically for youths. In general, they are covered along with other groups in the labor market and not treated as some form of special case. One area where their treatment does differ concerns the provision of redundancy payments. Under the terms and conditions of the Employment Protection (Consolidation) Act of 1978, an employer is required to make a lump sum compensation to an employee who is dismissed because of redundancy after at least two years' reckonable service since the age of 18. This automatically excludes those aged between 16 and 18 years from entitlement to redundancy compensation which makes them more vulnerable to dismissal. Furthermore, the increased cost of dismissal associated with older workers does nothing to improve the hiring and retention prospects of youth.

Trade Unions. Despite a professed interest on the part of trade unions in recruiting young people, for a variety of reasons youths have tended to participate less frequently and actively than older workers (Wray 1957). Unpublished data from the National Training Survey for 1975 indicate that over half of males 25–65, but only 42 percent of young adult males and 19 percent of teenage males were union members. Among females, however, the young adults showed the highest proportion, 22 percent compared to 18.5 percent for the total. According to the results from the 1978 New Earnings Survey both male and female manual/nonmanual workers under 18 years of age are considerably less likely than the total to be covered by collective agreements. It is no surprise that few teenagers are members of the predominantly white collar unions because many of the occupations they cater for, like teaching, require schooling throughout most of the teens and beyond. It is, however, slightly surprising that there are not more teenagers in the two general unions, and in the construction workers union. This suggests that low union membership rates among teenagers are not entirely due to the composition of the industries and occupations in which they work. Rather, younger workers are simply less likely to be unionized whatever the sector in which they work.

Government Programs for Unemployed Youth. The Youth Opportunities Program (YOP) was started in 1978 as a response to rising levels of school-leaver and youth unemployment. The general aim from 1981 to September 1983 was to guarantee places to school-leavers still unemployed at Christmas and to other unemployed youth under 18. In 1982–83, over 325,000 young people entered the program. Activities covered by YOP include work experience inside firms, community projects, training workshops, and employment induction courses. YOP was criticized both because the participants received little training and because it encouraged some substitution of young workers for adults. These criticisms led to the development of the New Training Initiative, described above. A lower priority has been accorded older unemployed youth, especially the long-term jobless who have been eligible for separate, smaller programs.

To stimulate employment of youth during their first year of full-time work and to reduce youth average wage levels, the Department of Employment offered a one-year wage subsidy to employers who hired youth at or below a fixed earnings level. Over 110,000 claims for subsidy under the Young Workers Scheme were approved in the initial period from January through September 1982 (DE 1950–82, Nov. 1982, p.488). It is not clear how many of these youth, mostly school-leavers, would have been hired without the subsidy, nor is it known how many substitutions were made of subsidized youth for existing employees. In addition, the Training Services Division of the MSC has directed programs toward unemployed youth and less qualified school-leavers. Some 145,000 young people were helped in obtaining long-term training over the four-year period 1975–79 at a gross cost of roughly £139 million with the net cost being considerably less due to the savings in supplementary benefit which would otherwise have been paid in the schemes' absence (Metcalf 1982; MSC 1981c).

Government Financial Assistance to Youth. Young people who have never worked and fail to find a job or a place on a youth program from age 16 can obtain Supplementary Benefit in their own right, subject to a means test. In some cases, they may receive these benefits while attending vocational courses at further education colleges, or while on government unemployment programs. The amount of benefit is small relative to youth earnings and is not usually a deterrent to job search (Layard 1982a). Unemployment, sickness, and disability benefits are available to youth who meet the eligibility requirements. Educational grants toward tuition and living expenses for those attending tertiary level institutions are made by local authorities. The amount of grant is based on family means and consists of a nationally determined and financed mandatory element and a discretionary amount which may vary according to individual local authority policy. Proposals have been advanced to extend such grants to needy youth in the upper secondary schools, but such a program has not been implemented.

Table 6.1　Type of First Employment of New Entrants, 15–18 Years Old, by Sex, Great
　　　　　　Britain, 1952–1974

Year	Number of new entrants	Appren- ticeships	Employment leading to professional qualification	Clerical employment	Employment with planned training[a]	Other employment
	(000)		Males (percentage distribution)			
1952	266.9	34.9	1.2	9.0	*	54.9
1956	246.9	37.7	1.3	8.0	*	53.0
1962	335.9	36.2	1.3	9.0	13.3	40.3
1966	270.2	42.4	1.3	9.1	13.1	34.1
1968	255.8	43.0	1.2	8.3	13.3	34.2
1972	258.9	38.7	1.3	7.1	16.5	36.4
1973[b]	140.5	47.0	2.3	12.7	14.5	23.5
1974[c]	274.8	43.0	1.3	7.0	17.1	31.6
			Females (percentage distribution)			
1952	256.1	5.9	1.2	31.4	*	61.6
1956	235.5	6.8	1.1	34.7	*	57.6
1962	321.3	6.6	1.1	35.3	10.0	47.0
1966	251.7	6.7	1.7	40.1	13.7	37.8
1968	232.4	7.3	1.8	38.8	14.4	37.7
1972	228.2	7.9	1.7	34.3	17.7	38.4
1973[b]	107.0	4.7	3.7	58.2	11.6	21.8
1974[c]	237.8	6.5	1.8	40.5	17.3	34.0

*Data for 1952 and 1956 included in "other employment."
[a]Originally training over one year; changed to training other than induction training.
[b]Affected by compulsory retention in school of all who turned 15 during the 1972–73
　school year.　[c]16–18 year-olds only.

Source: DE 1950–82, annual survey of Young Persons Entering Employment.

Dimensions of Youth Employment

The initial labor market experience of young people varies by race and
by geographic area. These dimensions of youth employment are considered below, but first we discuss trends in the jobs of school-leavers
as a whole, taking account of differences in sex and educational attainment.

There was a remarkable stability in the distribution of first jobs of
new entrants (15–18 years old) in the 20 years to 1974 (Table 6.1).
Although the annual data ceased to be collected thereafter, special
surveys indicate a continuation of the trends (DE 1980b, 1982a). Two-
fifths of the males went into apprenticeships and a similar proportion
of the women entered clerical employment. Fewer than 1 in 50 went
into employment leading to professional qualifications and around one-
third of each sex went into jobs with no training. During the postwar
years the qualifications held by school-leavers rose substantially, but

the rise in the average qualification level was not matched by a change in the composition of first jobs.

This accords with the detailed cohort analysis of Metcalf and Nickell (1982) who found that the later after 1930 that a cohort entered the labor market the higher the qualification required to enter any specific occupation. This is an important finding because it emphasizes that the distribution of jobs is determined by what people wish to spend their money on and by technology. Merely raising education levels is unlikely to alter the structure of jobs very much.

For example, the proportion of 15 year-olds in the 15–17 school-leavers cohort dropped from 78.6 percent to 68.7 percent for males and from 79.7 percent to 69.7 percent for females over 1961–66. These percentage point changes were matched by an equal reduction in the job opportunities for all 15–17 year-olds in the 40 less-skilled occupations, but an expansion occurred for the 18–19 age group. More significantly, among all females there was a 23 percent increase in the less skilled occupations which suggests that married women returning to work could have been plugging the gap left by young girls who had decided to stay on at school (DE 1969).

The industrial distribution of 16 and 17 year-old entrants into employment in England and Wales in 1979 showed that almost two-thirds of female and almost half of male first jobs were in distribution and other service industries, while manufacturing provided around a third of initial employment for both males and females. The occupational pattern of first jobs of 16 and 17 year-olds in England and Wales in 1979 showed a remarkable concentration for young women. Over 36 percent went into clerical and related occupations alone and three-quarters of first jobs were in four occupational groups—clerical, selling, catering, cleaning, hairdressing, and other personal services; and making and repairing (excluding metal and electrical). There was much less concentration among young men, the only noteworthy point being that a quarter entered processing, making, and repairing in the metal and electrical sectors, essentially occupations within the engineering industry (DE 1982a, p.118).

Many office jobs require higher school qualifications than manual jobs and it is noticeable that among both males and females more 17 than 16 year-olds enter clerical jobs, reflecting their higher average qualification level. Young men with no formal school qualifications (CSEs or GCEs) gravitate to the construction and mining and transport operating, material moving and storing occupations in tasks like general building laborer and driver's mate. Unqualified females are disproportionately represented in repetitive assembling and making and repairing (outside the metal and electrical sectors).

Quite clearly, the above suggests a relationship between educational achievement and first jobs. At the risk of oversimplification, the pattern which emerges suggests that those with "A" or "O" Level GCEs or equivalent are more likely to go into white collar jobs and those with

CSEs below grade one or no qualifications are more likely to go into blue collar jobs. The gravitation of the more qualified to the office-based industries may reflect the greater emphasis placed on formal qualifications as a method of screening young applicants. The stratified organization of the workforce and predetermined career paths known to exist in such sectors limits the choice of entrant to the better qualified, in the sense that these are seen as suitable material for "training-up" for middle and possibly senior management positions later in their working life. On the other hand, the possession of qualifications does not appear to be a prerequisite of entry to manual jobs which may indicate that such employers attach more weight to attributes such as personality and attitude to work rather than straightforward academic ability (see Ashton and Maguire 1982). Furthermore, the maximum age restriction on starting an apprenticeship automatically disqualifies the older and more qualified school-leaver who chooses to stay on and take GCE "A" Levels.

The amount of training received in the first jobs of 16 and 17 year-old entrants in England and Wales in 1979 ranged widely. While 31 percent of males and 42 percent of females received no training at all, over two years of training was anticipated for 36 percent of males and 6 percent of females. Short training of under three weeks was provided for 3 percent of males and 5 percent of females, training of three weeks to six months applied to 20 percent of males and 39 percent of females, and training of six months to one year was anticipated for 4 percent of each sex (DE 1982a, p.120). Unfortunately, no information is given to show whether training takes place on or off employers' premises or whether it is in the form of a continuous course or a day release over a longer period (if training is given for, say, only one day a week, the total period over which the training is given is recorded).

Not only are girls less likely to receive any training than boys, but the duration of their training is also shorter, reflecting the greater proportion of young men who enter apprenticeships and who pursue professional qualifications. The two occupations where over two-thirds of male entrants are in jobs providing at least two years of training are professional and related in science, and processing, making, and repairing in the metal and electrical trades. The extent and length of training is both a cause and an effect of the incidence and amount of labor turnover. Women have higher turnover rates than men and training-intensive occupations such as those in the engineering industry have lower turnover than jobs in the construction and transport sectors. However, the longitudinal analysis below does not suggest that individuals with a lot of job changing in their initial occupation end up in worse occupations later in life than more stable youth.

Although it is well known that young people have a higher rate of labor turnover than adults, virtually no cross-sectional empirical work has been undertaken to explain differences in turnover rates among youth with the same or varying levels of education. What little evidence there is (see MSC 1978b, pp.48–53) suggests that leavers with few or no qualifications had had more jobs than the better-qualified, though this could in part be due to the former having left school earlier and therefore been in the labor market longer. Most of the school-leavers who had had jobs since leaving school but were currently unemployed, had left their last job involuntarily; they had been dismissed, made redundant, or had been in a temporary position. Among those who left their jobs voluntarily, mainly the least qualified school-leavers, the most important motivations were to improve pay and working conditions. This may be the result of two factors. First, the least qualified accept that they will have less interesting jobs and so place a greater emphasis on pecuniary rewards. Second, the financial hardship of recurrent unemployment among such youth requires greater compensation while they are in work (MSC 1978b).

RACE AND EMPLOYMENT

Information on youth earnings or employment by race is limited by the paucity of national surveys and the small sample size in the few available sources. Results for 1975 from the National Training Survey tapes, also based on a small sample of nonwhites, do not show striking broad occupational differences between white and nonwhite youth, 16–24 (Table 6.2). Both male and female nonwhite youth were more highly concentrated in semiskilled manual occupations than white youth and white males had a considerably higher proportion than nonwhite males in skilled manual occupations. Drawing on a larger sample, the 1971 population census, and considering males of all ages, Mayhew and Rosewell (1978, p.229) found that immigrants suffered from occupational crowding into the undesirable, low-paying occupations and had more difficulty "in obtaining higher status jobs than their indigenous counterparts."

In terms of employment experience, there are several ways in which discrimination and disadvantage may produce a higher level of unemployment among racial minorities than whites. Discrimination in hiring and firing against blacks may, for example, lead to higher levels and longer durations of unemployment (which could be compensated for by more energetic job search or acceptance of a less attractive job than a white person would do). The concentration of minorities in particular kinds of jobs and industries may lead to a high level of unemployment if these jobs and industries are most vulnerable. The available information shows that in the early 1960s when immigration was at its peak the rate of unemployment was several times higher among the minorities than whites. This ratio followed a downward trend from 1963 such that by 1970 the rate among minorities was probably the same as among the general population.

The findings of the 1971 population census, and subsequent analyses since that date, unanimously echo the view that a change occurred; the

Table 6.2   Occupations of Youth, 16–24 Years Old, by Race, Sex, and
            Socioeconomic Group, Great Britain, 1975

	Males		Females	
	White	Non-white	White	Non-white
	(percentage distribution)			
Employer, large firms	0.0	0.0	0.0	0.0
Manager, large firms	0.8	0.0	0.1	0.0
Employer, small firms	0.3	1.0	0.0	0.0
Manager, small firms	1.0	1.0	0.6	0.0
Professional self-employed	0.0	0.0	0.0	0.0
Professional employee	3.0	2.0	0.3	1.0
Nonmanual intermediate	3.9	3.0	8.2	8.0
Nonmanual foreman	2.3	1.0	5.6	5.0
Nonmanual junior	13.6	14.5	50.6	49.0
Personal service	1.5	4.3	7.7	3.0
Manual foreman	5.4	6.0	1.2	0.0
Skilled manual	40.1	32.5	4.1	3.0
Semiskilled manual	19.6	29.1	19.2	30.0
Unskilled	3.3	5.0	1.3	1.0
Own account worker	1.4	1.0	0.3	0.0
Farmer	0.5	0.0	0.0	0.0
Agricultural worker	2.3	0.0	0.4	0.0
Armed forces	0.6	1.0	0.0	0.0
Total	100.0	100.0	100.0	100.0
Total number[a]	3,955	117	4,146	100

[a]Excludes individuals for whom there is no information on socioeconomic group.

Source: National Training Survey data tapes.

---

rate of unemployment has been higher among minority groups, for both
men and women, than among all groups. The National Dwellings and
Housing Survey carried out in 1977 showed an unemployment rate of
9.6 percent for minority groups compared with 5.2 percent for the
general population (Barber 1981). Among teenagers, the rate of unemployment, particularly for West Indian youths, is strikingly high; the
1971 census rate of 20 percent for those aged 15–20 exceeded the rate
for any other minority group and represented double that for all groups.

Although the incidence of unemployment is far higher among racial
minorities, survey evidence for 1979 suggested that the average duration
of male unemployment was broadly similar for whites and minority
groups in the same age group (Smith 1981). Duration was strongly
related to age. Men aged 25–34 had, on average, been unemployed for
twice as long as those aged 16–17, and almost one-third longer than
18–24 year-olds. Although such evidence is specific to the time of the
survey when total unemployment was itself at a high level, more
worrying is the disproportionate increase in unemployment suffered by

blacks when the general level of unemployment is rising. For example, between November 1973 and February 1976 when unemployment doubled, the number of blacks on the register more than quadrupled.

This is believed to lend support to the notion that minority groups function as a marginal source of labor in those industries which are most vulnerable when unemployment is high. The distribution of blacks across industries varies and these variations are associated with their special geographical distribution. The 1971 census reports that black males accounted for over 10 percent of the workforce in the textile, leather goods, clothing and footwear, other manufacturing and miscellaneous service industries (OPCS 1975). The first three are popularly recognized as being particularly adversely hit by the recession of the mid-1970s and thus could be cited as one cause of high unemployment among the racial minorities.

AREA DIFFERENCES

The share of youth in total employment varies across areas within Britain as do the employment:population ratios for youth and the composition of youth employment. Examination of the structure of labor force participation rates of males aged 15–20 across 83 towns (county boroughs) in England and Wales in 1971 suggested that four factors were particularly important in accounting for area variations in participation rates (Arman 1981). On the supply side, these were the absolute and relative size of the youth cohort in the town and the educational enrollment rates. Towns where a higher fraction of young people remained at school beyond age 16 had, not surprisingly, lower participation rates. A 10 percent increase in the size of a town's 15–20 year-old cohort was associated, other things being equal, with a fall in the youth participation rate of almost 1 percent, which reflects the difficulty that the labor market has in smoothly absorbing an enlarged teenage cohort into employment. The composition of occupations in the town and the unemployment rate in the area were two important demand side influences. The participation rate of 15–20 year-olds was lower in towns located in regions with substantial deficient demand and with a high demand and with a high fraction of unskilled and semiskilled manual occupations than in towns with opposite characteristics.

Data on regional differences in the distribution of new entrants to employment can be obtained from the annual survey of Young Persons Entering Employment, conducted through 1974. Comparing male and female distributions in 1972, by far the greatest proportion of boys entering apprenticeships was in Yorkshire and Humberside and the Midlands, predominantly in the engineering, construction and miscellaneous services industries; by 1979, two other regions had higher shares than Yorkshire and Humberside and the spread among regions had declined (DE 1950–82, March 1981, p. 152). Compared with Great Britain, the South Eastern region had a far smaller proportion of boys entering apprenticeships, but a considerably higher percentage entering employment with planned training (27.3 percent as against 16.5 percent) and clerical employment (13 percent as against 7.1 percent). For females, 34.3 percent went into clerical employment overall, but once again this varied regionally from 48.5 percent in London and the South East to 26 percent and 25 percent in Wales and Scotland, respectively. By way of contrast, the proportion of females entering apprenticeships, mainly in miscellaneous services and as hairdressers and beauticians, was almost three times greater in Scotland (8.4 percent) than in the South East (3.1 percent).

Such figures serve to underline the point that regional variations in first employment opportunities are mainly a reflection of the industrial structure of the regions which in turn will be revealed in such things as regional variations in youth unemployment, labor turnover rates, and geographical mobility. For example, over the 1966–80 period, the South East and North West accounted for 38 and 20 percent respectively of the total reduction in manufacturing employment while simultaneously providing 19 percent and 7 percent of the expansion in service employment. These changes were associated with twelvefold and sixfold increases, respectively, in youth unemployment.

Characteristics of Youth-Intensive Industries

The pattern of youth employment across major industrial groups differs from the pattern of all employment, as can be inferred from the analysis of youth-intensive occupations in Chapter 3. Identification of the youth-intensive industries and analysis of their characteristics can advance the inquiry into youth employment compared to that of other age groups. From age-sex group distributions of employment by industry in 1971 we have constructed ratios that show the relative youth-intensity of each major industry group (Table 6.3). The ratio of youth intensity for each major industry group is found by dividing each youth employment share by the respective all-age share. For example, 3.9 percent of male teenagers (15–19) and 3.5 percent of all males worked in one of the major industry groups, agriculture, forestry, and fishing; the ratio therefore is 1.11 and the industry group ranks as mildly youth-intensive.

Youth-intensity is more significant for teenage than young adult males both in the number of industry groups showing ratios above 1.0 and the amount of the excess. Thus 12 of the 27 major industry groups registered ratios over 1.0 and six had a ratio above 1.25 for teenage males. In the case of young adult males, nine of the 27 industry groups had ratios higher than 1.0 and none was over 1.2. The two age groups of young females were more alike. Among teenage females, 13 of the 27 industry groups qualified and five showed a ratio above 1.25. Young

Table 6.3 Youth Intensity of Employment, by Major Industry Group, Age, and Sex, Great Britain, 1971

	Males Relative youth intensity[a]		Females Relative youth intensity[a]	
	15-19 years	20-24 years	15-19 years	20-24 years
	(ratio)			
Agriculture, forestry, fishing	1.11	0.77	0.54	0.46
Mining and quarrying	0.76	0.64	1.00	1.00
Food, drink, tobacco	0.97	0.97	1.21	0.94
Coal and petroleum	0.33	0.67	1.00	1.00
Chemicals and allied	0.64	0.86	1.33	1.33
Metal manufacture	0.88	0.91	1.13	1.13
Mechanical engineering	1.18	1.03	1.10	1.29
Instrument engineering	1.00	1.17	1.00	1.17
Electrical engineering	0.86	1.06	1.00	1.14
Shipbuilding	1.27	1.00	1.00	2.00
Vehicles	0.73	0.84	0.92	1.17
Metal goods (n.e.s.)	1.32	1.04	0.95	0.89
Textiles	1.19	0.95	1.28	0.91
Leather and leather goods	1.50	1.00	1.00	0.67
Clothing and footwear	1.63	1.00	1.78	0.95
Bricks, pottery, glass (n.e.s.)	1.00	1.00	1.00	1.00
Timber, furniture	1.65	1.10	1.17	1.00
Paper, printing, publishing	1.00	1.00	1.52	1.35
Other manufacturing	0.93	1.00	1.07	0.86
Construction	1.15	1.18	1.09	1.27
Gas, electricity, water	0.70	0.85	0.70	1.00
Transport and communications	0.57	0.86	0.96	1.26
Distribution	1.35	0.95	1.21	0.78
Insurance, banking, finance	0.78	1.19	1.82	1.85
Professional and scientific services	0.42	0.90	0.47	0.95
Miscellaneous services	1.39	1.14	0.80	0.77
Public administration and defense	0.93	1.20	0.87	1.21
Industry inadequately specified	2.40	1.40	1.18	0.72
All industry groups	1.00	1.00	1.00	1.00

[a]Youth intensity is calculated by dividing the share for each industry group in total youth employment by the respective all-age share for the same sex.

Note: n.e.s. means "not elsewhere specified".

Source: Computed from OPCS 1975, Table 17.

adult females displayed 11 intensive industry groups and six of these had ratios over 1.25.

There was a tendency for the teenage-intensive industry groups to also be intensive in the employment of 20-24 year-olds of the same sex. In the case of males five industry groups and among females six industry groups were intensive for each youth age group. However, there was almost no overlap between the most important teenage-intensive male and female industry groups (Table 6.3). Only the clothing and footwear industry was among the top six teenage-intensive industry groups for both sexes. For males four of the industry groups were in manufacturing and two were services, while for females manufacturing dominated even more, incorporating five of the top six such industry groups. Although an absolutely large number and proportion of teenage women were employed in professional and scientific services and miscellaneous services, these industry groups were not counted as teenage-intensive because the teenage share was below the total share. And the biggest employer of female teenages, distribution, was only seventh when ranked by teenage intensity of employment.

The industry groups that had ratios above 1.0 accounted for 58.3 percent of total teenage male employment, 60.4 percent of total teenage female employment, 49.4 percent of total male young adult employment and 36.8 percent of total female young adult employment. In the six most teenage-intensive industry groups chosen for further analysis, the share of total employment was 31.1 percent for teenage males and 30.7 percent for teenage females. Therefore, the discussion which follows is based on a limited portion of teenage employment, roughly half of total teenage-intensive employment and under one-third of total employment for each teenage group in 1971. Moreover, teenagers did not constitute a significant fraction of total employment in any major industry group. A further limitation is the high level of aggregation of the data by major industry groups and, for teenage males, the inclusion of apprentices with young workers. Despite these reservations about the data, a test is deemed worthwhile.

A large number of statistical indicators has been computed for each of the six most teenage-intensive industry groups and for all industry groups. In most cases the indicators refer to both sexes, but for a few characteristics, the information is only for the sex under discussion. The fact that some of these data are drawn from a year other than 1971 is unimportant since the structure of the characteristics across industry groups is very stable over time.

The six male teenage-intensive industry groups lacked a clearly defined type of labor force (Table 6.4). The proportion who were unskilled, immigrants, receiving training, or unemployed in the six industry groups was not consistently above or below the corresponding average for total employment. These male teenage-intensive industry groups tended to have an above-average share of part-time males, but not markedly so. They also had relatively high rates of labor turnover; a larger than average fraction of male employees had job tenure durations of less than a year. Data on the characteristics of firms are mainly available for the four manufacturing industries in which a clear pattern emerged. Those who worked in teenage-intensive industry groups were disproportionately located in small firms and exhibited lower than average net output per worker. Overtime hours as a source of additional pay were also below average in three of the six industry groups and payment by results was higher than average only in metal goods n.e.s. The

Table 6.4 Characteristics of Six Most Teenage-Intensive Major Industry Groups, Males, Great Britain, 1971

	Timber and furniture	Clothing and footwear	Leather and leather goods	Misc. services	Distribution	Metal goods (n.e.s.)	All major industry groups
Ratio of teenage intensity	1.65	1.65	1.50	1.39	1.35	1.32	1.00
Employment characteristics, all ages, both sexes	(percentage, except where specified)						
Labor force							
Unskilled	9.5	1.9	7.6	8.8	3.7	6.9	7.5
Part-time[a]	2.7	3.6	3.8	6.5	6.5	1.7	2.3
Receiving training	5.3	4.7	3.5	n.a.	n.a.	6.2	4.6
Immigrants	4.6	9.2	10.3	2.9	3.5	7.5	5.8
Less than 12 months with employer[a]	20.5	13.1	20.8	22.3	20.6	16.7	14.5
Unemployment rate	3.2	1.8	3.1	2.9	2.1	3.7	3.2
Firms							
Employees per firm (average number)	32	72	33	n.a.	n.a.	49	105
Employees per plant (average number)	29	64	31	n.a.	n.a.	45	93
Net output per worker (£)	2,386	1,421	1,970	n.a.	n.a.	2,267	2,536
Labor intensity of production	54.0	59.0	54.0	n.a.	n.a.	55.0	53.0
Overtime as percent of total pay[a]	45.8	29.9	45.1	18.3	24.2	47.3	39.3
Payment-by-results[a]	15.6	8.1	15.0	12.1	14.3	16.9	16.3
Industrial relations							
Not covered by collective agreement[a]	22.8	42.6	18.0	46.4	45.9	25.1	16.8
Strikes per 100,000 employees	9.3	5.9	2.1	1.0	2.1	14.9	10.1

[a]Males only.

Note: n.e.s. means "not elsewhere specified."

Source: OPCS 1975, Table 33; DE 1971-1982, 1971 and 1973 Surveys; DE 1950-1982, July 1971, April 1972, September 1980, p.951-53; DE 1978b, Table 6; DE 1978a, pp.114-16; DI 1971, Tables 1,9.

industrial relations dimensions were quite sharp. The six teenage-intensive industry groups had a much higher than average fraction of their male labor force not covered by collective bargaining agreements, and they were not strike prone.

Because the characteristics vary across industry groups in a somewhat haphazard way it is difficult to discern a strong pattern. Nevertheless, the six male teenage-intensive industries do appear to have many of the characteristics associated with secondary employment or an inferior segment of the labor market. Compared with the all industry averages, they have, in general, lower collective bargaining coverage, higher turnover rates, smaller plants and firms, lower output per employee and more part-time workers. This is not necessarily to be condemned. These industries have such characteristics partly *because* they employ relatively large numbers of teenagers, and high turnover and lower unionization may well mean more job opportunities in total for teenagers. Since there will always be dispersion in employment characteristics, with some bad jobs and some good ones, the key factor when commenting on the impact on individual welfare is whether one can escape from that sector. The longitudinal analysis below, using somewhat different categories, addresses this issue and finds that significance should be attached to the level and characteristics of initial employment.

The characteristics of the six female teenage-intensive industries were even less clearcut than was the case for males (Table 6.5). There was no consistent pattern except for the much lower than average incidence of part-time female employment in these industry groups. The nature of the industry groups also varied, but it is noticeable that for the five manufacturing industry groups the majority of observations on firm size, plant size, and net output per worker are above the all industry average. From this analysis it does not appear that female teenage-intensive industries consistently have employment characteristics that diverge from the average, although data for individual industry groups do suggest the secondary labor market.

The nature of the foregoing analysis has precluded specific examination of the characteristics of teenage employment in comparison with those of adults in the same industries and occupations. Additional indicators and data are required to determine whether and how many young people are relegated to inferior jobs, who else holds these jobs, and what proportion of youth remain in the same type of jobs as they mature.

Relative Earnings

The earnings of youth relative to adults have been a source of much comment, anecdotal and otherwise, in the context of youths "pricing themselves out of jobs." Indeed, as described above, in an explicit attempt to encourage cuts in youths' relative earnings and to expand

Table 6.5 Characteristics of Six Most Teenage-Intensive Major Industry Groups, Females, Great Britain, 1971

	Insurance, banking, finance	Clothing and footwear	Paper, printing, publishing	Chemicals and allied	Textiles	Food, drink, tobacco	All industries, both sexes
Ratio of teenage intensity	1.82	1.78	1.52	1.33	1.28	1.21	1.00
Employment characteristics, all ages, both sexes	(percentage, except where specified)						
Labor force							
Unskilled	7.2	1.9	5.6	7.3	9.6	9.9	7.5
Part-time[a]	21.6	16.5	20.8	21.4	21.4	34.8	31.3
Receiving training	n.a.	4.7	5.4	4.2	2.5	2.6	4.6
Immigrants	4.4	9.2	3.5	4.5	8.8	6.0	-5.8
Under 12 months with employer[a]	24.7	21.8	21.2	24.8	19.4	23.9	22.8
Unemployment rate	1.6	1.8	2.1	2.2	3.8	3.0	3.2
Firms							
Employees per firm (average number)	n.a.	72	66	171	154	183	105
Employees per plant (average number)	n.a.	64	57	142	118	134	93
Net output per worker (£)	n.a.	1,421	2,700	4,435	1,955	3,269	2,536
Labor intensity of production	n.a.	59.0	54.0	36.0	56.0	38.0	53.0
Overtime as percent of total pay[a]	n.a.	44.0	38.2	30.1	48.6	31.6	32.8
Payment-by-results[a]	n.a.	1.7	5.1	2.8	2.8	5.8	3.8
Industrial relations							
Not covered by collective agreement[a]	n.a.	42.8	22.0	42.0	20.1	17.0	28.3
Strikes per 100,000 employees	0.4	5.9	4.9	9.4	11.3	9.7	10.1

[a]Females only.

Source: See Table 6.4.

employment, the Young Workers Scheme provides a subsidy to employers of youth whose gross earnings are quite low compared to the youth average; the subsidy has two levels, allotting the larger amount to the lower of the two designated earnings brackets.

It is of considerable interest that apprentices apparently do not earn much less than other youth. A calculation for 1978 showed that the annual earnings of apprentices and full-time trainees in manufacturing was 58 percent of the annual earnings of all manufacturing employees, and a few percentage points less if adults only are considered (DE 1950–82, March 1982, p. 133). At this time, male youth earned only a slightly higher percent of the adult male hourly wage (Table 6.6). If, as is likely, employers have net labor costs for apprentices exceeding those for other young workers, and if the output of apprentices over the course of their training does not exceed that of other young workers, as is also likely, then it is not difficult to see why employers may be careful about hiring apprentices.

Two clear facts stand out about relative earnings of young workers and adults (Table 6.6). First, among manual workers there has been a clear upward trend in the hourly earnings of males under 21 years old relative to those of adult males. The relative earnings of youth, on average, have risen by one-third in the thirty years, 1949–79. A considerable part of the rise during the 1970s is probably attributable to two elements: the sharp fall in the age of eligibility of males for adult wage rates in national collective bargaining agreements and the raising of the legal school-leaving age. In 1970, two-thirds of the agreements specified receipt of the adult rate on reaching age 21 or 22, but by 1979 only one-fifth of the agreements specified waiting till 21 or 22, and almost half the agreements provided adult rates at age 18 (DE 1972–82). Females have received the adult rate at 18 for some time.

The raising of the legal school-leaving age from 14 to 15 in 1947 removed a large number of teenagers from the labor market, which increased their relative earnings during the years of labor shortage and low growth of teenage population (O'Keefe 1975). The sharp rise in relative earnings in 1973 also can be related to the raising of the school-leaving age to 16 in 1972–73, but Layard (1982a) found that the rise in the teenage population from 1972 onward would have offset the effect of the change in the school-leaving age. To the extent that earnings are age-related, there would be a straightforward labor force composition effect which Makeham (1980) calculates might have added at least 5 percent to the average earnings of the under-21 age group.

The second point is that in the latter part of the 1970s the relative earnings of workers under 21 were fairly stable in relation to that of adults, while the earnings of both male and female 21–24 year-olds fell relative to adults (Table 6.6, Panel B). This suggests that the very large increase in teenage unemployment after 1973 cannot be mainly attributed to a rise in relative earnings, although a failure of youth pay levels to

Table 6.6 Hourly Earnings of Youth Relative to Adults, by Sex, Great
Britain, 1949-1980

	Manual workers, hourly earnings	
	Males under 21 relative to males 21 and over	Females under 18 relative to females 18 and over
	(ratio)	
1949	.45	.64
1959	.47	.63
1969	.52	.66
1979	.61	.67

	All Workers, hourly earnings					
	Males			Females		
	Under 18 relative to 21 and over	18-20 relative to 21 and over	21-24 relative to 21 and over	Under 18 relative to 21 and over	18-20 relative to 21 and over	21-24 relative to 21 and over
	(ratio)					
1974	.40	.63	.83	.58	.76	.98
1980	.41	.63	.80	.57	.76	.94

Note: All data refer to full-time workers. Manual workers include,
and all workers exclude the effect on earnings of both overtime hours
and absence from work.

Source: Manual workers: October data, published in DE 1950-1982,
February issues. All workers: April data published in DE 1971-1982,
1974 and 1980 issues.

fall sufficiently relative to those of adults may be related to age-group
differences in the increase of unemployment rates.

It is possible that fixed-amount increases across the board, stipulated
in the incomes policy guidelines of the mid-1970s, gave a boost to
relative youth earnings and therefore made youth less attractive to
employers. Public intervention in the collective bargaining process was
pervasive in the 1970s. Some form of incomes policy, voluntary or
statutory pay guidelines expressed either in cash amounts or percentages
or both, was in force for five-and-a-half years of the 1970 decade.
Earnings guidelines expressed in a fixed cash amount would, if strictly
adhered to, tend to narrow the earnings distribution. Although the
evidence above indicates that the earnings of all youth, as distinct from

manual youth only, did not rise in the latter part of the 1970s, it is worthwhile to examine the impact of incomes policy on the distribution of relative earnings.

The two phases of incomes policy which might have been expected to narrow the earnings structure occurred from July 1975 to July 1977 (stages I and II of the incomes policy instituted by the then Labour Government). From July 1975 to July 1976 there was to be a flat maximum cash increase to those earning under £8,500 a year. From July 1976 to July 1977, there was a combination of cash and percentage guidelines. If effective, these policies should have both squeezed youth earnings horizontally, the low paid youth gaining relative to the high paid, and vertically, youth gaining relative to adults.

The evidence for 1975–78 shows unambiguously that incomes policy had very little impact on horizontal or vertical equity in male earnings. Among both males under 18 and those 18 to 20 years old, the lowest decile and lower quartile did not experience an increase in gross weekly earnings relative to the upper quartile and highest decile. And, more importantly, there was not a vertical narrowing of the gross weekly earnings of youth relative to adults. If the incomes policy had been strictly observed for adults, there would have been a very substantial increase in youth earnings relative to adult, and a somewhat smaller compression within the employed youth group. Since the actual 1977 figures are substantially below the hypothetical figures, incomes policy cannot be blamed for pricing young men out of jobs. The results for females show a similar lack of impact of incomes policy on their earning distributions.

Within the youth group, relative earnings also have shifted over the years, leaving those with more years of education at a disadvantage. The starting salaries of male graduates from Arts and Social Science university courses fell from a 1968 level 2.18 times greater than the annualized weekly earnings of male youth under 21 to 1.26 times in 1974 and 1.44 times in 1978 (Freeman 1981, p. 7). Pissarides (1979) found that the starting salary of graduates fell by 35 percent relative to youth earnings 1969–76.

Analysis of the relative earnings and unemployment ratios of youth by sex in 1974 and 1980 suggests that relative unemployment among young females has risen at a time when their relative earnings have increased. This finding is in accord with economic theory that demand is responsive to price. The hourly earnings of females under 18 relative to males of the same age rose from .95 to .99 from 1974 to 1980, as the ratio of the same two groups' unemployment soared from .57 to .89. A similar movement appeared for the relative earnings of 18–20 year-olds and unemployment ratios of 18–19 year-olds (DE 1950–82, July 1979 and July 1980; DE 1971–82, 1974 and 1980, Table 124). Caution should be exercised when comparing the older teenage group because the 18–19 age definition for unemployment does not match the 18–20 earnings definition and so the measure of relative earnings is approximate. Nevertheless, the magnitude of the rise in relative unemployment among young females seems great, given the rather small change in their relative earnings, provided that this is the sole cause of the rising unemployment. A 4 percentage point increase in earnings was associated with a 32 percentage point increase in relative unemployment. These figures suggest that the demand for young female labor is highly elastic and any trend toward equal pay with adult women, which was almost achieved by the under-18s in 1980, will be reflected in levels of unemployment nearly identical to those of young males.

Hours of Work and Other Working Conditions

In 1960, youth and boys (under 21 years) worked for an average of 44.3 hours per week which was less than the corresponding adult male figure of 48 hours per week. Although females worked shorter hours than males, teenage females worked longer total weekly hours than adult females, the figures being 41.4 and 40.5 hours respectively. In 1979, teenage males had longer normal basic workweeks than prime-age males (aged 25–49) but worked less overtime, with 41.7 hours against the 43.2 hours average for all men. The majority of males under 18 worked over 38 hours but not over 40, while only a quarter of males over 18 were bunched in this range. For females overtime hours were low and hardly differed by age group and so the higher normal basic workweek of teenagers in 1979 (37.8 hours) was reflected in slightly higher total hours (38.3 hours) compared to the overall adult female figure (37.5 hours).

The obvious secular downward trend in hours over the 20 year period has not been evenly distributed by sex and age. The 10 percent reduction in adult male hours is almost twice that of the decline for young males, while the 7 percent reduction in female hours is the same for both teenage and adult groups.

Part-time work is not prominent among young Britons, either as an accompaniment during the school term to full-time or part-time educational enrollment or as a voluntary or involuntary activity of out-of-school youth. A recent survey in three representative British communities found considerable evidence of employer eagerness to hire part-time adult women, but not youth (Ashton and Maguire 1982). A survey by the European Communities in 1975 revealed that male teenagers in the United Kingdom accounted for 1.9 percent and female teenagers 0.4 percent of those with a part-time main occupation; the teenage groups showed much higher shares of those with a full-time main occupation. A similar discrepancy appeared for young adults (EC 1977, Tables I/4, III,6).

Further EC survey evidence on hours indicates that in 1975 U.K. teenagers of each sex and young adult males had a lower share of total shift work, night work, and Sunday and holiday work than they did of the total labor force of the same sex. On the other hand, young adult females showed a disproportionately large share of shift and night work and a somewhat smaller share of Sunday and holiday work than their fraction of the total female labor force. Thus, adverse working times did not excessively burden British youth, with the two exceptions mentioned for young adult females. Teenagers also were relatively less involved in work in noisy places or places with risks, and teenage females had a smaller fraction in unhygienic places than was compatible with shares of the total labor force. While young adults had a greater chance than teenagers of working in such places, it was still proportionate to their labor force share, except for young adult males in unhygienic workplaces (Reubens et al. 1981, Table 5.13). These measures of adverse hours and working conditions do not reveal British youth as disproportionately affected and teenagers were more protected than young adults.

Longitudinal Analysis

It is important to analyze not only cross-sectional data on youth employment, but also the interaction between initial employment and subsequent employment and unemployment experience. In Britain only the National Training Survey (NTS) permits such study for different cohorts. This retrospective longitudinal survey of the labor market experience of over 50,000 men and women was undertaken by the Manpower Services Commission in 1975 and offers data on the male and female cohorts which entered the labor market in 1930, 1940, 1950, 1960 and 1975 (Metcalf and Nickell 1982). The NTS presents 396 occupations, according to the list of KOS (Key Occupations for Statistical Purposes) (DE 1971–82, 1973 ed., pp.285–87). We have aggregated these occupations to either Socioeconomic Group (SEG) which has 19 categories or Social Class which has six categories. Although the sample size for each cohort is small, we believe that the results are reliable. A similar analysis of raw data from the much larger national longitudinal surveys of those born in 1946 and 1958 could provide a check on our findings for the most recent cohorts (Cherry 1976; National Children's Bureau, forthcoming).

SOCIOECONOMIC GROUP OF FIRST AND 1975 OCCUPATIONS

The distributions across socioeconomic groups of the first occupation held by our five male cohorts and where they had reached in 1975 tell us three things (Table 6.7). First, they indicate the distribution of first occupations according to year of entry into the labor market and describe how the distributions of the first occupations held by entrants have changed according to the year of entry of each of the five cohorts.

Table 6.7 First Occupation and 1975 Occupation, Males, by Year of Entry to Labor
Market and Socioeconomic Group, Great Britain, 1930–1975

	Year of labor market entry									
	1930		1940		1950		1960		1970	
	Socioeconomic group									
	1930	1975	1940	1975	1950	1975	1960	1975	1970	1975
	(percentage distribution)									
Employer, large firms	0.0	0.3	0.0	0.0	0.0	0.2	0.0	0.2	0.0	0.0
Manager, large firms	0.0	2.7	0.8	4.5	0.2	5.0	0.6	6.1	0.6	1.9
Employer, small firms	0.0	0.3	0.0	1.0	0.0	1.8	0.0	3.0	0.0	0.2
Manager, small firms	0.0	1.3	0.0	1.9	0.2	1.4	0.0	3.2	0.4	1.5
Professional self-employed	0.0	0.0	0.0	0.2	0.0	0.2	0.0	0.7	0.0	0.2
Professional employee	1.3	0.8	1.9	1.4	4.1	3.2	4.3	2.0	4.9	3.6
Nonmanual intermediate	0.3	1.3	2.1	2.1	2.3	3.2	3.7	3.0	5.9	6.2
Nonmanual foreman	0.3	1.6	0.6	1.2	0.2	1.6	0.2	3.9	1.3	2.1
Nonmanual junior	11.8	11.3	15.3	10.5	14.8	7.7	16.2	8.4	17.6	13.4
Professional service	1.3	0.8	1.2	1.0	1.1	1.1	1.5	0.4	1.1	0.8
Manual foreman	2.4	4.6	0.8	6.4	1.4	6.6	1.5	8.0	2.3	5.7
Skilled manual	23.6	22.0	27.6	21.6	36.0	26.4	37.2	24.0	32.9	30.8
Semiskilled manual	42.9	34.0	28.2	22.9	21.6	19.1	20.3	16.5	18.3	16.4
Unskilled	2.1	4.3	5.2	4.5	4.3	2.3	3.2	1.1	3.8	2.6
Own account worker	0.0	0.8	0.0	1.4	0.0	4.1	0.0	4.6	0.2	0.9
Farmer, employer, manager	0.3	0.5	0.0	0.2	0.7	0.2	0.4	0.7	0.2	0.6
Farmer, own account	0.0	0.0	0.0	0.4	0.0	0.0	0.4	0.4	0.6	0.6
Agricultural worker	8.6	5.4	9.1	6.4	8.2	3.0	5.8	1.5	3.4	2.1
Armed forces	0.5	0.0	3.9	2.3	2.3	0.2	0.7	0.4	0.6	0.9
No information	4.6	8.0	3.3	9.9	2.5	12.5	4.3	11.9	6.0	9.5
Total	100.0		100.0		100.0		100.0		100.0	
Total number	373		485		439		538		529	
Correlation between first and 1975 occupation (r)*	.64		.56		.47		.45		.68	

*Significant at 0.1 percent level.

Source: National Training Survey data tapes.

Second, for each separate cohort, they show the extent of net mobility
among SEGs, found by examining the pairs of distributions separately
for each of the five cohorts. Third, again for each separate cohort, the
correlation (r) between first occupation and 1975 occupation indicates
the stability or otherwise in the distribution of occupations held by
individuals over time. The correlations between the first and 1975
occupations are based on the detailed KOS classification, with occupational status in both years defined by 1975 hourly earnings in the
occupation (Metcalf and Nickell 1982).

The first occupations held by male entrants have been heavily
concentrated in skilled manual and semiskilled manual occupations.
Two-thirds of the 1930 cohort found their first employment in occupations covered by these two SEGs and even in 1970 over half of the
entering cohort were initially employed there. But within this concentration there has been a major change. The share finding their first job

in a semiskilled manual occupation fell by over half between 1930 and 1970, while the proportion initially entering a skilled manual occupation rose by nearly half over the period. The changing occupational and industrial composition in the whole economy is mirrored by the declining trend in the proportion whose first occupation was agricultural worker, down from 8.6 percent in 1930 to 3.4 percent in 1970, and the rising proportion initially employed in junior nonmanual occupations, up from 11.8 percent in 1930 to 17.6 percent in 1970. In each successive cohort a higher fraction has entered the labor market with some educational qualification. One consequence of this is the substantial rise in the proportions who find their first employment as professional employees and nonmanual intermediates. Many university and qualified upper secondary school graduates would enter such occupations.

The occupational mobility experienced over time by each cohort shows quite a clear pattern. As the cohort ages and gains experience in the labor market, the proportions in the two foreman SEGs rises sharply and this is accompanied by falls in the proportions in the corresponding lower SEGs, nonmanual junior, skilled manual, semi-skilled manual, unskilled manual, and agricultural worker. Indeed the drop in the skilled manual SEG is very similar to the increase in the manual foreman SEG. One other example of experience-related mobility is also straightforward. Thus the proportions who initially enter as managers in large and small firms, respectively, are minute, but as each cohort gains experience the shares rise substantially. As each cohort ages, the share of professional employees decreases, perhaps to feed the manager category.

The changes in the distribution over time for each cohort show rather little variation according to year of entry into the labor force. There is no strong evidence that those who entered in 1930 and, who have therefore accumulated the most work experience, had improved their SEG distribution by 1975 any more than those who entered in 1940, 1950, and 1960. *This strongly suggests that upward occupational mobility occurs in the first third of an individual's working life,* irrespective of the varying cyclical levels in overall employment and changes over time in the basic occupational structure.

In all cohorts, the correlation across individuals is positive and significant between the entry occupational status of members of each cohort and that status in 1975. *It seems clear that the occupation a British male first enters is the best predictor of the occupation where he ends up.*

The labor market experience of corresponding female cohorts shows some remarkably strong trends (Table 6.8). First, female cohorts from later years have been far more likely than males to enter into intermediate rather than skilled nonmanual jobs and skilled manual rather than semiskilled or unskilled manual jobs. This reflects the changing composition of occupations in the economy, the growth of educational

Table 6.8 First Occupation and 1975 Occupation, Females, by Year of Entry to Labor Market and Social Class, Great Britain, 1930-1975

	Year of labor market entry								
	1930		1940		1950		1960		1970	
	Social class									
	1930	1975	1940	1975	1950	1975	1960	1975	1970	1975
	(percentage distribution)									
Professional	0.0	0.0	0.0	0.0	0.0	0.0	0.0	0.0	0.0	0.0
Intermediate	1.0	4.0	4.0	6.0	9.0	13.0	9.0	14.0	12.0	16.0
Skilled nonmanual	14.0	11.0	7.0	5.0	10.0	8.0	11.0	9.0	7.0	8.0
Skilled manual	20.0	23.0	42.0	39.0	45.0	37.0	53.0	41.0	54.0	46.0
Semiskilled manual	55.0	44.0	40.0	36.0	32.0	27.0	25.0	26.0	23.0	25.0
Unskilled	8.0	14.0	4.0	8.0	1.0	8.0	1.0	5.0	1.0	1.0
No information	2.0	5.0	3.0	6.0	2.0	7.0	2.0	5.0	3.0	4.0
Total	100.0		100.0		100.0		100.0		100.0	
Total number	284		653		574		649		566	
Correlation between first and 1975 occupation (r)*	.64		.65		.65		.60		.70	

*Significant at 0.1 percent level.

Source: National Training Survey data tapes.

qualifications, and, possibly, an easing over time in the way employers classify jobs.

Second, as each female cohort ages, it appears that skilled nonmanuals feed the intermediate group. There is also a rise by 1975 in the proportion in each cohort classified as unskilled which presumably reflects the difficulty many mature women entrants have in carving out any subsequent career for themselves. The importance of a woman's first occupation on later status is very apparent. For example, 55 percent of the 1930s cohort entered as semiskilled manual workers and 44 percent of this cohort were still in this category in 1975. Similar proportions hold for the 1960 cohort, but for the skilled manual class. If there were real mobility in the female labor market there would be no reason for the 1930 cohort to have virtually the reverse distribution between skilled and semiskilled manual workers by 1975 to that of the 1960 cohort.

Third, *the key role played by the first occupation is indeed confirmed from the correlations.* In each cohort there is a strong positive association between the status of the first occupation entered and where the woman ended up in 1975. These correlations are even higher than the corresponding results for men. Except for entrants in 1960, the later the year of entry, the higher was the correlation, as might be expected since there were fewer years for career development.

IMPACT OF EARLY JOB-CHANGING ON LATER OCCUPATIONAL STATUS

The segmented market hypothesis emphasizes how initial employment experience might feed into subsequent achievements. The spirit of the segmented labor market is that an individual who begins in the "secondary labor market" and changes jobs frequently in the early years is likely to end up in a worse job later, perhaps because he or she has taken on the "unstable" attributes associated with the occupation even though the individual may not possess them inherently. In conflict with this view, not one single correlation coefficient between amount of turnover in the first occupation and where the individual ended up in 1975 is significant. There is no (raw) relationship. This is in line with the findings of Cherry (1976) who considered the first decade of labor market experience of young men in the 1946 birth cohort. While individuals who changed jobs frequently had more personal problems than their more stable peers, there was no evidence that their labor market experience was inferior.

IMPACT OF INITIAL UNEMPLOYMENT SPELL ON LATER LABOR MARKET STATUS

The NTS survey data show all unemployment spells with a duration longer than three months. This permits us to examine whether a prolonged spell of unemployment on labor market entry is associated with future occupational status and later unemployment experience. The male sample has been split into those unemployed for three months or above on entering the labor market and those who found employment with less than three months of unemployment, including no unemployment. Only 77 individuals out of the five male cohort samples of 2,364 had an initial spell of unemployment of three months or more, somewhat limiting the validity of this exercise.

The association between initial unemployment and future occupational status, using social class categories because of the small number of observations, indicates for each cohort that an initial spell of unemployment has no lasting effect on social class position. Combining all cohorts, exactly the same proportion, 43 percent, of those initially either employed or unemployed was in the professional, intermediate, and skilled nonmanual social class categories in 1975, leaving 57 percent in the three manual categories in both the employed and unemployed groups. If an initial spell of three months or more of unemployment had a strong association with later occupational status, proportionately more such individuals should be found in the lower social class categories in 1975 than those with less than three months of initial unemployment. Females have similar results to males: there appears to be no association between having an initial spell of unemployment and subsequent social class, either for the sample as a whole or individual cohorts.

An initial spell of unemployment may influence not only subsequent employment but also subsequent unemployment. Essentially the question is whether a prolonged spell of unemployment on entry to the labor force casts a lifelong shadow such that the individual is more prone to later unemployment. Our data do not, however, permit conclusions about the impact on later unemployment records of above average numbers of short spells (under three months) of early unemployment or of periods of withdrawal from the labor force. Nor can we measure the impact of all types of early unemployment on the cumulative amounts and types of unemployment over the working life.

The evidence from our data is rather striking and, in general, is very different between men and women. Calculating the mean number of spells of unemployment (of durations of three months or more) in 1965–75 by year of entry and initial unemployment position, we find that initial unemployment among males is strongly associated with subsequent unemployment. Males who were unemployed for three months or more on entry had, on average, three times as many such spells of unemployment in the 1965–75 decade as those who found an initial job with less than three months of unemployment or no unemployment. By contrast, none of the females who were unemployed for three months or more on entering in 1930, 1940, or 1950 had any similar spell of unemployment in the 1965–75 years; many of the most vulnerable may already have left the labor force. This pattern was overturned for a younger group, the 1960 cohort, in which those going to employment with less than three months or no unemployment had one-fifth of the number of unemployment spells in 1965–75 as those who were initially unemployed for three months or more. Men in all cohorts suffered, on average, over twice as many 1965–75 spells of unemployment as women.

None of this proves that among men initial unemployment causes subsequent unemployment. It may simply be that men at risk are unemployment-prone both on entry and later. The large discrepancy in subsequent unemployment experience between those initially unemployed for three months or more and those who were not does, however, seem to justify concern over high levels of youth unemployment and rising proportions of young men with longer spells of unemployment.

Summary

- The qualifications held by school-leavers have risen substantially since World War II. For example, 20 years ago only one in four school-leavers had any GCE "O" or "A" Level qualifications but now that proportion is one in two.
- The decision to remain in the education system is dominated by economic factors. These costs and benefits include starting pay, lifetime earnings profiles and maintenance grants.

- Two-thirds of British workers have no vocational qualifications and one-third of boys and girls enter occupations with no training at all. For males, craft apprenticeships are concentrated in engineering and for women, in hairdressing. Various initiatives to improve the apprenticeship system have not come to much but the *New Training Initiative* may be more successful. The new year-long Youth Training Scheme for unemployed school-leavers should also be instrumental in raising the skill level among youth.
- Despite the rise in average qualification level, the mix of first jobs held by school-leavers has changed little in the postwar period. Two-fifths of females go into clerical jobs and a similar proportion of males go into apprenticeships.
- Young black and brown workers have an inferior occupational structure to white youth.
- Employment prospects of young people vary across geographical area. If the region is one of relatively high deficient demand or if the local labor market provides few unskilled and semiskilled jobs, the prospects tend to be bleaker than in areas with opposite characteristics.
- There is no strong pattern in the characteristics of youth-intensive industries, but there is a hint that the six most teenage-intensive industries for males do have many of the characteristics associated with the so-called secondary segment of the labor market. Compared with the all industry averages, they have, in general, lower collective bargaining coverage, higher turnover rates, smaller plants and firms, lower output per employee and more part-time workers.
- Although the earnings of young male manual workers relative to adult male manual workers rose by some 15 points between 1949 and 1979, there is no evidence that the earnings of manual or nonmanual youth of either sex have risen relative to corresponding adult earnings since the mid-1970s. This suggests that rising teenage earnings have not been the major reason for the explosive growth of youth unemployment in the last decade.
- Longitudinal analysis suggests that upward occupational mobility occurs in the first third of an individual's working life. For any given cohort, there is also a high positive correlation between the level of the first job entered by each individual and the level the individual ends up at.
- Among men, individuals who have a spell of unemployment of at least three months duration on entering the labor market are more prone than other men to subsequent spells of unemployment. But initial unemployment on leaving school does not appear to be associated with subsequent occupational status.

References: Great Britain

Arman, D. 1981. "Male Youth Labour Force Participation in England and Wales 1971." MA (Econ.) dissertation. University of Kent, Canterbury, mimeo., November.

Ashton, D., and Maguire, M. 1982. *Youth in the Labour Market.* Department of Employment. London: Her Majesty's Stationery Office (HMSO).

Barber, A. 1981. *Labour Force Information from the National Dwelling and Housing Survey.* Research Paper no.17. London: Department of Employment.

Booth, C. 1980. *Education and Training in England: Some Problems from a Government Perspective.* Occasional Paper no.61. Columbus, Ohio: The National Center for Research in Vocational Education.

Cherry, N. 1976. "Persistent Job Changing—Is It a Problem?" *Journal of Occupational Psychology,* vol.49.

DE (Department of Employment). 1950–82. *Gazette.* London: HMSO, monthly.

_____. 1969. "Employment Changes in Certain Less Skilled Occupations, 1961–66." *Gazette,* April.

_____. 1971–82. *New Earnings Survey.* London: HMSO, annual.

_____. 1972–82. *Time Rates of Wages and Hours.* London: HMSO, annual.

_____. 1978a. *Strikes in Britain.* Manpower Research Paper 15. London: HMSO.

_____. 1978b. *The Role of Immigrants in the Labour Market.* Unit for Manpower Studies. London: HMSO.

_____. 1980a. "Learning the Job: Apprenticeship and Training in Manufacturing Industries." *Gazette,* September.

_____. 1980b. "First Off—16-Year-Olds Entering Employment in 1978." *Gazette,* December.

_____. 1981. *A New Training Initiative: A Programme for Action.* Cmnd. 8455. London: HMSO.

_____. 1982a. "First Employment of Young People." *Gazette,* March.

DES (Department of Education and Science). 1962–82. *Statistics of Education.* London: HMSO, annual.

_____. 1980a. *Education for 16–19 Year-Olds.* London: HMSO.

DI (Department of Industry). 1971. *Business Monitor PA 1002.* Report on the Census of Production, Summary Tables. London: HMSO.

Dolphin, A. 1981. "The Demand for Higher Education." Department of Employment *Gazette,* July.

EC (European Communities). 1977. *Working Conditions in the Community in 1975.* Luxembourg: Eurostat.

Freeman, R.B. 1981. *The Changing Economic Value of Higher Education in Developed Economies: A Report to the O.E.C.D.* Working Paper no.820. Cambridge, Mass.: National Bureau of Economic Research.

Layard, R. 1982a. "Youth Unemployment in Britain and the U.S. Compared." In Freeman, R.B. and Wise, D.A., eds. *The Youth Labor Market Problem: Its Nature, Causes, and Consequences.* Chicago, Ill.: University of Chicago Press.

_____. 1982b. *Youth Employment and Training.* Centre for Labour Economics, London School of Economics, mimeo.

Makcham, P. 1980. *Youth Unemployment.* Department of Employment. Research Paper no.10. London: HMSO.

Mayhew, K., and Rosewell, B. 1978. "Immigrants and Occupational Crowding in Great Britain." *Oxford Bulletin of Statistics,* August.

_____. 1979. "Labour Market Segmentation in Britain." *Oxford Bulletin of Statistics,* May.

Metcalf, D. 1981. *Low Pay, Occupational Mobility and Minimum Wage Policy in Britain.* Washington, D.C.: American Enterprise Institute.

_____. 1982. *Alternatives to Unemployment: An Examination of Special Employment Measures in Great Britain.* London: Policy Studies Institute.

Metcalf, D., and Nickell, S. 1982. "Occupational Mobility in Great Britain." In Ehrenberg, R., ed. *Research in Labor Economics,* vol.5. Greenwich, Conn.: JAI Press.

MSC (Manpower Services Commission). 1975. *Vocational Preparation for Young People.* London: MSC.

_____. 1978a. *Review of Youth Opportunities Programme.* Special Programmes Division. London: MSC.

_____. 1978b. *Young People and Work.* Manpower Studies no.19781. London: HMSO.

————. 1981a. *Manpower Review 1981*. London: MSC.

————. 1981b. *Corporate Plan*. London: MSC.

————. 1981c. *Review of Services for the Unemployed*. London: MSC.

————. 1981d. *A New Training Initiative*. Consultative Document. London: MSC.

NCB (National Children's Bureau). Longitudinal Survey, forthcoming.

O'Keefe, D.J. 1975. "Some Economic Aspects of Raising the School Leaving Age in England and Wales in 1947." *Economic History Review,* August.

OPCS (Office of Population Censuses and Surveys). 1975. *1971 Census of Population. Economic Activity,* Part II. London: HMSO.

Pissarides, C. 1979. *Staying-On at School in England and Wales—and Why 9 Percent of the Age Group Did Not.* Centre for Labour Economics, London School of Economics, Discussion Paper no.63, November.

Pliatzky, L. 1980. *Report on Non-Departmental Public Bodies.* Cmnd.7797. London: HMSO.

Prais, S. 1981. "Vocational Qualifications of the Labour Force in Britain and Germany." *National Institute Economic Review,* August.

Reubens, B.G.: Harrisson, J.A.C.; and Rupp, K. 1981. *The Youth Labor Force 1945–1995: A Cross-National Analysis.* Totowa, N.J.: Allanheld, Osmun.

Smith, D.J. 1977. *Racial Disadvantage in Britain.* London: Pelican (for PEP).

————. 1981. *Unemployment and Racial Minorities.* Report no.594. London: Policy Studies Institute.

Wray, J.V.C. 1957. "Trade Unions and Young Workers in Great Britain." *International Labour Review,* April.

Chapter 7

Youth Employment in Japan

Shun'ichiro Umetani and
Beatrice G. Reubens

The overall employment situation in Japan has changed roughly in proportion to the rate of economic growth in the postwar period. As the growth of real GNP entered the two-digit range in the 1960s, the balance between the demand and the supply of labor turned from a surplus to a shortage; following the oil shock of 1973 the shortage eased. Accordingly, the job opening/job applicant ratio for all ages, which is estimated by the public employment exchange offices, rose from almost two applicants per vacancy in 1960 to parity in 1964; this was the first time in the postwar period. It then climbed to a still higher point by 1973, just under two jobs per applicant. In subsequent years, the ratio declined, slipping well below one vacancy per applicant, but increasing slightly after 1978 (ML 1960–82).

Compared to adult or all workers, the situation of young people has been especially favorable. Since 1964, Japanese youth, especially teenage school graduates, have had little trouble in locating a job. This situation has persisted through the past two decades, even when the general demand for labor fell. The job opening/job applicant ratio for new school graduates gives evidence of the strength of the demand for youth relative to its supply. In every year from 1964 to 1981, at least three jobs were listed for each junior high school entrant to the labor force and in six of the years there were five or six jobs per applicant. For new high school graduates, the elevated level lasted from 1965 to 1975, but even in 1980 there were almost two jobs per applicant (ML 1960–82). While college and university graduates have not been so much in demand, they had fairly good prospects until the mid-1970s brought several years of slack demand, picking up again in the 1980s. At each educational level, the demand for new female graduates has been weaker than for males.

Opening applicant ratios for youth under 19, excluding new school entrants, exceed those of other age groups. The ratio rose from 0.7 in

1960 to 2.5 in 1964 to 5.1 in 1970. Though it declined after 1974, it remained at the 1964 level through 1981. Among young adults (20–24), on the other hand, the ratios were lower and showed less range, with a high of 1.3 in 1970 and a low of 0.7 in 1960. All other prime age-groups, up to 50 years old, had higher ratios than young adults in the boom years and usually slightly lower ratios in the other years. Above age 50, the ratios were decidedly inferior to those of all younger groups and almost always showed more applicants than jobs (ML 1960–82).

To the foregoing account of youth's advantage in the labor market should be added recent changes in youth unemployment rates and ratios. Unemployment rates of teenagers, usually very low and only fractionally higher than those of adults, began to rise very rapidly in the mid-1970s, touching 6.8 percent for males in 1978 and again in 1981, as the rate for 40–54 year old men reached only 1.7 percent. While the young adult male rate also increased more than those of most adult age groups, it did not exceed 3.8 percent. Among females, the teenage and adult rates grew strongly, but presumably withdrawal from the labor force restrained the advance (OPM 1956–82). Most observers see no structural change in the composition of unemployment, attributing the elevated rates more to longer duration of job search by youth than to a higher incidence of joblessness. Among youth, job-changers are more likely than new entrants to experience unemployment.

The phenomenal increase in the demand for labor after 1958 and its subsequent leveling off interacted with demographic change and the rise in educational enrollment rates of youth. Due to the postwar boom there was an expansion of the youth population toward the middle of the 1960s, but since then the rate of increase of the youth population has been declining with some fluctuations. The postwar growth in educational enrollments caused a drop in the proportion of an age cohort which has entered employment, although this has leveled off in the past few years.

Rising school attendance rates combined with demographic factors caused a severe shortage after 1960 in the supply of new junior high school graduates, called "golden eggs" by employers. Firms shifted to recruiting senior high school graduates, many of whom preferred white collar to the blue collar jobs they often were offered. The greatly increased number of college graduates has strained their labor market, causing many to take jobs that do not require a college education and some to refrain from work (Umetani 1977; Kato 1978). Changes in the absolute and relative numbers of youth at the several educational levels resulted in a compression of the differentials in starting wages between junior high school graduates and other educational levels, between college graduates and senior high school graduates, and between youth and adults; a slight reversal set in about 1975 (Umetani 1977; Freeman 1981; Nikkeiren 1980, p.26).

Future job prospects for young people will be shaped, on the one hand, by the known demographic trends which foretell a small supply of youth and an aging of the Japanese population and labor force. On the other hand, there is great uncertainty about the rate of economic growth, the employment effects of further technological change, and related factors on the demand side. Overlaying all of the developments will be the behavior of employers. Will they, on grounds of economic rationality or for other reasons, continue to favor the hiring of inexperienced young people straight from school? Or will they, also on grounds of economic rationality, alter their behavior to respond to new external conditions, as Shimada and Nishikawa (1979) suggest? These alternative possibilities in regard to levels of employment may also affect the composition and characteristics of youth employment, a subject to which we now turn, first providing some background information.

Educational System and Its Outputs

Compulsory education is provided from ages 6 to 15 in primary schools (six years) and junior high school (three years) and in particular departments of special schools for the blind, deaf, and otherwise handicapped. Postcompulsory education consists of three-year senior high schools, two or three-year junior colleges, four-year colleges and universities, and postgraduate studies. Also included in higher education are higher technical schools which admit junior high school graduates and provide training for five years. Beyond primary school, passage to the next educational level requires satisfactory completion of the prior stage, and an acceptable score on admission tests.

From an early age, competition is keen to attend those schools which have good records in gaining admission to the select schools at the next level. Direct connections exist between attendance at particular schools and universities and recruitment after graduation by the most highly regarded firms. Due to the highly demanding and competitive nature of Japanese education, intensive after-school and weekend classes and coaching begin early for those seeking admission to the more prestigious schools and universities (EPA 1980, p.158). Few teenage youth simultaneously have full-time school programs and hold paid jobs during the academic session, although some may work after school hours in family enterprises. University students engage in tutoring and other jobs, mostly in vacation periods (Kato 1978, p.47). A small proportion of youth combine work with specialized kinds of education or training, and a large share of the dwindling number of junior high school graduates who go directly to jobs obtain a high school diploma in night or correspondence courses or company schools (Kato 1978).

Private institutions play an important role, especially in higher education. As of 1980, 72 percent of the universities and colleges, mainly attended by males, 84 percent of the junior colleges, chiefly enrolling females, and 24 percent of the high schools were private institutions. National universities not only have much lower fees, but also greater prestige and more limited access than private universities; students at national universities constituted 17.3 percent of the total in 1965, dropping to 13.3 percent by 1975, with a slight recovery thereafter (EPA 1980, p.164).

The first nine years of formal education emphasize basic literacy and good citizenship. Senior high school divides into an academic curriculum and vocational curricula in such fields as industry, agriculture, fishery, business, nursing, and home economics. The selection of vocational courses in the rural areas may be limited. In 1980, over two-thirds of senior high school students were in the academic course, designed mainly for entrance to higher education; this proportion had risen over the years. Parental education, occupation, and income, together with geographic area, have been found to be highly correlated with students' subject choices (Bowman et al. 1970).

Enrollment rates at all levels of postcompulsory education have increased greatly during the postwar period. In 1955, just over half of those leaving compulsory education went on directly, mostly to senior high schools, but by 1980 the proportion had risen to 94 percent, with girls 2 percentage points ahead of boys. Before the 1970s, the reverse situation had prevailed for the two sexes. Virtually all who enter senior high school complete the course, usually at 18; the share in part-time courses has declined steadily (ME 1979a, p.91). Thus, this level of education is now the social norm for young people, with little variation according to socioeconomic class, parental education and occupation, or place of residence. In 1980, the standard deviation for the 47 prefectures in the percentage of both sexes proceeding from junior high school to higher levels of education was only 1.9 and represented a reduction compared to the period before 1975 (ME 1976a, pp.21–26). Prefectural differences were attributed to dissimilarities in the degree of urbanization, per capita income, and distances to major industrial-urban centers (Bowman et al. 1970).

The rate of transfer from senior high schools to higher education rose sharply from 1955 when it was 18 percent; only a small proportion combined college or university with a job. Twenty years later a peak transfer rate of 34.2 percent was reached, dropping to 31.9 percent by 1980 (ME 1981a). Inclusion of high school graduates of earlier years who finally passed their examinations or obtained admission to a selected university swells the proportion of the age group enrolled in higher education; in 1975, for example, a third of new university students and 10 percent of new junior college students were high school graduates of earlier years (ME 1976a, p.38). In addition, many high school graduates proceed to full-time special training and miscellaneous schools. Since 1976, the proportion entering such postsecondary education has offset the drop in the transfer rate to colleges and universities (EPA 1980, p.166). In all, about 50 percent of 18 year-olds continued their education in 1979.

Curriculum choice in senior high school has a decisive influence on additional education. In 1980, 42.2 percent of those completing the academic curriculum and 63.0 percent from special preparatory courses gained entrance to college and universities, while 24.6 and 18.3 percent, respectively, went on to special training schools. Much lower transfer rates were shown by graduates from vocational curricula. Averaging 9.6 percent for entrance to colleges and universities and 11.0 percent for special schools, only the two vocational curricula dominated by females, nursing and home economics, had transfer rates considerably above the overall vocational averages.

Increasing polarization of the sexes in higher education ensued even as the female rate of transfer began to exceed the male rate. Enrollments in junior colleges became increasingly female over the years, reaching over 90 percent in 1979. While junior colleges grew more rapidly than universities, they now have only about one-fifth as many students. On the other hand, the female share in university enrollments rose from 13.7 percent in 1960 to a mere 21.2 percent in 1979 (EPA 1980a). Thus, females are overrepresented in one type of higher education and underrepresented in the other.

Geographical differences in the rate of transfer from senior high school to advanced education diminished, with a standard deviation of 6.6 percent in 1980 among the 47 prefectures; Hiroshima had the highest transfer rate (42.3 percent) and Okinawa the lowest (19.1 percent). One cause of the convergence was the great decline in the transfer rate from high schools to universities in the largest cities; from 61.5 and 52.3 percent, respectively, in Tokyo and Osaka in 1975, the rates fell to 53.0 and 46.2 percent in 1979 (EPA 1980).

The drive for higher education continued in the face of a high cost to the family and diminishing returns to graduates. In 1979, 5.5 percent of total family expenditure went to children's education, chiefly for higher education (EPA 1980). As evidence that returns to higher education had declined, the Economic Planning Administration cited the rising proportion of graduates in blue and gray collar jobs, the fiercer competition for managerial posts, a dwindling income differential compared to high school graduates, and the length of time needed to recoup the costs of education and foregone earnings (EPA 1980, pp.159–62). Unlike the other educational levels, higher education has a dropout rate of over 10 percent (Kato 1978).

The phenomenal increase in educational attainment in the past 30 years has resulted in a sudden and wide educational gap between the generations and a much higher average level of education for youth entering employment (Table 7.1). The striking feature is that the number joining the labor force immediately after completing compulsory education has been decreasing rapidly, while the total joining after completing higher education has increased at an equally high rate; consequently, in 1980 twice as many of the new youth labor force had some higher education as had compulsory education only. All of these apparent

Table 7.1　Flows from Education into Employment, by Educational Level, Both Sexes, Japan, 1955-1980

	JHS	SHS	JC	C/U	Total new grad-uates[a]	Total employ-ment[b]	Employed new graduates as a share of total employment
			(000)				(percentage)
1955	634	332	14	70	1,050	41,119	2.5
1960	633	567	18	100	1,318	44,610	2.9
1965	549	690	35	135	1,409	47,480	2.9
1970	214	803	80	188	1,291	50,940	2.5
1975	63	577	103	233	984	52,230	1.8
1980	44	581	129	285	1,039	55,360	1.8
males	28	276	10	224	538	33,940	1.5
females	17	305	118	62	502	21,420	2.3
		Annual rate of change (percentage)					
1955-60	0.0	11.3	5.2	7.4	4.7	1.6	
1960-65	-2.8	4.0	14.2	6.2	1.3	1.3	
1965-70	-17.2	3.1	18.0	6.9	-1.7	1.4	
1970-75	-21.7	-6.4	5.2	4.4	-5.3	0.5	
1975-80	-6.9	0.1	4.6	4.1	1.1	1.2	
		(percentage distribution)					
1955	60.4	31.6	1.3	6.7	100.0		
1970	16.6	62.2	6.2	14.6	100.0		
1980	4.2	55.9	12.4	27.4	100.0		
males	5.2	51.3	1.9	41.6	100.0		
females	3.4	60.8	23.5	12.4	100.0		

[a]Employed as of June after graduation the previous March-April. Includes small number of entrants from technical college. Includes self-employed and family workers. Excludes entrants from postgraduate studies. Excludes employed who also continued education. [b]Includes self-employed and family workers.

Note: JHS: through junior high school; SHS: senior high school; JC: junior college; C/U: college and university.

Source: Entrants to employment: ME 1981a, pp.142,146,156,158; Labor Force: OPM 1956-82.

advances have, however, been accompanied by complaints about the quality of education and the performance of students as well as by dissatisfied students (Kato 1978; ME 1972a). Nevertheless, the educational system, especially through senior high school, inculcates and supports the qualities sought by employers, including a commitment to hard work.

Training System

Apart from the vocational courses in high schools, occupational skills are taught in special training and miscellaneous schools which the Ministry of Education licenses but controls less tightly than regular schools. The government offers low interest loans and tax exemption to the special schools which are run almost entirely by private profit-seeking organizations (Kato 1978, pp.37–41). Providing various types of occupational skills, in addition to courses in personal hobbies or cultural interests, these schools are important in vocational training and in some cases offer the major systematic means of training for such occupations as beautician, barber, typist, and technician jobs in the health, welfare and education fields. In 1976, the special training schools were divided into advanced and ordinary courses; the former are more important for vocational training and are obliged to comply with certain legal requirements. In 1980, there were 391,605 persons enrolled in postsecondary skill courses; they were mostly youth who had chosen such courses as an alternative to college or university (EPA 1980, pp.164–66).

Outside of schools, young people can obtain occupational training in public or semipublic vocational training centers or on the job. Managed either by local governments or public organizations commissioned by the central government, the public vocational training system offers a variety of training programs, geared to different types and levels of occupational skills and target groups. Semipublic vocational training is operated by nongovernmental bodies which are "authorized" by a government agency as capable of providing training equal in quality to that available in public institutions. Government provides some financial and other assistance to the sponsoring bodies.

The basic program in the public vocational training system teaches elementary occupational skills and knowledge, mainly to new junior and senior high school graduates, and facilitates achievement of skilled worker status after a few years' work experience. Thse courses primarily teach traditional craft skills that are taught under apprenticeship in other countries; few courses are offered in such rapidly developing industrial fields as microelectronics. Senior high school graduates have been a rising proportion of total entrants, reflecting the decreasing number of junior high school graduates entering the labor market, but the latter still are the large majority. Among trainees in the public nonbasic courses, 37 percent were 24 years old or younger in 1975, although these courses are not particularly designed for youth. Employers also are authorized and subsidized to offer training under the public system and small firms primarily participate.

All of the occupational skill training of youth in regular and special schools and in the public system is inadequate for employers' needs, both in number of places and types of training (Umetani 1980a). Many Japanese employers, especially the large companies, are willing to offer new recruits from school a considerable amount of informal on-the-job training and somewhat less formal training. It has been suggested that

> relatively rapid adoption of foreign technology and production methods probably has made employers even more motivated to develop work forces at their own cost, to fit their own specifications. If this is the case, the training is more the employer's task than the society's [Umetani 1980a, p.12].

A special feature of Japanese training is the development of a cohesive workforce which is deeply loyal and committed both to the parent company and the individual establishment. Under this aspect of training, such measures as QC (quality control circle) are training programs not only to establish a statistical technique of quality control, but also a more subtle way to develop a closeknit loyal work group (Ouchi 1982, Appendix Two).

Institutional Background

Vocational Guidance and Placement. The Employment Security Law of 1947 provides three modes of vocational guidance and placement for new school graduates. Under the first plan, the employment service, called public employment security office (PESO), has primary responsibility, working in cooperation with the schools. This system applies to 90 percent of junior high schools and less than 5 percent of senior high schools (Takeshi 1979). The second alternative permits the school principals or heads of colleges and universities to share part of the duties of PESO. Over three-fifths of the senior high schools and all remaining junior high schools are in this system which is currently the most common method for all school-leaver job placement and guidance at the high school level. In the third method, covering a third of the senior high schools and most colleges and universities, school principals and similar officials in higher education conduct a free placement service in agreement with the Ministry of Labor. Senior high schools tend to choose the latter two modes if many of their graduating students will be entering the labor force (Takeshi 1979).

Career guidance in the senior high schools varies considerably among schools, but most typically is left to the home room teacher. Each high school also has a chief guidance officer, an appointed regular teacher who is usually male and without prior training in guidance and who holds the guidance post for about three years, a brief term which "negatively affects both professionalization of this post and development of career guidance" (Izumi 1980). The provision of information about educational options and specific business firms that are recruiting is fairly well-developed in most schools, but information on occupations is only beginning to be produced and distributed by specialized groups. The success of individual guidance to students and parents often is measured by the proportion of students who gain admission to "famous universities or top-ranking companies" (Izumi 1980). Follow-up activity is undertaken by about 60 percent of the high schools and usually consists only of a mail questionnaire sent soon after graduation.

Job placement activities for new graduates are successful. In 1980, the schools and PESO placed 75 percent of new school graduates, a far higher proportion than official agencies claim in regard to other jobseekers (ML 1981a). Because employers generally compete with each other for the new crop of March graduates, many young people have jobs prearranged months before the final term ends. The competition has in fact been so keen that official rules have been laid down about how early recruitment may begin in the schools and universities. At the beginning of each fiscal year, PESO asks employers for information one year ahead of their recruitment plans for new school graduates. Coordinating these data with information about the number and type of pupils expected to seek jobs, PESO may advise employers to revise their recruitment plans. Employers notify job openings to PESO and the schools as much as nine months before graduation (Reubens 1977, pp.165–66). Large employers often contact the placement service of universities directly or students may arrange their own visits. University placement offices issue a formal letter of introduction to confirm the application of the student for employment and some send their staff to individual companies to solicit jobs for students.

Protective Social Legislation. Working conditions in the private sector are regulated by the Labor Standards Law of 1947. Employment is prohibited for youth under 15 as is employment of 15–18 year-olds in designated dangerous jobs and specific jobs, such as in bars. Legal restrictions seem to be a minor problem in youth employment, since the great majority of young people currently take their first job after age 18.

The standard work week consists of six full days of eight hours a day; extended hours of work are at overtime rates of at least one-and-a-quarter times the hourly rate. A five-day week through the month has been fully adopted in firms with 30 or more employees for only 24 percent of all industrial workers and 37 percent of workers in manufacturing (Hanami 1982, p.5). The larger the firm, the more likely it is to have a regular five-day week, but in 1977 only 42 percent of workers in firms with 1,000 or more employees normally worked no more than five days each week (JIL 1979a). The Labor Standards Law provides for six paid vacation days a year after one year of continuous employment and a daily attendance rate of 80 percent or higher. One additional paid day is provided for each year of service after the first year up to 20 days per year. Many firms offer additional time (JIL 1979a). However, only 19.6 percent of workers surveyed in 1977 used up more than 90 percent of their permitted vacation time (Hanami 1982, p.5). Protective measures on women's hours and maternity leave are said to raise the costs of employing women appreciably above those for men with equal qualifications and may partly account for the labor market discrimination against women (Umetani 1975).

Job security is not legally regulated and is only somewhat protected by the Civil Code or courts (Cole 1979; Suwa 1979). It is, nevertheless, well established for certain groups. Rapid economic growth has reinforced a commitment to continuous employment, called "permanent" or "lifetime employment," for key or core workers in large firms, with smaller firms attempting to maintain the principle in many cases. Although most collective bargaining agreements, which are typically vague and general, do not have provisions on job security or layoffs, unions are concerned about job security (Furuya 1980). When the need for layoffs occurs, management usually chooses the least skilled middle-aged and older workers, provided that the union agrees. All parties, however, favor mechanisms other than layoff or dismissal to adjust labor supply (Rohlen 1979; Cole 1979; Shimada 1980).

Wage Regulation. While wage levels are largely left to negotiation between labor and management, the Minimum Wage Law of 1959 provided for a floor to be set by each prefecture; this was accomplished by the 1970s. Minimum wages may also be set for specific industries and such regulations now apply to just over half of all employed persons, thereby exempting them from the prefectural minimum wage. Regional minima tend to be set at about 40 percent of the national average wage, while industry minima come close to 50 percent of each industry's average wage and have resulted in increased pay for 5 to 30 percent of the workers in the industries covered (Matsuda 1980). In keeping with the original function of the minimum wage to restrain the starting salary of new school graduates, the minimum is about the same as the starting wage for junior high school graduates (Okochi 1974, pp.148–50; JIL 1979a, p.20). More relevant to the present time, the minimum is about 30 percent lower than the average starting wage for senior high school graduates in most of the 47 prefectures. The workers mainly affected by the annual revision of the minimum wage are temporary or peripheral workers, often persons who had retired, and unskilled workers, typically employed in small enterprises (ML 1977, Table 7). Trade unions and management are increasingly concerned about the general impact of the minimum wage on wage negotiations, but discussions of possible adverse employment effects have centered on older workers rather than youth whose starting wage rates are set by vigorous market competition (Nikkeiren 1980, pp.21–22, 26).

Trade Unions. Overall, almost one-third of Japanese wage and salary workers are organized in trade unions. Enterprise trade unions, in which manual and nonmanual "regular" employees belong to the same union, are the predominant form in Japan, accounting for over 93 percent of all trade unions. Therefore, age and sex differences in trade union membership arise only from higher rates of trade union membership in the larger firms, in the industrial sector, and among male workers (ML 1975–82). Thse factors tend to make the rate of organization among male youth slightly higher than among male adults and the organization rate for female youth lower than for similar males. Trade union bargaining, usually conducted separately in each company, establishes conditions for each firm and is reinforced by the Spring Offensive of the trade union federations which make a concerted drive to obtain a share of business profits for workers.

Government Programs for Youth and Financial Assistance. A government subsidiary, the Japan Scholarship Foundation, provides financial aid to needy students. In 1976, it distributed $160 million among 330,000 students (Kato 1978, p.46). Like all workers, youth can obtain unemployment benefits that range from 60 to 80 percent of the daily wage, with a duration of up to one year; benefit duration can be extended for those undertaking a public vocational training course. Special government loans to young people who take public vocational training courses were initiated in 1972. Various employment promotion benefits and programs also are open to young unemployed persons. Welfare measures assist the substantial number of young people who take jobs at some distance from their homes, mostly in the large urban centers, supplementing similar efforts by the employers who actively recruited the young people.

Youth Employment

The rapidity of economic change in Japan requires frequent updating of employment data and trends. As recently as the 1950s, junior high school graduates, then the largest category of new graduates entering employment, were mostly recruited from farm families by small firms operating in local labor markets in which "recruitment had been regulated by territorial and kinship relations" (Okochi 1974, p.147). This compartmentalization resulted in large wage differentials for young workers in the same industry or region. With the breakdown of traditional labor market systems during the late 1950s and 1960s came greater standardization of wages and working conditions, a shift of new, more highly educated entrants into larger enterprises, and reductions of earnings differentials according to educational level, sex, age, size of enterprise, length of work experience and whether in blue or white collar jobs (Okochi 1974, pp.141–62).

Moreover, the diversity of actual youth experience should be distinguished from the stereotypical model of the operation of the Japanese labor market. In the model, Japanese companies are characterized by highly internalized labor markets with few ports of entry and exit. Workers are recruited straight from school and stay with the company until retirement age, thus making it economically feasible for companies to invest in general and firm-specific training, including a heavy emphasis on organizational training that instills devotion among workers to a company's interests and fortunes. Enterprise trade unions are part of the scheme. In return, the company offers "permanent" or "lifetime" employment; general and specific training; an age-seniority wage structure that rises with age and peaks at retirement age; substantial wage bonuses; non-cash fringe benefits; a wide range of goods and services, such as housing; and a variable payment at or after retirement which is mandatory at 55–60 years of age.

Seen as a process, the model implies continuous training over the worker's lifetime according to the skill needs of the firm. The career path in terms of occupation, qualification, and certification is under-developed and vague and the course of career development is not always predictable. Length of service in the firm is assumed to correlate with individual productivity, and thus determines wage levels, subject to individual performance rating. This system enables the employer to transfer workers from one job to another and even to shift them to a lower grade of work without reducing their pay or prospects. Male youth straight from school are prized under this system because of their relatively low wage and non-wage costs to firms, their geographic and occupational mobility, their adaptability to rapid technological change, their trainability in the specific ways of a particular company, the length of the potential working life in the company, and, when drawn from the farms, their docility (Okochi et al. 1974, pp.142, 145, 434).

The model is most viable in periods when the supply of inexperienced youth is ample, economic growth is sustained, and fluctuations in employment are minimal. It is most suited to government employment or companies that are sufficiently large and financially secure to offer extensive training and stable employment. Under these circumstances, it can be argued that the system reflects economic rationality and need not be interpreted in terms of the cultural factors cited by Western observers (Yashiro 1979; Shimada 1980). At any time, however, the model overemphasizes the experience of males, "permanent regular" employees, managerial levels, large companies, and the public sector, and the technologically advanced firms. Youth and adults actually have exhibited far more mobility and diversity of employment patterns than is compatible with the stereotype of lifetime employment.

Only a portion of male Japanese youth and few females have entered or remained in firms which operate under the employment model described above. The small proportion of youth who become self-employed, family workers, or homeworkers would not be included in the system. Many small companies, important in the employment of new school-leavers, are not able to maintain all of the features of the lifetime employment system. Companies of all sizes hire workers with previous job experience when a sufficient number of suitable new graduates are unavailable. These midcareer or halfway workers usually, but not always, have a lower wage scale and less job security than their contemporaries who joined the company as new graduates. Even the larger companies have not extended the system to all employees. To achieve flexibility in the number and allocation of workers, companies hire temporary, casual, and part-time workers who are not given the same pay, conditions, or security as regular employees. Employees of small subcontractors who supply components to the parent company also tend to be excluded, as are the workers of outside contract companies which provide guard, cleaning, trucking, and similar services.

Recent developments, especially since the oil crisis of 1973, have limited the coverage and viability of the "lifetime" employment system (EPA 1980a, pp.166–67). Among these are the change from a high to a stable growth rate, the aging of the work force, and the rising average educational attainment of entering cohorts of the labor force. Over a longer period, higher turnover rates and the advance in the wages of youth relative to adults have been deterrents. An increasing number of firms, modifying their basic policies of manpower development and personnel management, are eliminating general skills from internal training, excluding the unskilled workforce from internal training for organization skills, and reducing the number of employees in the internal labor market. Simultaneously, the system is being weakened by the increased importance workers attach to home and leisure as living standards improve.

With or without a commitment to lifetime employment, many employers have looked to new school-leavers as the main source of "permanent regular" employees, viewing this recruitment as their major hiring activity of the year. But as far back as the 1950s, when the number of new graduates seeking jobs exceeded employers' demand, new graduates did not constitute the majority of new hires, although they may have been a majority of new regular employees. From 1960 to 1970 new graduates and leavers shrank from 41.7 percent to 22.6 percent of all persons hired in a year. This was due to demographic factors, the enlarged number of new hires resulting from economic growth, and rising job-changing rates. After 1973 the proportion rose slightly (Table 7.2). Among teenagers, new school graduates and leavers have outnumbered other occupationally inexperienced and experienced new hires; in every age group, the proportion of graduates among new hires is higher in the larger than the smaller firms (ML 1964–82). Firms

Table 7.2   Newly Hired Employees, by Prior Work Experience, Age, and Sex,
            Japan, 1965-1980

	1965	1970	1975	1978	1980
Males, All Ages					
Total number of new hires[a] (000)	1,890	2,576	1,681	1,588	1,857
Of which: (percentage distribution)					
New school graduates and leavers	30.3	20.6	21.9	22.7	23.2
Others without work experience	35.0	9.2	10.2	14.0	13.1
With work experience	34.7	70.2	67.9	63.3	63.7
Females, All Ages					
Total number of new hires[a] (000)	1,718	2,341	1,681	1,604	1,955
Of which: (percentage distribution)					
New school graduates and leavers	34.9	24.7	24.7	26.7	24.8
Others without work experience	30.9	32.6	32.4	35.4	37.0
With work experience	34.3	42.7	42.9	37.9	38.1
Males, 15-19 years					
Total number of new hires[a] (000)	687	623	319	302	345
Of which: (percentage distribution)					
New school graduates and leavers	69.2	61.3	66.8	68.9	67.4
Others without work experience	11.0	9.9	12.3	15.7	14.7
With work experience	19.8	28.7	20.9	15.4	17.9
Females, 15-19 years					
Total number of new hires[a] (000)	783	736	417	371	421
Of which: (percentage distribution)					
New school graduates and leavers	73.0	67.5	74.7	78.7	77.8
Others without work experience	10.4	9.0	9.7	10.8	10.4
With work experience	16.5	23.5	15.6	10.5	11.7
Males, 20-24 years					
Total number of new hires[a] (000)	471	751	440	408	499
Of which: (percentage distribution)					
New school graduates and leavers	20.7	19.9	32.5	34.5	36.6
Others without work experience	13.9	11.6	13.5	15.6	15.4
With work experience	65.3	68.4	54.0	49.9	48.1
Females, 20-24 years					
Total number of new hires[a] (000)	393	663	452	433	472
Of which: (percentage distribution)					
New school graduates and leavers	6.9	12.3	22.6	32.6	32.6
Others without work experience	31.7	23.8	23.6	22.7	22.3
With work experience	61.3	64.0	53.8	44.7	45.1

[a]Includes public enterprises and excludes construction industry.

Source: ML 1964-82.

located away from the major metropolises have been more able to hire new school graduates, other things equal. Some urban companies have, however, spent large sums to recruit new school graduates, at times failing to utilize other sources of available labor (Glazer 1976, pp.868–69).

Continuing interest in new graduates also is demonstrated in recent surveys of employers' intentions and views which vary by size of enterprise, industry, occupation, and area; differences also appear among companies of the same size and industry. An inquiry in 1979 among companies with 30 or more employees on the criteria used in hiring indicated why new graduates were so competitive with workers having job experience. While skills readily useful in jobs were about equally desired with general intelligence and adaptability in recruiting for professional and technical work and in production and manual work, general intelligence and adaptability were the most desired traits for clerical and sales workers. For all four job categories, the emphasis on intelligence and adaptability rose as the size of firm increased, and in the largest firms (1,000 or more), general intelligence and adaptability far exceeded all other qualities desired for each type of work (ML 1980a). Another inquiry showed that those employing high school graduates valued "cooperativeness" above all else, while employers of college graduates look for the ability to make judgments beneficial to the company. Trainability in the specific ways of the company and potential company loyalty rate very high, especially in the large companies. This factor sustains preference for young people without work experience despite the greatly reduced flow of youth from rural areas, the wage premium to inexperienced young workers compared to their contemporaries with work experience, and the decided preference in other industrialized countries for youth with work experience.

For their part, many young people are more concerned about the size and prestige of the company which offers them their initial job than about entering any specific occupation. Perhaps the recent views of youth which put great weight on the content of jobs and little on the size and reputation of the enterprise are a harbinger of change (EPA 1980, pp.193–94), but altered behavior is not yet widely visible.

Educational attainment, sex, and the size of firm of the first job have a pervasive and long-lasting influence on the work life of young people: the nature of their first and later jobs, the training they receive, their initial and life-time earnings, their promotion opportunities, their job-changing patterns, and other aspects of employment. In addition, holding constant educational level, sex, and size of firm, there are differences among youth according to the size and type of community in which the youth first seek work, with some equalizing influence due to youth migration. Finally, the very small group of non-Japanese youth, mainly Koreans and Chinese, "are not likely to be given equal opportunities. They are, in spite of their Japanese citizenship, more or less discriminated against by employers as well as by the general public"

(Kato 1978, p.9). Much the same might be said about the native minority group (*burakumin*).

STATUS OF GAINFULLY OCCUPIED YOUTH

Youth, described as "mainly working" to distinguish them from the small number who hold jobs while attending school or caring for a household, were overwhelmingly ordinary employees in agricultural and nonagricultural industries in 1979. Under 1 percent of male teenagers (15–19) were self-employed, 7.2 percent were family workers, and a negligible number were home workers (OPM 1980a, Table 11). Among young adult males (20–24), the respective percentages were 1.6, 7.0, and 0. Some 8.9 percent of teenage and 5.2 percent of young adult males were temporary or day laborers; the survey defined the former as "those who are employed under contract of employment for at least one month but less than one year" and day laborer as "those employed on a daily basis or under contract for less than one month," including those who actually worked over one month under such a contract. Many Japanese analysts believe that the official statistics understate temporary and day workers. Among teenage females, the proportion of self-employed, family, home, temporary, and day workers was even lower than among corresponding males, with ordinary employees accounting for 93.5 percent of all who were "mainly working." Young adult females also were more apt to be ordinary employees, 91.2 percent, than their male counterparts, 86.1 percent. Over the years, the proportion of wage and salary employees has risen. Japan's youth are now only marginally different from those in other industrialized countries.

OCCUPATIONS

Although occupations in the Western sense are not strongly embedded in Japanese consciousness or management practices (Cole 1979, p.220; Glazer, pp.880–81), the national statistical agencies publish occupational data on new graduates that clearly indicate the influence of educational level and sex on first jobs. Details on the particular courses elected in high school and college and the prestige of the institution as well as specifics about the first jobs would reveal further impacts of type of education on job characteristics.

In 1980, the 44,000 entrants to work from junior high school, of whom 63 percent were males, overwhelmingly were operatives and laborers in production industries, with a somewhat higher representation of males, as had been the case in 1975 (Table 7.3). Females compensated by their higher relative representation in service occupations. Compared to the distribution of junior high school graduates in 1956–60, when over 600,000 entered work each year, by 1980 farming, forestry and fishing had dropped from one-fifth of junior high school graduates' jobs

Table 7.3 Occupations of Employed New Graduates, by Educational Level and Sex, Japan, 1980

	Junior high school[a]		Senior high school		Junior college		College and university	
	Males	Females	Males	Females	Males	Females	Males	Females
			(percentage distribution)					
Professional, technical	*	*	3.0	3.8	32.7	35.2	35.8	55.9
Managers, officials	*	*	*	*	0.9	0.1	0.7	0.2
Clerical and related	0.4	1.7	11.0	54.3	19.8	58.5	33.0	36.6
Sales	6.2	4.6	17.6	17.9	14.6	3.7	25.8	5.1
Farming, fishing, mining	5.8	0.9	3.4	0.3	5.2	0.1	0.3	*
Transportation and communications	1.5	0.4	4.7	0.6	2.2	0.1	0.3	*
Crafts, operatives, laborers	70.4	61.9	46.8	12.9	15.5	0.4	0.4	*
Protective services	0.7	0.1	5.9	0.3	1.4	0.1	1.5	0.2
Services	11.3	27.1	5.8	9.2	5.0	1.2	1.1	1.3
Other	3.8	3.3	1.7	0.7	2.7	0.7	0.9	0.5

*Less than 0.5 percent.
[a]1975 data.

Note: Includes those also attending school.

Source: OPM 1965-82; ME 1980a.

to less than 5 percent, and the share of sales workers also declined, while the share of production and service workers rose over the quarter century.

Senior high school graduates, who had an excess of females among the 580,000 entering work in 1980, exhibited greater sex disparity as well as the expected superiority over junior high school graduates attributable to increased age and added education (Table 7.3). Senior high school males were most heavily represented in production, while the females' largest share was in clerical work. Compared to 15 year-old junior high school graduates, the 18 year-olds were much more concentrated in gray or white collar jobs and even had a small representation in the professional and technical category, although for males the share had been higher in 1956-60 when fewer entered work. Other changes in first jobs for the senior high school graduates over the quarter of a century were the drop in the share of farming and clerical jobs (males) and the rise of production, transport (males), and service workers (males).

The use of high school graduates as blue collar workers, especially in the companies introducing new technologies, was a major development accompanying economic expansion and rising educational levels. This trend was not always what the youth expected or desired from their added years of schooling (NIVR 1974), since they were aware of the status gulf between blue and white collar workers, the limited promotion ladder for the former, the inferior employment conditions, and the difficulty of moving from blue to white collar status (Okochi 1974, p.413).

Junior college graduates of 1980, some 129,000, were overwhelmingly female. Among the females, over 35 percent of those with jobs in June 1980 were in professional and technical occupations and 58.5 percent entered clerical occupations (Table 7.3). This concentration marks a striking departure from the distribution for senior high school females. Compared to 1956–60, when the 15,000 junior college graduates were more evenly divided by sex, the occupational distribution for females had changed only slightly. Male junior college graduates showed a relative drop in clerical positions and a rise in sales, services, and blue collar jobs; the small increase in numbers of male graduates over the quarter century was accompanied by a slight occupational downgrading, similar to the trend for male university graduates.

Of the 285,000 graduates of colleges and universities in jobs shortly after receiving their degrees, almost 80 percent were males. Female graduates had a higher proportion in professional and technical and a lower proportion in clerical occupations than female junior college graduates; for males, the share in all white collar occupations was larger for senior than junior college graduates (Table 7.3). A considerably higher proportion of female than male college or university graduates was in professional and technical jobs. However, this reflects both selectivity and restriction: the small number of women university graduates, the lower proportion entering work, and the confinement of most such women to a narrow range of low-ranked jobs such as primary school teachers. A survey by the Women's Studies Society of Japan indicated that the few female graduates of the prestigious, male dominated national universities have a high employment rate, as do graduates of such institutions as the Kobe Women's College of Pharmacy where specialized training, career guidance, and good job prospects prevail. All in all, however, women are not competitive with similar men for most of the jobs entered by graduates of colleges and universities.

The importance of clerical jobs for male college graduates is related to personnel practices in Japanese enterprises and the occupational definitions used in official statistics. Newly recruited graduates, except perhaps for engineering and scientific graduates, are assigned to routine office work and are regarded as clerical workers unless and until they are promoted to a supervisory position, such as the chief of a section or a division. In large organizations, public or private, it usually takes ten or more years to reach that level in the organizational hierarchy. Meanwhile, staff with higher education will be given more important assignments and a higher level of pay than noncollege office workers, although the latter are also classified as clerical workers in the official statistics. Since 1973 there has been a deficiency of line managerial positions into which college graduates might be promoted and some enterprises have created staff specialist posts to absorb part of the surplus, a not entirely satisfactory solution. Other graduates face even less promising outcomes as the competition for supervisory posts stiffens (EPA 1980, pp.181–88).

The work history of a university graduate at a major bank, while not entirely typical, illustrates a career progression unfamiliar in other countries. Recruited as a bank clerk, the young man spent the first two years as a bank teller and clerk and the next two years in the customer's department. The personnel division then selected him to study for two years at the Japan Economic Research Center, with a subsequent year at the National Bureau for Economic Research in the United States. After returning to Japan, he served as a bank researcher for two years and then was elected deputy chairman of the enterprise trade union, holding office for two years. There followed two years as an officer in the bank loan department. He was currently president of the enterprise trade union, with an office on the premises. In two years he expected to return to a high bank position. Other work histories such as his lead one to predict promotion to the bank's board of directors.

Over a fourth of college and university graduates take first jobs that do not require that level of education and do not offer the prospects of advancement implicit in the work history described above. For example, some male university graduates are becoming stock clerks in supermarkets in hopes of rising to manager or becoming self-employed. More pronounced among males, nontraditional initial employment has become prominent among higher education graduates as their numbers and share of new entrants soared in the past quarter of a century; however, the 1956–60 distributions already showed a substantial share of such jobs for new graduates.

The differences observed in occupational distribution by educational level also are reflected in 1975 cross-sectional census data for single years of age. For males, each increased year of age fron 15 to 24 causes the proportion in the white collar occupational categories to rise and the share in each blue collar category to fall. Females show more irregularity and greater change with a year of age, but the general trend is the same (OPM 1978b, Tables 4, and 8).

SIZE OF ENTERPRISE

The importance of very small enterprises has not altered much in the postwar period despite the shift out of agriculture which is dispropor-tionately composed of small units. When nonagricultural industries only are considered, 41.6 percent of all private firms' employment was in establishments with fewer than ten workers in 1957, dropping in the 1960s, and rising again to 34.9 percent in 1978, according to the census of establishments. Firms with 1,000 or more employees had 7.2 percent of the total in 1966, but only 5.3 percent by 1978, due to the absolute and relative growth of services which tend to be organized in smaller units than manufacturing (ML 1965–82; JLB Feb. 1980, p.2).

Within each industry, a substantial gap exists between the larger and smaller enterprises in productivity and working conditions. Despite a considerable narrowing of wage differentials by size of firm since the 1960s, hours, prospects for training, promotion, and long-run earnings, company welfare benefits, and social status are superior in the larger firms; moreover, the chance to become a master, which once was an attraction of very small firms, has diminished. In the smallest enterprises, under five workers, average earnings were found to be only 55.6 percent of those in firms with 500 workers or more, while the latter worked 2.6 days less per month on average (JLB April 1981, p.3). Equally telling is the gap between large and small firms in expenditure per capita on wages plus all fringe benefits. In 1975 firms with 100 to 499 employees spent less than three-fourths as much as firms with 5,000 or more employees, while those with 30–99 employees fell below the 65 percent mark (EPA 1980). It may be assumed that still smaller firms, not tallied, would show an even smaller proportion. The variation in firm expenditure meant that in 1977 95.7 percent of the largest enterprises (over 5,000 employees) had facilities for physical training, moving downward by size to only 26.9 percent of enterprises with 30–99 employees. Similar advantages for large firms applied to company reading rooms, cultural clubs, social work consultation and assistance, housing provision and purchase loans, employee stock ownership plans, medical and health facilities, and company restaurants (EPA 1980, p.168).

Because of these factors, the distribution of new graduates and young workers by size of enterprise provides an important measure of disparity within youth employment. At any given educational level and for each sex, new graduates are widely distributed among the various size classes, with a substantial proportion in the smallest reported size category, under 30 employees (Table 7.4). The variations in new entrants' working conditions within an educational level may thus be as great as between the averages for different educational levels. Higher proportions of junior high than senior high school new graduates are found in the smallest size class, while other data for senior high school and college-university graduates suggest that a larger share of the former might be found in the under-30-size class. It is important to qualify size of firm data by industry, since some young people deliberately choose small firms in the services in preference to larger manufacturing establishments.

The desire and success of employers in hiring new graduates has not been uniform by size of enterprise. In 1967, the largest enterprises had the highest success rate in hiring junior high school graduates, but in 1980 all rates were much the same, except for the 500–999 employee size which had a rate almost twice as high as the others (ML 1965–82). With regard to high school graduates, 65 percent of all firms reporting to the employment service in 1967 sought senior high school graduates, ranging from 85 percent of the firms in the largest size classes to 53 percent in the smallest. The largest firms also were more successful than any others in 1967, but in 1980, firms with 500–999 employees

Table 7.4   Employment of New School Graduates, by Size of Enterprise, Educational Level, and Sex, Japan, 1961-1980

	Number of employees in enterprise						
	1,000 and over	500- 999	300- 499	100- 299	30- 99	Under 30	Number of placements
	(percentage distribution)						
JHS males							
1961	20.6		30.2		34.9	14.2	163,717
1967	15.7	8.7	26.0		22.3	27.3	131,478
1971	20.6	9.1	9.5	18.6	17.6	24.7	74,468
1980	6.2	3.0	4.0	18.0	27.2	41.7	22,823
JHS females							
1961	39.6		29.4		19.8	11.3	165,934
1967	25.1	15.1	27.1		14.1	18.6	158,934
1971	24.5	17.7	10.9	18.0	12.3	16.6	91,187
1980	7.7	20.5	14.0	19.3	14.3	24.1	23,082
SHS males							
1961	30.1		34.5		28.4	7.0	147,127
1967	27.0	13.3	31.2		17.8	10.7	171,524
1971	32.7	15.2	13.5	17.9	13.5	7.3	141,446
1980	27.5	10.7	10.2	20.9	18.0	12.7	208,928
SHS females							
1961	25.3		32.0		30.8	11.9	169,058
1967	25.3	13.2	28.0		19.8	13.7	247,605
1971	29.1	13.9	13.5	18.7	14.7	10.1	225,605
1980	28.1	11.3	10.3	20.1	17.1	13.4	283,072
C/U both sexes							
1970	48.5		27.8	23.7	*	*	n.a.
1975	53.0		27.3	19.7	*	*	n.a.
1980	31.2		22.7	17.3	12.8	16.0	313,000
All new graduates							
1980 males	26.3		20.2	18.5	15.7	19.3[a]	408,600
1980 females	36.3		17.8	16.4	14.4	15.2[a]	466,600

*Data do not cover this size group.
[a] 5-29 employees.

Note: JHS: through junior high school; SHS: senior high school; C/U: junior college, technical college, and university.

Source: ML 1960-82; JLB March 1979, p.3; ML 1964-82.

filled almost 90 percent of their demand while enterprises with under 30 employees achieved only 35 percent (ML 1960-82).

Although large firms currently are disproportionately interested and successful in recruiting new school graduates, as Table 7.4 shows, many graduates still enter small firms. However, relatively fewer new entrants than youth of the same age and sex with work experience enter small

firms. In 1978, males aged 15–19 who had already worked were twice
as likely as new school graduates in the same age bracket to find jobs
in the smallest firms and only one-fourth as likely to be hired by the
largest size firms. Among teenage females, experienced workers' chances
of moving to one of the smallest firms was three times greater and
their chances of being accepted by one of the largest firms was less
than half as good as for new school graduates (ML 1964–82).

Unlike teenagers, among young adults those with work experience
outnumbered new entrants and the disparity in size of firm distribution
therefore was more serious. Five times as many experienced male
workers as new graduates entered the smallest firms and less than one-
third as many were taken on by the largest two sizes of firms. For
young adult females the gap was less marked, but experienced workers
were not even half as likely to be in the two largest size firms and
were one and a half times more likely to be in the smallest firms (ML
1964–82).

Whether these discrepancies are the result of discriminatory hiring
practices associated with the lifetime employment system or reflect
objective differences among the two groups of young people that make
one group more attractive to large employers, the outcome is that a
fairly large number of youth are disadvantaged through employment
in smaller firms.

TRAINING

There is a widespread belief that most Japanese workers receive considerable training in the enterprise, but this is not supported by data
on formal training by the firm. Moreover, an important element in
training is the inculcation of loyalty to a particular company, an activity
not usually associated with vocational training in other countries. Most
training appears to be informal on-the-job training and its extent and
character vary greatly among enterprises, according to the type of output,
worker, and the size of firm. The costs of on-the-job informal training
are usually so perfectly meshed into general costs of production that
even the most cost-conscious employers do not try to measure them,
although they behave as though these training effects can be achieved.
For example, large enterprises often do not subject new college graduate
recruits to performance evaluation in the first two or three years on
the ground that no matter what their attained educational level or job
assignment, they are basically "trainees." Japanese companies also
transfer new graduates, mostly those with higher education, from one
job to another at relatively short intervals, thus providing a type of
training. Blue and gray collar new recruits are less likely to have this
experience, but some do in the more advanced companies.

Measurement has been applied only to formal company training.
The amount is not impressive, compared, for example, to formal

apprenticeship training of youth in other countries. Size of firm is a critical factor in the proportion of Japanese firms offering formal training to young people. In 1980, when 87 percent of firms employing 30 or more workers trained new graduates and 50 percent trained job-changers, the range for new graduates was from 95 percent in firms with 1,000 or more employees down to 66 percent in firms with 30 to 99 employees, while the range for job-changers was from 71 to 28 percent (ML 1981a). In 1974, when firms with 5 to 29 workers had been included, 65 percent of firms trained new graduates and the range by size of firm was 87 to 15 percent. For other new hires, the 1974 figures were 26 percent overall, with a range by size of 62 to 5 percent (Shimada 1980, p.21). Clearly, fewer firms offer formal training to young people who have changed employers than to those who have come straight from school.

Among new graduates, employers favor training males over females and higher education over senior or junior high school graduates. In 1974, 70 percent of all firms trained new college and university graduates, two-thirds of firms trained high school graduates, and 55 percent trained junior high school graduates; the larger the size class, the higher the proportion of firms offering training. Larger firms, however, were slightly more prone to train senior high school than higher education graduates (Shimada 1980, p.21).

In spite of the large proportion of firms offering formal training, the proportion of all workers receiving training is fairly small. In 1976, only 24.2 percent of new graduates received training (Umetani 1980a, p.89). However, 1979 data show much higher proportions (ML 1981a, Table 2). Few other young workers receive training. The duration of formal internal training also is brief. In 1980, two-thirds of all firms (30 or more workers) offered new hires training lasting no more than ten days, and in a substantial portion of the firms, it was five days or less. Only 3.8 percent of firms had a duration of six months or more. The differences by size of firm were consistently in favor of the larger firms (Table 7.9). Estimates by private companies of expenditures on educational and vocational training, probably confined to formal programs, ran only to 2.1 percent of all labor costs in 1972 and 1975 and fell to 1.7 percent in 1978 (EPA 1980, p.170). Even the addition of the costs of informal training, a difficult task, would not raise the share of this activity to the level of other nonwage costs. Further investigations are required to establish the extent and type of formal and informal vocational training given to young people, by age, sex, industry, and previous work experience.

EARNINGS

Monthly earnings, the sum of various complex elements, are said to provide management with flexibility and control over labor costs, since only the basic wage is fixed (Sakurabayashi 1972). A basic contractual wage in which age, educational level, and length of service automatically establish a rate of regular pay from the time of hiring to retirement forms the heart of the system for regular permanent employees. Modifications of the basic wage may result from evaluations of individual productivity or ability. Special additions are made for supervisory or other functions, and skill allowances may be paid to qualified workers who do not hold positions that reward them with supplements. Incentive allowances and dirty or hazardous work allowances as well as supplements for good attendance are paid. Overtime pay and miscellaneous work allowances may swell the pay packet by as much as 15 percent.

The monthly wage also includes a series of allowances related to the cost of living, varying for individuals according to area of residence, number of dependents, type of housing, travel to work costs, and related factors. It has been said that the "cost of living approach is incompatible with the principle of competition and cannot be explained without referring to paternalism and enterprise loyalty" (Sano 1977, p.57). In addition to the basic monthly contractual wage, Japanese workers receive substantial bonuses twice a year, a form of deferred wage payment that varies within an enterprise according to the basic wage and other personal characteristics and among enterprises mainly according to the profitability of the previous period. The bonuses may equal three to four months' pay.

Total cash wage payments in 1975 divided 68.6 percent for regular pay, 5.4 percent for overtime, 25.1 percent for bonuses and 1.0 percent for other payments. The share of bonuses and overtime in the total declined consistently as the size of firm decreased (JLB Feb. 1977, p.6). Over and above cash wages and bonuses, Japanese workers receive a wide set of benefits, including legally required and non-obligatory benefits, all of which have an actual or imputed cash value. In 1965 and 1975, surveys placed these benefits at about 15 percent of total remuneration with variations by size of firm (JLB April 1978, p.6). In short, the advantages employees of large firms enjoy in basic earnings are enhanced by the superiority of such firms in regard to bonuses and other benefits as well.

One Japanese economist has said that the (complex) wage system

> is a shrewdly devised scheme of exploitation which can function only at the sacrifice of employees of subcontractors, women workers, and part-time or temporary workers, who can be regulated easily over business cycles [Sano 1977, p.55].

Others treat the wage system as useful and economically rational with outcomes that closely parallel the wage profiles of other countries where individual productivity and payment for the job rather than for personal characteristics are thought to predominate (Shimada 1980).

A two-tier wage structure exists for youth. New graduates and leavers and other occupationally inexperienced youth begin at a monthly wage which is fixed annually by each employer, usually outside of collective

Table 7.5   Relative Starting Salaries of New Graduates, by Educational Level and
Sex, Japan, 1955-1980

	Senior high school		College and university				
	Males	Females	Males	Females	JHS	SHS	C/U
	(ratio[a] to junior high school graduates)				(ratio[a] of males to females)		
1955	1.64	1.58	2.63	2.28	1.05	1.09	1.22
1960	1.38	1.31	2.21	2.24	1.06	1.12	1.04
1965	1.25	1.18	1.74	1.63	0.99	1.05	1.06
1970	1.19	1.14	1.54	1.33	1.03	1.08	1.20
1975	1.21	1.20	1.44	1.42	1.05	1.05	1.06
1980	1.14	1.21	1.41	1.49	1.10	1.05	1.05

[a]All industries.

Note: JHS: through junior high school; SHS: senior high school; C/U: junior college, technical college, and university.

Source: ML 1954-76, 1955-82.

bargaining negotiations. Varying by educational level and sex, the average wage of employers is publicized to youth completing school and their parents. Differences among companies according to industry, size of firm, location, and other factors result in a range of starting wages and salaries for each educational level, divided by sex.

A separate determination is made of the monthly wage for young people who have previously worked in another enterprise. Such "mid-career" employees often receive lower basic monthly wages, allowances, etc. than their counterparts of the same age, sex, and educational background. Mainly due to the general shortage of young workers and the formation of new firms, the amount of reduction in the wage of job-changers of all ages has been shrinking and among those under 30 the wage differential is now negligible (JPC 1982, Table C-15).

The gap in the average starting basic monthly wage of new graduates at different educational levels has narrowed for each sex over the years, notwithstanding a slight reverse movement after 1974 which Table 7.5 shows for females (OE 1980, p.16). Differences in average starting pay also arise from type of industry, size of firm, and geographical location. Average starting pay of graduates, adjusted for age, vary little by level of education, implying that the return to private investment in education, if any, is long deferred.

Surveys of leading Japanese corporations in 1979 revealed they offered a wide range of starting salaries to male university graduates entering clerical posts, from a low in a textile company to a high almost one-and-a-half times greater in a broadcasting company. Also, the starting salaries of 18 year-old senior high school graduates in oil, coal, broadcasting, telecommunications and service corporations exceeded or equaled the starting salaries of 22 year-old university graduates in other industries

(OE 1980, pp.11, 16). The official survey for 1979, however, showed a much smaller dispersion of average starting pay by industry and no overlap between male high school and college graduates (JLB Feb. 1980, p.3). A longitudinal follow-up of a cohort of male junior high school graduates found that four-and-a-half years after graduation, those who had gone straight to work earned more than those who entered work three years later, after graduation from senior high school. Females did not show this relationship, but the advantage of the better educated girls was slight (NIVR 1974).

Size of firm also influences starting pay. A series (1956–72) for male junior high school graduates in manufacturing indicates a 1956 starting wage in firms with 500 or more employees was a third more than in firms with 30–99 workers. By 1964, the initial wage was higher in small than large firms. Subsequently, the ratio fluctuated, but the scarcity of such youth again drove small manufacturing firms to offer higher wages (Galenson 1976, p.606). Data for all industries in 1971 and 1978 indicate that at each educational level and for each sex, except male junior high school graduates in 1978 and similar females in 1971, firms with 10–99 employees started graduates at slightly lower monthly contractual wages than firms with 1,000 or more employees. In 1978, the finance, insurance and real estate industry was notable for its better pay in the small than the large firms for senior high school graduates of each sex and female junior college graduates (ML 1955–82). Geographical differentials in average monthly starting pay for each sex in 1978 showed a range among the 47 prefectures of about 20,000 yen at each educational level (ML 1955–82).

Sex differences, while reduced over time, persist in starting salaries at the same educational level and partially reflect differences in specific educational preparation, divergent industrial distributions by sex and varying ability of industries to pay (Table 7.5). Residual sex differentials bear further examination as an aspect of employer discrimination against women, since the sex disparity in earnings increases as young females gain work experience. The earnings ratios of adult females to adult males are far lower than those of younger females compared to their male peers (Table 7.10). Furthermore, over the female worklife adverse effects are exerted by limited access to many occupations, inferior training and promotion possibilities, smaller seniority pay increases and other cash and non-cash benefits, and earlier retirement. Females also are disproportionately part-timers with earnings and other work disadvantages (JLB Nov. 1980, p.2).

Over time, the average earnings of teenage and young adult males have become compressed as earnings differentials due to education, age, industry, size of firm, years of service, and geographical location have eroded (Table 7.6). The earnings of male 18–19 year-olds in relation to 20–24 year-olds rose from 71.9 percent in 1958 to 82.5 percent in 1975. Similar females showed almost no trend (ML 1955–82).

Table 7.6 Monthly Earnings of Youth in Enterprises with 10-99 Employees Relative to Earnings of Youth in Enterprises with 1,000 or More Employees, by Educational Level, Age, and Sex, Japan, 1958-1980

	Males			Females		
	1958	1974	1980	1958	1974	1980
	(ratio)[a]					
JHS graduate						
Under 18	.78	.90	1.03	.79	.83	1.00
18-19	.79	.92	.97	.81	.84	1.01
20-24	.85	1.01	1.05	.71	.78	.88
SHS graduate						
18-19	.77	.90	.95	.71	.85	.92
20-24	.83	.98	.97	.71	.84	.88
JC graduate						
20-24	.80	.94	.97	n.a.	.88	.92
C/U graduate						
20-24	.80	.98	.96	n.a.	.88	.95

[a]Includes overtime. Excludes bonuses.

Note: JHS: through junior high school; SHS: senior high school; JC: junior college; C/U: college and university.

Source: ML 1955-82.

Earnings data for youth that show the distribution across income classes indicate substantial concentration of youth in a narrow earnings band. Among male teenagers (15-19), almost half reported annual earnings of 1.0-1.49 million yen in 1979 (OPM 1980a, Table 19). The range was from 5 percent who earned under half a million yen a year to 0.2 percent who earned 3.0 to 3.99 million yen; besides the general factors making for differences in earnings, variations among companies, individual variations in ability, status as self-employed or family worker and, some would say, luck affect the dispersion. Male young adults (20-24) show somewhat higher median earnings in 1979 than teenage males; 37 percent of young adults had the same annual earnings as the teenage mode, while 10 percent fell below that mode; over 70 percent of young adults were concentrated in two rather low earnings classes, 1.0-1.99 million yen (OPM 1980a, Table 19). A larger proportion of young adult males in manufacturing had high earnings than in services and wholesale and retail trade.

Starting wages by educational level and the earnings of youth (15-25) demonstrate significant relative improvement in the postwar period for younger, less well-educated males, due to demographic factors and shifts in the output of the various educational levels. Although the same factors affected young females, the demand for them by employers was not as strong and the female time trends are less marked. Educational decisions already show the effects of the wage compression among youth, but lifetime earnings differentials by educational level have not worsened sufficiently to make sharp inroads in higher education enrollment rates.

HOURS OF WORK

Long, though declining, weekly and yearly hours of work have characterized postwar Japan, due to the late and partial introduction of the five-day work week, very low absenteeism rates, few paid holidays plus workers who do not take all of their holidays and vacations, and a slow growth of part-time and part-year work. Japanese youth are accustomed to long work weeks and little differentiation from adults.

Youth in nonagricultural employment in 1978–79 typically worked 43 hours or more per week and mostly worked for 200 days or more a year. Teenage and young adult males both showed about 88 percent of those with 200 days of work in the year working 43 hours or more per week, while slightly lesser proportions had such long hours among the small minority who worked for less than 200 days. Teenage and young adult females were much the same; over three-quarters of those with 200 or more work days in the year, and 58 percent of teenage and 49 percent of young adult females in the small proportion working less than 200 days put in, on average, 43 hours or more per week. Relatively few youth worked under 35 hours a week. In the 200 days and over category, only 1.6 and 0.9 percent of teenage and young adult males and 1.9 and 2.5 percent of corresponding females were part-timers, while 4.3 and 8.6 percent of young males and 6.0 and 18.2 percent of young females who worked under 200 days a year were part-timers (OPM 1980a, Table 14).

Youth in agriculture, forestry, and fishing, less than 10 percent of the total, worked even longer hours. In keeping with the findings for all employees by size of establishment, it is likely that the average weekly hours of youth would decline as the size of firm rose and that hours would be especially long for those employed or self-employed in enterprises with fewer than ten persons (JIL 1979a, p.22).

JOB–CHANGING

The Japanese view of job-changing has economic, ethical and institutional elements that distinguish it from the attitudes and practices in other industrialized market economies. Contrasting the two approaches, a distinguished Japanese labor economist writes:

> The neoclassical theories seem to tell us that instantaneous inflow and outflow of any production factor in response to changed market situations

are desirable to keep the system efficient. . . . However, human capital theory . . . tells us that employers can be benefited most from longer service of employees once intra-firm on the job training systems have been developed . . . it can be said that the Japanese lifetime employment system is the most efficient method [Koshiro 1979].

In keeping with this approach, companies rarely recruit openly among the employees of other companies. Workers who have obtained jobs through personal recommendation, an important method, feel that leaving the job may dishonor their backer. Other pressures also lead to loyalty to the company and guilty feelings over leaving. However, where bankruptcy occurs or employment opportunities become scarce, or changes in sectoral employment distribution require changes, job-changing is accepted and encouraged and is regarded with concern only if the pay and other conditions of the job-changers deteriorate (ML 1963–82).

Specific factors have held down job-changing and separation rates, although, as Cole (1979) observes, European countries show rates of much the same magnitude, leaving the higher rates in the U.S. and Australia as exceptional. Among the factors in Japan are: the high proportion of relatively stable self-employed and family workers among the gainfully occupied, the lifetime employment system and its psychological influence beyond those fully included in such a system, and the form of organization of companies which facilitates intra-firm job-changing that might be inter-firm in other countries.

Although it is commonly believed that the rate of inter-firm job-changing by Japanese youth has accelerated in the 1960s, the triennial Employment Status Survey, which includes the self-employed and agriculture, indicates only a small rise for each sex up to 1979 from a fairly modest base in 1959 (Table 7.7A). Significantly, the peak was reached in the late 1960s, the period during which special concern was expressed; thereafter, the rate of youth job-changing slowed down, apparently in response to the oil crisis and a diminished rate of economic growth. Young adults had a higher rate of job-changing than teenagers for each sex and at each survey (OPM 1960–78, 1980a). Although data on separations offer only a rough guide to job-changing since some separated individuals fail to take new jobs or leave the labor force, they refer only to employees and hence give a more accurate idea of the level of job-changing (Table 7.7B). From 1963 to 1980, male teenagers had a higher separation rate than female teenagers or young adult males, except for two years when the young adults included 25–29 year-olds. The young adult female rate far exceeded that for young adult males because the female separation rate includes a high proportion of withdrawals from the labor force.

How have job-changers fared? In terms of the size of the enterprise, in 1970 about half of teenage inter-firm job-changers of both sexes moved to larger firms; over one-fourth moved to firms of the same

Table 7.7A Job-changers Within One Year, by Age and Sex, Japan, 1959-1979

	15 years and over		15-19 years		20-24 years	
	Males	Females	Males	Females	Males	Females

(job-changers[a] as percentage of total employed)[b]

	Males	Females	Males	Females	Males	Females
1959	2.5	1.9	4.6	4.4	n.a.	n.a.
1962	3.4	2.8	5.6	5.1	6.2	5.9
1965	3.5	2.9	5.9	4.9	6.4	6.4
1968	3.9	3.3	5.7	5.5	7.3	7.7
1971	3.8	3.5	4.7	4.3	7.1	8.2
1974	4.2	4.0	5.3	4.4	8.0	9.4
1977	2.9	2.8	4.1	3.6	6.1	6.7
1979	3.3	3.2	5.7	3.4	7.6	7.1

[a]Job-changer is one who changed enterprises during the year. [b]Total employed and job-changers include self-employed, family workers, homeworkers, mainly employed, and secondarily employed. Includes agriculture.

Source: OPM 1960-78 (1975, Historical Series, Tables 3 and 44; 1978, Tables 1 and 40). OPM 1980a, Tables 1 and 53.

Table 7.7B Annual Separation Rates, by Age and Sex, Japan, 1955-1980

	15 years and over		Under 20 years		20-24 years	
	Males	Females	Males	Females	Males	Females
	(percentages)[a]					
1955	18.0	30.0	n.a.	n.a.	n.a.	n.a.
1958	20.4	32.4	n.a.	n.a.	n.a.	n.a.
1960	30.0	42.0	n.a.	n.a.	n.a.	n.a.
1965	16.0	30.3	29.2	25.3	22.6	37.5
1968	15.9	29.9	30.0	24.7	24.5	39.7
1970	16.5	30.9	28.6	24.1	27.5	42.9
1973	14.7	27.4	23.0	18.0	22.6	40.6
1975	11.9	23.2	19.9	15.9	35.2[b]	52.3[b]
1978	10.7	20.2	21.0	16.2	14.0[b]	28.4[b]
1980	10.7	20.1	27.8	20.5	36.4[b]	45.7[b]

[a]Total number of employees separated in a year, voluntarily or involuntarily, as a percentage of total number of regular employees at the beginning of January or July. Data cover all industries 1955-60 and exclude construction 1965-80. [b]Includes 25-29 years old.

Source: 1955-60: ML 1951-82; 1965-80: ML 1964-82.

size and under one-fourth moved to smaller firms. About 46 percent of job-changers 20–34 years old of both sexes moved to larger firms, 30 percent to the same size and 24 percent to smaller firms. In 1980, the rate of upward mobility declined to 41 percent for teenagers and those 20–29 years old, while 31 percent of both age groups moved horizontally. Moves to smaller firms were made by 28 percent of teenagers and 20–29 year-old job-changers (ML 1964–82).

With respect to changes in earnings, teenagers have a better chance than those 20–29 years old to improve their position by an inter-firm move. In 1980, the pay of 39 percent of job-changing teenagers of both sexes increased by 10 percent or more, compared to about 33 percent of 20–29 year-olds. Half the job-changers in each age group had a wage change of less than 10 percent in either direction. Finally, 11 percent of teenagers and 17 percent of the 20–29 year-olds suffered a reduction in wages of 10 percent or more. Over the last few years, the proportion obtaining higher pay by inter-firm moves has declined; for example, in 1975, 46 percent of teenage and 36 percent of 20–29 year-old job-changers had been able to raise their pay by 10 percent or more (ML 1964–82).

Special studies of youth began in the 1960s. A survey of the experience of over two million junior and senior high school graduates in 1966–69 indicated that more than 25 percent had changed jobs during the first year out of school and over half had changed once or more within the first three years. Job-changing rates were inverse to the size of the firm, falling from 70 percent in firms with under five employees to 38 percent in firms with 1,000 or more (JLB May 1969, p.2; March 1970, pp.2–3).

Concerned by these findings, the Ministry of Labor sponsored a ten-year longitudinal follow-up of a sample of junior high school graduates from the classes of 1969, 1970, and 1971 (NIVR 1974). Of those who took jobs immediately, one-third felt that they had not made good choices because they had been given only one or two employers' names; 65 percent had been placed in jobs by PESO and the schools. During the first 18 months, 23 percent had left their first jobs and 40 percent of the separations occurred within the first six months; almost all were voluntary departures and one-third made the decision without consulting any other person. A majority of the separated took new jobs, with 17 percent of the males and 30 percent of the females remaining in the same occupations and skill level. The remaining 83 percent of males changed occupations, divided into 19 percent who were downgraded in skill level and 8 percent who were upgraded. About 70 percent of females who changed occupations contained 20 percent with downgraded, and the same share with upgraded skill levels. Over half of the entire male and 60 percent of the female sample expressed the view that they either might in future change employers or did not know whether they wished to remain in their present firm (NIVR 1974).

The survey conducted 42 months after the completion of junior high school determined that job satisfaction had declined progressively with the passage of time and that those who had remained with their original employers were most dissatisfied, chiefly because of wages (NIVR 1974). A year later the follow-up covered both junior and senior high school graduates who held jobs. When they were 20 years old, 45.7 percent of male junior high graduates had never changed jobs, 26.1 percent had changed once, 9.4 percent had changed twice, 7.3 percent had changed three times, and 11.6 percent had changed jobs four or more times. In the shorter period of 18 months, 82 percent of male senior high school graduates were in their initial jobs, 16.2 percent had one and 1.8 percent had two job changes (Adachi and Oneda 1977, Table 2).

Most job leaving up to age 20 had been voluntary (NIVR 1980a, p.73). Four-and-a-half years after leaving school, the average length of continuous service with the current employer for junior high graduates was 2.5 years for males and 2 years and 2 months for females. One-third of the females had been in their present job for less than a year, but a higher proportion of females than males had over four years of service. Senior high graduates appeared more stable, since for each sex the average length of service was 1.3 years at a time when only 1.5 years had elapsed since leaving school (NIVR 1974).

Decisions on leaving jobs in the first four-and-a-half or one-and-a-half years were not weighed for more than one month in advance in the majority of cases; 41.5 percent of junior and 32.1 percent of senior high graduates already had another job promised when they left an employer, and another 9.2 and 7.6 percent, respectively, had applied for jobs. Over 18 percent of junior and 24 percent of senior high graduates had not thought of their next job as they quit, while 6.2 and 13.2 percent, respectively, did not intend to seek a job, and 18.5 and 13.2 percent, respectively, had not applied but expected to seek work (Adachi and Oneda 1977, Table 4.6). Substantial proportions of the female junior high graduates who had worked during the first 30 months had no work experience in the next two years, reflecting marriage preparation in many cases (NIVR 1974). In addition, some girls changed jobs after they completed part-time senior high school and qualified for clerical and sales jobs.

Many had moved from their home areas, mostly in order to obtain work; during the four-and-a-half year period, 86 percent of the junior high school graduates had moved, of which three-fourths had left their home prefectures. For senior high school graduates, only 18 months had elapsed; 59 percent had moved, of which 82 percent went beyond their prefectures (NIVR 1974). This is an extraordinary rate of geographic transfer for young persons, resulting from the disparity between the residence of the youth and the location of the available jobs, together with highly organized efforts to bring the youth to the jobs.

Few junior high school graduates saw opportunities or benefits from intra-firm transfers, confirmed by the small size of the firms they had entered and the limited scope of their jobs. Senior high school graduates, questioned on their feelings about changing employers after 18 months, expressed great uncertainty and reluctance, but the two attitudes supposedly typically Japanese were not strongly voiced, namely, "I see merit in staying with one company for a long time" and "changing employers is not easy because of the close human relations in the present company" (NIVR 1974). Over three-fourths of the males, who were then mostly 19 years old, said they had decided on a lifetime job or were searching for such a job; three-fourths of the one-third who had decided on such a job felt it was connected to their present job. Females, on the contrary, showed almost two-thirds of junior and 44 percent of senior high school graduates as never having thought of a lifetime job (NIVR 1974). At age 26, over one-fourth of a small sample of male senior high graduates felt that their current jobs would be permanent until retirement (Watanabe and Yoshitani 1980).

Roughly eight or five years after entering work, male junior and senior high graduates reported 38 and 68 percent, respectively, still with their first employer. Those who had changed employers once over the period constituted 26 percent of male junior and 20 percent of senior high graduates, while 12 percent of male junior and 8 percent of senior high graduates registered two changes of employer; the remaining 23 percent of junior and 4 percent of senior high graduates showed three or more employers (NIVR 1980b, p.72). In clerical, sales, and production jobs, male senior high graduates have substantially longer job tenure than junior high graduates (NIVR 1980b, p.72). Occupational mobility and change of employer are associated, especially for junior high school graduates in blue collar service and clerical jobs. Service jobs show much shorter job tenure in the firm for male junior and senior high graduates alike than in any other major occupation (NIVR 1980b, p.72). Reflecting previously discussed advantages of jobs in large firms, length of job tenure is substantially greater in the public sector and large firms (100 or more employees in wholesale and retail trade, finance, insurance, real estate, and services, and 500 or more in other industries) (NIVR 1980b, p.66). The continuation of job-changing into the young adult years suggests that a certain portion of youth cannot find, or reject, the types of jobs and training that lead to the Japanese ideal of early attachment to a firm. Alternatively, such youth may lack the characteristics that are sought by the employers who offer these jobs. Much of the increased teenage unemployment of the 1970s may be due to job-changers.

Furthermore, the prolongation of education since 1969–71, the time of selecting the longitudinal cohort, may have increased the job-changing rates of senior high school graduates who now represent a larger share of the age group. In addition, job-changing may have been stimulated by the growth of service and similar jobs entered by teenagers since it is difficult to structure such jobs in the traditional style. Job-changing patterns of those with no more than a senior high school education may be another factor undermining employer preference for new school graduates. A new longitudinal cohort is needed to check on trends.

Comparisons of Youth and Adult Employment

The Japanese "employment system" and progression of "model wages" make it acceptable that some young and adult workers may be in exactly the same jobs, with the youth more productive, but the adults receiving considerably more pay. All youth have not, however, been content with this situation, nor can it be assured that the wage structure will be maintained intact. Such a wage system, together with the division of adults into pre-retirement and post-retirement workers at an earlier age than in other countries, has been distinctively Japanese.

STATUS OF GAINFULLY OCCUPIED

Employees have remained steady at about three-fourths of all gainfully occupied persons in nonagricultural industries since 1959. Including agriculture, employees have risen from under half of the total in 1959 to two-thirds in 1979. Thus, secular changes in the distribution of the total gainfully occupied are almost entirely attributable to the decline of agriculture's share. In nonagricultural industries, the only trends 1959–79 were a drop in the proportion of the self-employed without employees and a slight rise in the percent of the gainfully occupied who were corporation directors (OPM 1960–78; OPM 1980a).

Within this framework, age comparisons of status in 1979 are fairly straightforward. Whereas teenagers and young adults were overwhelmingly employees, prime age adults and the total exhibited a somewhat smaller share and adult females in particular had a lower proportion in employee status. Homeworkers also were a larger share of the adult female gainfully occupied than of teenage or young adults, but for males the category was unimportant for all age groups. Family workers constituted a fifth of the 40–44 year-old female group, much more than for young females or males 40–44 years-old. While female family workers tended to form a rising proportion of the gainfully occupied with age, the reverse occurred in the case of males. Temporary and day workers were less significant for adult males than for young adults or teenagers, but for females, adults were most likely to be in this category, due to a return to the labor force after a period of homemaking.

OCCUPATIONS

According to the 1975 census, a higher proportion of gainfully occupied adult (25 and over) than young males were in the following major occupational groups: professional and technical, managerial, transportation and communication, mining and farming, forestry and fishing

(OPM 1978b, Table 9). The opposite age relationship was shown for two broad categories: crafts workers, production process and nonfarm laborers, and service workers. Since almost three-fourths of teenage males, over half of young adult males, and two-fifths of adult males were in the two latter occupational groups, it appears that occupational upgrading of teenage males at present largely involves movement out of these occupations. While adult males exhibited considerably more balance among the occupational categories than teenagers, they were only marginally different from young adults.

Clerical workers were the single most important category for teenage and young adult women, with 40 and 47 percent of the totals in 1975, but for adult women the share fell to 17.5 percent, largely because agriculture rose to over one-fifth, in contrast to its insignificant role for the younger women. In three important categories, professional and technical, service workers, and crafts and production workers and nonfarm laborers, teenage and adult females showed much the same proportions. Young adult females, however, had a higher share in the first occupational group and a lower share in the other two. Overall, adult women have a less favorable occupational structure than young adult females due to reentry problems for those who have taken time out from work, including changes from employee to family worker or self-employed, and from manufacturing to agriculture or low level services. Adult women rarely obtain the type of job they previously held due to employer policy on age and marital status or the women's desire for part-time work and they usually do not make up for their lost years of work experience. Currently, an increasing proportion of young women, whose labor force participation rate is very high upon completion of their education, are continuing to work after marriage or the birth of a child. If this trend continues and employers respond by removing some of the barriers to female retention and advancement, future female youth-adult occupational comparisons may display less variability than at present.

SIZE OF ENTERPRISE

Gainfully occupied adults (35–44) had a different distribution by size of enterprise in 1979 than youth (15–24), controlling for educational level and sex (Table 7.8). Youth were less prone than adults to be in the smallest enterprises (1–9 persons). Except for junior high school graduates, youth also were more likely than adults to be in firms with 1,000 or more persons, but this did not carry over into government employment. The 1979 data imply that life-cycle changes involve net movement into smaller enterprises with less favorable conditions, but also may reflect occupational and employment status shifts with more complex effects.

Table 7.8   Gainfully Occupied, by Size of Enterprise, Educational Level, Age, and Sex, Japan, 1979

| | Number of persons in enterprise[a] | | | | | | |
	1–9	10–29	30–99	100–499	500–999	1,000 and over	Govern-ment
	(percentage distribution)						
Males							
All levels, all ages	35.1	12.0	11.5	11.7	3.5	16.6	9.6
JHS, all ages	50.0	14.0	11.6	8.8	2.0	9.5	4.1
15–24	44.2	21.1	13.8	10.5	1.9	7.6	0.9
35–44	46.0	14.9	12.4	10.4	2.4	10.5	3.4
SHS, all ages	30.0	11.8	11.8	12.7	3.9	19.9	9.9
15–24	23.1	13.0	13.1	16.5	4.5	22.2	7.6
35–44	30.2	11.3	11.5	12.5	4.0	21.2	9.3
JC, C/U, all ages	19.0	8.9	10.7	14.9	5.6	22.2	18.7
15–24	15.6	11.0	14.8	20.7	6.7	16.9	14.3
35–44	19.0	8.0	9.9	14.0	5.0	26.8	17.3
Females							
All levels, all ages	36.4	12.9	12.6	11.8	2.8	12.7	10.8
JHS, all ages	49.0	13.3	13.8	10.7	1.8	6.5	4.9
15–24	29.5	14.0	15.1	18.9	4.6	16.5	1.4
35–44	45.6	14.2	15.6	12.2	1.7	6.3	4.4
SHS, all ages	32.0	12.9	12.6	13.2	3.6	17.2	8.5
15–24	13.6	11.6	13.9	19.2	6.5	30.0	5.2
35–44	42.9	13.5	12.3	10.2	2.1	9.7	9.3
JC, C/U, all ages	18.4	12.1	9.4	10.7	3.1	14.6	31.7
15–24	13.6	11.6	13.9	19.2	6.5	30.0	5.2
35–44	24.3	11.8	7.7	7.0	2.2	7.3	39.7

[a]Persons whose main activity was work, including self-employed and family workers. Excludes persons mainly in school, household work, or other activity who also worked. Excludes persons without a job.

Note: JHS: through junior high school; SHS: senior high school; JC, C/U: junior college, technical college, college, and university.

Source: OPM 1980a, Table 9.

TRAINING

Adults receive much less formal training in the enterprise than young people, especially than new graduates; females are largely excluded from formal training. The proportion of employers offering formal training and the proportion of employees receiving training falls sharply as the category shifts from new graduates to other newly hired workers or the existing workforce; the age composition of the latter two groups is older than that of new graduates. Finally, the duration of the training given

Table 7.9 Duration of Formal Internal Training, by Type of Employee
and Size of Enterprise, Both Sexes, 15 Years and Over,
Japan, 1980

	Number of employees in enterprise				
	30 and over	30–99	100–499	500–999	1,000 and over
	Number of enterprises in sample				
	832	245	231	187	169
	(percentage distribution)				
New recruits					
5 days or less	43.4	53.5	48.4	42.4	38.4
5–10 days	23.6	21.4	26.1	26.6	19.9
10 days–1 month	15.8	13.9	11.2	18.3	17.0
1–3 months	8.5	5.3	7.9	6.6	11.4
3–6 months	5.0	2.7	4.3	3.8	6.9
6 months or longer	3.8	3.2	2.1	2.3	6.3
Total	100.0	100.0	100.0	100.0	100.0
Other workers					
5 days or less	74.1	78.7	77.1	74.6	70.4
5–10 days	9.7	11.4	11.4	9.7	8.1
10 days–1 month	5.4	4.8	4.9	5.7	5.7
1–3 months	2.8	0.5	1.3	1.7	5.1
3–6 months	3.0	1.4	1.3	2.8	4.7
6 months or longer	5.1	3.2	3.9	5.5	6.1
Total	100.0	100.0	100.0	100.0	100.0

Note: Sample enterprises are drawn from the whole country and
represent industries such as manufacturing, construction, wholesale and retail trade, communications, transportation, and
services.

Source: ML 1981a, Table 8.

to other workers is considerably shorter than that offered to new graduates
which in itself is brief (Table 7.9). Nor is it clear that informal on-the-
job training is as favorable to adults as to youth. By their distribution
of formal company training, Japanese companies may underestimate
the capacity of adult production workers to be upgraded or retrained
for changing technological developments and new skills.

RELATIVE EARNINGS

The earnings of various age groups are of considerable concern in Japan
because the age-seniority wage system is an important feature of internal
labor markets. External labor market variables enter mainly through

wage differentials for given age-sex groups by size of firm; little attention is paid to industry and occupational wage differentials (Ono 1979). In measuring age differentials, the usual practice in Japan has been to take the earnings of 20–24 year-olds as 100; by this standard, age differentials are far wider for males in Japan than in other countries (ML 1963–82; JLB September 1979, p.6). Making the 25–29 year-old group the base reduces, but does not eliminate, the Japanese divergence from other nations (Sano 1977).

For purposes of this book, earnings of adults 25 and over have been taken as the base for relative earnings by age. This method directly confronts the relative cost to employers of youth vs. adults and the employment impact of various levels of relative earnings, central concerns of this book. We computed a series for 1958–80 on the earnings of youth relative to adults by sex and educational level (Table 7.10).

There has been a striking increase in the earnings of teenagers of each sex relative to similar adults (25 and over) over the period of 22 years, but especially from 1958 to 1965. A less marked rise appears for young adults relative to adults. Although several groups display a slight downturn after 1974, 1980 ratios are higher than 1958 in each age comparison group. On grounds of wage costs alone, the earnings ratios suggest that employers' preference for new school graduates is questionable in regard to females for the entire period and from the 1960s onward for males. If instead of adults 25 and over, we use as the base the earnings of a prime-age group, 30–39 or 35–39, the ratios for young females are not much affected, but the ratios for young males are somewhat reduced, especially for teenagers.

Another type of measurement frequently used in Japan pits peak earnings against starting pay: controlling for sex, educational level, and size of firm. Ratios of peak to starting pay in 1978 for male senior high school graduates, for example, were 2.82, 2.52, and 2.24 for enterprises with 1,000 or more employees, 100–999 employees and 10–99 employees, respectively, whereas the corresponding female ratios were 2.19, 1.83, and 1.48. Firms with 1,000 or more employees showed ratios of 2.66, 2.82, 3.17, and 3.49 for male graduates of junior high schools, senior high schools, junior colleges, and universities, respectively, whereas for similar females the ratios were 2.10, 2.19, 2.16, and 2.53 (ML 1955–82). These ratios suggest that starting pay for youth is relatively low and that employers may still have a good economic rationale for recruitment of new graduates and lifetime employment. But is peak pay the proper standard of comparison if the issue is a potential substitution of labor?

A comparison of the dispersion of annual earnings for male youth and adults in 1979 shows that 50–54 year-olds, those at the peak of their earnings and on the brink of retirement, have a much wider dispersion across the range of earnings than youth. The mode for the older men is three income classes higher than the mode of the two youth groups. Over half of the 50–54 year-olds fall in still higher earnings

Table 7.10 Monthly Earnings of Youth Relative to Adults, All Industries, by Age, Sex, and Educational Level, Japan, 1958–80

	Educational level[a]	1958	1965	1970	1974	1978	1980
				(ratio)[b]			
Males							
Under 18/25 and over	JHS	.26	.41	.46	.49	.47	.48
18–19/25 and over	JHS	.41	.52	.57	.59	.55	.56
20–24/25 and over	JHS	.57	.68	.72	.74	.70	.70
18–19/25 and over	SHS	.36	.45	.49	.53	.49	.49
20–24/25 and over	SHS	.50	.57	.60	.64	.60	.59
20–24/25 and over	JC	.36	.39	.42	.49	.51	.51
20–24/25 and over	C/U	.47	.54	.52	.54	.51	.51
Females							
Under 18/25 and over	JHS	.59	.77	.82	.85	.76	.75
18–19/25 and over	JHS	.70	.86	.91	.93	.85	.83
20–24/25 and over	JHS	.85	.96	1.00	1.00	.96	.92
Under 18/25 and over	SHS	n.a.	n.a.	n.a.	n.a.	n.a.	.73
18–19/25 and over	SHS	.56	.64	.71	.76	.73	.71
20–24/25 and over	SHS	.70	.74	.80	.84	.83	.81
20–24/25 and over	JC	n.a.	n.a.	n.a.	.63	.73	.72
20–24/25 and over	C/U	n.a.	n.a.	n.a.	.69	.68	.67
Females/Males							
Under 18	JHS	1.01	.98	.93	.95	.92	.89
18–19	JHS	.76	.86	.84	.87	.87	.85
20–24	JHS	.66	.73	.73	.74	.78	.75
18–19	SHS	.84	.92	.89	.92	.95	.93
20–24	SHS	.78	.83	.83	.84	.89	.88
20–24	JC	n.a.	n.a.	n.a.	.89	.94	.93
20–24	C/U	n.a.	n.a.	n.a.	.93	.94	.95
25 and over	JHS	.44	.52	.52	.55	.56	.57
25 and over	SHS	.55	.64	.62	.64	.64	.64
25 and over	JC	n.a.	n.a.	n.a.	.68	.66	.65
25 and over	C/U	n.a.	n.a.	n.a.	.72	.71	.73

[a]JHS: through junior high school; SHS: senior high school; JC: junior college; C/U: college and university. [b]Includes overtime pay. Excludes bonuses.

Source: ML 1955–82.

brackets, in contrast to none of the teenagers and 0.1 percent of the young adult males. Yet, 11.4 percent of the men about to retire had annual earnings at or below the mode for the youth groups (OPM 1980a, Table 19). The effect of the size of the firm on the distribution of earnings in 1978 among 50–54 year-old males by educational level is as follows: The third quartile for junior and senior high school graduates was comparable to the median for senior high school and college graduates, respectively (ML 1955–82). Among small firms, dispersion of salary by age is somewhat more compressed than among medium and large firms, but men of 50–54 show less compression than youth in all size firms.

At age 50–54 male monthly earnings are positively correlated with the level of education, presumably due to the higher likelihood of promotion for the more highly educated. Within an educational attainment level, the dispersion of earnings is the composite result of the length of service in the company, age, and performance evaluation. When work experience is divided into the number of years in the firm of current employment and the number of years in other firms, the former is a more powerful variable in explaining the level of earnings (Shimada 1981, p.44; see also, Sano 1977). Controlling earnings data for age and length of service, males with the longest service, and especially those who did not change their employer since leaving school, have the highest earnings.

Wage dispersion data for female junior and senior high school graduates in different age groups display much greater compression than males show, particularly in medium and small-size firms (ML 1955–82). Contrary to male experience, education has a very small effect on female earnings which show a great deal of overlap for women with different educational backgrounds. In small and medium-size firms, the effect of age on female earnings is negligible, while it is moderate in large firms. In other words, differences among women in inherent and acquired abilities and productive capacity are poorly rewarded, and age, length of service, and experience do not bring the delayed benefits that men are supposed to obtain as compensation for starting at relatively low pay.

HOURS OF WORK

Hours of work per week and over the year have been declining for all age groups. Monthly work hours declined from 202.7 in 1960 to 177.4 in 1979 (EPA 1980, p.189). Between 1959 and 1979, the proportion of the gainfully occupied who worked fewer than 200 days a year increased from 5.5 percent to 15.7 percent. The rise was more notable for females than males. Much less change and no real trend over the two decades occurred for the group that worked under 35 hours per week and over 200 days a year, while those working part-time and part-year showed an increase (ML 1960–75; ML 1980a).

Differences between age groups are less marked in weekly hours than in days worked per year. Gainfully employed males in nonagricultural industries worked 50.6 hours on average in 1979, while teenage and young adult males showed 45.8 and 48.6 hours, respectively. For females, average hours were 41.9 for all females, 43.6 for young adults, and 44.3 for teenagers, giving female youth a longer work week than other female age groups (OPM 1965–82, Table 24). Among gainfully occupied males in nonagricultural industries who were mainly working, the proportion working less than 200 days over the year was lower for 40–44 year-old men than for young adults or teenagers. Adult females, with 6.7 percent having a short work year, exceeded the 5.4 percent shown by teenagers and 4.2 percent for young adults. The proportion of teenage males working less than 200 days a year was considerably higher than the teenage female share; young adult rates were similar for the two sexes, while the female 40–44 year-old rate was almost twice that for similar males (OPM 1980a,Table 14). Deliberate efforts by government are under way to reduce worktime in Japan, partly in response to foreign charges of unfair competition and failure to conform to the standards set by the International Labor Office.

JOB-CHANGING

Adults are less prone to leave their employer during any particular year than teenagers or young adults (Table 7.7A,B). Adult females are only slightly less likely than adult males to have changed a job or left during the year. Both job-changing and separation rates confirm these statements. Voluntary as well as involuntary job-changing rates are lower for adults than for youth. For example, 22.2 percent of youth (15–24) as against 18.7 percent of 35–44 year-olds who changed jobs in 1978–79 wished to do so. However, the gap is not so great as to suggest that voluntary job-changing is confined to the under-30 age group. Longitudinal data from the National Institute of Vocational Research indicate that male workers, as they aged from 30 to 55, continued to change jobs. Adults who change jobs are less likely than youth to move to a larger size firm or to gain in earnings (ML 1964–82). Changes of occupation and place of residence, frequent but not necessary accompaniments of job-changing, also are exhibited less by adults. While no clear-cut time trend emerges from the data for 1959–79, adults as much as youth show an accelerated job-changing response to favorable economic circumstances, or vice versa (Table 7.7A,B).

Longitudinal Surveys

The longitudinal survey of youth which began in 1969–71 studied three annual cohorts of male and female graduates from 71 junior high schools in seven prefectures. Each participant was followed for ten years; the final survey was made in 1981. Information about the enterprises where the 2,820 young people worked was obtained from the Employment Security Offices (NIVR 1974). Information on those who became high school and college graduates was separately recorded (Watanabe 1981). Full data on first occupations and occupations ten years later were not available at the time of writing. Therefore, we present data from a

Table 7.11 First Occupation and 1973 Occupation, Males, by Age in 1973, Japan

	20-29 years		30-39 years		40-54 years		55-59 years	
				Occupation				
	First	1973	First	1973	First	1973	First	1973
	(percentage distribution)							
Professional, technical	7.1	8.0	6.7	7.8	6.3	6.5	5.1	4.1
Managers, officials	0.3	1.1	0.5	8.6	0.6	13.3	0.6	7.7
Clerical	18.7	19.2	16.9	15.7	15.7	12.2	9.0	8.5
Sales	12.5	11.8	12.4	11.6	6.8	8.5	10.0	10.0
Farming, forestry, fishing	6.1	4.9	16.2	9.4	28.6	17.8	40.2	28.4
Mining, quarrying	0.2	0.1	0.2	*	0.4	0.5	0.4	0.5
Transportation and communications	4.3	9.5	3.1	8.3	4.0	4.9	1.2	1.0
Crafts, operatives, laborers	43.4	38.3	37.0	33.3	29.5	31.5	24.6	23.2
Protective services	1.8	1.8	1.7	1.5	1.4	1.6	1.5	1.4
Services	3.8	3.3	3.2	3.4	1.2	2.4	2.6	3.6
Unclassifiable	1.8	1.9	2.0	0.5	5.5	0.9	4.9	11.5
Total	100	100	100	100	100	100	100	100
Total number	1,013		1,186		1,514		781	
Correlation between first and 1973 occupation (r)**	0.99		0.93		0.85		0.94	

*Less than 0.5 percent. **Significant at 0.1 percent level.

Source: NIVR 1979, Table I-12.

retrospective longitudinal survey, conducted in 1973 by the National Institute of Vocational Research (NIVR) among over 4,600 males aged 20–70. Table 7.11 shows the distribution of first occupations and occupations in 1973 for four age-cohorts of males. Restricted occupational mobility is demonstrated in each cohort and is notably lacking for those in professional and technical occupations. Differences among the cohorts in the distribution of first jobs reflect the changes in employment composition over the years, for example, the decline in farming and the growth of manufacturing. The expected effects on occupations of an increased average educational attainment between 1920 and the late 1960s is not, however, visible. The 1973 occupations combine both life cycle and cohort effects and are more difficult to interpret. Those who changed firms often remained in the previous occupation, especially if they did not leave employee status.

Further information on occupational change over the life cycle was produced for 793 males who were 25–64 years old in 1973. Male senior high school graduates who began as production process workers showed a high probability of leaving their first occupation by age 25. Many of the leavers had, however, shifted to other blue collar jobs such as laborer, construction, or communication and transportation worker; in 1973, 42, 49, 58, and 67 percent, respectively, of 55–64, 45–54, 35–44, and 25–34 year-old males who started as production workers were in blue collar jobs. Self-employment or family work in nonagricultural industries was the most common 1973 position of those who had left production work; white collar occupations had absorbed much smaller shares (NIVR 1979, Table I–34(1)).

Relatively few male senior high school graduates who began as sales and service workers remained in this occupation as they aged. They exhibited a dramatic shift into self-employment, especially in the age groups of 45–54 and 35–44 where only 3 and 19 percent still were in sales and service jobs as of 1973. About 45 percent of the leavers, 35–44 and 45–54 years old in 1973, had become self-employed or family workers in nonagricultural industries, while a fourth had changed to blue collar occupations, and some 13 percent in these two age cohorts had moved into professional and technical occupations, managers and officials, and clerks (NIVR 1979, Table I–34(2)).

Males whose first occupation was clerical worker had diversified experience according to their educational level and age cohort. Senior high school graduates showed a marked propensity to change occupations, mainly from clerical to other white collar occupations—managers and officials, with a smaller proportion becoming professional and technical workers. Self-employment or family work in nonagricultural industries was again the major destination of those who left white collar employment, but many also went into sales and service and blue collar occupations. Nearly 10 percent were engaged in blue collar occupations in all phases of their life cycle among males under 55. Sales and service occupations were negligible for men who were 35 or more in 1973, but for those 25–34 it accounted for 9 percent at age 25 and 7 percent in 1973, comparable to the proportion in blue collar occupations and substantially higher than the share in nonagricultural self-employment (NIVR 1979, Table I–34(3)).

College graduates starting as clericals had a low propensity to leave such work or the white collar occupations; they left clerical work mainly due to promotion into managerial or professional and technical jobs. The substantial retention rate of college graduates in clerical work is largely attributable to the survey's narrow definitions of managers, officials and professional and technical workers, identical to definitions used in the Population Census. As a result, these clerical workers included workers with a wide range of responsibility, qualifications, and salaries. Unlike the noncollege clerks, a negligible proportion moved into sales, service, or blue collar occupations. Among men under 54, a higher proportion with than without college education were found in self-employment or family work in nonagricultural industries (NIVR 1979, Table I–34(4)).

Longitudinal records indicate that the first job substantially determines the subsequent occupation, except for sales and service workers. Those who changed occupations show both upward and downward movement. Survey data suggest that sales and service occupations as initial jobs were not viewed as permanent by a majority. However, the jobs in these occupations have become more challenging, and have improved in relative income and social prestige, and past occupational mobility patterns may not apply in the future.

If occupational mobility is motivated by differentials in income and in stability of employment, the NIVR data imply that nonagricultural self-employment yields substantially higher income or other advantages over other occupations. Since there is no independent evidence that these advantages have been large enough to provide as strong an attraction as the 1973 NIVR data indicate over such a long period of time, further research is required.

References: Japan

Adachi, N., and Oneda, M. 1977. "The Early Stage of Careers of Japanese Young Males." *ARAVEG Bulletin,* no.5.

Bowman, M.J.; Ikeda, H.; Tomoda, Y.; and Harker, B. 1970. *A Theoretical and Empirical Analysis of Vocational Preparation in Japan.* Chicago, Ill.: Department of Economics and Comparative Economics Center.

Cole, R.E. 1979. *Work, Mobility and Participation: A Comparative Study of American and Japanese Industry.* Berkeley, Cal.: University of California Press.

EPA (Economic Planning Agency). 1980. *The Changing Society and How Poeple Are Facing It.* Annual Report on National Life. Tokyo: EPA.

Freeman, R.B. 1981. *The Changing Economic Value of Higher Education in Developed Economies: A Report to the O.E.C.D.* Working paper no.820. Cambridge, Mass.: National Bureau of Economic Research.

Furuya, K. 1980. "Labor-Management Relations in Postwar Japan: Their Reality and Change." *Japan Quarterly,* June.

Galenson, W. 1976. "The Japanese Labor Market." In Patrick, H. and Rosovsky, H., eds. *Asia's New Giant.* Washington, D.C.: The Brookings Institution.

Glazer, N. 1976. "Social and Cultural Factors in Japanese Economic Growth." In Patrick, H. and Rosovsky, H., eds. *Asia's New Giant.* Washington, D.C.: The Brookings Institution.

Hanami, T. 1982. "Worker Motivation in Japan (1)." *Japan Labor Bulletin,* February.

Izumi, N. 1980. "The Practice of Career Guidance in Japanese High Schools." Paper prepared for the Tenth World Congress of the International Association for Educational and Vocational Guidance (IAEVG), Manila.

JIL (Japan Institute of Labour). 1979a. *Wages and Hours of Work.* Tokyo: Japan Institute of Labour.

JLB. 1965–82. *Japan Labor Bulletin.* Tokyo, monthly.

JPC (Japan Productivity Center). 1982. *Katsuyō Rōdō Tōkei (Practical Labor Statistics).* Tokyo: Japan Productivity Center.

Kato, H. 1978. *Education and Youth Employment in Japan.* Berkeley, Cal.: Carnegie Council on Policy Studies in Higher Education.

Koshiro, K. 1979. "Labor Productivity and Recent Employment Adjustment Programs in Japan II." *Japan Labor Bulletin,* January.

Levine, S.B. 1980. "Careers and Mobility in Japan's Labor Markets." Paper prepared for the Annual Meeting of the Association for Asian Studies. Washington, D.C., March.

Matsuda, Y. 1980. "Minimum Wage System in Japan." *Japan Labor Bulletin,* May.

ME (Ministry of Education). 1966. *Nihon no Kyōiku Tōkei (Educational Statistics of Japan).* Tokyo: Ministry of Education.

――――――. 1972a. *Basic Guidelines for the Reform of Education.* Report of the Central Council for Education. Tokyo: Ministry of Education.

230   *Youth Employment in Japan*

————. 1976a. *Educational Standards in Japan 1975.* MEJ4257. Tokyo: Ministry of Education.

————. 1979a. *Statistical Abstract of Education, Science and Culture.* Tokyo: Ministry of Education.

————. 1980a. *Gakko Kihon Chōsa* (*1980 Basic School Survey*). Tokyo: Ministry of Education.

————. 1981a. *1981 Mombu Tōkei Yōran* (*1981 Summary Statistics of Education*). Tokyo: Ministry of Education.

ML (Ministry of Labour). 1951–82. *Maitsuki Kinrō Tōkei Chōsa* (*Monthly Labor Survey*). Tokyo: Ministry of Labour.

————. 1954–76. *Shinki Gakusotsusha Shoninkyū Chōsa* (*Survey of Starting Salaries and Wages of New Graduates*). Tokyo: Ministry of Labour.

————. 1955–82. *Chingin Kozo Kihon Chōsa* (*Basic Survey of Wage Structure*). Tokyo: Ministry of Labour.

————. 1960–82. *Shokugyo Antei Gyomu Tōkei* (*Annual Report on Employment Exchange*). Tokyo: Ministry of Labour.

————. 1963–82. *Rōdō Hakusho* (*White Paper on Labor*). Tokyo: Ministry of Labour.

————. 1964–82. *Koyō Dōkō Chōsa Hōkoku* (*Annual Survey of Employment Trends*). Tokyo: Ministry of Labour.

————. 1965–82. *Rōdō Tōkei Nempo* (*Yearbook of Labour Statistics*). Tokyo: Ministry of Labour.

————. 1975–82. *Rōdō Kumiai Kihon Chōsa* (*Basic Survey on Labour Unions*). Tokyo: Ministry of Labour.

————. 1977. *Wagakuni no Saitei Chingin-sei* (*Minimum Wages in Japan*). Tokyo: Japan Institute of Labour.

————. 1980a. *Shokugyō Nōryoku no Kaihatsu ni Kansuru Chōsa Kekka Hōkoku* (*Survey Report of Occupational Skill Development*). Tokyo: Ministry of Labour.

————. 1981a. *Jigyō nai Kyōiku Kunren Jisshi Jyōkyō oyobi Hiyō ni kansuru Chōsa Kekka Hōkoku* (*Survey on Employee Training and Training Costs*). Tokyo: Ministry of Labour.

Nikkeiren (Japan Federation of Employers' Associations). 1980. *Preventing the Resurgence of Inflation and Insuring Jobs for Older Workers.* Tokyo: Nikkeiren.

NIVR (National Institute of Vocational Research). 1974. *A Follow-up Study on the Vocational Aajustment of Young Workers.* Tokyo: NIVR.

————. 1979. *Nihonjin no Shokugyō Keireki to Shokugyō-kan* (*Occupational Mobility and Personal View of Occupations in Japan*). Tokyo: Shiseido.

————. 1980a. *Jakunen Rōdōsha no Shokugyō Tekiō ni Kansuru Tsuiseki Kenkyū. Sono 10. 20-sai Chōsa Kekka Deta-shū* (*Follow-Up Survey of Occupational Career of Young Workers. No.10. 20-Year-Old Survey*). Tokyo: NIVR.

————. 1980b. *Jakunen Rōdōsha no Shokugyō Tekiō ni Kansuru Tsuiseki Kenkyū. Sono 11. 23-sai Chōsa Kekka Deta-shū* (*Follow-Up Survey of Occupational Career of Young Workers. No.11. 23-Year-Old Survey*). Tokyo: NIVR.

————. 1982. *Jakunen Rōdōsha no Shokugyō Tekiō ni Kansuru Tsuiseki Kenkyū. Sono 12. 26-sai-Chōsa Kekka Deta-shū* (*Follow-Up Survey of Occupational Career of Young Workers. No.12. 26-Year-Old Survey*). Tokyo: NIVR.

Okochi, K.; Karsh, B.; and Levine, S., eds. 1974. *Workers and Employers in Japan.* Tokyo: University of Tokyo Press.

OE (*The Oriental Economist*). 1980. "Start of Age of Moderate Wages." January.

Ono, T. 1979. "Trends in Internal Wage Structure of Japanese Firms." *Japan Labor Bulletin,* November.

OPM (Office of the Prime Minister). 1956–82. *Rōdōryoku Chōsa* (*Annual Report on the Labour Force Survey*). Tokyo: OPM.

————. 1960–78. *Shūgyo Kōzō Kihon Chōsa Hōkoku* (*Employment Status Survey*). Tokyo: OPM, Triennial.

————. 1965–82. *Japan Yearbook.* Tokyo: OPM, annual.

————. 1967–79. *Jigyōsho Tōkei Chōsa* (*Statistical Survey of Establishments*). Tokyo: OPM.

————. 1978b. *1975 Population Census of Japan,* part 1, division 1, vol.5. Tokyo: OPM.

————. 1980a. *Shūgyo Kōzō Kihon Chōsa Hōkuku (1979 Employment Status Survey. Whole Japan).* Tokyo: OPM.

Ouchi, W.G. 1982. *Theory Z: How American Business Can Meet the Japanese Challenge.* New York: Avon.

Reubens, B.G. 1977. *Bridges to Work: International Comparisons of Transition Services.* Montclair, N.J.: Allanheld, Osmun.

Rohlen, T.P. 1979. " 'Permanent Employment' Faces Recession, Slow Growth, and an Aging Work Force." *The Journal of Japanese Studies,* Summer.

Sakurabayashi, M. 1972. "Wages in Today's Japan (1)." *Sophia Economic Review,* December.

Sano, Y. 1977. "Seniority-Based Wages in Japan." *Japanese Economic Studies,* Spring.

Shimada, H. 1980. *The Japanese Employment System.* Tokyo: The Japan Institute of Labour.

————. 1981. *Earnings Structure and Human Investment: A Comparison Between the United States and Japan.* Tokyo: Kogakusha.

Shimada, H., and Nishikawa, S. 1979. "An Analysis of Japanese Employment System and Youth Labor Market." *Keio Economic Studies,* no.1–2.

Suwa, Y. 1979. "Recent Cases on Dismissals by Reason of Redundancy: Economic Depression and Labor Law in Japan." *Japan Labor Bulletin,* February.

Takeshi, S. 1979. *Present Situation of Vocational Guidance by Employment Exchange Organizations.* Tokyo: NIVR.

Umetani, S. 1975. "The Japanese Women in the Labor Market." *Japan Labor Bulletin,* January.

————. 1977. "The College Labor Market and the Rate of Return to Higher Education in Postwar Japan, 1954–73." Ph.D. dissertation, University of Wisconsin–Madison.

————. 1980a. *Vocational Training in Japan.* Mittcilungen des Instituts für Asienkunde, no.114. Hamburg: Institut für Asienkunde.

Watanabe, A.M., and Yoshitani, J. 1980. "A Longitudinal Study on Vocationalization of Japanese Adolescents." Paper prepared for the Tenth World Congress of IAVEG, Manila.

Yashiro, N. 1979. "Why Do Japanese Workers Work So Hard: An Interpretation of the Internal Labor Market of Japan." Unpublished.

Chapter 8

Youth Employment in Sweden

Anders Björklund and

Inga Persson-Tanimura

During the 1950s and 1960s, public debate and manpower policy in Sweden were mainly concerned with the employment problems of the adult labor force. Young people were seen as the favored ones, the beneficiaries of the gradual expansion of the educational system who had better opportunities than did their parents. But the situation gradually changed. As the baby boom cohorts of 1943–48 entered the labor market in the late 1960s and early 1970s, some signs of stress appeared among arts and sciences graduates of universities who found that demand was not expanding fast enough to match the rapid increase in their supply. The tendency toward excess supply was, however, not a general phenomenon. High economic growth rates meant that, on the whole, the baby boom cohorts could be absorbed without any major problem.

It was not until economic growth slowed in the 1970s that a general concern about the employment problems of young people arose; in the public debate since the 1970s, youth unemployment has been treated as a major problem. While the rate of unemployment has increased over time for both teenagers and young adults, no such negative trend has appeared for adults. The percentage point increase in unemployment rates has been higher for young females than for young males and is particularly large for female teenagers (Persson-Tanimura 1980).

The development of employment between 1963 and 1980 gave less cause for concern than that of unemployment. The number of employed teenagers declined from 1963 to 1972 and then fluctuated around a slightly higher level. The number of employed young adult males rose until 1970, declined during the early 1970s and then remained roughly unchanged. But the large and consistent increase in employed young adult females, with few setbacks, meant that the 16–24 age group as a whole showed almost no change in total employment in 1980 compared to 1963. Today the likelihood of being employed is almost the same for young men and women. Two aspects of the employment of youth, however, offset the apparent stability in total numbers. One is the decrease in the number of youth working full-time (35 hours or more) during the 1970s and the rise in voluntary and involuntary part-time work, both as an absolute and as a share of the total. The expansion of part-time work reflects increased job-holding during the term and in vacations by young people enrolled in educational institutions and a greater proportion of young adult females in employment because they have fewer children than earlier cohorts and because young mothers are more likely to work. The second point about the steady total for youth employment is that it was achieved, particularly during the recessionary periods of the second half of the 1970s, only by counting the expanded number of temporary jobs under a government program (*Beredskapsarbeten*) as part of youth employment.

Concern about youth employment will probably be warranted during the 1980s as well. By the end of 1982, there were no real signs of an economic recovery, and a second baby boom, comprising the 1964–67 cohorts, will be entering the labor market during the 1980s. Young people can thus be expected to continue to face keen competition for education, jobs, and career advancement.

Educational and Training Systems and Their Outputs

During the postwar period the educational system has expanded at all levels and also has undergone a number of fundamental changes (Rehn 1980). At the base is a nine-year compulsory school (*Grundskola*) for 7 to 16 year-olds which is comprehensive and non-vocational. Some separation takes place in grades seven to nine as pupils choose elective subjects that prepare for different streams in upper secondary school. Subject choices vary according to social background and sex, influencing both later studies and occupational choices (SCB 1980a, pp.36–39). To reduce differences among socioeconomic groups, some entrance requirements for the academic streams of upper secondary school were removed in 1982. In the higher social groups both sexes make much the same subject choices, but in the lower social groups boys and girls tend to choose sex-biased subjects (for example, boys in technology and girls in languages or art). Thus, some sex differentiation starts in compulsory school.

About 5–10 percent of pupils leave compulsory school without full completion; children of workers and immigrants are overrepresented among the non-completers (SCB 1981a, p.57; SOU 1981a, p.56; SCB 1980a, p.38). The majority of school-leavers proceed directly to upper secondary school (*Gymnasieskolan*), reorganized in 1971 as an integrated school instead of three separate schools. In 1979, 94 percent of school-leavers applied for a place in upper secondary school, but only 79 percent were accepted and started directly; some of the remaining 21 percent will resume school after a year or two. The continuation rate is about 92 percent for those whose parents have higher education, but only 75–80 percent for children of unskilled workers. Immigrant youth had a 1977 continuation rate 10 percentage points lower than the total rate (SCB 1982a, pp.23, 32; SCB 1980a, pp.41–43). Well over 50 percent of immigrant young adults with non-Swedish citizenship have no more than compulsory education, compared to about 30 percent of all young adults (SCB 1981c, pp.40–41). A study of 1979 school-leavers found that, within the heterogeneous immigrant group, poor knowledge of Swedish was an important factor in non-continuation. Among immigrant children in whose homes a language other than Swedish was spoken, those with good knowledge of Swedish had a continuation rate of 74 percent, while for those with a deficient knowledge of Swedish the rate was only 46 percent (SÖ 1981a, p.1).

Regional variation in school continuation rates is small. In 1979, the highest continuation rates, 84 percent for females and 78 percent for males, occurred in the forest regions of the north, probably because education was chosen as an alternative to particularly high youth unemployment. The lowest rate of 72 percent was in two big city regions (Malmö and Gothenburg) for females and outside the big cities in the middle of Sweden for males (SCB 1982a, pp.31–32).

The upper secondary school offers two, three, and four-year theoretical and two-year vocational programs as well as shorter vocational courses. The three and four-year theoretical programs mainly prepare for tertiary education as do two of the four two-year theoretical "lines"; the other two mainly prepare for work. The 15 two-year vocational "lines" (e.g., agriculture, construction, communications, distribution and clerical, consumer, nursing), like the 400 shorter special vocational courses, prepare for work. Students in the special courses are older than students in the lines; in 1978, 42 percent of students in special courses were over 22 years old, compared to only 4 percent among students in the lines (SCB 1981a, p.136). In contrast to the special courses, the vocational lines provide general education (SOU 1981c, pp.60–62). Most students in the vocational lines and courses get some training in firms or institutions. The schools supervise the quantity and quality of such on-the-job training (SOU 1981b, pp.126–27).

The dropout rate from upper secondary school is about 20 percent, but some dropouts return later or attend another institution (SCB 1981a, pp.139–41). At present, about 70 percent of an age cohort eventually completes an upper secondary school program and another 15 percent completes vocational special courses of varying length. In 1979, 30 percent of the graduates of upper secondary schools came from the three or four-year theoretical lines, 17 percent from the two-year theoretical lines, 44 percent from the two-year vocational lines, and 10 percent from vocational special courses (SCB 1980a, pp.45,50).

A much larger share, almost 70 percent, of youth whose parents had higher education than of children of workers (10 to 15 percent) graduate from the three and four-year theoretical lines (SCB 1980a, p.51). In contrast, it is about five times as common for children of unskilled workers as for children of parents with higher education to graduate from vocational lines or courses. The marked increase in the proportion of youth choosing vocational lines during the 1970s mainly reflected change among children of workers, particularly females (SOU 1981c, pp.180–84). A smaller proportion of immigrant than Swedish youth are in upper secondary schools, and of these, 58 percent of males and 43 percent of females chose vocational lines or courses, as opposed to 48 percent among all males and 42 percent among all females (SCB 1981a, p.563). It is particularly common for immigrant youth with a deficient knowledge of Swedish to choose vocational lines (SÖ 1981a).

Most of the vocational lines in upper secondary schools are heavily dominated by one sex. About 60 percent of male students and 50 percent of female students graduate from lines in which one sex comprises at least 80 percent of the total number of students. The technical lines are dominated by males, while the female-dominated lines lead to jobs in the social services, other services, and office work (SCB 1980a, pp.50–51). Thus occupational segmentation by sex for this group largely occurs before labor market entry. Reforms of upper secondary education, expected in the 1980s as a result of the work of a special commission, are likely to increase the general education elements in the vocational lines and the work-oriented elements in the theoretical lines, so that all study programs will prepare both for work and further studies (SOU 1981a).

Apart from the vocational training offered through the educational system, a limited number of apprenticeships, subsidized by government, are available in a few of the traditional artisan, construction and personal service occupations (SCB 1981a, pp.239,243). Their number declined as the vocational lines and courses in upper secondary school were expanded, but they are also used to complete a basic vocational training obtained from a vocational line. Some youth also receive practical and theoretical vocational training in a small number of government-subsidized company schools (SOU 1977, p.12). In 1980, a trial program was set up to revive employer-based training as an alternative form of training; it is administered by the local governments and tied to the local upper secondary schools (SOU 1981b, p.129).

The labor movement, opposing basic vocational training by employers as too brief and excessively firm-specific, has advocated extension of the vocational lines and courses. This view may be changing in response to criticism that some 16–18 year-olds might be better served by some form of industry-based training. A complement to traditional schooling in the form of industry-based vocational training supervised by the secondary schools may evolve from the government's recent provision of a vocational introduction course and special youth jobs.

About a fourth of all employees in the private and public sectors participate annually in organized, employer-provided on and off-the-

job training that adds to basic vocational and other skills. In the private
sector, such training is about half as common among 16–24 year-old
males and females as it is among 25–34 year-old males (SOU 1977,
p.123). Organized training is particularly common in banks and insurance
companies, about average in incidence in manufacturing, and less
frequent or briefer in construction, hotels and restaurants, commerce,
and transport (SOU 1977, p.11).

Higher education was reformed during the 1970s and given a new
structure in 1977, when a number of shorter and more vocational
programs were incorporated into the traditional university system. Most
programs for a first academic degree require three to four years, but
many students take longer to complete their degree. A marked development during the 1970s, intended by the reforms, has been the increase
in the number of students who are not studying toward a complete
degree, but take a limited number of courses, often on a part-time basis
(SOU 1981c, p.170). The reforms also included changes in admission
policies. Eligibility was widened, quotas were set for different groups
of applicants and new rules for ranking applicants were applied (SOU
1981c, pp.168–73). The changes favored older applicants and the proportion of students in higher education who were recent upper secondary
graduates declined. In 1978, only 40 percent of students were under
25 (SCB 1981a, p.34). Changes in the quotas and ranking rules in 1982
are intended to favor those who are recent graduates from upper
secondary school (SCB 1980a, p.69).

Of those who completed the three and four-year upper secondary
course in 1977, 32 percent of males and 43 percent of females entered
higher education institutions within two years; the higher female rate
is related to compulsory military service for males. The continuation
rate was highest (49 percent for males and 57 percent for females) in
the natural science specialization and lowest (about 20 percent) in the
economics and four-year technical specializations. Among graduates
from the two-year theoretical and vocational lines, 12 percent and 6
percent, respectively, proceeded to higher education within two years.
Since the consumer and nursing specializations have a relatively high
continuation rate, it was more common for females (10 percent) than
males (2 percent) to enter higher education from the vocational lines
(SCB 1982b, pp.56–57).

Among those graduating from compulsory school in 1971, only a
fifth had participated in higher education up to 1978 (SOU 1981c,
p.164). Social selection in the schools is reinforced in higher education.
While a ratio of about 10:1 exists in the population between the number
of youth whose parents are workers and those whose parents had higher
education, the ratio is only about 1.5:1 among students in higher
education. Students whose parents had higher education are even more
overrepresented in certain long, high-status lines of study, such as
medicine, dentistry and engineering (SCB 1980a, p.60). As an offset, a

more even regional access to higher education has been provided recently (SOU 1981c, p.163).

Compared to their parents, the younger generation brings substantially more human capital to the labor market. Among 16–17 year-old males in the labor force in February 1980, about 80 percent of the males and 70 percent of the females had nine to ten years of education, compared to only 4.2 percent of 45–54 year-old males and 10.1 percent of females. Of the 18–19 year-olds in the labor force, 45.1 percent of the males and 48.9 percent of the females had up to two years of upper secondary schooling, including labor market training courses of at least two months' duration. In contrast, only 15.9 percent of males and 22.5 percent of females 45–54 years old had this level. For the young adult group, 8.2 percent of males and 11.8 percent of females had up to two years of higher education, against 4.0 and 5.1 percent, respectively, for the 45–54 age group (SCB 1981a, p.31).

In summary, while females in the labor force have a slightly higher *level* of attained education than males, there are great differences in the *type* of education followed. The vocational orientation differs between males and females, and, within educational levels, males tend to have taken part in longer programs than females. Educational differences between youth in cities and elsewhere and in the various regions have decreased over time. Social background remains an important determinant both of level and type of educational achievement. Educational attainment is also substantially lower among immigrants than the whole population.

Institutional Background

Although Sweden has wide-ranging labor legislation, there also is a strong tradition that management and labor should reach agreement on many issues without government interference. Trade union and employer organizations take public positions on education, training, and labor market issues, and are in most cases represented on the numerous government commissions that have an important influence on policy. They are also represented and active in the National Labor Market Board (AMS) and similar quasi-public agencies which execute policy. Their influence on employment conditions is pervasive.

Preparation for Work, Vocational Guidance, and Job Placement. Responsibility for vocational guidance is shared between the school authorities and the local employment service offices of the National Labor Market Board (Rehn 1980, pp.103–07; SOU 1981b, pp.131–41). In compulsory school, pupils in the sixth year or earlier receive information about training and education opportunities and job possibilities from counselors or trained teachers. An established feature of the last year of compulsory school has been that each pupil should spend two weeks in one or more private and public workplaces, mainly in work observation (PRYO). Starting in 1982, PRAO (Practical Working-life Orientation) will provide six to ten weeks in a variety of firms and will begin before ninth grade. The revised scheme has the aim, among others, of counteracting sex-stereotyped occupational choices. The upper secondary school organizes orientation courses in the vocational lines and special occupational guidance weeks for students in the theoretical lines. Experimental programs are underway for students in the theoretical lines (SOU 1981b, p.128).

In 1980, the compulsory schools became responsible for outreach and follow-up of school-leavers under 18 who are not in upper secondary school. Each youth is to be offered an educational, training, practical work experience, or job opportunity under the terms of "the youth guarantee." The school authorities also head the local planning councils for youth, a recent innovation which includes representatives of the municipal authorities, the employment service, employer and trade union organizations, thus representing School-Society-Working Life (SSA).

The public employment service (ES) retains many important functions in regard to teenagers. Vocational guidance officers from the ES give talks in the schools and students can be sent to the ES for guidance. The ES cooperates with the schools and the social partners in finding PRAO places, training places for the vocational lines, and special youth jobs. The ES also administers the government's measures for unemployed youth, and registration at the office is required to establish eligibility for unemployment benefits. A major task is to help youth find jobs, using specialist officers. Because employers are required to notify all job vacancies of more than 10 days' duration to the ES, these offices have a comprehensive view of the demand side of the market; their position is strengthened because private employment agencies are banned. Among 16–19 year-olds who were unemployed during 1980, 43 percent used only the ES in their job search and another 31 percent used the ES plus other methods of job search. The corresponding figures for 20–24 year-olds were 48 and 33 percent, respectively, and for 25–74 year-olds, 57 and 22 percent. Employed youth also heavily utilize the ES when they wish to change jobs (SCB 1981b). Actual job-finding involves the ES less heavily. Among youth who held jobs a year after leaving compulsory school in 1974, only 17 percent of the men and 25 percent of the women had found their jobs through the ES (SCB 1978a, p.45). The rate was about 20 percent of each sex for the two-year theoretical lines in upper secondary school and 13 percent for men and 18 percent for women from the vocational lines (SCB 1976a, pp.96–99).

Protective and Related Legislation. The Working Environment Law of 1978 (*Arbetsmiljölågen*) and the ordinance of 1980 on Minors in Working Life (*Minderariga i arbetslivet*) regulate the hours and type of work of youth under 18. During the school term, 13–15 year-olds are allowed to work only 12 hours a week on light work that does not harm their health, development, or schooling. Outside of term, they are limited to an eight hour day, 40 hour week with no night work. For 16–17 year-olds work is forbidden between 10 p.m. and 5 a.m. and their jobs must not be too physically, psychologically, or socially demanding; no youth under 18 may work in places with high health or accident risks. Workplaces with more than four employees must have a safety supervisor who is elected by the employees and is informed by the employer when a minor is employed. Under the guidance of the National Board of Occupational Safety and Health, the industrial inspection officers of the Labor Inspectorate, cooperating with the elected safety supervisors, enforce the laws.

By law (*Semesterlagen* 1978), all employees are guaranteed a minimum annual vacation of five weeks a year. Collective agreements give many white-collar employees longer annual leave, often increased with age or salary level. The legal right to paid leave to take care of small children, administered through the social security system, enables parents of either sex to take six months paid leave on the birth of a child and another six months leave, half at full pay and half at reduced pay, until the child is eight. Since 1975, all employees have a legal right to unpaid educational leave after a minimum of six months on the job.

Employment Security and Related Legislation. The Codetermination Act of 1977 (*Medbestämmandelagen*) and related agreements between employers and unions have given employees a potential for greater influence on hiring and other areas of personnel policy. If, and how, this will influence youth employment remains to be seen. The Employment Protection Act of 1974 (*Lagen om anställningsskydd* LAS), placed legal restrictions on the freedom of employers to employ, lay off, give notice to, or dismiss employees. Employment can only be terminated on such grounds as redundancy or grave personal misdemeanor; minimum periods of dismissal notice are provided, rising with age. The employee is entitled to his normal pay during the period of notice, even if the employer is partly or wholly unable to offer him employment. LAS defines and regulates the terms of employment, making the norm "employment until further notice." An employment contract for a limited time period, a fixed season or a specific task may only be concluded if it can be individually justified; LAS has sanctioned employment for a limited period in connection with vocational practice or the temporary replacement of a regular employee. Probationary employment and temporary employment to meet temporary periods of high work pressure were not allowed by LAS, but could, and in many cases were, allowed by union contract (Ds A 1980:2). The effects of LAS on employment in general, and youth employment in particular, have been widely discussed, but Holmlund (1981) did not find any negative impacts on aggregate employment. However, in response to criticism by employers and others that the restrictive provisions on probationary and temporary employment have hindered the employment of tens of thousands of people, especially youth, the provisions were changed in April 1982 to allow probationary employment contracts of up to six months and temporary employment contracts, when work pressure requires, for a maximum of six months out of a two-year period. It remains to be seen whether the relative employment position of youth will be improved.

Trade Unions. Almost all employees belong to a trade union and most employers are organized in their own associations. Over two-thirds of employed males under 25 and almost two-thirds of employed young females are members of a union; the rate is even higher for adults. Unions view youth in school as future members to be trained and integrated into the organized way of working in the Swedish labor market. Potential conflicts in union policy arise mostly during periods of slow growth when the protection of jobs for older members might put the main burden of deficient labor demand on youth.

Wage Regulation. There is no minimum-wage law in Sweden. Under wage contracts, negotiated between trade unions and employers' associations, member employers agree to pay the negotiated wage rates, etc. to *all* of their employees, whether or not they are union members. Contracts provide special wage rates for those under 18 years, but youth 18 and over are given the adult rates.

Government Labor Market Programs and Government Financial Aid to Youth. The main programs for youth have been temporary jobs in the public and the private sector and labor market training in special centers, educational institutions, or firms. The number of youth under 25 in temporary jobs rose very rapidly in the 1970s, and there also was an increase in the number of youth in labor market training (Björklund et al. 1979; Johannesson 1981). Originally conceived as a Keynesian work-relief program, the temporary job program came to be used to help unemployed youth enter the regular labor market by providing them with work experience and an opportunity to try out jobs. Labor market training, originally conceived as a retraining program to overcome structural unemployment, was now also used for youth that did have access to a well-developed educational system. As the number of youth in the programs increased, it came to be felt that when used for youth, the programs were too economically attractive and tended to draw them away from upper secondary school training. It was decided that for 16–17 year-olds the programs would be replaced as of autumn 1980 by a new program, called vocational introduction. This program places out-of-school 16–17 year-olds in subsidized workplaces for a maximum of 40 weeks under supervision and with a vocational training program; the participants receive normal student aid plus any additions offered by local governments. In early 1982, youth job contracts were negotiated between employers and trade unions in the private and the public sector, creating subsidized jobs at about $15 per day for 16–17 year-olds which are not to decrease the number of ordinary jobs. Negotiations for similar contracts for older youth are underway.

Entering youth with upper secondary training are eligible for special unemployment benefits (KAS) after three months' unemployment. The benefits are set at about $12 a day which is significantly lower than the rates paid via the unemployment insurance system covering those who have been employed for a certain minimum period. In 1980, about 35 percent of unemployed 16–24 year-olds as compared to about 50 percent of unemployed 25–54 year-olds belonged to the unemployment insurance system (SCB 1963–82, 1980).

Student Workers

Today it is common that young people will have had some part-time and/or vacation work experience during their school years. The employment-population ratio for teenagers goes up from about 45 percent to over 70 percent during the summer months and an increase of about 5 percentage points occurs for young adults (SCB 1963–1982, 1980). Vacation jobs mostly are low-level jobs in the service sector, agriculture, and forestry, but they also are found in manufacturing, health care, clerical and commercial work.

Many students work during the term. Among students who left compulsory school in 1976 without directly proceeding to upper secondary school, about 20 percent of both male and female students had worked during the term in their last school year (SCB 1981a, pp.57,102). Almost two-thirds worked less than 10 hours per week while only 3 percent worked more than 20 hours per week. Of students who left the three and four-year theoretical lines of the upper secondary school in 1976, 33 percent had worked during the term (SCB 1981a, pp.136,221). The work week was short; 63 percent worked less than 10 hours per week while 6 percent worked more than 20 hours per week. Work during the term was least common among students in the natural science line (26 percent) and most common among students in the economics line (39 percent). Similar or higher rates of job-holding probably prevail among full-time students in higher education under 25 years old, but data are not available. Local studies indicate that the percentage of students in upper secondary school who work during the term has increased since 1976, in spite of a general worsening of the employment situation (SOU 1981b, pp.118–22).

The jobs of student workers during the term vary somewhat with education and age but tend to be low-level. Among those who worked during their last year in compulsory school in 1975–76 and did not directly proceed to upper secondary school, female students worked mainly as retail salespersons and assistants, retail cashiers, babysitters, and assistants in restaurant kitchens. Male students were farm workers, delivery workers, retail salespersons and assistants, warehouse and stores laborers, and machine assemblers and repairers. While all student workers were concentrated in a few types of work, the ten most common occupations for each sex accounted for about 90 percent of the females, but only some 70 percent of the males (SÖ 1979a).

Students in the three and four-year theoretical lines who worked during the term were also concentrated in low-level jobs in a few occupational areas. The most common occupations of the female students were the same as for the younger group, except for nurse's aide. Male students worked as mail delivery workers, retail salespersons and assistants, gas-station workers, agricultural workers, and warehouse and stores laborers. The five most common occupations accounted for 63 percent of female employment and 52 percent of male employment (SÖ 1979b, pp.11–12).

That these two surveys are representative of the kind of jobs held by student workers is confirmed by 1975 census data on young (16–24) part-time workers. Many of the same occupations as in the above surveys also are found among the ten most common occupations. Additional occupations, such as motor vehicle driver, secondary school teacher, typist, secretary, and office clerk, appear in the census as important part-time occupations for youth. These are mostly better-paid jobs likely to be held by older student or non-student part-time workers.

Jobs of Out-of-School Youth

An easier process of entering the labor market and a better type of first job are likely to be found among youth with higher educational attainment, males, youth in cities and the southern areas, and natives or Swedish speakers. Follow-up surveys of school-leavers from different educational levels provide specific information on some of these points.

ENTRY JOBS FROM COMPULSORY SCHOOL

Of those leaving compulsory school in 1979, 24 percent of the males and 21 percent of the females were not in upper secondary school in spring 1980 (SCB 1982a, pp.31,43). Seventy-nine percent of the out-of-school males were gainfully employed, 8 percent were in created jobs, 4 percent were unemployed or out of the labor force, and 8 percent were in courses, mainly in labor market training. Almost two-thirds of the females were gainfully employed, 14 percent were in created jobs, 10 percent were unemployed or out of the labor force, and 10 percent were in courses, mostly in labor market training. High proportions of those in regular or created jobs, 70 percent of the males and 50 percent of the females, held a permanent job (SCB 1982a, p.36). Temporary training posts and jobs as substitutes for regular employees were more common among females than males. The percentage employed temporarily in created jobs or other types of temporary work varied greatly among the regions, being highest in the north of Sweden for both males and females.

Youth who have only compulsory education and no specific skill or vocational training can obtain a limited range of jobs. An occupational division by sex takes place at entry. Of the males employed in 1980 in regular or created jobs, 62 percent worked in manufacturing, 7 percent in commerce and 7 percent in service (about half of them as home and office cleaners); work in agriculture and in transport and communications was also fairly common. Only 18 percent of the females worked in manufacturing, while 35 percent were in the service sector; a majority worked in child care, cleaning, restaurants, etc. Some 10 percent worked in commerce, 10 percent in offices and 7 percent in health care; young females employed in health or child care were almost all employed through the created job program (SCB 1982a, pp.37–40).

Young males with no more than compulsory schooling thus faced fewer problems than similar females. A larger proportion of males found regular jobs and a larger share of such jobs were permanent; the jobs of females often involved varieties of temporary work. The sex difference may arise from the divergent occupational aims of the two sexes, and/or the existence of separate labor markets and job discrimination. The female labor market may require that young female school-leavers, unlike their male counterparts, must become older in order to obtain access and in order to get permanent employment. Leave of absence for child care will be more common in the female labor market and the openings available for entrants can thus to a greater extent than in the male labor market be expected to be as temporary substitutes. Females of 16–17 might also face keener competition for unskilled jobs from older females than similar males do from older males.

Immigrant youth with good knowledge of Swedish entering the labor market directly after compulsory school do not diverge greatly from entering Swedish youth in occupational distribution. The problems arise among immigrant children with another home language than Swedish and a deficient knowledge of Swedish. In this group, 38 percent of those who completed compulsory school in 1979 entered the labor force. Of these, 74 percent had regular or created jobs and 18 percent were unemployed a year later; these were more adverse proportions than for immigrants with Swedish spoken in the home, or Swedish youth. Employed immigrant male youth with a deficient knowledge of Swedish had a lower share of office and commercial jobs and a larger share of restaurant and cleaning jobs than males with Swedish as the language at home. Male youth in both groups were mostly employed in manufacturing (68 percent of those with Swedish as home language, 62 percent of those with poor knowledge of Swedish), but those with deficient knowledge of Swedish had a lower share (18 percent versus 25 percent) in the more skilled, better paid engineering industry. Female immigrant youth with a deficient knowledge of Swedish had a larger share than females with Swedish as the home language in household work, including child care in the home, restaurant and cleaning work (46 percent versus 35 percent) and in manufacturing (34 percent versus 21 percent), and a lower share in clerical and commercial work (9 percent versus 21 percent) and in health care, sick care and teaching (0 versus 13 percent) (SÖ 1981b, pp.45–46).

ENTRY JOBS FROM UPPER SECONDARY SCHOOL

In contrast to youth entering the labor market after compulsory school, many of those entering after upper secondary school at 18–20 years of age have a basic vocational training. Consequently, their entry process is somewhat easier and their entry jobs are superior. Furthermore, youth graduating from different lines in upper secondary school vary in their jobs. The latest follow-up of leavers from upper secondary school, undertaken in 1979 for students who had completed the upper secondary level in 1977, showed that among out-of-school female graduates from the three and four-year lines, 95 percent were employed in regular or created jobs and 2 percent were unemployed in 1979 (SCB 1982b). The corresponding figures for female graduates from the two-year theoretical lines were 93 percent and 3 percent, and for female graduates from the two-year vocational lines 90 percent and 3 percent (SCB 1982b).

The picture for out-of-school male graduates is complicated by compulsory military service; about 40 percent of graduates from the two-year lines were doing their military service in the spring of 1979, against only 12 percent of the graduates from the three and four-year lines, since most had done it in 1978. Among male graduates from three and four-year theoretical lines who were not in education or military service, 95 percent were in regular or created jobs and 4 percent were unemployed in 1979. The corresponding figures for males from the two-year theoretical lines were 92 percent and 4 percent and for males from the two-year vocational lines 96 percent and 2 percent. About 30 percent of all 1977 male graduates and 36 percent of all female graduates had experienced some unemployment during the two years since graduation. This varied between different lines, with the largest variation shown by some of the female vocational lines (from a low of 16 percent with unemployment experience in the nursing line to about 50 percent in the consumer and the distribution and clerical lines).

The level of disaggregation in Table 8.1 is insufficient to establish the clear superiority of the early jobs obtained by upper secondary school graduates over compulsory school graduates, but it suggests that

Table 8.1 Type of Job, Permanency of Employment, and Earnings in 1979, Upper Secondary School Graduates of 1977, by Sex, Sweden

Type of job	Occupational distribution Male	Female	Permanent employment Male	Female	Monthly earnings of more than 4,500 Swedish crowns Male	Female
	(percentage distribution)		(percentage)			
Technical	7	1	79	*	32	*
Health care	5	29	60	65	24	19
(nurse's aide)	(4)	(23)	(54)	(65)	(13)	(15)
Teaching	6	6	24	14	*	38
Other scientific, technical, etc.	3	4	45	53	*	11
Administrative	0	0	*	*	*	*
Clerical	7	28	65	66	6	5
(secretary, typist)	(3)	(20)	(45)	(61)	(6)	(5)
Commercial	6	6	74	78	25	*
(shop assistant)	(3)	(5)	(81)	(80)	(6)	(*)
Agricultural, etc.	4	2	72	57	16	6
Mining and manufacturing	46	5	86	81	36	15
Transportation and communications	7	3	68	75	29	18
Service	7	17	47	59	31	12
(child care)	(1)	(8)	(*)	(54)	(*)	(11)
Military, non-identifiable, no response	3	1	*	*	*	*
Total	100	100	73	63	31	12

*Not statistically reliable.

Source: SCB 1982b, pp.40–41,42,44.

this was the case. Sex differences were marked in the job distributions. Females were concentrated in a few service occupations with only 5 percent in manufacturing. For males, manufacturing, accounting for 46 percent, was the main source of employment. Males also had larger shares than females in technical jobs, agriculture, and transport and communications. The sex-biased subject choices in upper secondary school thus carry over into occupational segmentation by sex. The majority of graduates of either sex whose line has a clear vocational profile work in that vocational area and graduates recruited into specific vocational areas come mainly from closely related vocational lines (SOU 1981c, pp.145–46).

Two years after graduation 73 percent of the employed males, but only 63 percent of the females had a job described as permanent (Table 8.1). This is partly because males have a larger share of employment than females in the occupations with high rates of permanent jobs (e.g., technical work and manufacturing). Within individual occupations males or females may have the higher rate of permanent employment.

Males earned more than females; 31 percent of full-time males, but only 12 percent of full-time females earned over 4,500 SW.cr. Women earned less in all occupational areas where comparisons can be made (Table 8.1). One study indicates that male graduates from the two-year lines with an economic orientation obtained jobs of higher level than comparable females; the differences were less marked between male and female graduates from the three-year economics line (SOU 1981c, p.144). Another study, however, shows that women with education in economics end up in lower-paying jobs than similar men at all levels of education (Gladh et al. 1981). Studies by Gustafsson (1981) have also shown significant superiority of earnings of men compared to women, even after controlling for educational attainment and work experience. Table 8.1 indicates that these differences start with entry jobs and pervade all occupational areas.

ENTRY JOBS FROM HIGHER EDUCATION

A follow-up in 1980 of students who received their degree in autumn 1979 covers the main study programs in higher education and clearly indicates the advantages of this group over those with less education (SCB 1982c). One year after receiving a degree, 89 percent of the female and 85 percent of the male graduates, a minority of whom are likely to be under 25, had employment as their main activity, while 1 percent of the female and 2 percent of the male graduates were unemployed. The majority of those employed, 64 percent of the women and 59 percent of the men, had a job at graduation and another 23 percent of the women and 19 percent of the men found a job within one month. Differences both in the percentage unemployed and in the duration of job search appeared for graduates from different study programs.

Some 89 percent of the females and 85 percent of the males employed indicated that they were working in an occupation corresponding to their study program. About 90 percent were in technical, scientific, social science, and administrative jobs. At entry to the labor market secondary school graduates have low representation in such jobs. Over two-thirds of the employed women from higher education and almost three-fourths of the employed men had permanent employment. Median monthly earnings for full-time women were 5,600 SW.cr. as compared to 6,000 SW.cr. for full-time men. The sex difference in median earnings partly reflects the inclusion of graduates from shorter female study programs (e.g., nursing and primary education teaching). Men were ahead in the high earnings bracket; 23 percent, compared to only 5 percent of the women, had monthly earnings over 7,000 SW.cr.

The follow-up surveys demonstrate that youth entering the labor market from the lowest educational levels had greater difficulty than others in entering employment and found less rewarding entry jobs in the late 1970s. Educational *level* was, however, not the only factor at work. Female gender, poor knowledge of Swedish, and choice of certain educational specializations also were associated with longer periods of entry unemployment and less desirable jobs. These findings raise two questions; what happens to different groups over time and did the experiences of youth in the late 1970s differ significantly from those of earlier cohorts of youth.

DEVELOPMENTS OVER TIME

Information about employment and unemployment over time is available for a cohort of youth who finished compulsory school in 1971 (SCB 1973; SCB 1978b; SCB 1980b). At the 1978 follow-up they were about 23 years old; those with no more than compulsory school had been in the labor market for six to seven years and those with no more than upper secondary school education had been economically active for three to five years. Many of those who had continued to higher education had not yet completed their degrees. By 1978, differences persisted between the unemployment rates of those who had less than a completed upper secondary school education and those who had completed it. The unemployment rate for male (female) non-completers was 7 percent (6 percent) as compared to 4 percent (1 percent) for male (female) completers. Some 15 percent of male and 21 percent of female non-completers had been unemployed more than twice between 1971 and 1978, against 10 percent of male and 11 percent of female completers. The non-completers, particularly females, also had had longer spells of unemployment than the completers. Another marked difference was that 16 percent of the female non-completers were housewives, compared to only 6 percent of the female completers.

The expected differences in occupational distribution between the educational levels do appear (Table 8.2). Seven years after leaving compulsory school, many male non-completers (to a greater extent than females), were in the same occupational groups as at entry. However, many males probably had advanced occupationally, for example, moving from cleaning work into other service jobs, and from packing, storage etc. into other manufacturing jobs. Female non-completers seem to have moved out of such entry jobs as child care in the home into health care and clerical work. Our hypothesis that female non-completers face a "waiting-period" before entering their later occupational area is supported by the data. The occupational distribution among non-completers of both sexes did not change much after 1975, indicating that, at this educational level, occupational advance from entry jobs to more demanding occupations occurs early and then pauses (SÖ 1980a, p.97). Also, by age 23 the completers had made few inroads into technical, scientific, and administrative work. Information on subsequent years is needed to round out the picture.

Seven years after leaving compulsory education, a person's length of time in the labor market appeared to give better job security and higher

Table 8.2   Jobs Held in 1978 by Compulsory School Leavers of 1971, by Type of Upper Secondary School Program and Sex, Sweden

	Males			Females		
		Completers			Completers	
			3-4 year			3-4´year
		Voca-	theo-		Voca-	theo-
	Non-com-	tional	retical	Non-com-	tional	retical
Type of job	pleters	lines	lines	pleters	lines	lines
	(percentage distribution)					
Technical	2	2	17	1	1	2
Health care	1	3	5	17	43	13
(nurse's aide)	(0)	(2)	(2)	(11)	(31)	(5)
Teaching	0	1	6	3	4	15
(primary school)	(*)	(0)	(0)	(*)	(**)	(9)
(pre-school)	(0)	(**)	(0)	(3)	(2)	(3)
Other scientific,						
technical, etc.	*	2	5	*	2	15
Administrative	*	0	1	*	**	2
Clerical	3	3	12	18	19	39
(secretary)	(1)	(1)	(3)	(12)	(14)	(26)
Commercial	7	4	9	9	4	2
Agricultural, etc.	6	4	2	2	2	1
Mining and manufacturing	61	72	26	19	8	2
Transportation and						
communications	12	7	7	3	1	2
Service	6	1	4	21	15	8
(maid, child care)	(*)	(**)	(1)	(*)	(9)	(4)
(cleaner)	(**)	(0)	(**)	(4)	(2)	(0)
Military, non-identifiable						
no response	4	3	5	6	2	1
Total	100	100	100	100	100	100

*No separate figures for the occupation for noncompleters.   **No entries.

Source: SCB 1980b, pp.36,46-47, and 53-54.

earnings than did a higher educational level. In 1978, 95 percent (88 percent) of male (female) non-completers, 92 percent (85 percent) of male (female) completers from vocational lines, 88 percent (84 percent) of completers from two-year theoretical lines and 86 percent (76 percent) of completers from three and four-year theoretical lines had permanent employment or were self-employed. Earnings followed the same pattern, but sex differences in earnings were more pronounced than sex differences in job security. Among males, 21 percent of non-completers, 21 percent of completers from vocational lines, 14 percent of completers from two-year theoretical lines, and 17 percent of completers from three and four-year theoretical lines earned over 5,000 SW.cr. per month in 1978. For females the respective percentages were only 2, 21, 14, and 7. With the passage of time, these job security differences should disappear and the completers from the theoretical lines will probably have a steeper earnings profile than the non-completers or the completers from the vocational lines.

Longitudinal studies indicate that the educational system functioned as a sorting system for youth in the 1940s, 1960s and 1970s (SOU 1981c, pp.30,43, 134–35). On average, those with more education obtained the jobs requiring more qualifications. There was, however, also substantial overlap so that some years after leaving education, many non-completers held jobs classified as requiring more formal education than they had and many completers held jobs classified as requiring less formal education (SÖ 1980, pp.81–92). For the non-completers the explanation might be in part that they had later training, on-the-job or in institutions. For example, in the 1978 follow-up, 21 percent (13 percent) of the male (female) non-completers indicated that they had taken part in training of more than one month's duration arranged by their employer while 11 percent (13 percent) had taken part in AMS labor market training. Completers showed lower proportions—10 percent (12 percent) and 5 percent (4 percent), respectively (SCB 1980b).

CHANGES DURING THE 1970s

Youth unemployment has increased during the 1970s and youth have also increasingly come to be employed via special labor market programs. In this sense, youth entering the labor market in the late 1970s and early 1980s have clearly had a more adverse experience than earlier cohorts. Youth with only compulsory school have been overrepresented among the unemployed, but recently the number and share of unemployed with completed upper secondary school training has grown, especially among female graduates from some two-year vocational and theoretical lines which prepare for female dominated service occupations (SÖ 1981c). A slow growth rate in the private sector and a deceleration of the formerly high growth rate in the public sector are the main factors behind these developments.

However, the question also arises whether other changes have taken place that have tended to worsen the employment situation for youth or subgroups of youth. While the employment situation for youth with less than a completed upper secondary education has become more difficult over time, many jobs still do not require more than compulsory school. The qualifications needed to carry out specific jobs do not in general seem to have increased over time (SOU 1981c, p.133). A study comparing the jobs held in 1970 and 1978 by 20–24 year-olds with no more than a compulsory education revealed no tendency for the jobs to become concentrated in fewer or lower-level occupations (SÖ 1981d). What seems to have happened is that youth with no more than a compulsory education are at more of a competitive disadvantage in seeking jobs now. A lack of an upper secondary education has become a negative signal to employers, whereas for earlier cohorts, a completed upper secondary education functioned as a positive signal (SOU 1981c, p.135). The introduction of the vocational upper secondary school in 1971 might also have led to the "professionalization" of additional occupations, so that a completed and specific vocational education came in practice to be required for an entry job. Such a tendency might not have become prominent until the competition for entry jobs increased from the late 1970s. A tendency toward professionalization also could explain the increased difficulty that female graduates from certain lines have in finding entry jobs, even though the actual work tasks in the desired entry jobs may not really require any more training than these young women have.

The recruitment behavior of employers may also have adjusted to the growth of the upper secondary school system, so that entry level jobs into the career ladders of internal labor markets are no longer offered to under 18 year-olds or those without basic vocational education. The increase in relative youth wages during the 1970s (see below) has given an economic incentive to employers to make such an adjustment to the changed educational system. When it turned out that there remained a significant share of a cohort of youth that did not want to (or was not able to) proceed to upper secondary school, jobs with training had become rare for youth under 18. At the same time, there seems to have been a growth of temporary jobs with low training content and no clear career path, perhaps suitable for students, but increasingly the chief type of job now available to out-of-school youth under 18. Their structure of unemployment is consistent with this, since it has been shown to consist of many relatively short spells of unemployment, interrupted by temporary jobs, and periods in created jobs through labor market policy measures (SOU 1981c, pp.115–19). A selection also seems to be occurring *within* the group that enters the labor force with no more than compulsory school, as is confirmed by local studies of youth unemployment (SOU 1981c, pp.115–23).

At the same time, however, the follow-up of the 1979 compulsory school-leavers, reported above, indicates that many found a job with permanent status within one year of leaving school and that their permanency rates were higher than those of the 1971 cohort (69 percent for men and 39 percent for women in the 1971 cohort compared to 70 percent for men and 50 percent for women in the 1979 cohort). In addition, the 1978 occupational distribution of the 1973–75 completers from upper secondary school, shown in Table 8.2, largely duplicates the 1979 distribution of 1977 graduates, shown in Table 8.1. This suggests that youth who obtained stable jobs suffered no marked deterioration in relative position in the 1970s. More research is needed on this subject.

Youth and Adult Employment Compared

Some differences in the types and characteristics of jobs held by youth and adults might be natural and desirable and have to do with progress over the life span. Youth may change jobs more often than adults, as part of a voluntary search process leading youth to better and more suitable jobs. Youth might also have lower earnings and less job responsibility than adults, but larger amounts of on-the-job training that would enhance later earnings and advancement possibilities. On the other hand, many youth may leave jobs involuntarily and not advance as they change jobs. Some job differences by age group may be the outcome of wage rigidities, institutional or legal restrictions, or discrimination.

JOB STABILITY AND JOB-CHANGING

The familiar decomposition of unemployment into a turnover and a duration component indicates that the unemployment differential between youth and adults can be ascribed to a higher turnover component for youth; youth experience more, but shorter spells of unemployment than other workers (Björklund 1981). One reason may be that it is much less common for youth than for adults to have stable jobs. Rates of job stability of 88 percent for adult men and 87 percent for adult women in 1974 compare with 56 percent for teenage males, 69 percent for young adult males, 41 percent for teenage females and 67 percent for young adult females. No drastic changes in these rates occurred between 1968 and 1974 according to tapes of the Level of Living Survey.

How important differences in job stability are for explaining unemployment rate differentials between age-sex groups can be seen from unemployment rates by labor market status (Table 8.3). A large part of the unemployment rate differential between young and adult workers of the same sex is due to differences in entry and reentry unemployment. Differences in entry unemployment also account for part of the adverse female differential in youth unemployment rates, which agrees with our earlier finding from the follow-ups of school-leavers that the entry process for females, particularly those with only compulsory school, is more difficult than for males. In addition, the end of temporary jobs accounts for a large part of the youth-adult unemployment rate differentials. This was the case for young women in 1975 and 1980 and for young men in 1980. Youth unemployment for this reason increased for both sexes between 1975 and 1980, but young women remained more affected than young men. Entry and reentry unemployment was about the same in 1980 as in 1975, which means that the increase in youth unemployment reflected increased difficulties of finding *permanent* jobs rather than increased difficulties of finding any job at all (regular

Table 8.3   Unemployment Rates by Labor Market Status, Age, and Sex,
            Sweden, 1975 and 1980

	Males				Females			
	16–24 years		25–74 years		16–24 years		25–74 years	
	1975	1980	1975	1980	1975	1980	1975	1980
	(percentage)							
New entrants	0.6	0.7	0.0	0.0	0.7	1.0	0.0	0.1
Reentrants	0.7	0.8	0.2	0.2	1.4	1.0	0.5	0.5
Temporary layoff	0.0	0.1	0.1	0.1	0.1	0.0	0.1	0.0
Permanent layoff	0.2	0.4	0.2	0.3	0.3	0.3	0.3	0.2
Temporary job	0.5	1.6	0.3	0.3	1.2	2.3	0.2	0.4
Other	0.8	0.9	0.3	0.3	1.1	1.0	0.3	0.4
Total	2.8	4.5	1.1	1.2	4.8	5.6	1.4	1.6

Source: SCB 1963–1982, 1975 and 1980 annual averages.

or created) at entry. Youth are not excessively burdened by unemployment in connection with layoffs, temporary or permanent. No
separate information is available about voluntary quits, which are
included in "other" in Table 8.3.

Youth also might have higher rates of voluntary and involuntary
job turnover than other age groups without intervening spells of unemployment. In 1980, 12 percent of male teenagers and 19 percent of
female teenagers who were employed at some time during the year
searched for new jobs while employed; these rates compared to 22 and
21 percent, respectively, for young adults, and 10 and 7 percent,
respectively, for adults (SCB 1981b). Of those who were in the labor
force during all of 1980, 21 and 31 percent of male and female teenagers,
respectively, 20 and 16 percent of young adults, and 8 and 6 percent
of adults had two or more employers during the year (SCB 1981b).
The lower rates of adults were present in earlier years as was the higher
rate of female teenagers than young adults. Teenage and young adult
males, however, showed a fluctuating relation.

The youth groups were clearly less stable than adults, which may
reflect both higher rates of involuntary quits due to jobs with limited
duration and higher rates of voluntary quits either as a response to
more attractive job offers or as a spontaneous reaction to unsatisfactory
jobs. Male teenagers and young adults indicate a great similarity in
job-changing, while female teenagers had almost double the job-changing
rate of female young adults. The difference might be explained by the
waiting-period hypothesis discussed above and a higher incidence of
temporary jobs in the female labor market.

The improved job security for older workers provided by the 1974
Employment Protection Act might, to some extent, have been at the

expense of younger or recently hired workers and might also have stimulated labor hoarding, thus depressing recruitment in economic upturns. These effects could, however, be regarded as a desirable redistribution of burdens from older to younger workers. But the law might also have had other effects. According to a study of recruitment behavior during 1977, many employers indicated that LAS had led them to be more cautious and selective when recruiting and many also said that LAS had meant that it had become more difficult for youth to get employment in their firms (Ds A 1980:2). Thus, improved job security combined with prohibitions on probationary and temporary employment caused employers' recruitment decisions to assume the character of a risky, fixed investment decision. The effect of the Act could have been for some youth to end up with better job security than they otherwise would have had, but for other youth to end up with no jobs at all.

Temporary employment is still very common; in 1979, such vacancies constituted 48 percent of the total. Temporary employment vacancies were more common in public and other services (54 percent) than in manufacturing (31 percent), and also more common for low-skill than high-skill jobs (Henning 1982). Such data supports the conclusion from Table 8.3 that part of the youth-adult unemployment differential is attributable to termination of temporary jobs and that young women, who are overrepresented in public and other services, would have more of this type of unemployment than young men. It may even be that the desire to circumvent the Employment Protection Act has led to an increase in temporary replacements and other forms of temporary jobs permitted by the Act. Increased legal rights to obtain leave for studies, care of small children, etc. during the 1970s must have resulted in an increased need by firms for temporary replacements, also affecting the kind of openings available to new entrants.

TYPE OF JOBS

Chapter 3 has shown significant differences between the occupations of Swedish youth and adults. These differences are also reflected in the age distribution of employment in various industries. In 1965, male teenagers were overrepresented in manufacturing and construction and underrepresented in banking and business services and public and personal services. Young adult males had about the same overrepresentation as teenagers in manufacturing and construction; in both industries, male youth were more overrepresented than male adults. In contrast to male teenagers, male young adults were overrepresented in transportation and communications, and had a much higher representation in banking and business services. Male teenagers had a higher representation than male young adults in agriculture and forestry, and trade, restaurants, etc. Male young adults were underrepresented in public and personal services, but less so than teenage males.

Between 1965 and 1980, the share of male youth in total employment decreased, mainly due to increased educational enrollment rates; there were also some changes in the character of male youth employment. Both teenagers and young adults became more overrepresented in manufacturing. In construction there was a marked decrease in the overrepresentation of teenagers, whereas the overrepresentation of young adults remained roughly unchanged. Teenagers still had a higher representation than older males in trade, restaurants, etc. and a lower representation than older males in transport and communications, banking and business services, and public and private services.

In 1965, female teenagers, young adults, and adults were underrepresented in agriculture and forestry, construction, transportation and communications, and manufacturing. All female age groups were overrepresented in trade, restaurants, hotels, banking and business services, and public and private services. Between 1965 and 1980, female teenagers and young adults remained underrepresented in the same industries as in 1965, and their underrepresentation did not increase, except in manufacturing. Female teenagers lost out heavily in banking and business services, becoming underrepresented. The overrepresentation of female teenagers in trade, restaurants, and hotels increased, whereas there was a decrease for young adults and adults. The overrepresentation of females in public and personal services declined, but more so for teenagers than for older women.

The age distribution of employment by industry confirms that there are significant differences between teenage and adult employment, whereas the employment of young adults bears a closer resemblance to that of adults. Marked changes in youth representation by industry occurred between 1965 and 1980. In certain industries, the divergent developments for teenagers and young adults might have stemmed from such factors as altered relative wages, technological change, new legislation, and changes in educational requirements before entry. For example, certain categories of teenagers who in 1965 would have been in occupations with on-the-job training might in 1980 instead have received their training before entry in the vocational lines of *Gymnasieskolan,* thus changing the age distribution in certain industries.

Another measure of youth-adult differences is shown in Table 8.4. As expected, adults are more likely than youth to be employers, and fewer teenagers than young adults are employers. Employer status is about twice as common among young adult males as among young adult females. Private sector employment, outside of agriculture, is more common among youth than adults. While there were no major changes in the share of the private sector in male employment between 1965 and 1980, for women in all age groups a large decrease occurred in the importance of the private sector; by 1980, only female teenagers found over half of their jobs there. The local government public sector, responsible for health care, child care, and social services, has greatly increased its employment share in all age-sex groups since 1965, especially

Table 8.4 Occupational Status of Employed Population, by Age and Sex, Sweden, 1965 and 1980

		Total	Agriculture, forestry, etc.	Employees			Nonagricultural employers and self-employed	Paid and unpaid family workers
				National government	Local government	Private sector		
		(number)	(percentage distribution)					
Males								
16-19 years	1980	118,200	7.4	6.1	8.1	77.9	0.2	0.1
	1965	158,500	11.9	7.4	3.0	76.2	1.1	0.3
20-24 years	1980	231,600	5.0	8.8	10.8	73.8	1.6	0.1
	1965	239,900	6.6	11.3	2.5	77.4	2.0	0.1
25-74 years	1980	1,977,000	8.0	11.7	10.6	63.1	6.6	0.0
	1965	1,945,400	14.7	10.1	5.2	60.5	9.5	0.1
Females								
16-19 years	1980	110,900	2.5	5.9	35.3	56.2	0.0	0.0
	1965	135,100	1.7	9.0	10.5	78.6	0.1	0.1
20-24 years	1980	213,100	1.2	8.2	48.4	41.4	0.8	0.0
	1965	178,400	1.4	11.8	20.6	64.8	1.2	0.4
25-74 years	1980	1,581,500	3.4	9.1	43.3	41.3	2.8	0.2
	1965	1,039,600	9.0	9.3	21.0	54.6	4.7	1.6

Source: SCB 1963-1982, annual averages 1965 and 1980.

for females. But the national government share declined for all age-sex groups except adult males (Table 8.4).

HOURS OF WORK AND OTHER JOB CHARACTERISTICS

The decline in average weekly hours worked from 1970 to 1980 affected both sexes and youth and adults alike. Among males, average hours worked in the 1980 survey week increased with age, but among females, adults had a shorter average work week than either youth group. Growth in the proportion of part-time workers from 1970 to 1980 was one of the main reasons for declining average hours. Teenage males were more likely than older males to be part-time workers. Of males in the labor force in 1980, 16 percent of teenagers, 5 percent of young adults, and 3 percent of adults (25–54 years old) worked part-time (1–34 hours per week). Among females in the labor force in 1980, 16 percent of teenagers, 5 percent of young adults and 9 percent of adults (25–54 years old) worked 1–19 hours per week, while 40 percent of adults, 20 percent of young adults and 17 percent of teenagers held part-time jobs of 20–34 hours. Working part-time is in most cases a voluntary choice for youth, reflecting a desire to combine jobs with studies and/or household work. Among young males working part-time in 1980, only about 5 percent indicated that it was involuntary; the rate had been the same through the 1970s. About 10 percent of the young females who worked part-time did so involuntarily, but by 1980 it was up to 20 percent (SCB 1963–82).

Among youth working full-time, the incidence of inconvenient working hours is in most cases about the same or lower than among all full-time workers (16–74 years old) of the same sex. Early morning, evening, and night work are below average for young men. Young women also have a below average incidence of night work, but the incidence of early morning work is slightly higher and of evening work markedly higher than average (SCB 1976b). Higher proportions of youth than of all workers indicate that their jobs are physically demanding. Dirty work is markedly above average for young men and somewhat above average for young women. Slightly higher proportions of youth than of all workers regard their work as very or rather dangerous. Psychologically demanding or stressful jobs involve older workers to a greater extent than youth, but a higher than average proportion of young workers find their jobs monotonous (SCB 1978c). As expected, the proportion holding supervisory jobs increases with age. Computations from the tapes of the Level of Living Survey indicate that almost no teenagers of either sex hold supervisory positions, whereas about 10 percent of young adult and 30 percent of adult males, and 8 percent of young adult and 16 percent of adult females have supervisory tasks.

Youth under 25 are not the most favored group for on-the-job training; the proportion holding jobs with high possibilities of learning new abilities was higher for 25–34 year-old than 16–24 year-old male workers and also higher for 25–34 year-old than 16–24 year-old female workers in both 1975 and 1979. In all age groups, the training content of jobs is lower for females than for corresponding males. An improvement in the training content of jobs from 1975 to 1979 affected both sexes. Among males the improvement was concentrated on adults 35–64 years old, resulting in a deterioration of the relative position of male youth. Among women the improvement was more evenly distributed so that female youth kept their relative position (SCB 1978c; SCB 1982d).

The Level of Living Survey gives information about the educational prerequisites of youth and adult jobs in 1968 and 1974. While only 40 percent of all jobs were said to require more than compulsory education in 1968, the proportion reached 51 percent by 1974. The increased requirements were, however, concentrated on adult jobs; the proportion of teenage males holding jobs requiring more than compulsory education declined from 34 percent in 1968 to 27 percent in 1974, while the proportion for young adult males decreased from 55 to 49 percent. For young women, the proportion holding jobs requiring more than compulsory education remained at about 25 percent for teenagers and increased from 46 to 51 percent for young adults. Though the above data about the development of on-the-job training and educational requirements in youth jobs should be treated with care, they give cause for concern and point to the need for further research.

The hypothesis that there has been a deterioration in the quality of youth jobs is also supported by a rise from 1975 to 1979 in the proportion of youth, particularly male, indicating that they work only as a means of earning money, contrary to a decrease among adults (SCB 1978c; SCB 1982d). One factor behind such a change could be that the available jobs for youth have become less satisfactory. Another could be that youth have changed their life style and value leisure activities more highly than before, while adults have changed less (see also, Rehn 1980).

RELATIVE EARNINGS

An important and widely discussed feature of the Swedish labor market since the 1960s has been rising relative earnings of youth (Table 8.5). The same pattern can be found for both blue and white collar workers of each sex. This development is attributable either to market forces or the wage policy of the trade unions, or to a combination of both. The central wage agreements for both blue and white collar workers negotiated during the 1970s were primarily intended to decrease wage differentials among all workers, but also to raise the relative wages of new entrants. Among the methods used to achieve this aim was the negotiation of across-the-board absolute wage increases instead of per-

Table 8.5   Earnings of Youth Relative to Adults, by Age and Sex, Sweden, 1960–1980

	1960	1964	1968	1970	1974	1978	1980
				(ratio)			
Males							
16–17/18 and over[a]	.56	.58	.58	.63	.65	.70	.72
16–17/20 and over[b]	n.a.	n.a.	n.a.	.27	.30	.38	.39
18–19/20 and over[b]	n.a.	n.a.	n.a.	.37	.40	.49	.48
16–19/25 and over[c]	n.a.	n.a.	.46	n.a.	.58	n.a.	n.a.
20–24/25 and over[c]	n.a.	n.a.	.75	n.a.	.82	n.a.	n.a.
Females							
16–17/18 and over[a]	.69	.71	.71	.75	.74	.80	.81
16–17/20 and over[b]	n.a.	n.a.	n.a.	.47	.49	.54	.58
18–19/20 and over[b]	n.a.	n.a.	n.a.	.59	.61	.68	.68
16–19/25 and over[c]	n.a.	n.a.	.51	n.a.	.53	n.a.	n.a.
20–24/25 and over[c]	n.a.	n.a.	.83	n.a.	.87	n.a.	n.a.
Females/Males[c]							
16–19	n.a.	n.a.	.79	n.a.	.70	n.a.	n.a.
20–24	n.a.	n.a.	.80	n.a.	.81	n.a.	n.a.
25 and over	n.a.	n.a.	.72	n.a.	.77	n.a.	n.a.

[a]Blue collar workers. Average hourly earnings, including overtime.
[b]White collar workers. Average monthly earnings for full-time work, excluding overtime. [c]All employed. Average hourly earnings.

Source: SCB 1960–80 for ratios for blue collar and white collar workers (footnote a or b); tapes from Level of Living Survey for ratios for all employed (footnote c).

centage increases. Youth 18 years and over were treated as adults for this purpose, while special wage agreements for minors (under 18) gave high wage increases to this group also. Thus, the intentions of the central wage agreements were reflected in actual earnings outcomes for youth. The rising unemployment rates for youth seem to cast doubt on the market explanation of the observed increase in relative earnings, unless the effects of market influences in the 1960s and early 1970s, when the youth labor supply decreased because of higher school enrollment and the demand for labor was generally high, persisted into the late 1970s (Rehn 1980, pp.75–76). Moreover, during the 1970s, Swedish youth increasingly brought more human capital with them at entry, which should tend to give higher relative earnings for those who did find employment.

To what extent has this increase in relative earnings been responsible for the recent worsening of the employment situation of youth? The lower productivity and higher non-wage costs of youth, due to such things as less experience, higher turnover rates, etc. must be offset by lower wage rates if youth are to compete for jobs. This will particularly be the case during periods of general labor market slack when adult workers are available. A relative earnings increase, without offsetting increases in productivity, can lead to a decrease in the youth employment growth rate; the losers are those who do not find jobs. These are likely to be youth whom employers consider least likely to display the productivity implicit in the increased relative wage; such youth tend to have no more than compulsory school or difficult social backgrounds, etc. However, employed youth may also be affected, if they have to accept jobs with less favorable characteristics than would be the case without the relative wage rise. They might, for example, end up in jobs providing less on-the-job training or less stability. Though there is much discussion in Sweden about the impact of relative wages on youth employment and indications that the relative wage rates for youth may be reconsidered, empirical evidence is lacking to support the divergent viewpoints. The only available econometric study found youth labor (under 18 years old) to be complementary with adult labor in production, but also found youth labor to be easily, much more so than adult labor, substituted for by capital (Ekberg 1979). The precision of the estimates was, however, low and the results must be regarded as tentative.

Table 8.5 also shows that a sex differential in earnings exists for all three age-groups. The relative earnings for adults in 1968 put females at a greater disadvantage in comparison to males than was the case for young adults and teenagers. By 1974, the ratio for adult women had advanced, that of young adults had barely risen, and that for teenagers had decreased by almost 10 percentage points. This may be another indication of a difficult employment situation for teenage females; those who do find employment are more likely than teenage males to hold jobs not covered by union contracts and their wage development therefore probably reflects market forces to a greater extent. The earnings trend also indicates that the greater deterioration in the employment of female teenagers compared to males cannot be explained by an increase in female relative wages. This is not so surprising, given the rather strong division into male and female occupations described above.

A Longitudinal Perspective

How important is the early labor market experience of youth for their subsequent labor market prospects as adults? Do entry level and subsequent jobs simply replicate the personal attributes of youth or do they reinforce and perpetuate the traits and qualifications youth have on entry? Tables 8.6–8.8 present some descriptive analysis based on longitudinal data from the Level of Living Survey. The labor market position in 1967 or 1968 of individuals, grouped as youth (16–24) and adults (25 and over), is compared with the position of the same

Table 8.6 Distribution of Hourly Earnings in 1968 and 1974 of Persons Employed in Both Years, by Age and Sex, Sweden

Youth

16-24 years old in 1968	Males 22-30 years old in 1974					Females 22-30 years old in 1974				
	Quartiles					Quartiles				
	Lowest	2nd	3rd	Highest	Total	Lowest	2nd	3rd	Highest	Total
	(percentage)					(percentage)				
Quartiles[a]										
Lowest	9.9	5.0	4.6	4.6	24.1	7.7	5.5	5.8	5.9	24.9
Second	6.9	7.6	6.8	4.2	25.5	8.3	7.8	5.2	4.1	25.4
Third	6.1	6.9	8.4	4.2	25.6	7.7	5.4	7.0	5.3	25.4
Highest	1.9	5.0	6.1	11.8	24.8	1.2	4.3	9.3	9.5	24.3
Total	24.8	24.5	25.9	24.8	100.0 n=262	24.9	23.0	27.3	24.8	100.0 n=169

Calculated $\chi^2_{(df=9)}$=37.4; significant at 1% level.

Calculated $\chi^2_{(df=9)}$=18.2; significant at 5% level.

Adults

25 years and over in 1968	Males 31 years and over in 1974					Females 31 years and over in 1974				
	Quartiles					Quartiles				
	Lowest	2nd	3rd	Highest	Total	Lowest	2nd	3rd	Highest	Total
	(percentage)					(percentage)				
Quartiles[a]										
Lowest	14.4	6.9	2.2	1.5	25.0	14.4	6.7	2.3	0.9	24.3
Second	6.2	10.8	6.9	1.1	25.0	7.8	10.0	6.5	1.2	25.5
Third	2.8	5.7	12.3	4.2	25.0	2.1	6.1	12.2	4.5	24.9
Highest	1.6	1.6	3.6	18.2	25.0	0.4	1.8	4.7	18.4	25.3
Total	25.0	25.0	25.0	25.0	100.0 n=1,006	24.7	24.6	25.7	25.0	100.0 n=575

Calculated $\chi^2_{(df=9)}$=649.9; significant at 1% level.

Calculated $\chi^2_{(df=9)}$=380.7; significant at 1% level.

[a]In 1968, quartiles ranged from under 6.99 SW.cr. to 10.56 and over for 16-24 year-old males, from under 5.87 SW.cr. to 8.21 and over for 16-24 year-old females, from under 9.75 SW.cr. to 14.79 and over for adult males, and from under 7.38 SW.cr. to 11.55 and over for adult females. [b]In 1974, quartiles ranged from under 16.27 SW.cr. to 21.89 and over for 22-30 year-old males, from under 13.89 SW.cr to 17.29 and over for 22-30 year-old females, from under 17.05 SW.cr. to 23.57 and over for males 31 years and over and from under 13.94 SW.cr. to 18.96 and over for females 31 years and over.

Source: Computations from the tapes of the Level of Living Survey.

individuals six years later. The distributions show to what extent those who had an unfavorable position in 1968, also had such a position in 1974. The null hypothesis, to be evaluated by the chi-square test, is that the distribution of positions in the labor market in 1974 is independent of the distribution six years earlier.

A priori there are many strong arguments for the view that poor entry to the labor market can have longer run deleterious welfare effects on youth. Availability of jobs is a necessary condition to obtain on-the-job training, but the characteristics of the initial jobs are crucial too, since all entry jobs do not provide training and upward mobility

Table 8.7   Unemployment During 1967 and 1973 of Members of
the Labor Force in Both Years, by Age in 1968,
Both Sexes, Sweden

| | 16-24 years old in 1968 | | |
	Unemployed any time in 1973	Not unemployed any time in 1973	Total
	(percentage)		
Unemployed any time in 1967	1.5	5.1	6.6
Not unemployed any time in 1967	8.2	85.2	93.4
Total	9.7	90.3	100.0
			n=728

Calculated $\chi^2_{(df=1)}$=10.12; significant at 1% level.

| | 25 years and over in 1968 | | |
	Unemployed any time in 1973	Not unemployed any time in 1973	Total
	(percentage)		
Unemployed any time in 1967	1.3	3.4	4.7
Not unemployed any time in 1967	3.0	92.3	95.3
Total	4.3	95.7	100.0
			n=2,354

Calculated $\chi^2_{(df=1)}$=148.4; significant at 1% level.

Source: Same as Table 8.6.

in earnings and status or access to other jobs with these features. A difficult labor market entry can have deleterious consequences via other mechanisms too. Lack of information might mean that employers use "statistical discrimination" and treat those who are unemployed or have a low status job unfavorably. Furthermore, the problems experienced in the labor market might have negative effects on the attitude and ambitions of young people. Here we have chosen to classify entry experience in terms of job availability (unemployment experience), earnings, and other job characteristics.

The analysis is of the positions in the wage distributions by quartiles in 1968 and 1974 (Table 8.6), unemployment in 1967 and 1973 (Table

Table 8.8 Degree of Job Security and Attainment of Supervisory Position in 1968 and 1974 of Persons Employed in Both Years, by Age, Both Sexes, Sweden

Job Security Reported by Workers

16-24 years old in 1968	22-30 years old in 1974			
	Stable job	Plan to quit	Expect lay-off, temp. job, other	Total
	(percentage)			
Stable job	57.6	5.7	3.4	66.7
Plan to quit	10.7	2.1	2.0	14.8
Expect layoff, temp. job, other	15.5	0.7	2.3	18.5
Total	83.8	8.5	7.7	100.0
				n=439

Calculated χ^2(df=4)=13.65; significant at 5% level.

25 years and over in 1968	31 years and over in 1974			
	Stable job	Plan to quit	Expect lay-off, temp. job, other	Total
	(percentage)			
Stable job	81.8	2.9	4.1	88.9
Plan to quit	3.8	0.4	0.6	4.8
Expect layoff, temp. job, other	5.0	0.4	1.0	6.3
Total	90.6	3.7	5.7	100.0
				n=1,619

Calculated χ^2(df=4)=34.52; significant at 1% level.

Self-reported Job with Supervisory Position

16-24 years in 1968	22-30 years old in 1974		
	No	Yes	Total
	(percentage)		
No	80.0	2.2	82.2
Yes	13.3	4.5	17.8
Total	93.3	6.7	100.0
			n=439

Calculated χ^2(df=1)=56.9; significant at 1% level.

25 years and over in 1968	31 years and over in 1974		
	No	Yes	Total
	(percentage)		
No	61.6	11.6	73.3
Yes	7.4	19.3	26.7
Total	69.0	30.9	100.0
			n=1,619

Calculated χ^2(df=1)=336.0; significant at 1% level.

Source: Same as Table 8.6.

8.7), and distributions by the characteristics of jobs held in 1968 and 1974 (Table 8.8). Data are presented separately for youth and adults. In all cases the null hypothesis that the distributions are independent is rejected. The deviations from independence also reveal a systematic pattern. Those who had a strong (weak) position in 1968 (1967) tended to have a stronger (weaker) position in 1974 (1973) than the position they would have had if the distributions were independent.

There is, however, a non-negligible amount of mobility between positions in the labor market. Table 8.6 reveals, for example, that almost 20 percent of those young men who were in the lowest wage quartile in 1968 were in the highest quartile six years later. It appears that a majority of those who were unemployed at any time during 1967 were not unemployed at any time during 1973, although those who were unemployed in 1967 had a higher risk of being unemployed in 1973 than those who were not unemployed in 1967 (Table 8.7). In the same way, most of those who had a temporary job in 1968 had a stable or permanent job in 1974. But still, those with a temporary job in 1968 had a higher probability of having a temporary job in 1974 than those who had a permanent job in 1968 (Table 8.8).

Another common feature, indicated by higher chi-square statistics for adults, is that the youth labor market is characterized by greater mobility in earnings, job stability, etc. than the adult one. What general conclusions can be drawn from this analysis? First, the rather high amount of mobility for youth between positions in the labor market shows that all who start their labor market career with a low-paying job, unemployment experience, or a job with "bad characteristics" are not predestined to have an adverse position as adults too. The risk of having an unfavorable position as adults is, however, higher for these groups. Consequently, our data are compatible with the common view in the Swedish political debate that a difficult entry to the labor market can have serious long run consequences. Nonetheless, we have not shown that there are any causal mechanisms between the labor market situation during youth and the adult situation. It might also be that those who have unfavorable positions both in youth and as adults have adverse personal characteristics. To discriminate between these two explanations requires more controls for a number of variables than are available for this data. Björklund (1981) investigated whether the occurrence of unemployment and the duration of unemployment have any deleterious effects on subsequent wages. The results were not completely conclusive, but there were some indications of "duration effects" of unemployment, i.e. the longer a person has been unemployed, the lower the subsequent wage will be. This result clearly supports the emphasis in Swedish labor market policy on the importance of availability of jobs.

Summary and Conclusions

Swedish discussion and policy concern in the area of youth employment have focused mainly on the inadequacy of the number of jobs open to Swedish youth. There has been much less concern with what happens to youth once they have found employment, that is the types of jobs they obtain and their occupational and earnings mobility as they age. In this chapter, we have examined the character of Swedish youth employment with a view to identifying the problem areas, if any, and the relations and interactions between the educational and institutional systems and youth employment, and between youth unemployment and the character of youth employment.

Swedish youth today bring substantially more human capital with them at labor market entry than did their parents. Increasingly, 11 or 12 years of schooling, i.e., completion of an upper secondary school program, theoretical or vocational, is becoming the norm. At the same time, however, the percentage leaving compulsory school without full completion increased during the 1970s. It may be that the negative sorting function of the educational system is becoming more pronounced and that there is an increased polarization between youth who continue and advance in the educational system and youth who do not. Differences in the work histories of these two groups, at entry and later in life, will be an important area for future research.

Swedish youth seem to be well prepared for the world of work. Programs for occupational orientation and practical work experience cover all students and almost all youth have worked during vacations and/or terms while in school. The allegation, sometimes made in the discussion of Swedish youth unemployment, that today's youth are not well enough prepared for working life thus needs further discussion. If anything, youth get more preparation for the world of work than did earlier generations. This means that the relevant question is why employers demand more preparation than before and why they are not willing to supply such preparation as part of the on-the-job training of youth. One possible explanation could be the increased relative costs of youth labor.

The problems experienced at entry differ by educational attainment and by sex. Entry problems, as reflected in unemployment rates and incidence of unemployment experience, are most pronounced for youth with no more than compulsory school. Among such youth, males fare better than females; a larger proportion of males find regular jobs at entry and a larger share of their jobs are permanent. Among youth with upper secondary school training, entry problems vary considerably according to the study program followed. There are great differences in unemployment incidence during entry among graduates from various programs, but the differences in unemployment rates two years after graduation are much less marked. Differences in unemployment by educational level, on the other hand, persist over time, as is shown by the longitudinal follow-up on the 1971 cohort of compulsory school-leavers and cross-sectional labor force survey data on unemployment rates by age and educational attainment. Youth with only compulsory school thus seem to have not only more severe entry problems but also more severe permanent labor market problems. Consequently, policy measures to improve the permanent labor market position of this group might also be called for.

The initial jobs held by youth also vary with educational level. There is, however, an overlap and some years after entry many of those with only compulsory school hold jobs classified as requiring more formal education than they have and many of those with upper secondary school hold jobs classified as requiring less formal education than they have.

Among youth with only compulsory school, and thus no specific vocational training, an occupational division by sex takes place at entry. At the same time, a similar division takes place among their former classmates who continue their education in vocational lines and make sex-biased choices of educational programs that are later carried over into sex differences in entry jobs. The overall picture emerging is one of divergent occupational aims of the two sexes and of separate male and female labor markets. It seems that both the sex difference in entry problems and the significantly higher unemployment rates for young women than for young men might be explained by this segmentation into different labor markets and differences in the ways they operate. When men and women with the same educational background are found in the same occupations, the women earn less. Since this is true of entry jobs also, other factors than differences in human capital must be at work.

The distribution of youth employment between industries and between sectors of the economy differs from that of adult employment. Employed Swedish youth seem to be fairly well off. Their relative wages are rather high and increased substantially during the 1970s. Youth report a higher incidence of certain job characteristics such as physically demanding work, risky work and monotonous work, but, on the other hand, they are less likely than adults to find their jobs psychologically demanding. Signs of a negative development of training content and educational requirements in youth jobs do, however, give cause for concern.

The Swedish youth labor market is characterized by greater mobility in earnings, job stability, etc. than is the adult one. Youth with unfavorable entry experience are thus not predestined to have adverse positions as adults. Their risk of having an unfavorable position as adults is, however, higher than it is for youth with more favorable entry experience.

As can be expected, part of the unemployment rate differential between youth and adult workers of the same sex is due to differences in the incidence of entry and reentry unemployment. But there are also characteristics of youth employment that seem to make for high unemployment rates. Termination of temporary employment accounts for a substantial part of the youth-adult unemployment differential and its tendency to widen. A significant part of the unemployment differential between male and female youth is also attributable to temporary employment and its reflection, in part, of differences in the functioning of male and female labor markets. Thus, the problem for Swedish youth, particularly female, seems to be not so much that of finding a job (regular or created) as that of finding a permanent one.

Since there are no signs of a decrease in the proportion of employed youth holding permanent jobs, what seems to be happening is that youth in temporary jobs are having a more difficult and prolonged transition into permanent employment. This is what can be expected to happen during a period of slow growth, but the problems probably have been accentuated by increases in the relative wages of youth and changes in job security legislation. The exact weights to assign to slow growth, increases in relative wages, and legislative changes as causal factors behind the changes in entry problems and job characteristics of Swedish youth does, however, remain a controversial and unsettled issue.

References: Sweden

Björklund, A. 1981. *Studies in the Dynamics of Unemployment.* Stockholm: The Economic Research Institute, Stockholm School of Economics.

Björklund, A.; Johannesson, J.; and Persson-Tanimura, I. 1979. *Labour Market Policy and Labour Market Development in Sweden During the 1960s and 1970s.* IIM papers no.14. Berlin: International Institute of Management.

Ds A 1980:2 *Anställningsformer m.m.* (*Employment Types etc.*). Reports from the Department of Labor. Stockholm: LiberFörlag.

Ekberg, J. 1979. *Sysselsättningseffekter av lönesubventioner* (*Employment Effects of Wage Subsidies*). Växjö: Department of Economics, Växjö University.

Gladh, L.; Lantz, P.; and Saro, I. 1981. "Var finns det kvinnliga ekonomer?" ("Where are Female Economists to be Found?"). In *Kvinnor och ekonomi* (*Women and Economics*). Stockholm: Affärsförlaget.

Gustafsson, S. 1981. "Male-Female Lifetime Earnings Differentials and Labor Force History." In Eliasson, G., Holmlund, B., and Stafford, F.P., eds. *Studies in Labor Market Behavior: Sweden and the United States.* Stockholm: Almqvist & Wiksell International.

Henning, A. 1982. *Tidesbegränsad anställning.* (*Temporary Employment*). Lund: Department of Law, Lund University.

Holmlund, B. 1981. "Determinants and Characteristics of Unemployment in Sweden: The Role of Labor Market Policy." In Eliasson, G., Holmlund, B., and Stafford, F.P., eds. *Studies in Labor Market Behavior: Sweden and the United States.* Stockholm: Almqvist & Wiksell International.

Johannesson, J. 1981. *On the Composition of Swedish Labour Market Policy.* Stockholm: Expert Group for Labour Market Research, Department of Labor.

Persson-Tanimura, I. 1980. *Studier kring arbetsmarknad och information.* (*Studies in Labor Markets and Information*). Lund Economic Studies no.19. Stockholm: LiberFörlag.

Rehn, G. 1980. "Sweden." In *Education and Youth Employment in Sweden and Denmark.* Berkeley, Cal.: Carnegie Council on Policy Studies in Higher Education.

SCB (Central Bureau of Statistics). 1960–80. *Löner*. (*Wages*). Stockholm: SOS (Official Statistics of Sweden).
_____. 1963–82. *Arbetskraftsundersökningen, Årsmedeltal*. (*Labor Force Survey*, Annual Averages). Stockholm: SCB.
_____. 1973. *SM U* (*Statistical Reports, Educational Statistics Series*). 1973:1. Stockholm: SOS.
_____. 1976a. *SM U* 1976:43. Stockholm: SOS.
_____. 1976b. *Levnadsförhållanden*. (*Living Conditions*). Report no.2. Stockholm: SOS.
_____. 1978a. *SM U* 1978:29. Stockholm: SOS.
_____. 1978b. *SM U* 1978:21. Stockholm: SOS.
_____. 1978c. *Levnadsförhållanden*. (*Living Conditions*). Report no.12. Stockholm: SOS.
_____. 1980a. *Information i prognosfrågor*. (*Forecasting Information*). 1980:4. Stockholm: SOS.
_____. 1980b. *SM U* 1980:16. Stockholm: SOS.
_____. 1981a. *Utbildningsstatistisk årsbok 1980*. (*Yearbook of Educational Statistics 1980*). Stockholm: SOS.
_____. 1981b. *Årssysselsättningen 1980 och utbildningsnivån februari 1981*. Tilläggsfrågor till Arbetskraftsundersökningen i februari 1981. (*Employment During 1980 and Educational Level in February 1981*. February Retrospective Labor Force Survey 1981). Stockholm: SCB.
_____. 1981c. *Levnadsförhållanden*. (*Living Conditions*). Report no.26. Stockholm: SOS.
_____. 1982a. *SM U* 1982:6. Stockholm: SOS.
_____. 1982b. *SM U* 1982:3. Stockholm: SOS.
_____. 1982c. *SM U* 1982:12. Stockholm: SOS.
_____. 1982d. *Levnadsförhållanden*. (*Living Conditions*). Report no.32. Stockholm: SOS.
SOU (Swedish Government Official Reports). 1977. *Utbildning i företag, kommuner och landsting*. (*Training in the Private and the Local Government Public Sector*). 1977:92. Stockholm: LiberFörlag.
_____. 1981a. *En reformerad gymnasieskola*. (*A Reformed Upper Secondary School*). 1981:96. Stockholm: LiberFörlag.
_____. 1981b. *Undersökningar kring gymnasieskolan*. (*Research About Upper Secondary School*). 1981:97. Stockholm: LiberFörlag.
_____. 1981c. *Studieorganisation och elevströmmar*. (*Study Organization and Student Flows*). 1981:98. Stockholm: LiberFörlag.
SÖ (National Board of Education). 1979a. *Förvärvsarbete parallellt med studier på grundskolans högstadium*. (*Gainful Employment Among Students in Compulsory School*). P 1 1979:1. Stockholm: SÖ.
_____. 1979b. *Förvärvsarbete vid sidan av studierna. Elever på gymnasieskolans 3- och 4-åriga linjer*. (*Gainful Employment Among Students in the 3- and 4-year Theoretical Lines of Upper Secondary School*). P 1 1979:6. Stockholm: SÖ.
_____. 1980. *Ungdomars studie- och yrkesverksamhet under de sju första åren efter grundskolan*. (*Studies and Labor Market Activity Among Youth During the Seven First Years After Leaving Compulsory School*). P 1 1980:3. Stockholm: SÖ.
_____. 1981a. *Elever med annat hemspråk än svenska, som gick ut grundskolan 1979. Delrapport 1*. (*Comprehensive School Leavers in 1979 with Another Home Language than Swedish. Part 1*). P 1 1981:1. Stockholm: SÖ.
_____. 1981b. *Elever med annat hemspråk än svenska, som gick ut grundskolan 1979. Delrapport 1*. (*Comprehensive School Leavers in 1979 with Another Home Language than Swedish. Part 3*). P 1 1981:1. Stockholm: SÖ.
_____. 1981c. *Arbetssökande ungdomars utbildningsbakgrund hösten 1980*. (*Educational Background Among Unemployed Youth in Autumn 1980*). P 1 1981:11. Stockholm: SÖ.

————. 1981d. *De grundskoleutbildades sysselsättning 1970 och 1978. En jämforelse av grundskoleutbildade ungdomars (20–24 år) yrken 1970 och 1978. (Employment Among Youth with Comprehensive School in 1970 and 1978. A Comparison of Occupations in 1970 and 1978 Among Youth 20–24 Years Old*). 1 1981:13. Stockholm: SÖ.

Vuksanović, M. 1979. *Kodbok för 1974 års levnadsnivåundersökning. (Codebook for the Level of Living Survey 1974*). Stockholm: Swedish Institute for Social Research.

Chapter 9

Youth Employment in the United States

Stephen M. Hills and Beatrice G. Reubens

Youth employment in the United States encompasses both in-school and out-of-school youth because so many students participate in the labor force. An overview shows a deterioration in the labor market position of youth in the past quarter century relative to workers 25 years and over. Unemployment rates for in-school and out-of-school youth alike began to rise around 1958 and, except during the Vietnam years, 1965–69, have continued to rise (DOL 1981a, Table B-12). Youth unemployment rates have also risen in relation to adult rates, with blacks most affected (Freeman and Medoff 1982, p.41). In 1954 the unemployment rate for black teenagers was almost four times the adult rate for both races, but by 1981 the ratio reached 7:1 (Freeman and Wise 1982, p.5; DOL 1982b, Tables 2 and 4).

Rates of employment (population divided by employment, excluding armed forces from employed) also depict worsening conditions, but only for some subgroups of youth (DOL 1981a). Employment rates dropped for out-of-school male youth, while in-school males showed some increase over the 1960–80 period. Employment rates for in-school female youth have risen steadily for two decades and the male-female gap has closed. Rates grew equally dramatically for out-of-school females, but a significant male-female gap remains.

Black American youth fared poorly despite legislation requiring equal employment opportunities. While employment rates for young men as a whole were negatively affected only in the last few years, rates for black young men have fallen steadily for two decades. Black male teenage employment rates that were over 40 percent in the early 1960s fell to 30 percent in 1980. Black young adult males, who experienced a peak employment rate of 82 percent in 1965, registered a rate of only 61 percent in 1980. Rates for black female youth, although slightly higher in 1980 than they had been in 1959, compared unfavorably with the growth in employment for all young women. Between 1959 and 1980 the employment rate rose 18 percentage points for all young women aged 16–24, but only 6 percentage points for comparable blacks (DOL 1981a). Employment indicators thus point to serious problems for black youth, male and female. High and rising unemployment rates further reinforce the picture of deteriorating market conditions for black youth across the entire period.

Three societal developments could help to explain postwar youth employment trends. First, the baby boom generation of the late 1940s and early 1950s were entering the labor force in the 1960s and 1970s. Second, significant changes occurred in attitudes regarding women's work roles. Finally, U.S. policy makers took cognizance of the serious employment problems faced by minority youth. The baby boom and changes in attitudes on job-holding by young wives and mothers are reflected in youth labor market trends, but equal employment policy is not. As a result of the baby boom, markets strained to absorb the abnormally large influx of youth seeking jobs, and youth unemployment rates rose (Easterlin et al. 1978; c.f., Russell 1982, pp.61–68). As Table 9.6 shows, earnings of youth were also depressed relative to those of other age groups, creating the economic position for the postwar generation described by one analyst as the "baby boom's financial bust" (Welch 1979). Rising female labor force participation rates plus a change in the occupational distribution of the post-school jobs held by females accompanied changes in attitudes. But for black youth, national equal employment policy was ineffective or overshadowed by other government policies or by demographic and other factors which had negative impacts on employment.

In the future, the U.S. must adjust to a demographic change from baby boom to baby bust. The ratio of men aged 15–29 to men aged 30–64, for instance, reached a peak of .74 in 1975. Projections indicate that this ratio should fall to .64 in 1985, .55 in 1990, and .47 in 1995 (Easterlin et al. 1978). Thus, some trends characteristic of youth labor markets in the 1970s may be reversed in coming years.

Education and Training Systems

American primary and secondary education is overwhelmingly in schools that are governmentally funded and operated (NCES 1981b, p.7). Youth typically spend twelve years in elementary and secondary schools, from age 6 to 17–18, though the compulsory school attendance laws of the 50 states most commonly set the legal leaving age at 16. This age does not coincide with educational sequences and to leave at the legal age, even if in good academic standing, labels a youth as a "dropout," unless senior high school has been completed. In 1980, about three-quarters of the appropriate age group were senior high school graduates, a constant percentage since 1965 which had risen steadily from 60 percent in the mid-1950s (NCES 1981b, p.67).

Racial/ethnic differences in high school graduation rates vary considerably. In October 1979, the proportion of 18–19 year-olds who were senior high school graduates was 75 percent for whites, 57 percent for blacks, and 54 percent for Hispanics (Young 1981a, p.45). Further subdivisions show that Asians have the highest completion rates. Cubans fall above the Hispanic average, which is higher for white than black Hispanics, and American Indians are at the low end (NCES 1982a).

Despite the high proportions completing an upper secondary education, there is much dissatisfaction with the levels of math and English competency among American youth and some concern that performance levels may have declined over time (GAO 1982). It is estimated that 12 percent of high school students are functionally illiterate and that the proportion is much higher among blacks than whites and dropouts than graduates (CBO 1982, pp.xv,14). About 30 percent of 1980 high school seniors were in remedial English and/or math courses, with overrepresentation of most minority groups (NCES 1981c, p.8). These seniors reported few hours spent on homework; 68 percent spent less than five hours a week and 7 percent admitted to no time at all (NCES 1981c, p.7). A recent report called "Labor Market Problems of Teenagers Result Largely from Doing Poorly in School," identifies these youth as disproportionately from families that are poor, minority, and have low educational achievement of other members (GAO 1982).

The curriculum chosen by a high school student reflects expectations and influences subsequent education and employment. Curricula are divided into academic courses, generally required for postsecondary education; vocational courses, including skill training for jobs and training for farm or household living; and general education, usually a watered-down version of academic courses. General education plays an important role, encompassing 37 percent of high school seniors in 1980. Another 39 percent were academic, and the remaining one-fourth were in vocational programs. Sex differences in choice of curriculum were minor, but females took fewer years of math and science (NCES 1981c, Tables 1 and 2). Private schools had more than twice the public school rate in an academic curriculum, half the proportion in the general curriculum, and one-third in a vocational curriculum (NCES 1981c).

Regional differences were marked in the curriculum choices of 1980 high school seniors, with the Northeast showing a much higher share in the academic curriculum and a smaller share in the general curriculum than the other three regions. The vocational curriculum had the lowest proportion in the West and highest in the South, but the spread was only 8 percentage points. In various parts of the country and in different school districts, either the vocational or the general curriculum ranks second to the academic in prestige. In 1980, about two-fifths of white high school seniors were enrolled in an academic curriculum compared with only 32 percent of blacks and 26 percent of Hispanics. Though black and Hispanic enrollments in academic programs differed significantly, the proportions enrolled in vocational programs were identical.

The 31 percent of either minority group enrolled in vocational programs exceeded by 9 percentage points the enrollment of whites (NCES 1981b, Table 62).

Since students are free to enroll in individual courses from each of the curricula, the divisions are not rigid. While 1980 high school seniors in the vocational curriculum were most likely to have had two or more years of vocational courses, substantial proportions in the other two curricula also had such courses, especially in business and sales (NCES 1981c, Table 8; O'Neill and Braun 1981, pp.92–95). Some vocational curriculum students, especially in courses in the distributive trades, spend part of their time in workplaces. In 1980, a little less than one-fourth of high school seniors, chiefly from the vocational curricula, were in such cooperative education or work-study programs (NCES 1981c, p.8, Table 7). Sex divisions are very prominent in vocational course choices. Male high school seniors in 1980 were disproportionately represented in drafting, carpentry, machine shop and auto mechanics courses, while females were concentrated in office work, home economics, practical nursing, sales/merchandising, and quantity food production programs (NCES 1981c, p.8). Assessments of the later earnings of vocational curriculum graduates compared to others of the same high school graduation class have generally shown little benefit, with slightly more advantage to females than males, but only in the initial work years (O'Neill and Braun 1981, pp.93–98).

For some years, the proportion of high school graduates proceeding to higher education has been 45–50 percent. In October 1981, 54 percent of the over 3 million high school graduates of the previous June were enrolled in two- or four-year colleges, overwhelmingly as full-time students. The male enrollment rate exceeded the female by only 1.7 percentage points, while the white rate, slightly above average, was only 2.5 percentage points above the Hispanic rate; blacks, however, with a rate of 43.0 percent, were considerably below the other two groups (DOL 1982c, Table 7).

Because postsecondary occupational skill training in the U.S. is not highly formalized and much of it takes place informally on the job, it is difficult to give precise information. Such training takes place through five main mechanisms: junior or community colleges or public technical institutes; private, profit-seeking training institutions; registered and unregistered apprenticeship; formal on-the-job training by employers; and government employment and training programs for the unemployed, discussed below.

In 1978, 1.8 million students of all ages were enrolled in occupational training programs in postsecondary public and private institutions, chiefly the latter (NCES 1981b, p. 169). While only slightly more males than females were enrolled in such postsecondary training, the two sexes attended different types of schools. The four main types for women were: business/office schools, 34 percent; vocational/technical, 27 percent; cosmetology/barber, 14 percent; and hospital and allied health, 12 percent. Institutions for men were: vocational/technical schools, 37 percent; business/office, 25 percent; trade schools, 17 percent; and flight schools, 8 percent (NCES 1981b, Table 157).

Apprenticeship, a relatively small program, is privately financed by employers who are encouraged to register their programs with the Bureau of Apprenticeship and Training of the U.S. Department of Labor. In most cases, joint union and management apprenticeship training committees determine apprenticeship policy for each industry, including the length and content of training. In 1980, an estimated 420,000 registered apprentices, overwhelmingly male, received training, including 125,000 first-year apprentices (DOL 1981a, p.45). Registered apprentices are concentrated in the construction industry (57 percent in 1979). A number of unregistered apprenticeships are offered by employers, perhaps half as many as registered, but these are not reflected in official statistics. Apprenticeship is not open to many teenagers; the average age is about 25 (Marshall and Glover 1975). Upon completion of an apprenticeship, journeyman or skilled status is achieved, but the journeyman's card also is granted to individuals who have obtained their training outside the regular apprenticeship program.

Formal on-the-job training is also an important part of the skill acquisition process of American youth. When young men aged 24–34 were asked to report all types of training they had received, either in school or out, formal company training programs accounted for 16 percent of all training programs reported. This compared with 9 percent of all programs accounted for by apprenticeship and over 40 percent for the training acquired through public or private schools (Hills 1982b).

The multiple, cumulative, and haphazard nature of skill training in the U.S. becomes clear in a recent study of how craftsmen whose average age was 26 had obtained their skills. It revealed complex combinations of training methods as well as heavy reliance on purely informal means of skill acquisition; two-fifths had not acquired their skills through apprenticeship or any other formal training program (Hills 1982b). In a second study of a national sample of men aged 28–38 with less than three years of college, three-fifths chose informal on-the-job training as the training method most helpful in acquiring the skills used on jobs. Apprenticeship accounted for 11 percent of the responses and formal schooling for 8 percent; only 4 percent selected formal on-the-job training (Hills 1982c).

Institutional Background

The United States has less legislative regulation of employment than most industrialized market economy nations, having no statutes on minimum vacations, parental leave, educational leave, dismissal, job security, works councils, or co-determination. Far from moving toward adoption of any of these measures, American political sentiment leans toward a reduction in existing government regulation. Joint action by management and trade unions or tri-partite bodies including government are less common than in other industrialized market economy countries.

Preparation for Work, Vocational Guidance, and Job Placement. In recent years an attempt has been made under the Career Education program, federally sponsored and financed in part, to infuse all subject matter courses in schools with occupational information, beginning at a very early age. Definitive evaluations have not yet been made. The federal government has also sponsored and in part financed computerized systems of educational/occupational information to aid counselors and students in making educational and occupational choices. Counselors are appointed by schools and school districts, with consequent disparities around the country in the ratio of counselors to students. Moreover, counselors are poorly trained to dispense educational/occupational information, have a bias toward students planning to attend college, are overburdened with disciplinary and routine tasks, and have too little time to serve each student more than perfunctorily (Reubens 1977b; CBO 1982, p.16).

Structured work experience programs have been mainly for vocational education students. Others held special part-time employment under CETA (Comprehensive Employment and Training Act); in 1980, 9 percent of high school seniors participated, with a 17 percent rate for those of low socioeconomic status and a 3 percent rate for those of high status (NCES 1981c, p.8, Table 7). The contribution of such programs to later performance has not been determined. Job placement services in schools or through the Employment Service are variable in effectiveness, and subject to frequent reorganization and change in priorities. The official agencies place relatively few students leaving school for work (CBO 1982, pp.69–76; Reubens 1977b).

Protective Legislation. Under the Fair Labor Standards Act of 1938, children under 14 are prohibited from working, with explicit exceptions such as agriculture. Youth of 14 or 15 may only be employed for stipulated hours on school days, with slightly longer hours on nonschool days. They are limited to designated occupations, primarily in retail and food industries, gasoline service stations, and school-supported or administered work experience and career-exploration programs. Youth of 16 or 17 are excluded from jobs in hazardous industries (Blackburn et al. 1982, p.468). In mid-1982 the Department of Labor proposed to extend the hours of work of 14–15 year-olds to 9 p.m. instead of 7 p.m. on school nights, permit up to 24 hours of work on four days of the school week, allow longer hours and work weeks in nonschool periods, and reclassify some occupations as open to this age group, chiefly in the fast food industry. Because of opposition to the proposals in Congressional hearings and elsewhere, the Department of Labor did not publish the proposed regulations, deferring action until 1983.

For youth 16 and over and adults, hours in excess of a 40 hour week must, under the Fair Labor Standards Act, be paid at an overtime rate of one-and-one-half times the normal hourly wage. States typically have supplemented the Act by passing a variety of other restrictions on employment. In cases of conflict, Federal law prevails, thus, for example, negating protective state legislation that limits women's jobs, since this is contrary to the Civil Rights Act of 1964.

Wage Regulation. A national uniform hourly minimum wage rate was established in 1977 by amendment of the Fair Labor Standards Act of 1938, replacing earlier differentials for low wage industries. Coverage has been expanded gradually, from 53 percent in 1950 to 84 percent of private, nonfarm, nonsupervisory wage and salary workers when the 1977 amendments took effect. About 80 percent of low wage workers are covered. Teenagers constitute less than half of all minimum wage workers and about half of all teenagers earn the minimum wage (Brown et al. 1982, pp.490,502). Lowest coverage is in agriculture, private households, and service industries, all important sources of teenage employment. Over 97 percent in construction and manufacturing and 80 percent in wholesale and retail trade are covered (DOL 1981b, Table 7). The minimum wage rate in 1980 was 46 percent of average hourly earnings of production or nonsupervisory workers in the private nonagricultural sector; between 1960 and 1980, the minimum wage varied as a proportion of hourly earnings in the private nonagricultural sector from a low of 41 percent in 1973 to 56 percent in 1968 (DOC 1955–82; DOL 1982b). A subminimum wage rate for youth, rejected in 1971 after heated debate, was introduced again by President Reagan in 1983.

Certified employers may currently hire full-time students in specified occupations at 85 percent of the Federal minimum. In 1979–80 3 percent of students with jobs were employed under this certification, and three-fourths of such student workers were employed by colleges and universities (GAO 1983). Learners and apprentices are exempted from the minimum by Federal law. State minimum wage laws invariably set rates below the Federal standard and supplement the Federal law for those within-state businesses not covered by the liberal court interpretation of "engaged in interstate commerce."

Trade Unions. American workers have fairly low rates of unionization and these have been declining as the share of white collar jobs has risen. In 1980, 19 percent of employed male youth (16–24) were union members, compared to 35 percent for adult males (25–64) (BLS 1982a, Table 12). Female rates were lower, 10 percent and 22 percent, respectively. Trade unions have not been notable for special efforts or organizational arrangements on behalf of either their younger members or youth in general. It has been calculated for male workers that "a

10 percent rise in rates of unionism among all blue-collar workers would raise overall wages of young blue-collar whites by about 5.5 percent and those of young blacks by almost 10 percent. [The same rise] would lower young white employment by about 2 percent and young black employment by almost 4.5 percent" (Holzer 1982, p.404).

Government Programs and Financial Assistance to Youth. Since the mid-1960s the Federal government has financed a substantial number and variety of youth unemployment programs or programs in which youth participated. The Youth Employment Demonstration Projects Act (YEDPA) of 1977 supplemented other government training programs operated cooperatively between the federal government and local administering agencies. Many provisions of the act, including an independent set of experimental programs, were incorporated into the 1978 reauthorization of CETA, adding to the availability of publicly funded training. In 1978–79, some 2.4 million youth under 22 were said to have participated in the key Federal employment programs (GAO 1982, p.41). Over three-fifths were in work experience programs, mainly the summer programs for youth on vacation from school. Created jobs and subsidized employment accounted for another 13.5 percent. Survey data for 1979 show that 6 percent of 15–21 year-olds participated in at least one program, with heavier participation by black, Hispanic, and other youth whose family income fell below the poverty line (Crowley 1981, p.75). As efforts were made to cut federal expenditures, the proportion of youth participating fell and the mix of services shifted from subsidized employment to training (Crowley 1981, p.83). The Targeted Jobs Tax Credit, an employment subsidy for disadvantaged youth 18–24, cooperative education students, and others, has been judged as ineffective in increasing the employment of disadvantaged youth and possibly as unnecessary for cooperative education students (CBO 1982, pp.31–34).

Financial assistance to youth by government is fairly limited, since educational loans, the major form, are fully repayable. Payments on youth employment programs generally are at or below the minimum wage, except for subsidized private employment. Few youth receive direct payments that discourage search for work.

Public assistance is not payable directly to needy young people unless they are disabled or responsible for a child, and relatively few teenagers qualify for unemployment insurance (U.I.) benefits. In the first six months of 1979 (the last period for which data are available), the ratio of U.I. recipients to the total number of unemployed was .18 for male youth and .12 for female youth (16–24). By contrast, the ratios were .74 and .48 for male and female adults, respectively (DOL 1979b, Table 31; DOL 1979a, Table A–15). Youth still in school often do not receive U.I. because their earnings are insufficient to establish eligibility. Once out of school, this constraint is quickly removed, at least for young men. Within two years of leaving school, the proportion of young men who have established sufficient earnings to be eligible for U.I. is the same as among adult men (Hills and Thompson 1980). The low proportion of youth actually receiving U.I. must therefore be related to other tests of eligibility required by U.S. law. Those who leave jobs voluntarily, for example, are ineligible, and youth may be disproportionately affected.

Student Workers

American society encourages youth to work while still in school. The President's Science Advisory Committee in its 1972 Panel on Youth Report recommended a stronger mix of schooling and work to lessen the isolation of youth from adults and to provide "experience with responsibility affecting others" (Coleman 1972, p.160). Though not without its detractors (Behn et al. 1976), the report has been influential in encouraging special work experience programs which supplement the many part-time jobs youth hold during non-school hours.

In October 1980, 30 percent of all youth jobs were held by full-time or part-time students (16–24) at all educational levels (Table 9.1). Among 16–17 year-olds, students held 87 percent of all jobs while for 18–19 year-olds students held over one-third. The relative importance of student employment has increased with time; in October 1953 only 14 percent of youth employment was accounted for by student job holders. This increase reflects both a 4 percentage point rise in enrollment rates from 1953 to 1980 and a rising fraction of students holding jobs during the school term. Although recent trends have been slightly downward, in October 1980, 36 percent of teenage and 51 percent of young adult students were employed; in October 1953, corresponding percentages had been 28 and 32 (DOL 1981a, Tables B9 and B10).

Differences within the youth group were substantial in some cases. Among the 1.6 million high school graduates of 1981 enrolled in college in the following October, 36.3 percent held jobs in the survey week; the female rate was only 1.0 percentage point below the male. The black rate for both sexes, 17.5 percent, was less than half the white rate, while the Hispanic rate was just 4.7 percentage points below the white rate (DOL 1982c, Table 7). Racial differentials also were marked for all teenage and young adult student workers. In 1981, white teenage students had an employment rate of 38.6 percent, against a black rate of 12.6 percent and a Hispanic rate of 24.3 percent. Among young adult students, the white rate was 54.0 percent, the black 36.7 percent and the Hispanic 56.9 percent (DOL 1982c, Tables 4,5,6). These variations in student employment rates reflect the combined influences of racial differentials in labor force participation rates and unemployment rates. It has been noted that racial differences are wider among student than nonstudent youth (Iden 1980, p.14).

CPS rates may understate actual work by students because these official labor force survey data usually are collected for a whole household with a parent or older relative reporting on youth living at home; this

Table 9.1   Employment of Youth, 16-24 Years Old, by Enrollment Status,
            Age and Sex, United States, 1953 and 1980

	16-17 years		18-19 years		20-24 years		16-24 years	
	1953	1980[a]	1953	1980[a]	1953	1980[a]	1953	1980[a]
	(percentage distribution)							
In-school								
Males	33	45	9	16	3	9	9	15
Females	20	42	4	18	2	8	5	15
Out-of-school								
Males	28	8	45	35	51	44	46	37
Females	19	5	42	31	44	39	40	33
Total	100	100	100	100	100	100	100	100
Total employed (000)	1,347	2,863	2,170	4,384	5,149	13,650	8,666	20,897

[a]Revised data, based on the 1980 census of population, are fractionally lower (DOL 1982c).

Source: DOL 1981a.

source tends to underreport youth jobs, especially casual or short-term employment (Freeman and Medoff 1982; Lewin-Epstein 1981; Santos 1982; Hills 1982a). Special panel surveys among youth show much higher rates. For example, while the CPS rate for 18–19 year-olds in school in October 1980 was only 39 percent, 63 percent of high school seniors (17–18 years old) reported that they were employed during a survey week in Spring 1980; rates were higher for vocational than academic or general students and for whites and Hispanics than for American Indians, Asians, or blacks (NCES 1981c, p.18). Both the special survey among students and the regular CPS survey indicate that student employment rates rise as family income rises (NCES 1981a, Table 1; Young 1979, Table 4). This finding has been variously interpreted as evidence of the greater assistance that middle class families provide to their children, an indication of labor market discrimination against low income youth, or support for the belief that low income youth are less inclined to work than middle class youth.

When the weekly hours of student workers are added to their numbers, their significance in youth employment declines, since student workers are overwhelmingly part-timers (Young 1979, Table 2). In October 1980, the CPS survey found that average hours of student workers in non-agricultural industries were 15.8 and 14.1 hours per week for male and female high school students respectively, and 19.7 and 17.4 hours per week for male and female full-time college students. Only part-time college students had longer hours, 36.3 and 34.0 per week, respectively. Age composition and marital status of the three groups were partly responsible for the differences (Young 1981b). Somewhat longer hours are reported in surveys answered directly by students. With high school seniors (17–18 years old) reporting an average work week of 20.7 hours in 1980, 22.5 hours for males and 18.6 for females (NCES 1981c, p.18). Moreover, 10 percent worked 35 hours or more, a considerable burden added to a full-time school program (NCES 1981a, Table 2).

The jobs held by students are low paid. Average hourly earnings of high school seniors in 1980 were $3.18, just above the minimum wage; the female average of $2.99 was below and the $3.38 for males was slightly above the minimum. Asians and Hispanics had the highest average earnings, followed by whites, blacks, and American Indians, but the range was only from $3.23 to $3.10 per hour (NCES 1981c, p.18). A fourth of all seniors earned $3.50 or more per hour, half earned $3.10–$3.50, and a fourth earned less than the minimum wage (NCES 1981a, Table 3). Earnings below the minimum were possible through student exemptions, employer violation of the law, and private negotiations in such informal jobs as baby sitting or grass cutting.

The most common jobs held during the term by 1980 high school seniors were low level; food service and store clerks together accounted for 30 percent of male and 47 percent of female student jobs. Sex segregation begins early. Over 30 percent of male high school seniors but only 4 percent of females had jobs during the term in factories or in manual and skilled trades. Clerical positions and baby sitting accounted, respectively, for 18 and 9 percent of female jobs, but only 2 and 0.5 percent for males (NCES 1981a, Table 5). The array of jobs sounds like the classic description of "secondary" jobs, as applied to the youth group (Bowers 1979, p.5; Osterman 1980), with the important exception that students are often confident that such jobs are temporary. The quality of the jobs held by high school seniors can be judged from the statement by the great majority of employed students that they spent almost no time on job training. About 68 percent of the total and 62 percent of vocational students made this assertion. Asian students, with 58 percent, had the lowest proportion among racial/ethnic groups (NCES 1981c, p.18). Comparable information is not available for college student jobs, but it may be assumed that full-time students, not enrolled in occupational courses, hold jobs that are slightly superior on average to those of high school students.

A growing number of part-time jobs has enabled more students to be employed despite the increased supply of young workers caused by the baby boom. The distribution of teenage (16–18) part-time jobs in 1968 and 1980, drawn from NLS samples, reveals important changes in composition by sex and race. These data cover all paid jobs, including those created by special government and school programs. Teenage part-time workers of both races, almost all of whom were in school, showed a tremendous increase in part-time work in eating places, undoubtedly reflecting the rapid growth of fast food chains (Table 9.2). Black males also had substantial growth in other services, construction and manufacturing, and educational institutions, the latter representing mainly special youth programs. White males had small gains in construction and manufacturing and other services. Areas of relative loss were food

Table 9.2   Part-time Employment of Youth, 16-18 Years Old, by Industry, Sex, and Race, United States, 1968 and 1980

	Males				Females			
	White		Black		White		Black	
	1968	1980	1968	1980	1968	1980	1968	1980
	(percentage distribution)							
Food markets and gasoline stations	24	19	14	9	10	8	4	5
Eating places	12	21	16	21	8	28	4	24
Other wholesale, retail trade	19	16	15	8	20	15	10	13
Medical services	3	1	1	3	9	6	6	5
Educational institutions	6	4	13	17	9	4	26	20
Personal services	4	4	7	7	33	19	29	12
Other service institutions	9	11	5	13	4	9	7	7
Transportation, finance	5	3	8	4	2	3	6	6
Construction, manufacturing	11	13	8	12	3	5	*	4
Agriculture, mining	8	6	10	3	2	2	2	1
Government	*	1	2	3	*	1	7	4
Total	100	100	100	100	100	100	100	100
Total number	304	556	97	181	261	521	82	130
Percentage in school		99		99		99		95

*Less than 1.0 percent.

Source: NLS 1966-80, 1968-80, 1978-81.

markets and gasoline stations, wholesale and retail trade, agriculture, and transport and finance. White female teenagers, showing a rise from 8 to 28 percent in eating places, had relative losses in most of the other industry groups, except for other service institutions, construction and manufacturing, and transport and finance. Black females, displaying the largest gain in part-time jobs in eating places, also showed an increase in wholesale and retail trade. The sharp relative decline for both races in personal services reflects less employment in baby sitting and domestic household work. This evolution of part-time jobs for 16–18 year-olds, in which eating places rank first for all groups, with 21 to 28 percent of the totals, helps to explain the attempts to lengthen the permitted work day of 14–15 year-olds, described above.

For students 19–24 years old, employment in their own educational institutions was an important source of part-time jobs. Blacks, in fact, compensated for their underrepresentation in retail trade industries by a disproportionate share of jobs within educational institutions. In the early 1970s, over one-third of the part-time jobs held by blacks were in educational institutions, compared to only 20 percent for whites. The black proportion rose over a four-year period by more than ten percentage points, most likely a reflection of increased work-study assistance for blacks who were attending colleges or universities (NLS 1966–80, 1968–80).

American researchers have analyzed the immediate and longer-term benefits and costs of working while in school, with economists tending to take positive and educators and sociologists negative views. On the one hand, apart from immediate income, jobs provide early labor market experience to students, perhaps helping them to make wise and realistic career choices when they leave school. On the other hand, time spent working may detract from study time, and the jobs that are obtained may have few real linkages with full-time jobs acquired after completing school. A strong positive relationship between young men's work experience and the number of post-school weeks worked per year has been found by Meyer and Wise (1982). Male high school graduates who worked while in school and did not proceed to college also had higher post-school wages, all else constant. The combined effects meant that young men who worked 16–20 hours per week while in school (and with other characteristics matching the mean values for the sample) four years later earned 12–13 percent more than comparable students with no student work experience. Stephenson (1978), using another data base, has similar findings on the benefits of work while in school. Given the type of jobs students hold and the inherent difficulty of controlling for personal characteristics, some economists remain suspicious of these favorable results.

Using a sample of 531 tenth and eleventh graders from Orange County, California, Greenberger and Steinberg (1981) examined more intensively both the potential benefits and costs of student employment, going beyond the economic. Working students demonstrated measurable gains in self-reliance, and they described themselves as more able to persist at a task or derive pleasure from doing a job well than did nonworking students. Working students had somewhat more knowledge about business practices, financial concepts, and consumer matters than nonworking students, but students' jobs provided little opportunity to use cognitive skills acquired in school and little on-the-job training. Very little work time was spent talking with an adult supervisor or coworker, perhaps because student jobs did not require substantial new learning. Working was associated with less time for school study, less involvement in extracurricular activities, more absenteeism from school, and some decline in academic performance. Working was also associated with increased cigarette, alcohol, and marijuana use, each of which was used more frequently the greater the number of hours worked. The authors conclude that 15 to 20 hours of work per week in the term is a break-even point beyond which costs begin to outweigh benefits. They also note that some jobs are better than others for learning opportunities, responsibility, and contact with adults. Thus an undifferentiated conclusion that work while in school confers benefits is not warranted.

Employment of Out-of-School Youth

The labor market provides several broad types of work for youth once their formal preparation for work is complete. Youth may choose paid employment, military service, or unpaid work at home. For some, unemployment may be necessary before any of these choices are made. At any two points in time, youth flow from institutions preparing them for work to other institutions providing work. According to survey data for 14–21 year-olds who left school or post-school training during 1978 with 14 or fewer years of education, four-fifths of the flow into employment came directly from schools, 12 percent from technical institutes and proprietary schools, and 8 percent from government training programs or subsidized jobs for out-of-school youth. More than half of those coming direct from schools had also been on a government training or work experience program or held regular jobs during the school term. Very little difference in the flows is evident by sex, but 42 percent of the blacks moving to employment had no specialized training or work experience other than the final year of regular school, compared with 38 percent of the total (NLS 1979–81).

Quite different transitions from school to work appeared for white females and blacks of each sex compared with white males. A full year after leaving school or training institutions during 1978, three-fourths of the male and two-thirds of the female sample reported a full-time job as their most recent activity. Some 8 percent of the males and 1 percent of the females entered the armed forces. Twelve percent of males and 19 percent of females reported a part-time job as their most recent employment. About 4 percent of the males and 14 percent of the females had had no employment in the first full year after leaving school. The record for absorption into employment was worse among black than white youth. In the first year after school, 18 percent of black males and females combined had no employment, twice the figure for youth as a whole. Twice as many black as white young men opted for military service (NLS 1979–81).

Differences among youth groups in the flow into employment also are shown by the official CPS employment rates of high school graduates not entering college. Several months after graduation from high school, in October 1981, 70 percent of males, 62.1 percent of females, 71.8 percent of whites, 32.4 percent of blacks, and 51.4 percent of Hispanics were employed. For dropouts from high school during the 1980–81 school year, the employment rates were 52.5 and 27.0 percent for males and females respectively, and 48.3 and 13.3, and 45.1 percent for whites, blacks and Hispanics (DOL 1982c, Table 7). Not all without jobs were unemployed, since some did not enter the labor force after graduation.

In October 1981, the unemployment rate for all June high school graduates in the labor force was 19.7 percent; it was 16.7 percent for males, 22.6 percent for females, 16.0 percent for whites, 50.8 percent for blacks and 20.8 percent for Hispanics (DOL 1982c, Table 7). While the level of these rates for entrance unemployment varies considerably according to business conditions, with October 1981 rates among the highest on record, the differences among the subgroups have persisted and the relative position of blacks has worsened. Wise and Meyer (1982) using another data set on male high school graduates, find lower unemployment rates, as well as little racial difference on several labor market indicators.

Corcoran et al. (1980) suggest that information networks may be a serious barrier which differentiates black from white youth in finding jobs. Using the University of Michigan's Panel Study of Income Dynamics, they investigated the job search patterns and long-run wage outcomes of different job search methods for black and white men. Their analysis casts doubt on the hypothesis that restricted access to informal information networks helps explain early wage differentials among blacks and whites.

A Chicago labor market study conducted in the early 1960s reported a high use of informal channels of information to locate jobs, particularly blue collar positions. Furthermore, jobs found through informal methods tended to pay more than jobs located through more formal means. Since blacks, other disadvantaged groups and recent migrants had less access to informal sources of information, they were put at a further disadvantage compared to longer term, white residents (Rees and Shultz 1970). However, in the more recent study by Corcoran et al. (1980), black males were more likely to have heard about a job through informal channels, all else constant. Both black and white males gained short-run wage advantages from knowing someone on the job before taking it. Black males, in addition, earned a long-run wage advantage from hearing about a job from a friend and short-run wage advantages from receiving help in obtaining jobs. The authors conclude that "the effect of information and influence on wages do not provide a convincing story to explain early wage differences between blacks and whites" (Corcoran et al. 1980, p.35).

A reasonable way to identify further potential barriers to youth employment is to ask youth themselves. In the newest extension of the National Longitudinal Survey young men and women were asked the reasons why young people, have trouble getting a good job. A surprisingly prevalent response to this question was "lack of transportation." Thirty percent of young people and 46 percent of black males aged 14–21 agreed that transportation was an important problem. The most prevalent response, however, was "discrimination on the basis of age," which about 45 percent of youth recorded. This response was fairly constant across race-sex groups and was larger than responses of race discrimination among minorities or sex discrimination among women.

The proportions who felt race or sex discrimination to be a problem were substantial, nevertheless. About 15 percent of women felt discrimination on the basis of sex, and 18 percent of blacks perceived race discrimination as a problem. Rural blacks responded very similarly to urban blacks, but fewer rural than urban Hispanics felt that discrimination was a problem. Urban Hispanics and urban blacks were very similar in their perceptions of racial bias. Other barriers cited by youth tended to be associated with their insufficient training or experience. Perceptions of youth cannot always specify in detail what the employment barriers actually are, but they serve as a valuable impetus for further research.

COMPARISONS WITH STUDENT WORKERS

The 20 most common occupations of nonenrolled and enrolled 18–19 year-olds, by sex, indicate that the similarities between the two groups outweigh the differences, although the latter are significant. Using calculations of detailed occupations from the 1970 census made for Chapter 3, it appears that among employed male 18–19 year-olds, who were equally divided between the enrolled and nonenrolled, 13 of the 20 most common occupations were the same for each group. Since the top 20 occupations accounted for over half of all employment of both enrolled and nonenrolled 18–19 year-old males, a substantial part of the employment of each was accounted for by such jobs as warehouse and stores laborers, operative, n.e.c., garage and station workers, farm laborers, retail salespersons, janitors, freight handlers, delivery workers, and short-order cooks. The seven divergent occupations followed expected lines of division. Those of the out-of-school group consisted of more demanding and better paid jobs, such as truck driver, assembler, carpenter, precision machine operative, and textile operative. By the same token, the in-school group listed busboy, dishwasher, garden care worker, and newsboy, all low level occupations.

Females of the same age showed even less difference between the enrolled and nonenrolled. With 70 percent of employment accounted for by the top twenty occupations, both groups were predominantly retail salespersons, secretaries, waitresses, typists, clerical workers, n.e.c., and cashiers. Bookkeepers, file clerks, receptionists, office machine operators, telephone operators, nursing assistants and orderlies, and food counter workers also were represented on each list. Among the nonidentical occupations, the enrolled were baby sitters, library assistants, fast-food workers, counter clerks, fast-food cooks, and household workers. The nonenrolled were operatives, n.e.c., sewers and stitchers, assemblers, hairdressers, packers and wrappers, bank tellers, and stenographers.

Later data from another source, however, suggest that the jobs and pay after leaving school are quite different from those held while still in high school, especially for males. Corresponding differences are likely

Table 9.3   In-school and Post-school Jobs of a Cohort of Noncollege Youth, by
Occupation, Industry, and Sex, United States, 1979-80

	Males		Females	
	In-school	Post-school	In-school	Post-school
Occupation	(percentage distribution)			
Professional, technical	3	4	3	3
Managerial, administrative	2	3	1	3
Sales and clerical	13	14	48	50
Crafts	15	17	1	2
Operatives	22	19	6	11
Transport workers	7	6	*	*
Laborers	16	18	3	2
Farm laborers and managers	3	3	1	1
Services	20	16	36	29
Total	100	100	100	100
Industry	(percentage distribution)			
Agriculture, mining	4	8	2	1
Construction	5	12	*	1
Manufacturing	20	22	9	15
Transportation, communications	2	3	2	3
Restaurants, etc.	10	8	22	15
Retail, wholesale trade	29	21	23	23
Finance	5	3	3	11
Services	22	20	38	28
Public administration	3	4	2	4
Total	100	100	100	100

*Less than 0.5 percent.

Note: Noncollege youth were 14-21 years old in 1979 and completed 14 years or
less of education and/or post-school training. In-school jobs were held in
the last year of school and post-school jobs in the first year after leaving
school during 1979.

Source: NLS 1979-81.

to exist between the jobs of college and university sudents and the first
jobs of graduates of these institutions. Rates of pay of high school
graduates rise significantly compared to those of high school seniors.
Among youth (14-21) who were not college graduates, 10 percent reported
wages below the minimum in their first job after leaving school and
another 10 percent earned from $3.10-$3.49. Thirty-seven percent earned
between $3.50 and $4.99, 26 percent between $5.00 and $6.99, and the
remaining 17 percent $7.00 or more (NLS 1979-81). More post-school
than school employment is in the more secure and better paid unionized
sector of the economy.

Table 9.3 presents a distribution of the jobs held in the last year of
school and in the first post-school or post-training year by the same

cohort of 1200 youth (14–21). They all had 14 or fewer years of education and had left school in 1979. For both males and females, jobs in eating places accounted for smaller proportions of their out-of-school employment when compared with the jobs they held in their final year of school. Classified by occupation, service jobs fell for both males and females; classified by industry, jobs in service organizations fell dramatically for females but only slightly for males. The construction industry grew in importance for the employment of out-of-school males, and manufacturing became relatively more important for out-of-school females.

Favorable comparisons with jobs of students do not mean that a large proportion of these first post-school jobs would not exhibit the characteristics associated with "secondary" jobs (Bowers 1979). The data available from national surveys, presented above, do not permit judgments about jobs as such. However, small regional surveys, identifying the jobs and tasks of youth, suggest that many of those with no more than a high school diploma begin in menial jobs with low pay and poor prospects for training, continuous employment, or advancement (Osterman 1980).

Other employment differences between student workers and out-of-school youth distinguish the two groups. In October 1978, just under 85 percent of male and 75 percent of female employed out-of-school teenagers worked 35 hours or more per week; less than 13 percent of male and 9 percent of female student workers had full-time hours (Young 1979, Table 2). A similar diversity characterizes the number of weeks worked over the year. In a matched file of two years work experience, it was found that youth whose major activity in March 1975 and 1978 was reported to the CPS survey as "other than school" worked for many more weeks in 1974–75 and 1977–78 than those whose major activity was school; the gap was wider for the older than the younger groups. In 1977–78, a period of economic recovery, the results were remarkably close to those for 1974–75, a period of recession (Bowers 1982, Table 2).

Job turnover, as evidenced by the number of employers in a year, was more frequent among out-of-school than in-school youth during 1977, according to the same matched file from the CPS (Bowers 1981, Table 6). The proportion with two or more employers varied from 19.6 percent for 16–17 year-olds whose major activity was school to 38.0 percent for 18–19 year-olds whose major activity was not school; the remaining four age-school groups had rates of 27–29 percent. From one-third to a half of those with two or more employers in 1977 also had two or more employers in 1978; out-of-school teenagers had higher proportions than teenage students, but out-of-school young adults showed a much lower proportion than in-school. Among out-of-school youth, the probability of working for two or more employers in 1978, regardless of the number of employers in 1977, declined sharply by age, but among in-school youth, the probabilities for each age group were similar (Bowers

1981, Table 6). To the extent that young people did not have two or more employers because they were out of the labor force or unemployed, these data may be misleading about the propensity of employed youth to change employers.

Results might also vary in period with different general economic conditions. However, survey data for young men in the mid-1960s reinforce the mobility figures for 1977. One–half of out-of-school white males aged 15–20 changed employers between 1966 and 1967 (Zeller et al. 1970, Table 3.11). The proportion dropped to one-third among males 21–25 years old and was higher for blacks than for whites. Moreover, even among youth who did not change employers, a considerable amount of intrafirm occupational mobility occurred. Out of the two-thirds of the sample aged 21–25 who did not change employers between 1966 and 1967, 19 percent experienced an occupational change (Zeller et al. 1970, Table 3.13). If intrafirm mobility is combined with interfirm mobility, the total mobility rate becomes 46 percent for white young adult males aged 21–25. Some geographic mobility accompanies job mobility in the U.S., but the rates are considerably lower for geographic than for job changes. Little difference in geographic mobility rates was evident for the two age-groups of white young men in 1966–67; the mobility rate was about 12 percent for each group. Blacks had the same 12 percent overall rate of mobility though the younger group was less likely to move than the older (Zeller et al. 1970, Table 3.17).

Information about unemployment among those with work experience, by school status and age, are also analyzed by Bowers. In both 1974–75 and 1977–78, in-school youth in each of the three age groups had a lower incidence of unemployment than out-of-school youth; those with some unemployment as a proportion of those with some labor force experience ranged from about one-third to 48 percent, with a clustering around 35–40 percent (Bowers 1982, Table 1). The average number of weeks of unemployment in each two-year period, calculated by dividing total weeks of unemployment by the number experiencing unemployment at least once, also was lower for in-school than out-of-school youth and there were no regularities by age (Bowers 1982, Table 1). The probability of having extensive unemployment or an unemployment duration of 15 weeks and over in 1975 or 1978, if one had that length of unemployment in 1974 or 1977, was only marginally higher for 18–19 and 20–24 out-of-school youth than for similar students (Bowers 1982, p.14, Table 9).

Recurrent spells of unemployment were more likely to affect out-of-school than in-school youth, although, in both school statuses, only a small proportion in each age group had two or more spells of unemployment in 1977. The incidence and gap was highest for 18–19 year-olds, 12.4 percent of out-of-school and 4.6 percent for in-school (Bowers 1981, Table 4). Even the proportion with one spell was lower for in-school youth in each age group, perhaps because some students ended a job with a return to school and withdrawal from the labor force. The probability of having two or more spells of unemployment in 1978 was only slightly greater among teenage students with multiple spells in 1977 than among out-of-school teenagers with the same 1977 record; for young adults there was no clear difference in probabilities according to school status (Bowers 1982, Table 4).

Important evidence from the matched file sample concerns the concentration of unemployment on a small number of individuals who suffer either uninterrupted joblessness or many spells; the data do not distinguish between the two. Regardless of economic conditions, a small proportion of the youth labor force accounted for a large part of total unemployment in each of the four years, and out-of-school youth, 18–19 and 20–24, generally exhibited more concentration than their student counterparts (Bowers 1982, Table 7). Previously explored by Clark and Summers (1982), the extent of concentration is shown by the proportion of total unemployment accounted for by those with 15 weeks or more of unemployment. In 1978, these proportions were 69.5, 67.6, and 66.0 percent for 16–17, 18–19, and 20–24 year-old students, respectively. Among those whose major activity was other than school, the respective proportions were 73.8, 67.3, and 78.5 percent. The corresponding shares of the labor force with 15 weeks or more of unemployment are 7.2, 7.0, and 5.1 percent for in-school youth and 14.1, 9.7, and 9.8 percent for out-of-school youth (Bowers 1981, Table 3A).

On balance, the foregoing comparisons of hours and weeks worked and number of employers in a year reinforce the earlier job advantages discerned for nonstudents. However, the comparative record on unemployment, most of it occurring between jobs, suggests a more difficult labor market situation for nonstudents. The different unemployment experience for out-of-school youth may reflect different job search patterns once full-time, permanent jobs are sought, different propensities to leave the labor force for students and nonstudents, or other non-labor market factors which distinguish the two groups. Until it can be determined which, if any, of these explanations may be true, a relationship is hard to establish between the types of jobs held by each group and its unemployment experience.

LABOR MARKET STRATIFICATION

Are the initial and subsequent jobs held by out-of-school youth due to the stratification of the labor market? Education, of course, creates stratification stemming from the skills individuals acquire and has long run effects on earnings. Education may also perform a screening function, sorting individuals into various job segments of the economy regardless of their skills.

Striking differences exist in the occupational distributions of the first jobs of college graduates compared with youth who have completed high school or less (Reubens 1977a). For both males and females in the early 1970s, over 60 percent of college degree recipients entered professional or technical occupations, against less than 3 percent of high school graduates, though the gap may have shrunk recently. In the early 1970s little difference existed in occupational distributions of male high school graduates or dropouts. The data indicate the low value placed on attainment of the high school diploma, since 12 years of schooling is considered the minimum socially acceptable amount of education in the U.S., thus placing high school graduates near the bottom of the labor market queue (Reubens 1977a, p.18).

In addition to the level of educational attainment, the type of curriculum or major subject will influence initial job choice and placement. To the extent that societal factors or the structure of education causes different outcomes among youth with the same potential, education may establish a stratification pattern that is replicated in the labor market. However, differences in the initial job distribution of those with essentially the same educational qualifications indicate that other independent factors play a role as well. The influence of education on labor market outcomes wanes as work experience grows.

Other mechanisms of stratification into jobs also are present. Youth have little or no choice regarding their sex, race/ethnicity, or families into which they were born, the communities in which they were raised, or the part of the country in which they grow up, but such factors could influence whether initial and later jobs are in the well paid, unionized, and stable sectors of the economy. While data are lacking on out-of-school youth employment conditions by family income and background or place of residence, such information can be presented by sex and for minority youth.

MALE AND FEMALE OUT-OF-SCHOOL YOUTH

Even though young women increasingly participate in the labor force to the same extent as young men, the types of jobs they hold have changed only slowly, despite attitudinal changes (Mott 1981; Mott et al. 1981). Beginning with the jobs held in school, sex segregation persists in the initial and later jobs of the youth cohorts at all educational levels (Tables 9.2, 9.3, 9.7; Greenberger and Steinberg 1982; Reubens 1977a). Finer detail on jobs than are given in the broad occupational and industrial classifications of tables in this chapter reinforce the conclusion (see Chapter 3). The industries of first jobs after school were vastly different for males and females. Two-fifths of males entered jobs in construction and manufacturing, while trade and service jobs accounted for an additional 40 percent. Three-fifths of the females entered the trade and service sectors, while only 18 percent were in manufacturing and construction (Table 9.3).

Training on-the-job was far less available to young women than to young men. Both the proportion receiving training and the amount of training provided was substantially less for young females (18–25) than similar males, according to 1976 data from the Panel Study of Income Dynamics, a national survey of over 5,000 families (Hoffman 1981, Tables 2,3). Furthermore, males were more likely than females to enter the unionized sector of the economy. Unionized jobs accounted for 29 percent of the initial employment of noncollege male youth who left school or training in 1978. The comparable figure for females was only 18 percent (NLS 1979–81).

Due to union contracts, males were likely to have more favorable earnings, fringe benefits, training, advancement, working conditions, and job security provisions than females. These benefits are distinct from and additional to the advantages males enjoy from sex differences in the occupational and industrial distribution of their jobs. Thus, young women (16–24) who usually worked full-time had weekly earnings that were 76.8 percent of the earnings of their male counterparts in May 1967 and 80.4 percent in the second quarter of 1981, displaying an upward trend in ratios that exceeded the record for other age groups (O'Neill and Braun 1981; Russell 1982). 27.4 percent of full-time young females, but only 10.4 percent of similar males, earned under $150 per week; for the next earnings bracket, $150–199, the respective proportions were 32.0 and 22.3 percent. Part-time young women did better in 1981, earning 96 percent of the corresponding male weekly amount (Mellor and Stamas 1982, p.22, Tables 3,4).

As in the case of the comparisons between in and out-of-school youth, various indicators of employment and unemployment show gaps between young females and males. The shorter work-week of the females has already been cited in the school status comparison (Young 1979, Table 2). While data on the remaining indicators mostly refer to both in and out-of-school youth, the sex differentials probably are fully valid for out-of-school youth alone. As expected, males in each of three age groups, 16–17, 18–19, 20–24, had more weeks of employment than females in 1974–75 and 1977–78; weeks worked increased with age for each sex, but the sex gap was widest for young adults. The probability of working in both years of the two periods also was greater for males, except for 16–17 year-olds in 1977–78 (Bowers 1982, Table 2).

The propensity to quit a job voluntarily was found to be considerably higher for both white and black young females (aged 17–28) than for corresponding males (18–29) in an analysis of 1969–72 NLS data for out-of-school youth. When the values of the variables for males were substituted into female equations, however, the predicted female youth quit rate fell below that of young males, leading to the conclusion that actual rates

> may be, in part, a reflection of labor market discrimination . . . If women are confined to a worse set of jobs (in terms of wages, working conditions, etc.) than males, then a given set of job characteristics . . . constitutes on the average a better job for women than for men compared to the alternatives open to each group [Blau and Kahn 1981, p.573].

Table 9.4   Annual Mean Number of Employers for Employed Youth, 16–23 Years Old,
             by School Enrollment Status, Race, and Sex, United States, 1980

	In school[a]			Out of school[a]		
	Mean	SD	N	Mean	SD	N
White males	1.81	0.98	1,229	2.22	1.15	410
White females	1.83	1.00	1,062	2.14	1.08	475
Hispanic males	1.74	0.94	311	2.28	1.15	108
Hispanic females	1.76	1.09	280	1.89	1.12	115
Black males	1.65	0.81	458	1.89	0.93	158
Black females	1.59	0.80	443	1.94	1.03	152

[a]All data are weighted to account for over-sampling of blacks, Hispanics, and
poor whites. Data exclude youth with no employers during 1980.

Note: SD refers to the standard deviation and N to the number included in the
sample.

Source: NLS 1979–81.

The proportion of youth with two or more employers during 1977
was 4.5 to 6.0 percentage points higher for males than females among
16–17, 18–19, and 20–24 year-olds. Highest rates were shown by 18–19
year-olds among both sexes; 35.1 and 29.7 percent, respectively, and
lowest, 23.2 and 18.6 percent, by 16–17 year-olds (Bowers 1981, Table
4). The probability of working for two or more employers in 1978 also
was greater for males than females. According to another source, the
most mobile youth groups in 1980 were out-of-school white and Hispanic
males. In each racial group, young women were less mobile than men,
but the least mobile of all race and sex groups were blacks enrolled in
school, both male and female (Table 9.4). The greater mobility of all
out-of-school youth may in part explain the differences in unemployment
between students and nonstudents that were noted earlier.

The proportion of male youth with some work experience who had
some unemployment tended to exceed that for female youth, in the
study of matched files from the special CPS surveys in March 1974–75
and 1977–78 (Bowers 1982, Table 1). For all youth groups, the incidence
was high, ranging from 33 to 45 percent. Fairly high proportions also
had a probability of unemployment in both years of the two-year
periods. Males also exceeded females in each youth age group in the
duration of unemployment over the two years (Bowers 1982, Table 1).
The probability of having 15 weeks or more unemployment in 1975
(1978), if one had that amount in 1974 (1977), was greater for young
males than females (Bowers 1982, Table 8). Similarly, the proportion
of young males with two or more spells of unemployment in 1977
exceeded that of females, as did the probability of having multiple
spells in 1978 (Bowers 1982, Table 3). Finally, a concentration of
annual weeks of unemployment, without regard to number of spells,

in a small proportion of the youth age groups appears for both males and females, but was usually more marked for males in 1974, 1975, 1977, and 1978 (Bowers 1982, Table 5). The more favorable female unemployment experience cannot be understood without information for each sex on time out of the labor force. Therefore, preliminary conclusions stand that most aspects of the jobs of young females are inferior.

BLACK AND WHITE OUT-OF-SCHOOL YOUTH

More clear-cut results emerge for minority youth, controlling for sex and other differences. Because data are scarce or nonexistent for groups other than blacks, comparisons of blacks and whites represent the minority experience. Recent trends in employment for blacks suggest that minorities had less employment growth than whites and are channeled into low paying jobs through labor market stratification.

A sharp demographic change implies shifts in the shares of jobs held by workers of different age groups. Yet as demographic change swelled the numbers of youth relative to adults, black youth did not capture the same share of jobs as their white counterparts. Between 1959 and 1980 white young men (16–24) increased their share of total white male jobs from 13 percent to 20 percent, but young black males increased their share of the jobs held by all black men from 17 percent to only 19 percent. Black women also fared worse than white, their shares of jobs rising from 16 percent to 19 percent while white women's shares rose from 19 to 25 percent (DOL 1981a).

Structural changes in labor markets could account for black youth's relative disadvantage in employment growth. The main possibilities are: a shrinking pool of jobs in the secondary sector of the economy, the sector where blacks would usually obtain entry level positions; growth in the size of competing labor force groups, namely women, white youth of the baby boom generation, and illegal aliens; and the suburbanization of jobs without an accompanying reduction of black residential concentration in urban centers. Osterman (1980) finds some evidence that changes in the industrial structure have resulted in a modest secular decline in youth-intensive jobs within the economy. The effect is small, however, compared to the drop in black employment rates. He also finds that "white youths have been able to maintain their position in the labor market to some extent at the expense of black youth" (p.142). Again the effect is not strong. Most importantly, Osterman's analysis does not show that suburbanization of jobs has had a negative effect on the employment of black youth. He thus concludes that though "discrimination is difficult to prove . . . it is also difficult not to believe that much of the problem rests there" (Osterman 1980, p.147).

Cogan (1981) finds that much, if not all, of the decline in black teenage employment from 1950 to 1970 occurred in the South where technological progress in agriculture displaced large numbers of youth (see also, GAO 1982, pp.13–16). He presents evidence that the level of the federal minimum wage was an important barrier to absorbing black youth in the agricultural sector of the economy. He then observes that:

> In the relatively short span of 20 years the number of black teenagers living in the North increased by 215 percent. More than 90 percent of these teenagers took up residence in urban areas . . . the ability of Northern urban labor markets to absorb a massive influx of black teenagers is both surprising and impressive [Cogan 1981, p.9].

Whether Cogan's findings can be extended to the period 1970–80 is unclear. In the early 1970s, the teenage share of all jobs was still rising and urban labor markets may have been pressed beyond their limits (Bowers 1979; Newman 1979).

Osterman (1980) also found that the school enrollment rates of whites have fallen over time while black enrollment rates have risen. The difference explained to some degree why relative employment for blacks declined, but it was not a major reason. Increased enrollment rates themselves could have been in part a result of demographic pressures however: "When the potential youth labor supply increases without a corresponding expansion of demand, education becomes an attractive alternative either to unemployment or to a reduction in relative earnings" (Reubens et al. 1981, p.280). A second alternative to civilian employment is military service. Throughout the latter 1960s, white rates of entrance into military service exceeded black rates by 3 to 4 percentage points, but with the elimination of the draft, rates for blacks began to exceed those for whites by approximately the same amount (Reubens et al. 1981, p.287). Military service and additional schooling probably kept black rates of nonemployment from rising even higher in the late 1970s, but these two alternatives would also help to explain why black shares of all civilian jobs did not rise as fast as white shares (see also, Iden 1980, pp.12–14; Bowers 1979, pp.11–16).

Freeman (1980) suggested that the reduced earnings differentials between comparable black and white male youth in the postwar period might have adversely affected the demand for black youth, relative to white youth and black adult males. Another explanation is that blacks' reservation wages (the lowest acceptable wage at which a job will be taken) are too high and thus serve as an "obstacle" to employment from the supply side of the market. Osterman (1980) does not find racial differences in reservation wage equations. According to Borus (1982), black youth aged 14–22 are significantly more willing than comparable white or Hispanic youth to accept specified jobs at a wage below the minimum or not greatly above it. But, in a more detailed study, Kim (1981) concludes that while reservation wages do not differ by race, all else held constant, they are too high compared to what blacks can expect to earn, given the present discriminatory wage differentials between whites and blacks. Thus, whether blacks accept discriminatory wage differentials and discount their expectations is critical to making the value-laden judgment of whether reservation wages are "too high." In summary, minimum wage issues and discrimination, coupled with demographic changes, are still primary in understanding employment trends of out-of-school black youth.

The second issue concerns racial differences in the composition and characteristics of employment. That the first and later jobs held by young blacks are inferior to those of white youth is clearly indicated by the respective proportions in the professional, technical and managerial categories (Table 9.7). Whites of each sex had about three times the black share in these occupational classifications to begin with. Ten years later black females had improved their relative position, but black males remained underrepresented to the same extent. Further disaggregation of occupations and information about actual jobs would correct the apparently favorable position of white females in the professional, technical occupations by indicating that they occupy the lower ranks. Similarly, more detailed breakdowns for males by race, such as Osterman (1980) has made, reveal even greater racial disadvantage for blacks.

Differences among youth in on-the-job training provide important clues to the quality of their jobs and future prospects. Dividing youth (18–25) into four race-sex groups Hoffman (1981) made an analysis of responses from the 1976 interviews for the Panel Study of Income Dynamics. The proportion of whites receiving training far exceeded the proportion of blacks; for males it was 35.3 percent against 7.4 percent and for females it was 18.9 percent against 9.4 percent. The average length of training also was more favorable to whites, especially males, for whom it was 1.28 years against 0.50 years; females of each race received about the same amount as black males (Hoffman 1981, Tables 2,3). Hoffman does not attribute the weaker access to training of female and black male youth to lower educational attainment or earnings in these youth groups. As the cohort ages, he expects a widening of earnings differentials and a more permanent low-wage condition for black males and black and white females than for white male youth (Hoffman 1981, p.36).

While unionization rates are slightly higher for the black than the white male youth (16–24) labor force (Holzer 1982), the distribution of occupations of the two races implies that whites have better earnings, benefits and other working conditions. Earnings data confirm this. In 1981, the usual weekly earnings of full-time black males (16–24) were 86 percent and those of Hispanics were 87 percent of the earnings of white male youth. The ratios were 94 and 93 percent, respectively, for black and Hispanic females (16–24) relative to white female youth (Mellor and Stamas 1982, p.17).

Racial differences in other employment and unemployment indicators suggest additional disadvantages for blacks. CPS matched file samples of both in and out-of-school youth show a lower total number of weeks worked in 1974–75 and 1977–78 by blacks than whites. Against the 40–41 weeks of work in a two-year period for white 16–17 year-olds, blacks had less than 27 weeks. For 18–19 year-olds, comparable figures were about 53 weeks and 39 weeks. While a smaller difference separated young adults, in 1977–78, whites worked ten weeks more than blacks (Bowers 1982, Table 2).

The propensity to quit a job showed much the same racial differences in the analysis by Blau and Kahn (1981) as was described above for the sexes, and the authors' conclusions apply equally to young blacks as to young women. Somewhat contrary to expectations, lower proportions of black than white youth in each of three age groups changed employers twice or more during 1977 (Bowers 1981, Table 5). NLS data in Table 9.4 also show that the mean number of employers in a 12-month period is higher for white than black youth. The explanation is that blacks had fewer jobs and weeks of work than whites in which to change employers. Data on the incidence and duration of youth unemployment by race confirm this hypothesis.

Much higher proportions of black than white youth with work experience had some unemployment over a two-year period, according to the matched file study for 1974–75 and 1977–78 (Bowers 1981, Table 1). While the white percentages ranged from 33 to 42 for the three youth age groups in both periods, the blacks had a low of 48 percent and a high of 57 percent. Average weekly durations were correspondingly higher for 18–19 and 20–24 year-old blacks as were the probabilities of experiencing unemployment in each year of a two-year period. Extensive unemployment affected black youth more than white, both in the share of total weeks of youth unemployment accounted for by youth with 15 weeks or more and in the share of the youth labor force experiencing this amount. In 1975, 23 percent of the black 18–19 year-old labor force was unemployed for 15 weeks or more and accounted for 82.7 percent of total weeks of unemployment. The white percentages were 10.5 and 76.7, respectively (Bowers 1982, pp.9–10). The concentration of unemployment was thus more marked for black than white youth.

One explanation for the racial difference may be the change in the character of unemployment from the 1960s to the 1970s, as deduced from analyses of the experience of successive NLS cohorts. Rising unemployment and a concomitant decrease in employment stability characterized the 1970s. Pollard (1982), distinguishing between nonemployment due to high turnover rates of youth and long-term, chronic nonemployment associated with economic stagnation, found that over the 1970s "individual nonemployment patterns have changed for both black and white youth, the change having been much more drastic for blacks." High turnover was characteristic of the earlier part of the decade but toward the end of the period "blacks, much more than whites (moved) toward nonemployment characterized by stagnation" (Pollard 1982, p.39). As periods of nonemployment grew for youth in

1980, the increased burden was shared by a large portion of white males, but black nonemployment became more concentrated among those who had spent a relatively large portion of the year without work.

When combined with the rising concentration of black youth unemployment, the additional racial disparity in the number who are discouraged job seekers or who are otherwise not participating in the labor force produces an even more serious picture for young blacks. Overall, our analysis of the work experience of out-of-school youth shows substantial variation within the youth group in the composition and characteristics of employment, a fact which must be taken into account in comparing youth and adult employment. Males are in a more favorable position compared to females, as are whites compared to blacks. White males are favored relative to all three other race and sex groups. These distinctions are not easily explained away and will require further investigation.

Youth and Adult Employment Compared

For males and females alike, the distribution of occupations within an age group varied greatly between youth (14–24) and all employed persons (14 and over) (Table 9.5). Not surprisingly, unskilled positions such as operatives and laborers were relatively more important for young men than adults and clerical positions more common for young than adult females, either in 1958 or 1980. Also of little surprise is the shift over time in the total occupational distribution to larger shares of professional and technical workers. Both of these results confirm findings from Chapter 3 for a mid-point year, 1970. Nonetheless, changes occurred in the occupational distributions between 1958 and 1980 which were much more marked for youth than for the total. The crowding of the baby boom youth into the labor market affected certain occupational categories more than others.

Over successive years from 1958 to 1980, out-of-school young men (14–24) displayed rising shares of total employment in the craft, operative, laborer, and service occupational categories (Table 9.5). In professional, technical, and clerical occupations, young women's shares of the jobs held by all women fell during the 1958–80 period, while their shares rose in traditionally male occupations—managerial, administrative, sales, operative, service and craft positions; these expanded shares did not involve large numbers of young women, however. In spite of increasingly similar rates of employment for young men and young women, occupational segregation of females persisted. Four occupational categories, professional and technical, clerical, operative, and service, accounted for 84 percent of young women's jobs in 1980; the same four categories had accounted for 88 percent in 1958.

Voluntary and involuntary job-changing has been more frequent for youth than adults, according to the limited number of studies on the

Table 9.5   Share of Out-of-School Youth, 14–24 Years Old, in Total Employment, by Major Occupational Group and Sex, United States, 1958–1980

	Professional and technical	Managers and administrators	Sales	Clerical	Crafts	Operatives	Nonfarm laborers	Service	Farm managers and laborers	All occupations
				Males (percentage)						
1958	6	2	8	13	7	14	19	9	13	10
1961	5	3	8	13	8	17	22	12	13	11
1964	6	4	10	14	8	18	21	9	12	11
1967	8	4	9	13	8	17	19	10	9	11
1970	7	4	10	15	10	18	19	12	9	11
1973	8	6	10	16	14	22	26	11	12	14
1976	6	5	11	13	14	20	23	11	14	13
1979	7	5	11	14	16	23	29	14	14	14
1980	7	5	10	14	15	20	26	16	16	14
				(percentage distribution)						
1958 (14–24 years)	7	3	5	9	14	28	15	6	14	100
1980 (14–24 years)	7	5	5	7	23	25	14	10	5	100
1958 (14 years and over)	11	14	6	7	20	19	8	6	10	100
1980 (14 years and over)	15	14	6	5	21	17	7	9	4	100
				Females (percentage)						
1958	14	2	11	25	9	12	18	11	19	16
1961	13	3	10	24	8	15	14	13	17	16
1964	14	4	11	23	7	15	15	14	16	17
1967	17	4	12	25	10	16	14	12	11	17
1970	15	8	13	25	14	15	22	13	9	17
1973	11	7	15	25	16	19	24	16	8	19
1976	11	8	15	19	14	15	25	14	14	15
1979	12	12	15	21	16	19	25	16	11	17
1980	10	11	16	20	17	18	24	17	16	17
				(percentage distribution)						
1958 (14–24 years)	11	1	5	49	9	12	*	16	6	100
1980 (14–24 years)	11	4	7	42	2	11	2	20	1	100
1958 (14 years and over)	12	5	8	30	1	15	*	23	5	100
1980 (14 years and over)	17	7	7	35	2	11	1	20	1	100

*Less than 1.0 percent.

Source: DOL 1981a; BLS 1959–82.

subject (Reubens 1977, Table 9.4). Hall (1980) found that two-fifths of American workers 30 years old and over hold jobs in which their tenure will be twenty years or more, an approximation to "lifetime employment." Nevertheless, considerable mobility occurs before stable, long-term jobs are obtained. Less than 6 percent of male teenagers can expect that the jobs they hold will last even five years, and only one-fourth of young adult males can expect job tenure of five years or more (Hall 1980, Table 2).

Today's high mobility rate of young workers probably exceeds their rate in the past. According to a study of Detroit workers, young males (15–25) had the highest rate of job-changing, controlling for education and size of firm, and also had the largest increase in mobility rates over time. However, in all age groups and in each subperiod, the mean number of inter-firm job changes fell as the size of firm rose (Cole 1979, Tables 6,10,13). If relatively more young people than adults hold jobs in small firms, as appears to be the case, then this would contribute to the greater propensity of youth to change jobs.

Individual perceptions of jobs by race, sex, and age yield comparative value judgments about job satisfaction and job characteristics. Ratings are available for youth (16–22) and adults (26–36) with no more than 12 years of schooling in 1979 (NLS 1966–80, 1968–80, 1979–81). With the exception of white women, adult jobs were perceived as more dangerous, more injurious to health, more capable of transmitting valuable skills, and somewhat more likely to offer a chance to do the things they did best. Youth and adult jobs were rated fairly similarly on pay adequacy, friendly co-workers, and for whites, the pleasantness of surroundings. Youth perceived that chances for promotion and competent supervision were somewhat more characteristic of their jobs than was the case for adults, but greater variety and task significance were reported by adults. The largest disparity between youth and adults concerned the desire to continue in the same type of job, a good indicator of job satisfaction. Young white females were the least satisfied of the four race-sex groups, but relative to their white adult counterparts, their scores were more similar than any of the other groups. Black young men were relatively most dissatisfied compared to black male adults.

A recently developed index of relative occupational risk suggests that youth are more likely than adults to suffer job-related injuries, although specific age data are not yet available (Root and Sebastian 1981). Based on the age distribution in the occupations covered by the index and the briefer tenure of youth in jobs, itself a predisposing factor to a higher injury rate, the conclusion seems warranted that youth are more at risk than adults.

A calculation of on-the-job training for adults and youth, drawn from an inquiry in 1976 of the 5,000 families in the Panel Study of Income Dynamics shows that the proportion receiving on-the-job training was higher for youth than other age groups, but that racial differences were sharp. White youth of each sex (18–25) were more likely than white adults to receive on-the-job training, and the rate declined steadily after age 25 (Hoffman 1981, Table 3). For blacks, the lower proportions receiving training at each age were erratically distributed. Black youth (18–25) ranked third among both males and females in the five age classes; for each sex, 45–54 year-olds reported the highest training rate, followed by 25–34 year-olds. Findings for the duration of on-the-job training by age were the reverse of findings on the proportion receiving training, with youth receiving a shorter on-the-job training than any other age group (Hoffman 1981, Table 2). There were no racial differences in patterns. The duration of training lengthened for each age group, except for black males 55–64 and white females 45–54. Since job tenure rises with age, age differences in training duration within a race-sex group may be related to length of tenure in the job.

Noteworthy is the higher proportion of white male youth receiving on-the-job training compared with all adult white females and adult blacks of either sex. The length of training for white male youth, while shorter than for any other white male age group, also exceeded that of adult white women and blacks of either sex, except for black males 45–54 and black females 55–64 (Hoffman 1981, Tables 2,3). These race/sex differences persist across different educational groups and for high as well as low-wage jobs, with white males always favored in the proportion and amount of training. Hoffman also finds:

> some evidence that the low-wage jobs held by white men are very dissimilar from those of blacks and women. Many of these jobs for white men also provide training, so the low wage is probably only temporary; for the other groups, the proportion of low-wage workers receiving training is much less, suggesting a more permanent low-wage condition [1981, p.36].

Hoffman (1981) projects that, because of the differences in current training, racial-sex earnings gaps will be larger with increasing age, a finding not supported by others (Mellor and Stamas 1982, p.18 and fn.8,9). In any case, the training differences between youth and adults are significantly overlaid by persistent race-sex differences, a finding that may be applicable to other aspects of the youth-adult comparison of employment characteristics.

HOURS OF WORK

Some employment outcomes would be expected to vary between youth and adults as a result of differences in hours worked during the week and over the year. Average weekly and annual hours of work have declined in the postwar period, both for youth and adults. An important component in the overall drop in hours has been the relative and absolute expansion of part-time jobs; voluntary part-timers grew from 7 percent of all workers in 1959 to 13 percent in 1979 (DOL 1980, p.269; 1963, p.148). As the number of part-time jobs grew over the postwar years, the share held by young females rose while that of young males remained stable. Involuntary part-time work tends to fluctuate cyclically. In 1978, about one-fourth of all part-time workers were involuntary, one-half chose part-time status, and the rest had other reasons; about two-thirds of voluntary part-timers were female (Terry 1981). Among males, teenagers and young adults were more likely than adults (25–54) to be voluntary part-timers, due mainly to the presence of students in the youth groups. Among females, teenagers and adults (25–54) had a higher proportion of voluntary part-timers than young adults.

In October 1980, out-of-school young males (16–24) showed much the same proportions in full-time (51.7 percent) and overtime work (31.0 percent) as adult males (25 and over), while relatively more young females worked full-time (56.2 percent) than did adult women (50.7 percent). The latter, however, had a slightly larger share with overtime hours (Young 1981b, Table 3). In general, relatively more of the jobs held by youth, especially young adult males, than those held by adults require shift, night, weekend, and holiday work. While the benefits to industry and society and some advantages to individuals have been found, the balance of research on work during nonstandard hours reveals unfavorable effects (Finn 1981). If part-time work and nonstandard hours are associated with poorer jobs, then male youth sustain a worse position relative to male adults than do female youth in relation to female adults.

Adults consistently have more weeks of employment over the course of a year than out-of-school young people. This is clearly shown in 1974–75 and 1977–78, based on matched files from the CPS March survey of persons with some work experience in the previous years. In 1974–75, a period of recession, prime age adults of both sexes (25–54) worked 78.9 weeks on average over two years, compared to 48.8 weeks for 16–17 year-old nonstudents, 61.3 weeks for those 18–19 and 71.0 for those 20–24. In 1977–78, years of recovery and expansion, the range was almost identical (Bowers 1981, Table 8). Racial and sex distributions for youth and adults conformed to the general pattern of average number of weeks worked, but white (male) adults had more weeks of employment than black (female). The difference was, however, slight between white and black adults, in contrast to the record for younger groups.

NLS 1979 data for nonstudents show that females aged 16–22 worked on average 30 weeks compared to 37 weeks for women aged 28–36. Male youth worked much less than adult males, 35 weeks on average compared to 48 weeks (NLS 1979–82; 1966–80; 1968–80). A new measure of annual average hours of paid employment 1977–81 by age, sex, and race shows that the male labor force, both black and white, experiences a rise in average annual hours from age 16–17 to 35–44 and then a decline for subsequent age groups. For similar white females, the greatest number of hours are worked by 55–59 year-olds, while for black females the peak hours tend to occur either among 45–54 or 35–44 year-olds. In every age group, fewer hours are worked by females than males, whether black or white, with a minor exception in 1981 for black females 16–17 years old. There is less sex disparity in hours for youth than adults, apart from white 16–17 year-olds (Smith 1983, Tables 1,2). Overall, the record on number of hours and weeks worked over the year suggests a more favorable employment record for adults than out-of-school youth, but it is not clear how much of the explanation of the age differences should be allocated to the characteristics of jobs, the traits of the two age groups, or other circumstances.

RELATIVE EARNINGS OF YOUTH AND ADULTS

Information about relative earnings by age serves two purposes: it provides a standard for comparing youth and adult jobs and it underlies explanations of the demand for young workers. Data on changes in relative earnings over time, explored as to causes and effects, enhance the age comparisons. Assuming a fixed number of entry level positions, a rising proportion of jobs held by out-of-school youth implies sharp competition for jobs, leading to a concomitant drop in youth pay or a sharp rise in unemployment, or both. Similarly, a fixed number of jobs, whether entry level or not, may be suitable only for youth who would presumably demand less of their first jobs than workers who are older. In this case also, a decline in relative youth wages is an expected adjustment without which youth employment (unemployment) would be lower (higher).

Data from Table 9.6 do show a deterioration over time in the earnings of youth relative to adults. Over a ten year period, the teenage earnings ratio fell significantly. With the exception of black female teens, where data are incomplete, relative earnings fell sharply in 1975, followed by some degree of recovery by 1979 and further decline through 1982. Currently, white teenage earnings relative to adults are 44 and 61 percent for males and females, respectively. Corresponding ratios for blacks are 52 and 70 percent. Young adults, with their added work experience and skills, show higher earnings ratios relative to adults, ranging from 61–81 percent. For young adults, declines in earnings ratios over a ten year period were, at a minimum, 10 percentage points for each of the four race and sex groups. The decline in relative earnings was quite steady for most groups, irrespective of variation in the business cycle. Only in the case of black young adult women did earnings recover somewhat, once in 1978 and again in 1981.

To some extent the trend may reflect changes in the composition of the youth group—the demographic bulge that reduced the average age of the later cohorts and the increased proportion of student workers over time which would have tended to reduce the youth earnings. It is likely, however, that a genuine wage adjustment occurred for youth

Table 9.6 <u>Median Usual Weekly Earnings of Full-time Youth Relative to Adults,</u>
<u>by Age, Own Race, and Sex, United States, 1973-1982</u>

	16-19/25 and over				20-24/25 and over			
	Whites		Blacks[b]		Whites		Blacks[b]	
	Males	Females	Males	Females	Males	Females	Males	Females
				(ratio)[a]				
1973	.51	.71	.62	*	.71	.91	.81	.95
1974	.52	.71	.62	*	.71	.89	.81	.93
1975	.49	.67	.55	.69	.68	.84	.78	.85
1976	.47	.68	.56	*	.66	.88	.75	.85
1977	.45	.67	*	*	.66	.88	.69	.83
1978	.46	.67	.51	.76	.67	.86	.76	.86
1979[a]	.48	.69	.55[b]	.72[b]	.67	.84	.70[b]	.83[b]
1980	.48	.66	.52	.73	.67	.83	.69	.79
1981	.45	.64	.62[c]	.69	.64	.81	.72	.85
1982	.44	.61	.52	.70	.61	.81	.69	.80

*Not available because base was less than 75,000 persons.
[a]Prior to 1979, relative earnings were for May. In 1979 and thereafter, relative earnings are the second quarter average. [b]Beginning in 1979, earnings are for blacks only. Prior to 1979, earnings are for blacks and other minorities. The change in definition meant that in 1978, the ratio for blacks alone was one percentage point higher than for blacks and others combined. [c]Though reflecting the actual CPS data, this ratio appears to be an anomaly. First quarter figures for 1981 yield a ratio of .55. For black males, 20-24, relative to adults, first quarter figures yield exactly the same ratio as in the second quarter.

Source: BLS 1982b.

and that the reduction in relative earnings made possible the substantial expansion in youth employment shown in Tables 2.2 and 2.3. Perhaps some change in the composition and characteristics of youth jobs compared to those of adults also is reflected in the earnings trends.

Freeman (1979) used cross-sectional measures of annual earnings in 1969 and 1978 to fit a linear regression model to data on young males. Comparing the regression coefficients for older workers with younger, he concluded that age-earnings profiles had fallen over time, particularly for more highly educated males. The depression in relative earnings appeared to stem from a demographic increase in the numbers of young men, since changes in the amount of capital and in the number of female workers competing for entry-level jobs had a weaker impact when aggregate production functions were estimated. Freeman concluded:

> Apparently because younger and older male workers are imperfect substitutes in production, changes in the number of young male workers relative to older male workers substantially influence the ratio of the earnings of younger men to the earnings of older men [1979, p.291].

In a second study, Freeman (1982) rejects claims that the gains of black males subsequent to passage of the Civil Rights Act of 1964 disappeared in the sluggish economy of the 1970s, but the picture was mixed depending on age and experience. For young black males, 18–24 at the outset, and for those with little labor market experience, earnings fell relative to those of whites, reflecting again the severe employment problems of young black males. As the black male cohort 30–34 years old aged over the decade, some improvement occurred in their earnings relative to white males. Among those 25–29 in the initial period, little change occurred in the relative position of black and white males. The question whether their early earnings disadvantage would persist later for the baby boom generation was addressed directly by Welch (1979) who concluded that, though the income-depressing effects of cohort size should decline over the career, such effects would not vanish altogether.

Smith and Welch (1981) concluded that since 1940, lifetime earnings might vary by 4 percent between the smallest and largest cohort of high school graduates and 10 percent for college graduates; the heaviest impact of cohort size was felt in the initial years of work. The converse may also prove true in the future. As demographic patterns shift to a relatively smaller cohort of youth, employment and earnings may favor youth, particularly the highly educated, on the assumption that demand does not fall behind the youth labor supply. If, for young men, a limited number of entry level jobs and sharply increased labor supply explain the decline in relative earnings, for young women, occupational segregation further adds to pressure on wages.

Concurrently with the demographic changes of the labor force, changes in the minimum wage law have tended to restrain relative wage depression and have had a negative effect on the volume of youth employment. A review of minimum wage studies concluded that for teenagers a 10 percent increase in the minimum wage is associated with a decrease in employment of between 1 and 3 percent. Time series studies typically fall within this range of estimates, but the preferred estimates lie at the lower end. Cross-sectional studies produce a broader range of estimates, with the most plausible between a 0 and 0.75 point decrease in employment. The employment effect on youth aged 20–24 is negative and smaller than for teenagers (Brown et al. 1982).

JOB TURNOVER AND UNEMPLOYMENT DIFFERENTIALS

It is well established that young people change employers more frequently than adults. Data for 1961, 1966, and 1977, reflecting different economic circumstances, confirm the relationship (Reubens 1977b, Table 9.4; Bowers 1981, Table 4). Hall (1980) has calculated the probability that a newly employed worker will ultimately achieve a five year tenure in the same job. For teenagers the probability is less than 2 percent and for workers aged 20–24, it is 6 percent, but it peaks at about 25 percent for workers in their early fifties. In 1977, 12.1 percent of adult males (25–54) and 10.4 percent of adult females had two or more employers, using the matched file from the CPS March survey of persons with some work experience in 1977 as the base. This proportion was under one-half to almost one-third of the rates for 16–17, 18–19, and 20–24 year-olds, taking each sex separately and including in and out-of-school youth (Bowers 1981, Table 4). The data may understate the age difference since youth who wished to find a new employer remained unemployed or left the labor force to a greater extent than adults during 1977 (Bowers 1982). The probability of working for two or more employers during 1978 for those with two or more employers in 1977 also was considerably lower for adults than youth of each sex (Bowers 1981, Table 4). The greater occupational mobility of youth within a year is one source of the age difference (Rosenfeld 1979).

The extent to which the higher youth job mobility rates reflect less satisfactory jobs for youth than for adults cannot be determined without focusing on the minority of out-of-school youth who change jobs very frequently and boost the rate of their whole age group. Bartel (1980) analyzed age differences in job quits among two age groups of male, nonstudent workers who were 14–24 and 45–59 years old in 1966. Their experience in 1967–69 and 1969–71 revealed job-related causes of quits and variation by age. While wages had a negative and significant effect on the quit decision for both age groups, fringe benefits were not a significant factor for the young men. Young men were more likely to accept and remain on physically demanding, stressful, nonrepetitive jobs and jobs providing control of an entire activity. Older men were induced to quit by bad working conditions, but not by repetitive work. The more rapid growth of wages in the strenuous jobs with bad working conditions was a prime consideration for the young men. Variations in job-changing rates among youth also may be greater than among adults due to differences in jobs held and jobs available by race, ethnic group, region of the country, or state of the local economy.

The relation between differential rates of job-changing by age and age differences in unemployment rates is not straightforward. A substantial proportion of job-changers do so without any intervening unemployment, especially if they have left voluntarily after making their job search while employed (Reubens 1977b, pp.179–86). As a result, the proportion of the labor force with two or more spells of unemployment in a year tends to be much smaller than the proportion with two or more employers in a year, a reasonable standard of frequent job turnover. In 1977, for example, the matched file from the March CPS survey showed that three times as many males and five times as many females had two or more employers as had two or more spells of unemployment. Moreover, the ratios for youth and adults were much the same, omitting 16–17 year-olds since most were in school (Bowers 1981, Table 4; Bowers 1982, Table 3).

Is there any connection between the types of jobs youth hold and unemployment experience? Brown (1982), attempting to study the relationship between lack of opportunities for advancement and youth unemployment, concluded that his results were "too weak to justify either a confident yes or a confident no." Another investigation is suggestive, although data by age are not available. Ryscavage (1982) studied the total work force and those living in families below the poverty line as part of a pioneering attempt to investigate multiple employment problems. He found an association between adverse employment conditions and unemployment in experimental tabulations from the March 1980 CPS in which the unemployed who had other employment problems during 1980 were separated from those who were unemployed without such problems. The designated adverse employment conditions were involuntary part-time jobs, low hourly earnings, and fewer than 40 weeks of employment. Excluding year-round full-time workers and those who had no work experience in 1979, there were 15,243,000 persons, of whom 83.1 percent had unemployment accompanied by one or more of the three specified employment problems. However, 38 percent of all unemployed persons reported that having fewer than 40 weeks of work in the year was their only employment problem. Since much of this group may consist of students and others voluntarily working part of the year, the proportion of unemployed with other employment problems probably lies between a half and two-thirds of all unemployed. The unemployed who lived in poverty families were disproportionately represented among those who had experienced all three employment problems, only two of the problems, or just low hourly earnings (Ryscavage 1982, Table 5).

Longitudinal Surveys and Analyses

Longitudinal data and analyses are well developed in the United States and analytic methodology is constantly being debated and improved. At a minimum, such data permit a descriptive account of changes in the occupations and industries, hours, earnings, and other employment aspects of cohorts of youth as they age. The longitudinal data sets also contain enough information on individuals to permit analytic issues to be tackled in which the outcomes are allocated between effects due to the variable being investigated (state dependence) and the effects due to the diversity among the individuals being investigated (heterogeneity). These and other distinctions are crucial to any conclusions about the "scarring" effects of early experience in the labor market (Corcoran 1982a). Moreover, careful consideration must be given to the amount and character of the early experience which is being tested and the general economic circumstances under which it occurred; six months of unemployment after leaving school would have a different meaning if the youth unemployment rate was 5 percent than if it was 20 percent.

Table 9.7   First Jobs of Youth, 16-24 Years Old, Leaving School in 1968 and
            Jobs Held Ten Years Later, by Occupation, Industry, Sex, and Race,
            United States, 1968 and 1978

| | Males | | | | Females | | | |
| | White | | Black | | White | | Black | |
	1968	1978	1968	1978	1968	1978	1968	1978
Occupation[a]	(percentage distribution)							
Professional, technical	15	15	7	7	21	21	6	11
Managerial	3	20	*	6	1	7	1	1
Clerical	9	6	9	6	43	40	39	31
Sales	4	5	1	1	6	6	3	3
Crafts	9	26	5	17	*	*	1	1
Operatives	21	15	30	30	8	10	16	26
Services	4	5	8	10	15	11	17	20
Household services	*	*	*	*	5	2	13	3
Farm managers	1	3	*	*	*	*	*	*
Farm laborers	4	*	5	2	1	2	4	*
Other laborers	11	3	19	11	*	1	*	4
Armed forces	19	3	17	10	*	*	*	*
Total	100	100	100	100	100	100	100	100
Total number	466	462	126	126	339	280	123	95
Industry[a]	(percentage distribution)							
Agriculture, mining	5	5	6	3	1	3	4	1
Construction	8	13	4	8	*	1	*	*
Manufacturing	27	26	38	37	18	19	13	25
Transportation	4	8	4	8	7	6	6	7
Retail, wholesale trade	20	16	15	13	19	18	18	14
Finance	2	6	*	1	9	5	4	7
Business, personal services, and entertainment	4	6	3	3	12	9	21	15
Professional services	9	11	11	12	30	33	29	26
Public administration	2	8	2	5	4	6	6	5
Armed forces	19	2	17	10	*	*	*	*
Total	100	100	100	100	100	100	100	100
Total number	465	462	126	125	339	276	123	96

*Less than 1.0 percent.
[a]Includes armed forces.

Source: NLS 1966-80, 1968-80.

It is also important to have longitudinal data for a reasonable number
of years; conclusions drawn from changes over a two or even a four-
year period are not adequate documentation.

The descriptive statistics from one sample of longitudinal data reflect
the changes from 1968 to 1978 in the occupational and industrial
distribution of a cohort (16-24) which left all levels of education in
1968 (Table 9.7). Though sample sizes are small, the data may be more
accurate than cross-sectional data based on larger samples. Nevertheless,

for the purposes of this book, the most serious limitation is the high degree of aggregation in the age group and in the occupational and industrial categories. Even at this level of aggregation, 70 percent of the males had changed occupational categories by 1978 and 60 percent had changed industries, including the armed forces as an occupation and industry. Fifty percent of females changed occupations and 57 percent changed industries. Few racial differences were evident among males, but black women changed occupations and industries with greater frequency than whites.

Upward mobility is implied by many of the moves, but some of the movement was downward. The usual pattern for males was to move from the armed forces, operative, and laborer positions to craft and managerial jobs. In the male industrial distributions, construction, transport, finance, and public administration grew in importance. Females moved into managerial and operative positions and out of clerical and service jobs. With some decline in the finance industry matched by an increase in professional service institutions, industrial distributions for females remained relatively stable.

Despite their longitudinal nature, descriptive data such as those in Table 9.7 have serious limitations for measuring the degree of segmentation in youth labor markets and persistence in later years. Empirical tests based on a hypothesis, such as dual or segmented labor markets (see Chapter 1), also are difficult. After a review, Griffin et al. (1981), judge earlier empirical tests of the dual labor market thesis "inconclusive and tentative." In retesting the dualism thesis, they used four years of longitudinal data on over 8,000 young men and women leaving high school in their senior year in 1972 and not proceeding to college. Classifying respondents' jobs into a primary or a secondary sector, they measured mobility between the sectors from 1973 to 1976 and found that although 84 percent of those originally in the primary sector still were in that sector in 1976, only 35 percent of those beginning in the secondary sector were still there in 1976. However, females and black males were much less mobile than white males; the rates of initial assignment to the secondary sector were higher for these groups and so was the rate of staying. The rates of remaining in the secondary sector were: white males 24 percent, black males 38 percent, white females 42 percent, and black females 55 percent. In spite of these differences, the study found that:

> initial entry into labor market segments was almost a random process ... few systematic patterns of determination (were observed), especially with regard to initial sectoral placement in 1973. Three years later, in 1976, greater stability is apparent, but even here there is considerable indeterminancy in workers' occupational positioning and attainments. Although we do, for example, observe linkages in sector location over this period, sector boundaries appear surprisingly permeable, and sector location relatively unstable [Griffin et al., p.219].

The specification of only a primary and secondary sector in an empirical test is open to question, as is the reliance on occupation as the sole indicator of segmentation. Nevertheless, another empirical study which uses cross-sectional data, a far more complex segmentation model, and several relevant variables instead of occupation alone, comes to much the same conclusions about rates of escape of youth from the least desirable jobs (Freedman 1976). This latter study, however, finds consistent patterns of assignment and retention in the "bad" jobs throughout working life, as well as a disadvantaged position of youth vis-à-vis adults.

Osterman (1980) contends that mobility between the segments is not the relevant issue, since most young men exhibit such mobility. He does find that "many, and probably most, youths spend their initial years after (high) school in secondary jobs," which are unskilled and casual (Osterman 1980, p.23). Successful young men move into stable primary jobs after a lengthy "moratorium" period of weak labor market attachment and they also adopt behavioral patterns that indicate "settling down." In the process, they have held a succession of jobs that do not follow career patterns. Overall, their job mobility is heavily influenced by the structure of labor market opportunity, access to contacts, and chance.

The empirical studies to date have not been definitive, particularly in so controversial a subject as labor market segmentation. Further research on dualism should be more precise in specifying the "mechanisms which create and maintain the job structures implied by the dual labor market and other segmentation theories" (Griffin et al. 1981, p.222).

Earnings profiles also are more usefully described through longitudinal than cross-sectional data. Ten-year earnings profiles have been constructed for two youth groups. The first consists of 320 males and 200 females (16–19) who were enrolled in school in 1968 and left school or entered the military in 1969; few had gone beyond high school and some were dropouts. In the second group there were 130 men and 85 women (20–24), virtually all of whom had been enrolled in college, leaving with or without a degree between 1968 and 1969. Steeper profiles for median weekly earnings are typical in the initial years for both males and females, but age-sex differences become quite pronounced after 1971 (Table 9.8). Making allowance for a temporary dip in 1976, earnings of young adult men rose about 3.5 percent after 1971 for each year of experience, using 1978 dollars in all years. Teenage males, however, had a smoother profile which rose at about 8 percent per year. Young adult women, in contrast, exhibited a falling profile, despite the fact that those who had no earnings in a given year were excluded from the calculation. However, a shift to part-time employment as the women aged could produce this earnings pattern. The median weekly earnings of teenage women remained relatively constant after 1971.

Table 9.8   Median Weekly Earnings and Average Annual Change,
             Youth 16-24 Years Old on Leaving School in 1968,
             by Age and Sex, United States, 1970-1978

	Males		Females	
	Age in 1968			
	16-19 years	20-24 years	16-19 years	20-24 years
Median weekly earnings		($)		
1970	151	264	113	187
1971	161	282	121	199
1973	198	305	132	196
1975	212	326	128	172
1978	250	357	130	150
Average annual change		(percentage)		
1970-71	6.6	6.8	7.1	6.4
1971-73	10.9	4.0	4.4	-0.8
1973-75	3.5	3.4	-1.5	-6.3
1975-78	5.7	3.1	0.5	-4.3

Note: Median earnings are annual earnings divided by weeks
worked. If no weeks worked, the observation is excluded
from the calculation. All earnings expressed in 1978
dollars.

Source: NLS 1966-80, 1968-80.

These earnings profiles depict the immediate monetary costs to
females, arising either from labor market discrimination or their decision
to participate in paid employment less extensively than men. Mincer
and Ofek (1982) estimate that wages of women in their late 30s and
early 40s are 1.5-1.8 percent lower for each year of withdrawal from
paid employment in earlier years. For a more recent interruption, wages
would be 3.3-7.6 percent lower per year of interruption. Thus, a
significant rebound in female wages is found after reentry to paid
employment, double the rate estimated for men of similar ages at the
outset of their working lives. Shaw (1982), using the same data set,
finds an average rate of skill depreciation of only 1-4 percent, even in
the short-run. Corcoran (1978, 1982a), using another set of longitudinal
data, found somewhat different results for females with periods of
nonwork soon after leaving school; black women were less affected than
white.

    Longitudinal analyses have also dealt with the relationship between
differing amounts of early unemployment (or nonemployment) or job-

changing and later unemployment, employment, job-changing, and earnings. An important issue is whether early youth unemployment or nonemployment has lasting effects on later unemployment, employment and earnings. Ellwood (1982), Heckman and Borjas (1980), Meyer and Wise (1979), Osterman (1980), and Stevenson (1978) found that teenage unemployment or nonemployment in the 1960s had a "scarring effect" on subsequent earnings. Adjustments for heterogeneity in the sample, that is, the unmeasured individual characteristics which cause poor labor market performance both early and later in life, minimize the persistence effects among males and reduce them for female teenagers (Corcoran 1982a, 1982b). Black teenagers did, however, continue to show greater persistence than white (Osterman 1980; Corcoran 1982a).

Corcoran (1982b) states "there is consistent evidence that accumulating half a year or more of unemployment in the teen years may dramatically lower future wages—even as much as eight years later." She cites Ellwood (1982), Meyer and Wise (1982), Becker and Hills (1980, 1982), and Corcoran (1982a). Only Ellwood, however, controlled for heterogeneity. Furthermore, any "scarring" effects may vary considerably with the frequency and duration of unemployment. Thus, Becker and Hills (1980, 1982), found that teenage unemployment does not always have a negative influence on wages and, in fact, brief periods of unemployment, perhaps used to shop around for new jobs, were positively associated with wages nearly eight years later. The more recent of the two studies shows that job mobility in the year immediately after leaving school was positively related to wage rates eight to ten years later, both for black and white young men. Teenagers with more stable employment records in the transition period tended to have lower subsequent earnings than teenagers who experienced short-term unemployment. Among whites, individuals with longer term unemployment earned the lowest subsequent wages, but for approximately half the teenagers studied, job switching and short periods of unemployment (less than five weeks in the mid-1960s) reflected a positive labor market adjustment process (Becker and Hills 1982).

American studies of the possible "scarring" effects of youth unemployment, more numerous and sophisticated than in other countries, lend some support to the position that teenage unemployment in the late 1960s had longer-run harmful effects on an individual's subsequent earnings but little effect on longer-run employment stability. Though longitudinal, these studies still reflect labor market conditions in the 1960s. Until the studies are replicated for several cohorts, it will not be clear how much of the findings reflect specific historical context and how much represent underlying and persistent relationships.

Summary and Conclusions

Differences among groups of young people emerge as a more significant feature of our analysis of the characteristics of jobs than differences between youth and adults. The diversity within the youth group is powerfully and persistently associated with the inferior position and opportunities of females and minority youth. Poorer choices and market limitations, namely, the inability of minority youth to capture their fair share of employment during a period of demographic change and the continuing occupational segregation of young women, have occupied American policy makers in recent decades. But other sources of variation among youth also are present, attributable to school enrollment status, educational attainment, and place of residence and work. The last particularly needs further research.

Significantly diverse experience characterizes the various subgroups of youth. In 1980, 30 percent of employed youth aged 16–24 were students, double the proportion 25 years ago. Student jobs, differing from those held by nonstudents in a number of predictable ways, are largely part-time, have wage rates which cluster around the legal minimum, and show a growing concentration of work in over-the-counter eating places. For males, in particular, the composition of employment is quite different when comparing post-school with student employment, although many out-of-school youth initially take low level, dead end jobs. For females, sales and clerical positions appear to occupy much the same share of post-school as in-school employment. For all youth groups, rates of pay rise significantly on leaving school.

Overall contrasts in experience between male and female youth further add to the diversity associated with student and nonstudent status. Despite changes in attitudes regarding female employment and near equal student employment rates by sex, early sex differences in education, training, job aspirations, and jobs are characteristic. Occupational segregation begins with in-school employment and persists in subsequent jobs, regardless of the educational attainment of female youth. The industries in which youth find jobs are very different for males and females, with females more apt to find jobs in less unionized industries. Both the proportion of female youth receiving on-the-job training and its total duration are less than for male youth. Differences in occupation, industry, and training are part of the reason that the full-time earnings of female youth are only 80 percent of the earnings of their male counterparts.

Still more diversity is clear when contrasting the experience of white and minority youth, taking the experience of blacks as similar to that of Hispanics and other minorities. Three times as many white teenage students as black were employed in 1981, and one-and-one-half times as many white young adult students had jobs. While these differences by race were more pronounced for students than nonstudents, they persisted in both groups. Once out of school, the proportion of white youth who received on-the-job training was, for example, considerably greater than for blacks and white earnings were higher.

The gap in employment rates has been the most significant handicap of out-of-school blacks compared with whites. Although post-school youth in the aggregate captured a share of jobs in the 1960s and 1970s which matched the increased size of their demographic group, black post-school youth fared much worse than white and continue to do so. Military service and increased school enrollment rates for blacks have served as safety valves, but even so, current black employment rates have fallen to the lowest levels in two decades. The search for causes has more or less ruled out suburbanization of jobs, even though there was not a comparable residential shift by blacks. Continuing discrimination in employment coupled with reluctance on the part of youth to accept lower wages because of discrimination may explain why blacks have borne the brunt of the demographic strain on youth employment. Increases in the amount and coverage of the minimum wage may also have contributed to poor employment prospects for young blacks, particularly in the South.

While diversity among youth is related to sex, race and school enrollment, most of the divergence between youth and adult jobs appears to be the expected consequence of the extra years of maturation and work experience of adults. There are, however, several aspects that warrant more detailed analysis than is possible with currently available information. For example, it is not entirely clear that all jobs young people could perform are open to them or that seniority systems and other constraints do not operate restrictively against youth.

A life-cycle perspective suggests why age differences are to be expected. As youth move from initial post-school employment to longer term adult jobs, several trends become apparent. The quality of employment improves, the proportion who need and acquire training falls, employment patterns become more stable, and unemployment declines. None of the trends is as straightforward as might seem on the surface, even for white males, the favored group. Firstly, the movement of youth into higher quality jobs has been complicated by the negative influence of demographic change. Pressure from the baby boom has altered the composition of employment, compressed relative earnings, and raised rates of joblessness. Secondly, the prediction that larger amounts of training will be acquired by youth is qualified by actual data which do show larger proportions of youth than others acquiring training, but also show much shorter duration of training than for adults. Finally, dismissal and quit rates are interrelated with unemployment according to complex patterns which require careful interpretation of the relationship with age or the quality of employment of the various age groups.

Youth labor market experience is perhaps most distinguished from adult in terms of job mobility and unemployment. A surprisingly large number of American workers ultimately acquire jobs that could be considered permanent or "near-lifetime" in duration. However, a great deal of job mobility and unemployment occurs among youth before they find longer term, stable employment, and different types of unemployment contribute further to the diversity in youth labor markets.

Observed unemployment affects both youth who are upwardly mobile, searching for new employment possibilities, and youth who are working for firms which are themselves in a precarious market position, thereby increasing the probability of involuntary unemployment. The identification of youth in the latter category would be an important contribution to policy making which has tended to identify vulnerable youth by their personal characteristics, such as educational level, family income, and racial background, or by an undifferentiated measure of the rate of unemployment.

Does the diversity of youth labor market experience imply equally diverse outcomes for longer run earnings and employment? Given the low employment levels of in-school black youth, the question of potential long-run effects of early work experience is important. Economists tend to attribute positive later effects to in-school employment, whereas sociologists and psychologists draw more mixed conclusions, depending on the type of in-school employment, hours worked per week, and impacts on school performance and personal behavior. The jobs that women and blacks enter immediately following school appear to be strongly related to the jobs they have in years later. Yet much change underlies the stable distributions. Systematic research does not yield a strong confirmation of underlying dualism in jobs, since placement in various types of jobs and industries has a large random component. Occupational segregation, however, has persisted and little change has occurred in twenty years in overall occupational distributions by sex.

Youth unemployment is linked to significant long-run costs in the form of lower earnings later on, both for men and for women. Yet for some young men, short spells of unemployment in the early years may be better than remaining with one employer, particularly if it is in a dead-end job. For young women who interrupt careers to work in the home, research points to some depreciation of skills, though the degree of loss is a matter of debate. A rapid, though perhaps not full restoration of earnings tends to occur following the interruption.

Though U.S. research increasingly relies on longitudinal data to relate early youth experience to subsequent outcomes, the very diversity of experience complicates both the theoretical framework and the empirical tests. In no case is this more true than in the interpretation of youth unemployment. To some degree, unemployment is linked with job mobility which, in turn, can be favorable if it is part of a rational job search process or unfavorable if it is linked to a segment of the labor market characterized by high turnover rates, poor jobs, and little chance for job occupants to escape to more favorable market sectors. Short spells of unemployment are therefore an ambiguous indicator of later position. Studies which link unemployment to other measures of employment difficulty and economic hardship and which contrast youth and adult experience are increasingly necessary. The heterogeneity of youth labor market experience warns against easy generalization regarding subsequent earnings and employment.

References: United States

Bartel, A. 1980. *Wages, Nonwage Job Characteristics, and Labor Mobility.* Working Paper no.552. Cambridge, Mass.: National Bureau of Economic Research.

Becker, B., and Hills, S. 1980. "Teenage Unemployment: Some Evidence of the Long-run Effects on Wages." *Journal of Human Resources,* Summer.

─────── . 1982. "The Long-run Effects of Job Changes and Unemployment Among Male Teenagers." *Journal of Human Resources,* Spring.

Behn, W.H., et al. 1976. "School is Bad; Work is Worse." In Carnoy, M. and Levin, H., eds. *The Limits of Educational Reform.* New York: David McKay.

Blackburn, J.; Klayman, E.; and Malin, M. 1982. *The Legal Environment of Business.* Homewood, Ill.: Irwin.

Blau, F.D., and Kahn, L.M. 1981. "Race and Sex Difference in Quits by Young Workers." *Industrial and Labor Relations Review,* July.

BLS (Bureau of Labor Statistics). 1959-81. *Employment of School Age Youth.* Special Labor Force Reports. Washington: GPO.

─────── . 1982a. *Earnings and Other Characteristics of Organized Workers, May 1980.* Bulletin 2105. Washington: GPO.

─────── . 1982b. Unpublished tabulations for median usual weekly earnings of full-time wage and salary workers from the Current Population Survey, May 1973-78 and second quarter averages 1979-82.

Borus, M.E. 1982. "Willingness to Work Among Youth." *Journal of Human Resources,* Fall.

Borus, M.E., et al. 1980. *Pathways to the Future: A Longitudinal Study of Young Americans, Preliminary Report, 1979.* Columbus, Ohio: Center for Human Resource Research, The Ohio State University.

Bowers, N. 1979. "Young and Marginal: An Overview of Youth Employment," *Monthly Labor Review,* October.

─────── . 1981. "The Dynamics of Youth Labor Force Flows: An Empirical Examination of Data from the Current Population Survey." Unpublished paper, Bureau of Labor Statistics.

─────── . 1982. "Tracking Youth Joblessness: Persistent or Fleeting?" *Monthly Labor Review,* February.

Brown, C. 1982. "Dead-end Jobs and Youth Unemployment." In Freeman, R.B. and Wise, D.A., eds. *The Youth Labor Market Problem: Its Nature, Causes, and Consequences.* Chicago, Ill.: University of Chicago Press.

Brown, C.; Gilroy, C.; and Kohen, A. 1982. "The Effect of the Minimum Wage on Employment and Unemployment." *Journal of Economic Literature,* June.

Carnoy, M., and Levin, H., eds. 1976. *The Limits of Educational Reform.* New York: David McKay.

CBO (Congressional Budget Office). 1982. *Improving Youth Employment Prospects: Issues and Options.* Washington: GPO.

Clark, K., and Summers, L. 1982. "The Dynamics of Youth Unemployment." In Freeman, R.B., and Wise, D.A., eds. *The Youth Labor Market Problem: Its Nature, Causes, and Consequences.* Chicago, Ill.: University of Chicago Press.

Cogan, J. 1981. *The Decline in Black Teenage Employment: 1950-1970.* Working Paper no.683. Cambridge, Mass.: National Bureau of Economic Research.

Cole, R.E. 1979. *Work, Mobility, and Participation.* Berkeley, Cal.: University of California Press.

Coleman, J.S. 1972. *Youth: Transition to Adulthood—Report of the Panel on Youth of the President's Science Advisory Committee.* Chicago, Ill.: University of Chicago Press.

Corcoran, M. 1978. "Work Experience, Work Interruption and Wages." In Duncan, G.J., and Morgan, J.N., eds. *Five Thousand Families—Patterns of Economic Progress,* vol. 6. Ann Arbor, Mich.: Institute for Social Research, University of Michigan.

─────── . 1982a. "The Employment and Wage Consequences of Teenage Women's

Unemployment." In Freeman, R.B. and Wise, D.A., eds. *The Youth Labor Market Problem: Its Nature, Causes, and Consequences.* Chicago, Ill.: University of Chicago Press.

_____. 1982b. "Estimating the Long-run cost of Unemployment During a Recession." Paper for the National Commission for Employment Policy, Washington.

Corcoran, M.; Datcher, L.; and Duncan, G. 1980. "Information and Influence Networks in Labor Markets." In Duncan, G., and Morgan, J., eds. *Five Thousand American Families—Patterns of Economic Progress,* vol. 8. Ann Arbor, Mich.: Institute for Social Research, University of Michigan.

Crowley, J.E. 1981. "Government Employment and Training Programs: Comparisons of Characteristics, 1978–1979." In Borus, M.E., ed. *Pathways to the Future: A Longitudinal Study of Young Americans, Preliminary Report on the 1980 Survey.* Columbus, Ohio: Center for Human Resource Research, The Ohio State University.

DOC (Department of Commerce). 1955–82. *Statistical Abstract of the United States.* Washington: GPO.

DOL (Department of Labor). 1963–71. *Manpower Report of the President.* Washington: GPO.

_____. 1979a, 1982a. *Employment and Earnings.* Washington: GPO.

_____. 1979b. *Unemployment Insurance Statistics.* Washington: DOL.

_____. 1980. *Employment and Training Report of the President.* Washington: GPO.

_____. 1981a. *Employment and Training Report of the President.* Washington: GPO.

_____. 1981b. *Minimum Wage and Maximum Hours Standards Under the Fair Labor Standards Act, 1980.* Washington: GPO.

_____. 1982b. *Monthly Labor Review.* Washington: GPO, April.

_____. 1982c. "Student Participation in Work Force Slackens." *News.* Washington: BLS, May 20.

Easterlin, R.A.; Wachter, M.L.; and Wachter, S. 1978. "Demographic Influences on Economic Stability: The United States Experience." *Population and Development Review,* March.

Ellwood, D. 1982. "Teenage Unemployment: Permanent Scar or Temporary Blemish." In Freeman, R.B. and Wise, D.A., eds. *The Youth Labor Market Problem: Its Nature, Causes, and Consequences.* Chicago, Ill.: University of Chicago Press.

Finn, P. 1981. "The Effects of Shift Work on the Lives of Employees." *Monthly Labor Review,* October.

Freedman, M. 1976. *Labor Markets: Segments and Shelters.* Montclair, N.J.: Allanheld, Osmun.

Freeman, R.B. 1979. "The Effect of Demographic Factors on Age-Earnings Profiles." *Journal of Human Resources,* Summer.

_____. 1980. "Why Is There a Youth Labor Market Problem?" In Anderson, B.E., and Sawhill, I.V., eds. *Youth Employment and Public Policy.* Englewood Cliffs, N.J.: Prentice-Hall.

_____. 1982. "Have Black Labor Market Gains Post-1964 Been Permanent or Transitory." Working Paper no.751. Cambridge, Mass.: National Bureau of Economic Research.

Freeman, R.B., and Medoff, J. 1982. "The Youth Labor Market Problem in the United States: An Overview." In Freeman, R.B. and Wise, D.A., eds. *The Youth Labor Market Problem: Its Nature, Causes, and Consequences.* Chicago, Ill.: University of Chicago Press.

Freeman, R.B., and Wise, D.A., eds. 1982. *The Youth Labor Market Problem: Its Nature, Causes, and Consequences.* Chicago, Ill.: University of Chicago Press.

GAO (General Accounting Office). 1982. *Labor Market Problems of Teenagers Result Largely from Doing Poorly in School.* Washington: GAO.

_____. 1983. *Minimum Wage Policy Questions Persist.* Washington: GAO.

Greenberger, E., and Steinberg, L.D. 1981. *Part-Time Employment of In-School Youth: An Assessment of Costs and Benefits.* Final Report to the National Institute of Education. Irvine, Cal.: University of California.

_____. 1982. *Sex Differences in Early Labor Force Experience: Harbinger of Things to Come.* Irvine, Cal.: University of California.

Griffin, L.; Kalleberg, A.; and Alexander, K. 1981. "Determinants of Early Labor Market Entry and Attainment: A Study of Labor Market Segmentation." *Sociology of Education,* July.

Gustman, A.L., and Steinmeier, T.L. 1981. "The Impact of Wages and Unemployment on Youth Enrollment and Labor Supply." *Review of Economics and Statistics,* November.

Hall, R.E. 1980. *The Importance of Lifetime Jobs in the U.S. Economy.* Working Paper no.560. Cambridge, Mass.: National Bureau of Economic Research.

Heckman, J., and Borjas, G.J. 1980. "Does Unemployment Cause Further Unemployment? Definitions, Questions and Answers from a Continuous Time Model of Heterogeneity and State Dependence." *Economics,* August.

Hedges, J.N., and Mellor, E.F. 1979. "Weekly and Hourly Earnings of U.S. Workers, 1967-78." *Monthly Labor Review,* August.

Hills, S.M. 1982a. "Comment on Freeman and Medoff, Why Does the Rate of Labor Force Activity Differ Across Surveys." In Freeman, R.B. and Wise, D.A., eds. *The Youth Labor Market Problem: Its Nature, Causes, and Consequences.* Chicago, Ill.: University of Chicago Press.

————. 1982b. "How Craftsmen Learn Their Skills: A Longitudinal Analysis." In Taylor, R., Rosen, H., and Pratzner, F., eds. *Job Training for Youth.* Columbus, Ohio: National Center for Research in Vocational Education, The Ohio State University.

————. 1982c. "Longitudinal Analyses of Training Processes in the United States." Columbus, Ohio: Center for Human Resources Research, The Ohio State University.

Hills, S.M., and Thompson, J. 1980. "The Transition from School to Work." In National Commission on Unemployment Compensation and Research. *Unemployment Compensation: Studies and Research,* vol.3. Washington: GPO.

Hoffman, S.D. 1981. "On-the-Job Training: Differences by Race and Sex." *Monthly Labor Review,* July.

Holzer, H.J. 1982. "Unions and the Labor Market Status of White and Minority Youth." *Industrial and Labor Relations Review,* April.

Iden, G. 1980. "The Labor Force Experience of Black Youth: A Review." *Monthly Labor Review,* August.

Kim, C. 1981. "On the Determinants of Reservation Wages: An Empirical Specification." Working Paper. Center for Human Resource Research, The Ohio State University.

Lewin-Epstein, N. 1981. *Youth Employment During High School.* Washington: NCES.

Marshall, R., and Glover, D. 1975. *Training and Entry into Union Construction.* Manpower Research and Development Monograph 39. Department of Labor, Manpower Administration. Washington: GPO.

Mellor, E.F., and Stamas, G.D. 1982. "Usual Weekly Earnings: Another Look at Intergroup Differences and Basic Trends." *Monthly Labor Review,* April.

Meyer R.H., and Wise, D.A. 1982. "High School Preparation and Early Labor Force Experience." In Freeman, R.B. and Wise, D.A., eds. *The Youth Labor Market Problem: Its Nature, Causes, and Consequences.* Chicago, Ill.: University of Chicago Press.

Mincer, J., and Ofek, H. 1982. "Interrupted Work Careers: Depreciation and Restoration of Human Capital." *Journal of Human Resources,* Winter.

Mott, F.L., ed. 1981. *Years for Decision, Volume Five: A Longitudinal Study of the Educational, Labor Market, and Family Experiences of Women 1968-1978.* Report to the U.S. Department of Labor. Columbus, Ohio: Center for Human Resource Research, The Ohio State University.

Mott, F.L.; Statham, A.; and Maxwell, N. 1981. "From Mother to Daughter: The Transmission of Work Attitudes Across Generations." In Mott, F.L., ed. *Years for Decision, Volume Five.* Columbus, Ohio: Center for Human Resource Research, The Ohio State University.

Myers, S., and King, R. 1982. "Relative Earnings of Hispanic Youth in the U.S. Labor Market." Paper prepared for the Hispanic Labor Conference, Santa Barbara, Cal., February 4-5.

NCES. 1981a. (National Center for Education Statistics). Bulletin. *Gainful Employment Among High School Youth.* Washington: Department of Education.

_____. 1981b. *Digest of Education Statistics 1981*. Washington: GPO.

_____. 1981c. *High School and Beyond. A National Longitudinal Study for the 1980s: A Capsule Description of High School Students*. Washington: GPO.

_____. 1982a. Bulletin. *Hispanic Students in American High Schools: Background Characteristics and Achievement*. Washington: Department of Education.

Newman, M.J. 1979. "The Labor Market Experience of Black Youth, 1954–78." *Monthly Labor Review*, October.

NLS (National Longitudinal Surveys of Labor Force Experience). 1966–80. Data on Young Men 14–24 in 1966. Columbus, Ohio: Center for Human Resource Research, The Ohio State University.

_____. 1968–80. Data on Young Women 14–24 in 1968. Columbus, Ohio: Center for Human Resource Research, The Ohio State University.

_____. 1979–81. Data on Youth 14–21 in 1979. Columbus, Ohio: Center for Human Resource Research, The Ohio State University.

O'Neill, J., and Braun, R. 1981. "Women and the Labour Market: A Survey of Issues and Policies in the United States." Paper prepared for the International Institute of Management, West Berlin.

Osterman, P. 1980. *Getting Started*. Cambridge, Mass.: MIT Press.

Pollard, T.K. 1982. "Changes Over the 1970s in the Employment Patterns of Black and White Young Men." In Borus, M.E., ed. *Pathways to the Future, vol. 2: A Final Report on the National Longitudinal Survey of Youth Labor Market Experience, 1980*. Columbus, Ohio: Center for Human Resource Research, The Ohio State University.

Rees, A., and Shultz, G.P. 1970. *Workers and Wages in an Urban Labor Market*. Chicago, Ill.: University of Chicago Press.

Reubens, B.G. 1977a. "The Place of the Occupational Component in Education and Training." In *Entry of Young People into Working Life. Technical Reports*. Paris: OECD.

_____. 1977b. *Bridges to Work: International Comparisons of Transition Services*. Montclair, N.J.: Allanheld, Osmun.

Reubens, B.G.; Harrisson, J.A.C.; and Rupp, K. 1981. *The Youth Labor Force 1945–1995: A Cross-national Analysis*. Totowa, N.J.: Allanheld, Osmun.

Root, N., and Sebastian, D. 1981. "BLS Develops Measure of Job Risk by Occupation." *Monthly Labor Review*, October.

Rosenfeld, C. 1979. "Occupational Mobility During 1977." *Monthly Labor Review*, December.

Russell, L.B. 1982. *The Baby Boom Generation and the Economy*. Washington: The Brookings Institution.

Ryscavage, P.M. 1982. "Employment Problems and Poverty: Examining the Linkages." *Monthly Labor Review*, June.

Santos, R. 1981. "Employment Status of Youth—1980." In Borus, M.E., ed., *Pathways to the Future: A Longitudinal Study of Young Americans, Preliminary Report on the 1980 Survey*. Columbus, Ohio: Center for Human Resource Research, The Ohio State University.

Shaw, L.B. 1982. "Effects of Age, Length of Work Interruption, and State of the Economy on the Reentry Wages of Women." Paper presented at the annual meeting of the Western Economic Association, Los Angeles, July.

Smith, J.P., and Welch, F. 1981. "No Time to be Young: The Economic Prospects for Large Cohorts in the United States." *Population and Development Review*, March.

Smith, S.J. 1983. "Estimating Annual Hours of Labor Force Activity." *Monthly Labor Review*, February.

Stephenson, S.P., Jr. 1978. "The Transition from School to Work with Job Search Implications." In *Conference Report on Youth Unemployment: Its Measurement and Meaning*. Washington: Department of Labor.

_____. 1982. "Labor Market Turnover and Joblessness for Hispanic American Youth." Paper prepared for the Hispanic Labor Conference, Santa Barbara, Cal., February 4–5.

Stevenson, W. 1978. "The Relationship Between Early Work Experience and Future

Employability." In Adams, A., and Mangum, G.L., eds. *The Lingering Crisis of Youth Unemployment.* Kalamazoo, Mich.: Upjohn Institute of Employment Research.

Terry, S.L. 1981. "Involuntary Part-time Work: New Information from the CPS." *Monthly Labor Review,* February.

Wachter, M.L. 1977. "Intermediate Swings in Labor-Force Participation." *Brookings Papers on Economic Activity,* vol.2.

Wachter, M.L., and Kim, C. 1982. "Time Series Changes in Youth Joblessness." In Freeman, R.B., and Wise, D.A., eds. *The Youth Labor Market Problem: Its Nature, Causes, and Consequences.* Chicago, Ill.: University of Chicago Press.

Welch, F. 1979. "Effects of Cohort Size on Earnings: The Baby Boom Babies' Financial Bust." *Journal of Political Economy,* pt.2, October.

Wise, D.A., and Meyer, R.H. 1982. *The Transition from School to Work: The Experiences of Blacks and Whites.* Working Paper no.1007. Cambridge, Mass.: National Bureau of Economic Research.

Young, A.M. 1979. "The Difference a Year Makes in the Nation's Youth Work Force." *Monthly Labor Review,* October.

————. 1981a. *School and Work Among Youth During the 1970's.* Special Labor Force Report 241. Washington: Department of Labor.

————. 1981b. "Labor Force Activity Among Students, Graduates and Dropouts in 1980." *Monthly Labor Review,* July.

Zeller, F.A., et al. 1970. *Career Thresholds,* vol.2. Columbus, Ohio: Center for Human Resource Research, The Ohio State University.

Chapter 10

Overview and Implications

Beatrice G. Reubens

Concern about youth unemployment in the industrialized nations has given rise to a large body of descriptive and analytic studies which mainly concentrate either on the forces influencing the demand and supply of young workers or the nature of unemployment and the characteristics of the unemployed. Aiming to widen the scope of inquiry, this book has examined the composition and characteristics of the jobs held by youth and adults to discover whether differences in the types, conditions, and rewards of the jobs of young people and adults, and of various subgroups of youth, are associated with differences in the extent of unemployment.

To this end, we have drawn on the postwar experience and record of six industrialized market economy countries: Australia, the Federal Republic of Germany, Great Britain, Japan, Sweden, and the United States. Exhibiting a diversity of institutions, practices, and basic economic and social trends, these countries display both similarities and differences in the subject chosen for investigation.

Consisting of six chapters written by country experts and four cross-national chapters, the book attempts to establish for the six countries:

- The evidence for a distinct youth labor market, disproportionate shares of youth in "secondary" labor markets, "youth jobs," and labor market segmentation by age.
- The extent and nature of the variations in the composition and characteristics of the jobs of youth compared to those of adults, considering each sex separately.
- The extent and nature of the variations in the composition and characteristics of the jobs held by young people, subdivided by age and sex and further subdivided by school enrollment status, educational attainment, race or ethnicity, and place of residence.
- The relation between the type and conditions of early jobs and later employment.

- The interactions and repercussions of the types and conditions of jobs on the rate, incidence, and duration of youth unemployment.

On each subject, the current situation as well as the postwar trend is described, to the extent that data permit. The similarities and differences among the countries in experience and in interpretations offered by country experts are explicated in this final chapter, whose synthesis and summary cannot do full justice to the rich and wide-ranging country chapters.

Separate Youth Labor Markets

In customary usage, "youth labor market" is a somewhat pejorative term, but when applied to Germany and Japan, the term can be affirmative, describing a nurturing, protective situation in which competition with other age groups is severely limited. In documenting this point, the book has fulfilled a major purpose of cross-national studies: to present alternatives that might otherwise not be considered. At the same time, warnings about transferability are in order. Policy makers in other countries should not take the points made about Germany and Japan narrowly and literally. Rather, they should focus on the underlying spirit and the beneficial outcomes for youth. Transferability, if any, requires that ways, consistent with a country's own institutions, be utilized to accomplish the same results as are displayed elsewhere, taking full account of the costs as well as the benefits.

In Germany, apprenticeship shields the vast majority of 15–18 year-olds from labor market competition with other age groups. In Japan, employers strongly prefer new, inexperienced workers straight out of schools and colleges as the core of their regular, permanent employees, conferring advantages on youth over others seeking new jobs. The result in both countries is a certain amount of labor market segmentation arising from the distinct and separate youth labor market that operates through special recruitment institutions and patterns at given times of the year; labor market statistics in the two countries reflect the separate youth labor market. The consequence is that Germans who do not complete an apprenticeship, or alternative training, are excluded from a whole range of jobs open to youth completing apprenticeship. In the same way, experienced adult Japanese workers who have changed employers will be treated thereafter less favorably than those still in their first jobs; this practice, however, appears to be weakening as a result of the scarcity of young entrants from school.

Youth in the two countries have several specific advantages, albeit with differences according to national conditions. To begin with, the troublesome and protracted process of moving from education to employment which plagues certain segments of youth in other countries is very much easier in Germany and Japan; employers regard youth's literacy and numeracy as adequate. Initial jobs of all youth, but especially apprentices, are hedged by legal protection and require part-time education to age 18 in Germany. Japanese youth in first jobs benefit from larger amounts of on-the-job training, including job rotation, than other age groups receive. Job security is assured to many at the outset. The German apprenticeship system provides work socialization and job security during training; afterward, there is continuity of employment for a large proportion of apprentices. The manner of organizing apprenticeship training confers status and stability on jobs that, in other countries, tend to be low-level, dead-end, and often part-time. At the same time, relative earnings in such occupations in Germany are not lower than in other countries. The benefits of organizing work in this fashion merit attention, especially as low-level service jobs have become a growing part of total and youth job opportunities.

In Germany and Japan, the number of job openings for youth in recessions is maintained better than for other age groups. German employers, spurred by the government, have provided more apprenticeship places than firms deemed necessary for their immediate needs; government has supplied additional places. It is significant that German apprenticeship wages, relative to those of other youth or older workers, are considerably lower than those reported in Britain or Australia (see Table 4.6).

All youth who leave school at 15 or 16 do not benefit from German apprenticeship. Among the less than 10 percent of (out-of-school) 15–18 year-olds not in the system, females and children of foreign workers are disproportionately represented. The small proportion of apprentices who do not complete their training or pass the qualifying exams are not protected. Also, a share of those who obtain their skilled worker credentials subsequently are found in semi- or unskilled jobs, often because their apprenticeship was in an occupation with limited job opportunities. While unemployment is relatively rare for apprentices, in recession periods it may simply be shifted to the post-apprenticeship years and to the young adult group. It may, however, be preferable that unemployment be borne by those who have already acquired some occupational skills, work experience, and socialization to working life, instead of by teenage entrants.

Limitations of the Japanese situation are less easily specified. Young people who find jobs in the smaller firms in their industry usually have less favorable work conditions and a greater exposure to job-changing and unemployment than those who obtain jobs with the largest firms. Similarly, the beneficial status associated with lifetime employment is much more likely to be granted to male than female youth. The very small percentage of non-Japanese or aboriginal (*burakumin*) youth face discrimination in all aspects of life.

In both countries, an advantageous position for youth has been accompanied by disadvantage for older workers, especially compared to relative positions in other countries. It is not entirely clear, however, that this adverse situation for older workers is inextricably tied to the benefits enjoyed by youth. Therefore, the various forms of a fostering youth labor market should not be abandoned on this ground alone.

A "youth labor market," whether in its affirmative, neutral, or invidious connotations, has not been identified in the four remaining countries. The test is whether the detailed occupations (or industries) which account for most of the employment of young people also have a work force disproportionately composed of youth. Analysis fails to disclose a sufficient number of important detailed occupations with a heavy concentration of young workers to establish a distinct youth labor market. Nonetheless, in each country certain categories of jobs are youth-intensive, and some may be regarded also as entry-level jobs. Trainee positions tend to be youth-intensive, as are the armed forces, professional athletics, and other occupations where youth is an accepted prerequisite. On the other hand, specific occupations and industries are youth-intensive in one country but not in another; there is nothing inherent in the occupation to give it any concentration of young workers.

In addition, the term "youth jobs" has been coined to describe certain low-skill, poorly paid, possibly part-time or temporary jobs with little or no training and negligible career potential. Many of these jobs are youth-intensive, even though other age groups also compete for the jobs; particular jobs, such as newspaper deliveries, tend to be almost exclusively reserved to youth. Evidence is presented in several of the country chapters that the share of such jobs in total youth employment has increased over the years, especially in Australia, Sweden, and the United States. In these countries there was a combination of two complementary trends. There was a substantial rise in the share of service sector and part-time employment in total employment. At the same time, a growing share of youth sought such jobs, as their educational enrollment rates climbed and more students worked while attending school. There is spillover to out-of-school youth as well. In Germany, youth who do not enter apprenticeship are the main group affected.

The trend observed in regard to "youth jobs" is part of a more general trend affecting youth employment in all of the countries. As the level of educational attainment has risen and the average age of labor market entrants has increased, the array of jobs available has not altered sufficiently to match the qualifications young people bring to the labor market. This development caused the authors of the British chapter to caution that "merely raising education levels is unlikely to alter the structure of jobs very much." They also cite data that each cohort entering the labor market from 1930 onward has had to offer higher qualifications than its predecessors in order to enter any specific occupation.

The Swedish authors report that "the qualifications needed to carry out specific jobs do not in general seem to have increased over time," and that "youth get more preparation for the world of work than did earlier generations." They therefore ask "why employers demand more preparation than before and why they are not willing to supply such preparation as part of the on-the-job training of youth." This broader picture helps to explain why the issue of "youth jobs" or temporary jobs currently carries so much weight in the industrialized countries. The rise in the average educational level of young people increases their sensitivity to the type of job implied by "youth job," and if the share of such jobs in the total has also swelled, as it has in several countries, the issue is even sharper.

Secondary Labor Markets and Segmentation

Discussions about whether youth, or some part of youth, are working in a secondary labor market or are affected by labor market segmentation flourish in various countries to the extent that "youth jobs" are perceived as prevalent. In addition, the disproportionate representation of young workers in particular occupations or industries whose characteristics suggest secondary labor markets causes complaints about segmentation. Analysis in the British chapter of those industries in which male and female teenagers are employed in relatively great numbers shows that for male teenagers these industries

> do appear to have many of the characteristics associated with secondary employment or an inferior segment of the labor market. Compared with the all-industry averages, they have, in general, lower collective bargaining coverage, higher turnover rates, smaller plants and firms, lower output per employee, and more part-time workers.

The female teenage-intensive industries do not consistently diverge from the all-industry averages for the selected indicators, but "data for individual industry groups do suggest the secondary labor market." This finding reflects the adverse characteristics of all female employment, rather than the superiority of female to male teenagers.

Australian identification of secondary labor market traits is limited to the jobs held by most full-time students. While accepting this description of some student-workers, the U.S. chapter extends the category to some of the jobs held by full-time youth, especially those with no more than a senior high school education. Jobs taken by youth who have not completed a basic vocational education are viewed as secondary employment in Germany. The terminology has not been applied in Japan or Sweden, but some youth are in work situations which would be consistent with that label.

It is, however, a long step from acceptance of secondary labor market characteristics to agreement that labor market segmentation exists and that youth may be one of the groups trapped in inferior segments. Analysts divide into those who deny the existence of segments, those who perceive no systematic pattern of assignment of youth to labor market segments (however they are defined), and those who believe in the segments and hold strong views that youth are particularly prone to be in the inferior segments. The U.S. chapter points to specific mechanisms of stratification, holding constant the level and type of education:

> Youth have little or no choice regarding their sex, race/ethnicity, or families into which they were born, the communities in which they were raised, or the part of the country in which they grow up, but such factors could influence whether initial and later jobs are in the well-paid, unionized, and stable sectors of the economy.

In the other countries, the sorting function of educational and training levels is given an overwhelming role, tending to minimize the argument for sorting into distinct segments according to other attributes.

To some, the issue of blocked exits from the secondary to the primary labor market furnishes the chief argument against the segmented labor market hypothesis. Critics assume that the hypothesis is invalid if individuals in the secondary market do move to the primary. Advocates, however, accept a considerable amount of movement of individuals between segments over time, but expect that, at any given time, cross-sectional analysis will reveal a heavy concentration of certain groups, including youth, in the secondary segments. It is patently impossible to claim that youth are trapped in secondary segments in a longitudinal sense, since the specific characteristic of being young must disappear over time. But it is entirely possible to find a disproportionate number of young people in a cross-sectional view of secondary labor market segments.

Since the term "segment" seems to suggest to most doubters that there is an absolute absence of upward mobility of individuals as well as a polarization of jobs, proponents of the dual labor market paradigm must expect that their ideas will be interpreted literally and subjected to empirical tests focusing on the alleged impermeability of the barriers between segments. Such tests have, of course, rejected the lack of mobility hypothesis.

The idea of labor market segmentation continues to have considerable appeal, however, as witnessed by its spread from the United States to many other countries where adaptation to national circumstances has altered the original concepts. The proponents need to formulate their doctrines more explicitly with regard to the number of segments, the characteristics of segments, the process of sorting individuals into segments, the interactions of segment and individual characteristics, and movement between segments. Propositions amenable to empirical tests remain a high priority. For the foreseeable future, however, empirical tests will suffer from a dearth of detailed information about the types and conditions of jobs, such as enter into the conceptual discussions of segmentation.

At present, a more fruitful approach to youth employment studies is to recognize the range of jobs and variety of job conditions facing distinct age groups and specific subgroups of youth.

Youth and Adult Jobs

The most significant comparisons between the jobs of youth and adults relate to detailed occupations, relative earnings, job-changing, on-the-job training, and size of firm.

OCCUPATIONS

A high degree of occupational (or industrial) similarity between youth and adults of the same sex is indicated by the cross-national analysis of four countries (Chapter 3) and the country chapters. Indexes of occupational dissimilarity (IOD), computed for five countries, suggest a good deal of complementarity and/or substitutability between younger and older workers of the same sex, with considerably less indicated for youth and adults of opposite sex. It is acknowledged that substitutability cannot be judged exclusively from occupational data, no matter how detailed.

Such occupational differences as are observed between youth and adults of the same sex are attributed mainly to the effects of the length of work experience, the amount of on-the-job training, the occupational qualifications and certifications accumulated, and the length of tenure in specific jobs. By all of these criteria, adults are normally expected to rank higher in the occupational hierarchy than youth. The amount of divergence between the age groups in the several countries seems to be associated with the prominence of service sector employment, the extent to which it consists of low-level jobs, and the share of such jobs held by youth. Among males, the occupational variation between employed teenagers and adults appears to be greater in the United States than the other countries, reflecting the high employment rate of teenage students in addition to the factors mentioned above. Support for this interpretation comes from Australian data showing less industrial congruence between young and adult part-time workers than between similar full-time workers.

No evidence was presented for any country that young people are deliberately excluded from the more responsible or rewarding jobs that youth might perform as well as adults. Little information exists on this subject which merits further research. A decline in public sector employment among Australian 15–20 year-olds at a time when other age groups had increases in such employment is cited as a possibly important factor in the deteriorating labor market position of youth. Given that the occupational composition of total employment is fixed at any time, the manner in which occupations are distributed among the age-sex groups may be a neglected issue of social policy.

RELATIVE EARNINGS

Important new data in the country chapters on the levels and trends in the relative earnings of full-time youth to adult workers suggest several striking points.

First, the current level of the ratios of youth to adult earnings in the six countries, taken separately for each sex, fall within a narrow range. After rough adjustments for data measurement differences among the countries, but continuing to exclude apprentices in Germany, it appears that around 1980 the earnings of young males (under 25) were 55–60 percent of those of adult males (25 and over) in each country except Sweden, where the ratio exceeded .70. Current ratios for female youth and adults also fall in a narrow range. Clustering around 65–75 percent, relative earnings in Sweden again were highest, but other countries followed closely. While the Swedish chapter attributes its high ratios to the success of a strong trade union movement in raising disproportionately the pay of low-paid workers (including youth), the other country chapters offer no clues as to why ratios of relative earnings should cluster closely now, or why the dispersion was somewhat wider in earlier years.

Second, higher ratios for females than males, especially noticeable in Japan and the United States, appear to be a function of the flatter earnings curves of females than males as they mature, a development demonstrated in both cross-sectional and longitudinal data. The amount of spread between male and female ratios for youth to adult earnings in a country also reflects the earnings ratios of female to male youth.

Third, the fact that Japanese youth are no longer cheap relative to adult labor gives added importance to the continued preference of Japanese employers for young, inexperienced workers. The same point cannot be extended to Germany, because the inclusion of apprentices in the earnings data would reduce the current ratio of youth to adult earnings below the levels of other countries, especially to teenagers.

Fourth, the trend in each of the countries, except the United States, has been toward rising ratios of youth to adult earnings (Tables 4.7, 5.7, 6.6, 7.10, 8.5, 9.6). Compression of earnings differentials in the five countries has occurred at varying speeds, with or without interruptions, and at a different pace for males and females. But the upward trend has been clearly visible for each sex, in spite of cross-national differences in the absolute and relative growth of the youth and adult labor supply, rates of economic growth, changes in youth and total employment, levels of youth unemployment and similar factors. Further exploration of the causes of wage compression are needed, especially since the contrary trend in the U.S. is explained by the expansion of absolute and relative youth employment, the demographic bulge which increased numbers and reduced the average age of new entrants, the increased proportion of student workers among youth, and possible changes in the composition and characteristics of youth compared to adult employment.

Fifth, in Australia, Great Britain, and Sweden, where the compression of wage relativities between youth and adults has been a subject of public concern, the chapters report no straightforward or simple relationship to changes in youth employment and unemployment and no general agreement on the subject. In offering the conclusion of econometric studies that the rise in the relative earnings of youth have had "no significant influence on the demand for youth labor," the Australian chapter cites the possible offsetting impact of subsidies to wages by government training programs. The British finding is that in the latter 1970s

> the relative earnings of workers under 21 were fairly stable in relation to that of adults. [This] suggests that the very large increase in teenage unemployment after 1973 cannot be mainly attributed to a rise in relative earnings, although a failure of youth pay levels to fall sufficiently relative to those of adults may be related to age-group differences in the increase of unemployment rates.

In Sweden, whose youth earnings show the highest ratio, there is little empirical evidence and divergent viewpoints are voiced. Current indications are that the relative wage rates for youth may be reconsidered.

Sixth, the tendency of youth-adult earnings ratios to cluster despite divergent institutions and economic trends raises questions about the impact on youth employment of different methods of wage-setting, including minimum wage legislation. Such legislation exists in Japan and the United States, and in Britain is applied to selected low-paid industries on an individual basis. Germany and Sweden rely entirely on, and Britain largely utilizes, collective bargaining agreements, while Australia has its unique Awards system. It therefore appears that the particular way in which a country sets wage levels for its most poorly paid workers has relatively little impact on youth-adult earnings ratios. This may be due to the superior influence of other forces, or because, in the absence of legislation, other, voluntary wage-setting institutions tend to develop more strongly and perform the same function of elevating the lowest wages. The latter possibility should be weighed by those who wish to abolish or alter statutory wage-setting or minimum wage legislation in hopes of giving greater play to market forces, reducing relative and absolute earnings of youth, and increasing youth employment.

JOB-CHANGING

In each country, youth change jobs more frequently than adults, are more likely to change occupations, and have a greater propensity to change jobs voluntarily; the hazy line between voluntary and involuntary job-changing is recognized. Rising unemployment inhibits job-changing by all age groups, and the reverse is true of periods of full employment. In Australia it was observed that the reduction in job mobility rates from 1972 to 1979 "was greatest for those age groups which had the largest increase in unemployment rates." Thus, the youth-adult ratio for job-changing should decline in times of rising unemployment and be at its peak in times of full employment; Japanese data illustrate the point (see Table 7.7).

The ratio of youth to adult job-changing varies among the countries, but it is difficult to rank the countries accurately because of the paucity of comparable data. Overall job-changing rates appear to be highest in Australia, followed by the United States, Sweden, Great Britain, Germany, and Japan; possibly Germany should precede Great Britain. If account is taken of cross-national differences in the age composition of the employed, the ease of obtaining another job in a particular year, and the occupational composition of employment (particularly the importance of service sector employment and its rate of growth), there might be some adjustments of rank.

There is uncertainty about the proper weights to attach to the two main explanations of higher job-changing rates among youth than adults. The two factors are labor market conditions and characteristics of the youth. On the one hand, youth is seen as having a higher share than adults of unfavorable types of jobs, unpopular work conditions, and greater exposure to layoff or dismissal. They also have better prospects to obtain wage increases and improved conditions through changing jobs. On the other hand, a higher rate of job mobility by youth would be expected in light of youth's greater need to obtain knowledge about various types of jobs, to make decisions about long-term goals and aspirations, and to try to realize them. Youth also have fewer health problems or personal and family obligations and thus are able to take more risks, including occupational and geographical mobility. Youth are motivated to such change more than adults by registering lower rates of subjective job satisfaction.

These forces are all relevant in the six countries to some extent, but vary in significance. There is, however, no support from the other countries for a thesis popular with some American dual labor market economists, namely, that noncollege youth pass through distinct stages of instability in their internal development until, at age 25 and older, young workers begin to settle down into stable work patterns. Some individuals within the noncollege group in the other countries may display such unstable behavior, but it would be largely attributed to their exclusion from the early opportunities that bring stability to the rest of their cohort at a quite early age, matched by an attachment to the labor force equal to that of adults. Comparative research suggests that the U.S. view has not sufficiently questioned the origins of the so-called inherent stages in youth development. Are they inherent if a set of labor market conditions like those in Germany or Japan might soon alter the behavior patterns?

To the degree that analysts regard greater job-changing by youth primarily as a natural and desirable aspect of gaining valuable labor market experience, they may discount moderate amounts of intervening unemployment as a minor cost compared to the benefits. Both the U.S. and British chapters describe studies that indicate either no adverse effects on later occupations and earnings or even positive benefits to job-changers (who had a limited amount of attendant unemployment), compared to those who did not change jobs. In Japan, however, the human capital model specifies greater returns to those who remain with the original employer, and the facts seem to bear out the assumption. This discordance in interpreting the operations of the human capital model suggests that theory is influenced by practice, as observed locally.

ON-THE-JOB TRAINING

Youth appear to be the favored group in the amount and quality of on-the-job formal and informal training in most countries. In Australia, Germany, and Great Britain, the institution of apprenticeship is largely responsible for the advantage to youth, while Japan has a special system of youth recruitment-training. Rational calculation by employers would favor a concentration of training on youth because of the longer period to reap returns and the lower relative earnings of youth. These considerations seem to operate without regard to the particular training system or its division between general and firm-specific training. Employers have more incentive to offer youth large amounts of training if many employers engage in general training, with specific components, as in German apprenticeship, or if training is firm-specific, as in Japan. In Australia and Britain, the minority of employers who offer extensive training to youth fear poaching by other employers. Adult on-the-job training tends to be exclusively firm-specific, except for special circumstances.

In the United States, white youth of each sex are more likely than adults to receive on-the-job training, but black youth receive less than adults of either race. All youth groups, however, have a shorter training period than comparable adults. Swedish data on the proportion of various age groups holding jobs with a high potential for learning new skills show some adult groups as more favored than youth under 25. Each country has inadequate data and research on the quantity and quality of training by age and other characteristics, hampering comparative analysis, except in gross terms.

SIZE OF FIRM

The relation between size of firm and the characteristics of jobs and the differences in size of firm distribution between youth and adults are striking and important contributions of the Japanese chapter. The advantages of larger firms to their employees, industry by industry, are clear-cut in Japan and probably would also appear in the other countries, if suitable data were collected.

Cross-national differences in the prevalence and role of small firms influence the results; small firms are unusually important in Japan. In 1978, for example, 35 percent of Japanese employment was in firms with fewer than ten employees, compared to 14 percent in the United States; similarly, firms with 1,000 or more accounted for only 5 percent of Japan's employment, but 19 percent of American jobs. It is doubtful, however, that in other countries youth would have a higher proportion than adults in the larger firms, as they do in Japan. The small size of the firms that train apprentices in Germany would cause a departure from the Japanese pattern. It is likely that in all of the other countries, youth are employed in smaller firms, on average, than adults. Size of firm is a valuable but underutilized indicator which, with a fuller development of data, could enrich our knowledge of the pecuniary and nonpecuniary differences in job characteristics for youth and adults, as well as within youth subgroups.

Job Differences Among Youth

Variations among the subgroups of youth may be as great and more significant than the job differences between youth as a whole and adults. In each country, job differences between male and female youth are sharp and persistent, surviving further subdivision by student status, educational attainment and/or age, race or ethnicity, and place of residence. The confirmation of similar sex differences in countries whose attitudes toward women run the gamut from Japanese traditionalism to Swedish egalitarianism, and whose educational and preparatory systems are fairly undifferentiated to highly sex-specific is a major comparative finding.

The investigation of the composition and characteristics of youth employment reveals that the dispersion in job types within the youth group owes much to societal factors that have shaped opportunities and decisions prior to labor force entry. But a youth's initial place in the spectrum of jobs also is affected by labor market forces operating on both the demand and supply sides. Patterns of initial job dispersion in a youth cohort have great importance because of strong persistence effects over time; the position in which a youth starts out has a good deal to do with the place in which he or she ends up, despite a cohort's advances in average occupational status, responsibilities on the job, and earnings. Countries vary in the extent of the dispersion in job characteristics as a cohort ages, as well as in the extent of individual upward and downward mobility over time.

SEX DIFFERENCES IN JOBS

Young females hold different and often inferior jobs to those of young males, measured by occupational status, earnings, on-the-job training, hours, and job-changing. Indexes of Occupational Dissimilarity (IOD) from detailed occupational census data for five of the countries show that the occupational distributions for the two sexes are quite dissimilar in the youth age groups (Tables 3.7, 5.4). From 60 to 71 percent of the females in Germany, Great Britain, Japan, Sweden, and the United States would have to change occupations in order to match the corresponding male distribution; Sweden and Great Britain display slightly more dissimilarity than the U.S., Japan, and Germany. The high IODs are the result of the separation of males and females into occupations in which there are relatively few persons of the other sex and the crowding of women into few occupations, compared to men. The latter effect is in part attributable to the nature of occupational classifications.

Further discussion in the country chapters indicates that the type of educational and vocational preparation of a majority of youth is directly associated with sex differences in initial jobs. The German conclusion is that the training situation for apprentices is highly segregated, with only about 5 percent of female apprentices in female occupations. In Sweden, "most of the vocational lines in upper secondary school are heavily dominated by one sex." While the same point would be made in the other countries in regard to vocational education courses, only a minority of youth take these courses. Nevertheless, initial occupational choices are equally marked by sex differences among those whose education has not had a vocational slant; such differences exist at every level and in every type of education. The Swedish observation that there is considerable similarity in occupational choices between male and female youth who have completed academic upper secondary education is not borne out in other countries. In Germany, employment has not reflected the reduction in the disparity between the sexes in vocational education levels.

Over time, occupational progress and movement into the higher-status jobs is less marked for females than males. A British study discerns an increase in vertical segregation (that is, rank within an occupation), even as horizontal segregation seems to have declined; other countries have also observed such a decrease in segregation by type of occupation. Debate rages over the extent to which initial and later sex differences in occupations are due to personal choices and voluntary interruptions of work, on the one hand, and labor market segregation and discrimination, on the other.

Earnings records convey more clearly than any other indicator the inferiority of female jobs. Male youth with the same educational and vocational qualifications as female youth usually earn higher full-time wages in entry and early jobs, although the gap appears to have narrowed over time. Such sex differences in earnings, after allowance for the slightly shorter work week of full-time females, are attributed in the United States to occupational segregation of females, their more limited access to training in the firm, and their lower representation in unionized jobs. Japanese explanations center on sex differences in specific educational preparation, the divergent industrial distribution of the two sexes, along with the varying ability of different industries to pay, and the anticipated short work life of females. Swedish studies show inferior earnings for young females with precisely the same preparation as males and in the same kind of jobs.

Changes in wage relativities between young males and females in Australia and Great Britain are seen as increasing the competition for jobs between young ïnales and females. In the British case, however, the magnitude of the rise in female youth unemployment "seems great, given the rather small change in their relative earnings, provided that this is the sole cause of the rising unemployment." Swedish female teenagers suffered greater deterioration in their employment prospects than males, coupled with a decline in their relative earnings, so that the latter could not be the explanation of the former trend.

It might be expected that the earnings differentials between young males and females, especially new entrants to the full-time labor force, would be smaller than those between adult males and females, because youth have fewer differences in human capital investment and less difference between the sexes in total work time over a given period. Interruptions or anticipated interruptions of work affect earnings adversely via reduced on-the-job training and depreciation or obsolescence of accumulated knowledge and skills, particularly affecting women.

Three countries provide cross-sectional data on this subject which properly should be studied through longitudinal surveys. Japan, controlling for educational level, and Germany, controlling for vocational qualifications level, clearly show the expected relationship (Tables 5.7, 7.10). Sweden's more general data for a scattering of years are somewhat ambiguous and possibly reflect the high proportion of adult women at work, even if part-time (see Table 8.5). In addition, the official statistics for Britain and the United States indicate the expected relationship, with female youth earning an amount relatively close to male teenage earnings, while adult women show a lower ratio in regard to adult men. As the trend toward a closing of the sex gap proceeds, it seems that the younger cohorts are making greatest progress, in part because the erosion of sex differences in the continuity of work experience is proceeding most rapidly among the newest entrants to the labor force.

EDUCATIONAL ATTAINMENT AND JOBS

Educational attainment, in all of its ramifications, emerges as a major determinant of initial job distributions and a powerful life-long influence on career progress. Since educational attainment is assumed to be largely completed before labor market entry, the importance accorded to it naturally diminishes the role of labor market stratification or discrimination. In most of the chapters, the latter forces appear to be superimposed on a basic framework constructed from the variations in educational attainment levels. This approach is reinforced by the fact that the human capital theory underlying discussions of placements in the job hierarchy, and the data associated with analysis, deal with central tendencies, rather than dispersions at given levels of educational attainment. While greater detail and specificity may increase the ability of human capital theory to explain the job dispersion of youth entering with lower or upper secondary education, it is doubtful whether labor market influences will be eradicated.

Given the important role assigned to educational attainment, it is curious that the educational systems are more diverse in these countries than the structure and tasks on jobs and the shape of job hierarchies. Why does one set of jobs require different numbers of years of education and different types of studies in various countries? Accepting that some of the preparatory systems may be better than others for given jobs, judged by objective or subjective standards, the inflexibility of the outcomes, as described by the chapter authors, strengthens the sorting and screening role of education. In general, the cross-national overview conveys the impression that employers in each country distribute initial jobs by responding both to the relatively fixed basic structure of educational systems and to the rapidly changing outputs, absolutely and relatively, from the various levels and types of education.

Considerable evidence is presented of the diversity of initial jobs for youth with the same general educational qualifications. Delaying discussion of differences due to sex, race, and place of residence, we note that such diversity appears among youth of similar characteristics. Moreover, the consequences for those with unfavorable jobs are not only immediate, but also carry over into subsequent labor market experience. In Germany, for example, apprentices whose training occurs in small firms are more likely than other apprentices in that industry to change their jobs at the end of the training period and may experience more unemployment. Japanese junior and senior high school graduates, having a relatively undifferentiated education, nevertheless end up working in the smallest to the largest firms in particular industries, with many adverse job effects for those located in the smallest firms.

Skepticism about the relation of the amount of human capital investment to this distribution is reinforced by the fact that polls of Japanese employers reveal that a cooperative attitude is their primary requisite when they hire such young people. At college and university level also, Japanese employers, expressing the desire that their new hires should be able to make judgments, tend to pay as much or more attention to the status of the university as to the individual's academic record. The Swedish chapter, noting that, on average, those with more education obtain the jobs requiring more qualifications, also reports that some hold jobs classified as requiring more formal education than they actually have, while others are in the opposite situation. Although on-the-job training might explain some of the first group after a few years, no explanation is given for the initial dispersion.

The countries vary in the earnings differentials between various levels of education, the shape of the earnings curves over the years, and the length of time it takes for additional years of education to pay off. In Japan, for example, the pay-off period is long, but the differentials are very large in the prime ages for males. Moreover, the differentials established at the outset by educational level are maintained and reinforced by the differences in on-the-job training possibilities and advancement prospects according to highest educational level completed before entering work. Nevertheless, there is considerable dispersion in Japanese earnings, controlling for age, sex, and education. In other countries, it is assumed that individuals can change their fortunes after labor market entry because of choices they make about additional investments in their training on and off the job; initial effects from the sorting of the educational system are important, but are not fixed and irreversible for individuals.

RACE AND ETHNICITY

Unlike sex differences in jobs where the rate of growth of female youth employment is generally satisfactory, but the quality of female jobs is at issue, racial and ethnic differences in youth employment involve both the quantity and quality of jobs. Four countries discuss race or ethnicity. In the German and Swedish chapters, the employment problem of youth from immigrant or foreign worker families is viewed primarily in terms of insufficient general and vocational education and inadequate fluency in the language of the host country. For several reasons such youth, whether they have had some or all of their schooling in Germany or Sweden, show lower completion and advancement rates than other youth in both compulsory and postcompulsory education and training.

The consequence is a disproportionate share of such youth in unskilled jobs. Swedish data show that "immigrant youth with good knowledge of Swedish, entering the labor market directly after compulsory school, do not diverge greatly from entering Swedish youth in occupational distribution." It is assumed in both countries, in which the concern about minority youth is relatively recent, that the employment pattern of immigrant youth would be much the same as for native-born youth, if and when general and vocational education and language fluency are made equal. In effect, labor market stratification and discrimination are assumed to be negligible or absent.

These assumptions are no longer accepted in Great Britain, where Asian and West Indian youth, born in Britain, with good command of English, and equal or higher educational qualifications than their

British counterparts, are rejected more often by employers, take longer to find jobs, and are offered lower-level jobs. Discrimination in hiring and firing coupled with the concentration of such youth in particular low-paid industries that are especially vulnerable to recession are the main features of the employment problem, although some issues remain on the supply side as well.

American concern has centered on the failure of black youth to maintain their share of total youth employment as the black share of the youth population grew. In addition, a wide variety of indicators disclose the pervasive and persistent inferiority of the jobs and employment experience of many black youth. With the gradual closing of the educational attainment gap between the races, this source of difference has diminished as an explanatory factor, although residual questions remain about the quality of education. Explanations are sought for a trend toward greater divergence between the races, even as new research suggests that, controlling for all relevant factors among high school graduates, racial differences are smaller than has previously been thought.

Whether these four countries differ basically in regard to labor market discrimination, or whether Germany and Sweden still have to learn the limits of educational equalization as a measure against employment inequality, remains to be seen.

PLACE OF RESIDENCE

British data show marked geographical differences in the distribution of the jobs of new entrants (to 18 years of age). The underlying industrial structure of the regions and the rate and direction of change are the chief influences on the available employment opportunities, modified by regional variations in the size and composition of the labor supply, labor turnover rates, and geographic mobility rates.

In Japan, job opportunities for youth, quantitatively and qualitatively, are disproportionately concentrated in a few large urban areas, while youth disproportionately are raised and complete high school in rural areas and small cities. This disparity has been rectified by a high rate of voluntary and assisted mobility among teenage youth under the supervision of various institutions that look after their welfare. Young Japanese who fail to move have, on average, poorer jobs, although the youth may in all other respects be fully comparable to those who moved. More knowledge about this least-researched subject is needed in a number of countries and might assist in the formulation of policies for youth, especially in areas with low levels of economic activity or limited types of employment.

LONGITUDINAL EFFECTS

Several chapters investigate the effects of some years of labor market experience on the position of youth whose initial jobs had unfavorable aspects; though these might be characteristic of a secondary labor market, no attempts at categorization are made. The analysis of Swedish longitudinal data shows that youth who held a temporary job in 1968 "had a higher probability of having a temporary job in 1974 than those who had a permanent job in 1968," although most youth with temporary jobs in the earlier year had progressed to stable jobs in 1974. In the same way, Swedish youth in the lowest earnings quartile in 1968 had a greater chance of being in that quartile in 1974 than others. Nevertheless, almost 20 percent of males in the lowest quartile in 1968 had moved to the highest quartile six years later (Tables 8.6, 8.8). On the other hand, the overwhelming share of youth reported both in 1968 and six years later that their jobs were not supervisory (Table 8.8).

British longitudinal analysis of a succession of cohorts which entered the labor force 1930–60 produces a positive and significant correlation between the occupational or socio-economic status of each new entrant and the individual's status in 1975. The occupation first entered is the best predictor of where British workers will end up. Therefore, young workers who enter the least favorable occupations at the outset are more likely than others to continue to be toward the bottom of subsequent occupational distributions, although the whole cohort will tend to show progress over time, particularly among males. A similar Japanese analysis of first and 1973 occupations for four cohorts of males aged 20–70 in 1973 is notable chiefly for its remarkably high correlations between first and 1973 occupations, in comparison with the British correlations (Tables 6.7, 7.11).

STUDENT WORKERS

Students who hold jobs during the academic year are of consequence only in Australia, Sweden, and the United States, so far as can be judged by available research. Australian review of the causes of the rapid growth of student part-time work casts doubt on the supplementation of family income as a major motivation. To some extent, Australian student part-time workers fill the places of out-of-school youth who reject such jobs because the conditions and amount of unemployment benefits act as disincentives. Other reasons are the desire of students to gain work experience in advance of job search, the declining real levels of government financial assistance to students, and the search by youth for greater financial and social independence. Additional jobs have become available through the expansion of retail and service industries in which flexible work schedules are utilized.

The causes of student job-holding are not much discussed in the United States where the phenomenon is widely accepted, long established, and involves relatively more students and hours of work than in the other countries. Data on student workers show disproportionately low participation by low-income and black youth. This is variously interpreted as evidence that middle-class parents are better able to find jobs for their children, especially in the suburbs, that labor market discrimination is at work, or that low-income and black youth are less inclined to work while studying.

In the three countries, student workers are more concentrated in low-level jobs than nonstudents. Only limited job competition between teenage students and nonstudents is found in Australia. The characteristics of the student jobs, including low unionization rates, breaches of wage awards, and other violations, lead to the charge that "employed full-time students are concentrated in the secondary labor market" in Australia. Researchers in that country also doubt that the work experience of students will be of much subsequent benefit, although the need for longitudinal studies, such as those in the U.S., is recognized.

The American studies by economists regularly demonstrate later benefits in earnings levels and number of weeks worked for students who have worked compared to similar fellow-students who did not. This message has had more impact on opinion than the findings of sociologists and educators that excessive hours of work during the school week have current harmful effects. What has not been confronted by cither sct of analysts, sincc thcy havc confincd themsclves to individual outcomes, is the possibility that the standards and performance of the American educational system have been undermined by the adaptations made in the classroom to the needs of students who work.

The assignment of fewer hours of homework and the acceptance of non-compliance with assignments, the dilution of the content and difficulty of courses, the reduced offerings of science and math courses, the lower expectations of student performance in class and on examinations, and the policy of promotion and graduation without regard to grades—all of which prevailed until quite recently—may in part be attributable to recognition of the work activities of students who, in increasing proportions, have devoted longer hours per week to outside jobs, usually not structured to enhance studies in school or college.

Job Characteristics and Youth Unemployment

The opening chapter charged the authors of the six country chapters to explore a subject that has gained some prominence in the United States. It is the belief that the characteristics of the jobs held by youth (or a portion of youth) may in part explain the higher unemployment rates of youth as a whole and of subgroups of youth.

Such job characteristics as monotonous, simple, mostly unpleasant tasks, night, holiday, and other unpopular hours, low pay, and a lack of training or advancement opportunities, jointly referred to as "dead-end" jobs, might be expected to be disproportionately found among young people. Youth therefore might display more frequent voluntary and involuntary job turnover than other age groups, and some subgroups of youth would do likewise in relation to youth as a whole. In turn, higher job turnover rates might result in greater vulnerability to unemployment than if the same or similar youth held jobs with better conditions or greater promise. This hypothesis about linked events deliberately distinguishes the characteristics of the jobs from the attributes of the jobholders, while recognizing the confusion of the two in much of the available data.

Both the direct and indirect evidence provided in the country chapters enlarge the perspective and lead to a series of significant points. First, several additional dimensions of unfavorable job characteristics are identified, beyond those commonly cited in the United States. Even American research suggests that involuntary part-time or part-year work might be added to the list. In Sweden, temporary jobs of fixed duration would be listed. Noting that "there seems to have been a growth of temporary jobs with low training content and no clear career path" and that this is "increasingly the chief type of job available to out-of-school youth under 18," the Swedish authors speculate that the rise in such jobs may be associated with the job security protection afforded to established workers, leading employers to caution in hiring, and the dampening effect of the recession on new hires. Analyzing the contribution of unemployment attributable to temporary jobs, the authors find that "the end of temporary jobs accounts for a large part of the youth-adult unemployment rate differentials . . . but young women remained more affected than young men" (Table 8.3). Other European countries, especially France, report the same set of phenomena.

In the German view any unskilled job, not requiring apprenticeship or full-time vocational education, would be regarded as exposing youth to much more unemployment than those with jobs demanding training. British analysis would stress certain labor-intensive manufacturing industries, regional industrial structures, and racial differences in industrial concentration in declining fields with a high risk of unemployment. In Japan, small firms and the services would be singled out, but mainly in terms of youth unemployment resulting from voluntary turnover. These differences among the countries on the definition of unfavorable job characteristics suggest additions to a common list, rather than each country going its own way.

Second, we still do not know enough about the precise proportion of all jobs that would be classified as unfavorable in the various countries or what part of these are held by young people. It is clear, however, that many of the institutions and practices that have been described in the country chapters tend to reduce or augment the share of such jobs in total employment as well as the youth share of all unfavorable jobs. The latter seems to be lower in Japan. Within fairly similar occupational and industrial distributions, the way that individual countries structure jobs makes for significant cross-national differences in potential job turnover rates for youth and adults. This is on the assumption that job characteristics are an important influence on job-changing. While well-documented evidence for individual countries is lacking on this point, the cross-national material strongly suggests that certain job characteristics inhibit turnover; the Japanese information for all age groups and the German report on youth illustrate this.

Third, youth attitudes as a cause of job turnover or remaining unemployed instead of finding another job crop up in most of the chapters, but the subject is not fully developed and no firm conclusions are possible for individual countries, let alone the group. Obviously, this is a difficult subject to document objectively; further research to distinguish opinions voiced by youth and others from standardized measures of behavior can advance the discussion of a subject that does not go away.

Fourth, the relationships between turnover or job-changing rates and unemployment rates are not straightforward in any country or among countries. It appears that most job-changing takes place without intervening unemployment. In the United States in 1977, three times as many males and five times as many females had two or more employers as had two or more spells of unemployment, according to matched data. Moreover, the ratios were much the same for the two youth groups (18–19, 20–24) as for adults, separately for each sex. Raw data tend to show that young adults have higher job-changing rates than teenagers, but lower unemployment rates. This may be the consequence of shorter duration of unemployment for young adults. An Australian finding is that young unemployed job-changers have no more problem in finding another job than adult males, another indication that long duration unemployment is not the issue.

It remains to be determined whether the higher job-changing rates of youth are stimulated by the characteristics of their jobs, as intuitive judgment suggests, and result in a higher incidence of unemployment than adults experience. The fragmentary evidence currently available does not adequately identify either causes or results of the variations in job-changing rates by age, sex, or race. Turnover rates, often used instead of job-changing rates, are not fully satisfactory because they include those who leave a job in order to leave the labor force.

Fifth, youth in unfavorable jobs who experience more spells of unemployment than similar youth in the initial work years may also have inferior labor market outcomes later on, the "scarring" effect. The British analysis of longitudinal data for cohorts entering the labor force in 1930, 1940, 1950, and 1960 finds that

> initial unemployment among males is strongly associated with subsequent unemployment. Men who were unemployed for three months or more on entry had, on average, three times as many such spells of unemployment in the 1965–75 decade as those who found an initial job with less than three months of unemployment or no unemployment.

The opposite result for females may be due to the withdrawal from the labor force of the females who had initially been most vulnerable to unemployment. A similar Swedish exercise found that a majority of youth who had some unemployment during 1967 had no unemployment in 1973, but that those with 1967 joblessness had a higher risk of subsequent unemployment (Table 8.7). American analyses, controlling for the personal characteristics of the youth as neither the British nor the Swedish were able to do, suggest that teenage unemployment in the late 1960s was not associated with unemployment in the 1970s; for black youth the persistence effects were stronger. None of the data separate the unemployment occurring between jobs, the relevant subject here, from unemployment on entering, leaving, or reentering the labor market.

Impacts of early unemployment on later earnings or social class position are other possible scarring effects. In Britain, an initial spell of unemployment has no lasting effect on the social class position 15 to 45 years later, either for males or females. Swedish analysis found that the longer the duration of unemployment the larger was the adverse effect on subsequent wages. A summary of several related American analyses concludes that "there is consistent evidence that accumulating half a year or more of unemployment in the teen years may dramatically lower future wages—even as much as eight years later." Again, black youth show more persistence effects than white. Briefer periods of joblessness, however, perhaps utilized to shop around for better jobs, have a positive effect on later wages, according to one American study. More refined and fuller longitudinal data and an agreed-on methodology will throw further light on the later consequences of initial difficulty in the labor market, if adequate allowance is made for the changes in overall economic circumstances between the early and later periods.

Last, the three European countries and Australia are less interested than the United States in the policy implications of the relation between job characteristics and youth unemployment, because their problem for the past ten years has been a dramatic rise of youth unemployment from levels far lower than any the U.S. has ever recorded. They now have so many youth facing substantial periods of unemployment before they can find a first job (or the post-apprenticeship job in Germany) that the overall availability of jobs overrides all other policy issues. Japan would be affected in the opposite way—concerns about youth are mostly in terms of the paucity of their numbers for the future labor force and a tendency to focus on the good job conditions in the largest firms. Recession unemployment has not yet reached serious proportions, and it may not go much higher.

These differences from the other countries should reinforce the potential importance of adverse job characteristics of youth jobs in the United States. Instead of the usual approach in American programs, which takes the youth most likely to fill the unfavorable jobs and attempts to improve their ability to compete for the better jobs, a more-balanced and two-pronged attack could be made. One would continue present methods, while the other would look at the possibilities of changing the character of the unfavorable jobs. The reports from other countries suggest the diverse ways in which this might be accomplished. There also is the policy issue of which age groups, youth or older workers, should be the prime target for such improved jobs. Given the changing shares of the working population that lie ahead, youth may diminish in importance in national concern, especially if jobs are structured and improved so that they are appealing to various age groups. In any case, a reduction in the number of jobs with no redeeming features, especially in the burgeoning services sector, is a goal that seems achievable, using and adapting some of the practices that work elsewhere.

Index

Page numbers followed by *t* indicate material in tables.

Age:
  cross-national variation in jobs and, 14
  discrimination based on, in the United
      States, 283
  job type and, 10–13
    in Australia, 92–103
    in Germany, 125–29, 134*t*, 136*t*
    in Great Britain, 65–67, 160–70
    in Japan, 65–67, 195–203, 219–20
    in Sweden, 65–67, 244–50, 254–56
    in the United States, 65–67, 279–81,
        288–92, 306*t*, 312–13
  population group and, 15
Apprenticeship programs, 55
  in Australia, 88–89, 106*t*, 329
  in Germany, 3, 113, 117–23, 132*t*, 141–42,
      320–21, 329, 331
    jobs of young people and, 124–29, 333
    occupational status and, 130–37
    wages and, 137–39
  in Great Britain, 76, 150, 153, 157–58,
      165–66, 172, 182, 329
  in Sweden, 235
  in the United States, 76, 273
Australia, 86–110, 328
  adult and youth employment compared
      in, 29*t*, 98–103
  apprenticeship programs in, 88–89, 329
  education in, 4, 87–90, 92–96
  employment rates in, 18–19, 86–87
    total employment, 20–26
    youth employment, 22*t*, 23*t*, 26–37
  employment systems in, 5, 90–92, 329
  nonstudent workers in, 96–98
  occupational status in, 9
  relative earnings of young workers in,
      105–8
  sectoral distribution of employment in,
      6–8, 96–103, 325
  student workers in, 92–96, 323, 336–37
  teenage population of, 6
  unemployment trends in, 9–10, 24, 87,
      90, 92, 94, 102–3, 109–10

    working conditions in, 103–5
    young adult population of, 6

Björkland, Anders, 232–68
*Bridges to Work: International Compari-
    sons of Transition Services,* xi

Career guidance:
  in Australia, 90–91
  in Germany, 120–21
  in Great Britain, 155–56
  in Japan, 192–93
  in Sweden, 237–38
  in the United States, 274
CETA (Comprehensive Employment and
    Training Act—United States), 274,
    276
Civil Rights Act of 1964 (United States),
    303
Codetermination Act of 1977 (Sweden), 239

Discrimination:
  age, in the United States, 283
  racial:
    in Great Britain, 163–65, 182, 334–35
    in Japan, 199–200
    job type and, 334–35
    in the United States, 269–72, 276,
        279–84, 292–96, 303, 311–12
  See also Sex (gender)
Dismissal Protection Act of 1969 (Ger-
    many), 121–22

Earnings. *See* Wages/salaries
Education, 4
  apprenticeship programs as. *See* Appren-
      ticeship programs
  in Australia, 4, 87–90, 92–96
  employment statistics and, 35–36
  in Germany, 4, 114–20, 122–24, 333
  in Great Britain, 4, 149, 150–55
  in Japan. *See* Japan, education in
  job types and, 331–34

manpower training programs as. *See* Manpower training programs
sex differences in jobs and, 331
in Sweden, 4, 233–37, 242–50, 257, 265, 333–34
in the United States, 4, 270–73, 311
vocational. *See* Vocational education
Education Act of 1944 (Great Britain), 156
Employment and Training Act of 1948 (Great Britain), 156
Employment of Women, Young Persons and Children Act of 1920 (Great Britain), 157
Employment/population (E/P) ratios:
described, 22
for total employment, 22–24, 26
for youth employment, 28, 30, 33, 35, 149
Employment Protection Act of 1974 (Sweden), 239–40, 252–53
Employment Protection (Consolidation) Act of 1978 (Great Britain), 158
Employment rates:
in Australia, 18–37, 86–87
in Germany, 18–37
in Great Britain, 19–37
in Japan, 18–37
levels and growth of, 1960 to 1980, 20–26
in Sweden, 18–37
of teenage females, 23*t*, 28–30, 35*t*
of teenage males, 22*t*, 27–28, 29*t*, 35*t*
in the United States, 18–20, 22*t*, 23*t*, 26–37
of young adult females, 22*t*, 23*t*, 29*t*, 32–34, 35*t*
of young adult males, 22*t*, 29*t*, 30–32, 35*t*
Employment Security Law of 1947 (Japan), 192
Employment systems, 14
in Australia, 5, 90–92, 329
in Germany, 5, 120–23, 329
in Great Britain, 5, 155–59, 329
in Japan, 5, 192–95, 329
in Sweden, 5, 237–41, 329
in the United States, 5, 273–77, 329

Factories Act of 1961 (Great Britain), 156–57
Fair Labor Standards Act of 1938 (United States), 274–75
Federal Education Promotion Act of 1971 (Germany), 122
Federal Republic of Germany, *See* Germany
Female employment:
adult and youth occupations compared, 60–64
in Australia, 98–103, 106*t*, 107*t*
in Germany, 129–37, 142–43
in Great Britain, 60–61, 62*t*, 176–81

in Japan, 60–61, 62*t*, 219–26
in Sweden, 60–61, 63*t*, 251–60
in the United States, 60–61, 63*t*, 296–305
concentration of, in specific occupations, 7–9, 41–45
in Australia, 97–98, 99*t*
in Germany, 125–29, 136*t*
in Great Britain, 42*t*, 46*t*, 62*t*, 164*t*, 166–70, 171*t*
in Japan, 42*t*, 46*t*, 62*t*, 200–206
in Sweden, 43*t*, 47*t*, 62*t*, 65–67, 244–50, 254–56
in the United States, 43*t*, 47*t*, 62*t*, 285*t*, 288–92, 297*t*, 306*t*
growth of, 21–23
teenage females, 28–30, 35*t*
young adult females, 29*t*, 32–34, 35*t*
Indexes of Occupational Dissimilarity and, 70–72
wages and:
in Australia, 327
in Germany, 138*t*, 138–39, 326
in Great Britain, 170–75, 327
in Japan, 209*t*, 210, 211*t*, 222–25, 326
in Sweden, 245*t*, 246–49, 257–60, 265, 326–27
in the United States, 279, 294, 301–3, 308–10, 326–27

GDP. *See* Gross domestic product
Germany, 113–43, 328
adult and youth employment compared in, 29*t*, 129–37, 142–43
apprenticeship programs in, 3, 113, 117–23, 132*t*, 141–42, 320–21, 329, 331
education in, 4, 114–20, 122–24, 333
employment rates in, 18, 19
total employment, 20–26
youth employment, 22*t*, 23*t*, 26–37
employment systems in, 5, 120–23, 329
nonstudent workers in, 122, 124–29
occupational status in, 9, 129–37
relative earnings of young workers in, 137–39, 326–27
sectoral distribution of employment in, 6–8, 124–37
student workers in, 114, 121
teenage population of, 6
unemployment trends in, 3, 9–10, 24, 122, 126–29, 136–37, 321
working conditions in, 121–23, 139–40
young adult population of, 6
youth labor market in, 320–22
Great Britain, 149–82, 328, 334–36
adult and youth employment compared in, 29*t*, 56–64, 176–81, 219–26

apprenticeship programs in, 76, 150, 153,
157–58, 165–66, 172, 182, 329
education in, 4, 149, 150–55
employment rates in, 19
total employment, 20–26
youth employment, 22*t*, 23*t*, 26–37
employment systems in, 5, 155–59, 329
nonstudent workers, in, 160–70
occupational status in, 9
relative earnings of youth in, 170–75
sectoral distribution of employment in,
6–8, 160–70
student workers in, 151–53
teenage population of, 6, 149
unemployment trends in, 9–10, 152, 155,
172–74, 180–81, 332, 339–40
working conditions in, 156–57, 175–76
young adult population of, 6, 149
Gross domestic product (GDP), 5
employment growth and, 25
service sector growth and, 7

Harrisson, John A. C., 17–38, 39–85
Hills, Stephen M., 269–318

Income distribution, 5
Indexes of Occupational Dissimilarity (IOD),
67–72
computation of, 67
in Germany, 131, 133*t*
sex differences in jobs and, 331
for youth and adult jobs, 325
Industrial Training Act (Great Britain), 154

Japan, 185–231
adult and youth employment compared
in, 29*t*, 56–64, 219–26
education in, 4, 186–92, 206–7, 221–22,
333, 335
job characteristics and, 200–203
job mobility and, 216–19, 227–29
wages and, 209–10, 224*t*, 225
employment rates in, 18, 19
total employment, 20–26
youth employment, 22*t*, 23*t*, 26–37
employment systems in, 5, 192–95, 329
occupational status in, 9
relative earnings of young workers in,
207–12, 222–25
sectoral distribution of employment in,
6–8, 200–206, 219–20
size of firm and job characteristics in,
203–6, 220, 221*t*, 222*t*, 329–30
teenage population of, 6, 185–86
unemployment trends in, 3, 9–10, 24, 186,
195, 321, 340
working conditions in, 193–94

young adult population of, 6, 186
youth labor market in, 320–22
Job mobility:
adult compared to youth, 327–28
in Australia, 101–3, 108–9, 328
in Germany, 141–42, 328
in Great Britain, 176–80, 328, 329, 336
in Japan, 196–99, 212–19, 226–29, 328,
329
labor market segmentation and, 323–24,
337–41
in Sweden, 251–53, 260–63, 328, 335–36
in the United States, 287, 291, 295, 297–98,
303–5, 309–10, 312–13, 328, 329
Job types:
age and. *See* Age, job type and
cross-national variations in, 13–14
education and, 331–34
racial discrimination and, 334–35
unemployment levels and, 1–2
See also Occupation

Labor Standards Law of 1947 (Japan), 193–94
LAS. *See* Employment Protection Act of
1974 (Sweden)

Mackay, Keith, 86–112
Male employment:
adult and youth occupations compared,
56–60, 64
in Australia, 98–103, 106*t*, 107*t*
in Germany, 129–35, 142–43
in Great Britain, 56–60, 176–81
in Japan, 56–60, 219–26
in Sweden, 56–60, 251–60
in the United States, 56–60, 296–305
concentration of, in specific occupations,
8–9, 41, 45–51, 65–67
in Australia, 97–98, 99*t*
in Germany, 125–29, 134*t*
in Great Britain, 46*t*, 48*t*, 52*t*, 58*t*, 164*t*,
166–70
in Japan, 46*t*, 48*t*, 52*t*, 58*t*, 200–206
in Sweden, 47*t*, 49*t*, 52*t*, 59*t*, 248*t*,
251–60
in the United States, 47*t*, 49*t*, 52*t*, 56–60,
285*t*, 296–305
growth of, 21–23
teenage males, 27–28, 29*t*, 35*t*
young adult males, 29*t*, 30–32, 35*t*
Indexes of Occupational Dissimilarity and,
70–72
wages and:
in Germany, 137*t*, 138–39
in Great Britain, 170–75, 326–27
in Japan, 209*t*, 211–12
in Sweden, 245*t*, 246–49, 257–60, 265

in the United States, 279, 284–85, 294, 301–3, 308–10, 326–27
Manpower training programs:
in Australia, 92
in Germany, 122
in Great Britain, 154–55
in Sweden, 240–41
in the United States, 274, 276–77
Maternity Protection Act of 1968 (Germany), 121
Metcalf, David, 149–84
Minimum Wage Law of 1959 (Japan), 194
Minimum wages:
in Australia, 91
in Great Britain, 5
in Japan, 5, 194
in the United States, 5, 275, 303
See also Wages/salaries
Minority groups:
in Germany, 129
in Great Britain, 163–65, 182, 334–35
in Japan, 199–200
in Sweden, 234–35, 243–44
in the United States, 269–72, 276, 279–83, 284, 292–96, 303, 311–12

Occupation, 39–77
comparison of adult and youth, 325–30
in Australia, 98–103
in Germany, 129–137, 142–43
in Great Britain, 56–64, 176–81, 219–26
in Japan, 56–64, 219–26, 227t
in Sweden, 56–64, 251–60
in the United States, 56–64, 296–305
concentration of, by age and sex, 8–9, 51–56, 65–67, 331–32
in Australia, 92–103
in Germany, 125–29, 134t, 136t
in Great Britain, 42t, 65–67, 160–70
in Japan, 42t, 65–67, 195–206, 219–20
in Sweden, 43t, 65–67, 244–50, 254–56
in the United States, 43t, 65–67, 279–81, 288–92, 306t, 312–13
cross-national comparison of youth, 40–51
Indexes of Occupational Dissimilarity and, 67–72
job mobility and. See Job mobility
sectoral distribution of:
in Australia, 6–8, 96–103, 325
in Germany, 6–8, 124–37
in Great Britain, 6–8, 160–70
in Japan, 6–8, 200–206, 219–20
in Sweden, 6–8, 253–56, 265
in the United States, 6–8, 305–8
status differences in, 9, 57, 60–61, 129–37, 179–80, 200–203, 219
See also Job types

Part-time employment, 336–37
in Australia, 86, 92–96, 101, 103–4, 105–7
in Great Britain, 175
in Japan, 212, 220, 225
in Sweden, 233, 241–42, 256, 338
in the United States, 274–75, 277–82, 299–300, 311, 338
See also Student workers
Paterson, Paul, 86–112
Permanent (lifetime) employment, 194, 196–99
Persson-Tanimura, Inga, 232–68
Population of workers, 5–6, 149
designations of, 15
total employment rates, 20–26
youth employment rates, 26–37

Reubens, Beatrice G., 1–16, 17–38, 39–85, 185–231, 269–318, 319–41
Rivers, John, 149–84

Salaries. See Wages/salaries
Schober, Karen, 113–48
Sex (gender):
education and, in the United States, 272–73, 311
employment growth and, 21–23, 26–37
Indexes of Occupational Dissimilarity and, 70–72
occupational concentration by, 8–9, 65–67, 71–72, 200–206, 331–32
in Australia, 92–103, 97–98, 99t
in Germany, 125–37, 142–43
in Great Britain, 42t, 46t, 48t, 52t, 58t, 60–61, 62t, 160–70, 171t, 176–81
in Japan, 42t, 46t, 48t, 52t, 56–61, 62t, 200–206, 219–26
in Sweden, 43t, 47t, 49t, 52t, 56–61, 62t, 63t, 65–67, 244–60
in the United States, 43t, 47t, 49t, 52t, 56–61, 62t, 63t, 65–67, 279–81, 285t, 288–92, 296–305, 306t
wages and:
in Australia, 91, 327
in Germany, 137–39, 326–27
in Great Britain, 170–75, 326–27
in Japan, 209t, 210–12, 222–25, 326
in Sweden, 240, 245t, 246–49, 257–60, 265, 326–27, 336
in the United States, 279, 284–85, 294, 301–3, 308–10, 326–27
See also Female employment; Male employment
Sparr, Pamela, 17–38
Student workers, 336–37
in Australia, 92–96, 323, 336–37
in Germany, 114, 121

in Great Britain, 151–53
in Sweden, 238–39, 241–42, 336–37
in the United States, 269, 275, 277–82,
  284–88, 311, 336–37
See also Part-time employment
Sweden, 65–67, 232–66, 328, 335–36
  adult and youth employment compared
    in, 29*t*, 56–64, 251–60
  apprenticeship programs in, 235
  education in, 4, 233–37, 242–50, 257, 265,
    333–34
  employment rates in, 18, 19
    total employment, 20–26
    youth employment, 22*t*, 23*t*, 26–37
  employment systems in, 5, 237–41, 329
  nonstudent workers in, 242–50
  occupational status in, 9, 255*t*
  relative earnings of young workers in,
    257–60
  sectoral distribution of employment in,
    6–8, 253–56, 265
  student workers in, 238–39, 241–42,
    336–37
  teenage population of, 6
  unemployment trends in, 9–10, 24, 232,
    234, 238, 241, 244, 246–47, 249–51,
    258, 263–66, 340
  working conditions in, 238–39, 256–57
  young adult population of, 6

Teenagers:
  defined, 15
  employment growth of, 27–30, 35*t*
  employment rates of, 22*t*, 23*t*, 27–30, 35*t*
  occupational groups of, 41–56
  population of, by country, 6, 149
  See also specific countries
Temporary employment in Sweden, 252–53,
  266
Total working population, defined, 15
Trade unions:
  in Australia, 91–92, 96
  in Germany, 122–23, 139
  in Great Britain, 158
  in Japan, 194–96
  in Sweden, 237, 240, 257–58, 326
  in the United States, 275–76, 290, 294
Turnover, job:
  adult compared to youth, 2, 327–28
  in Australia, 101–3, 109
  in Germany, 141–42
  in Great Britain, 162–63, 176–80
  in Japan, 196–99, 212–19, 226
  labor market segmentation and, 323–324,
    337–41
  in Sweden, 251–53
  unemployment and, 1–3

in the United States, 287, 291, 295, 297–98,
  303–5, 309–10

U.K. (United Kingdom). *See* Great Britain
Umetani, Shun'ichiro, 185–231
Unemployment:
  in Australia, 9–10, 21*t*, 24, 87, 90, 92, 94,
    102–3, 109–10
  data adequacy on, 30
  employment versus, 1–3, 25
  in Germany, 3, 9–10, 21*t*, 24, 122, 126–29,
    136–37, 321
  in Great Britain, 9–10, 21*t*, 152, 155,
    172–74, 180–181, 332, 339–40
  in Japan, 3, 9–10, 21*t*, 24, 186, 195, 321,
    340
  job characteristics and, 337–41
  job turnover and, 1–3
  in Sweden, 9–10, 21*t*, 24, 232, 234, 238,
    241, 244, 246–47, 249–52, 258, 261*t*,
    263–66, 340
  in the United States, 3, 9–10, 21*t*, 24,
    269–70, 276–77, 282–84, 287–88,
    291–92, 295–96, 303–5, 309–10,
    312–13
United Kingdom. *See* Great Britain
United States, 269–313, 328
  adult and youth employment compared
    in, 29*t*, 56–64, 296–305
  apprenticeship programs in, 76, 273
  education in, 4, 270–73, 311
  employment rates in, 18–29
    total employment, 20
    youth employment, 22*t*, 23*t*, 26–37
  employment systems in, 5, 273–77, 329
  nonstudent workers in, 282–96
  occupational status in, 9
  relative earnings of young workers in,
    301–3
  sectoral distribution of employment in,
    6–8, 305–8
  student workers in, 269, 275, 277–82,
    284–88, 311, 336–37
  teenage population of, 6
  unemployment trends in, 3, 9–10, 24,
    269–70, 276–77, 282–84, 287–88,
    291–92, 295–96, 303–5, 309–10,
    312–13, 340
  working conditions in, 274–75
  young adult population of, 6

Vocational education:
  in Australia, 87–89
  in Germany, 114–20
  in Great Britain, 153–55, 182
  in Japan, 188, 189, 191–92, 195, 206–7,
    221–22

manpower training programs in. *See* Manpower training programs
in Sweden, 234–37, 240–41, 244–46
in the United States, 271–73
Vocational Training Act of 1969 (Germany), 117

Wages/salaries:
adult compared to youth, 105–8, 137–39, 170–75, 222–25, 326–27
in Australia, 91, 105–8, 109, 326–27
in Germany, 137–39, 326–27
in Great Britain, 5, 157–58, 170–75, 326–27
in Japan, 5, 194–95, 207–12, 222–25, 326–27
in Sweden, 240, 245*t*, 246–49, 257–60, 265, 326–27, 336
in the United States, 5, 275, 279, 284–85, 294, 301–3, 308–10, 326–27
West Germany. *See* Germany
Working conditions:
in Australia, 103–5
in Germany, 121–23, 139–40
in Great Britain, 156–57, 175–76
in Japan, 193–94
in Sweden, 238–39, 256–57
in the United States, 274–75
Working Environment Law of 1978 (Sweden), 238
Working hours:
in Australia, 92–93, 100*t*, 103–5

in Germany, 139–40
in Great Britain, 175–76
in Japan, 193–94, 212, 225–26
in Sweden, 238–39, 256
in the United States, 274–75, 299–301
Workplace Constitution Act of 1977 (Germany), 121

Young adults:
defined, 15
employment growth of, 29*t*, 30–34, 35*t*
employment rates of, 22*t*, 23*t*, 29*t*, 30–34, 35*t*
occupational groups of, 41–56
compared with adults, 56–64
concentration of, by age and sex, 65–67
Indexes of Occupational Dissimilarity and, 68–72
population of, by country, 6, 149
See also specific countries
Young Workers Protection Act of 1976 (Germany), 121, 140
Youth Employment Demonstration Projects Act of 1977 (United States), 276
Youth Labor Force 1945–1995, The: A Cross-National Analysis, xi
Youth labor market:
characteristics of, 320–23
common occupations of youth in, 41–72
definitions of, 11–12
secondary markets and, 323–24
youth-intensive occupations and, 51–56

About the Authors

Anders Björklund is Research Associate at the Industrial Institute for Economic and Social Research in Stockholm.

John A. C. Harrisson is Research Associate at Conservation of Human Resources, Columbia University.

Stephen M. Hills is Associate Project Director, National Longitudinal Surveys, Center for Human Resource Research, The Ohio State University.

Keith R. Mackay is Senior Project Officer of the Bureau of Labour Market Research, Department of Employment and Youth Affairs, Australia.

David Metcalf is Professor of Economics at the University of Kent, and Consultant at the Centre for Labour Economics, London School of Economics.

Paul R. Paterson is Principal Project Officer of the Bureau of Labour Market Research, Department of Employment and Youth Affairs, Australia.

Inga Persson-Tanimura is Research Associate at the Swedish Institute for Social Research, Stockholm, and Secretary, Expert Group for Labor Market Research (EFA), Swedish Ministry of Labor.

Beatrice G. Reubens is Senior Research Associate at Conservation of Human Resources, Columbia University.

John Richards is a Ph.D. student in economics at the University of Kent, England.

Karen Schober is Senior Research Associate at the Institute of Employment Research (IAB), Nürnberg.

Pamela Sparr is a graduate student in economics at the New School for Social Research, New York.

Shun'ichiro Umetani is Associate Professor of Economics at Tokyo Gakugei University, and Research Associate at the Japan Institute of Labour.